WWW.

D0343288

IRELAND

researcher-writers
Adeline Byrne
William Locke

staff writers
Holly Cao
Ronit Malka

research manager
Clémence Faust

editor
Mallory Weiss

managing editor
Mark Warren

ADELINE BYRNE. Addie, driven by wanderlust and an un-matched enthusiasm for Irish spirits, traversed the Emerald Isle and made it her own. Always living on the edge, she progressed from dodging junkies in Northside to teetering on cliffs at the end of the earth, and is probably still where we left her: bellowing drinking songs with old Irish men in a forgotten pub.

WILLIAM LOCKE. Will handled the island's northernmost cities, adeptly researching the best student and budget haunts on both sides of the border. From Belfast to Westport, this always good-natured researcher left a trail of lasting peace behind him, which we expect will be sung of for centuries.

CONTENTS

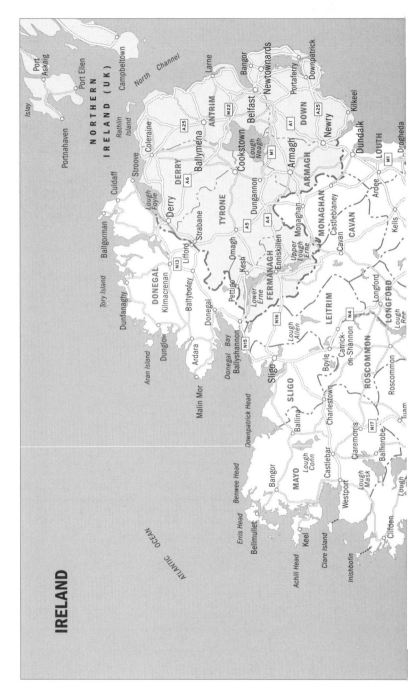

IRELAND

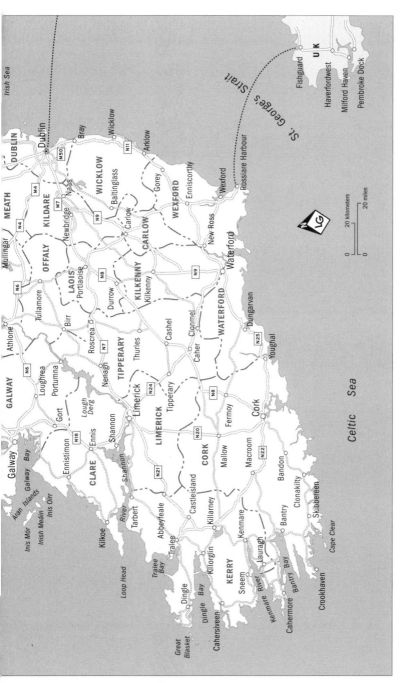

DISCOVER

IRELAND

Did you find a four-leaf clover? You must've, since you're lucky enough to be in Ireland, the land of leprechauns and pots o' gold. Okay, maybe that's just the Ireland in our heads and on cereal boxes. But, believe it or not, the real Ireland is better. What is better than tiny green men and rainbows, you ask? Well, full-grown Irishmen (with brogues) and fish 'n' chips. (Do rainbows leave you with the ever-satisfying food coma? I don't think so. But, then again, we've never eaten a rainbow before.) Ireland is chock full of castles and pubs, parks and Riverdance. There is a reason why a country that sees so much rain is full of so many happy people. So go see what those Irish eyes are smiling about.

1

when to go

Do you have an umbrella? Great! Then the seatbelt sign of your trip is turned off, and you can feel free to move about Ireland. If you're in Ireland, it will rain. The Irish didn't get so pale for nothing. But don't be discouraged; the weather is temperate year-round, making even winter a pleasant time to visit. But it isn't cloudy every day, so take the rain with a Guinness and enjoy the sunshine when it pokes its way through the mist.

Ireland is at its sunniest in May and June, though that isn't saying much. The island sees the most tourists in July and August, so expect accommodations and sights to be more crowded and the prices to increase slightly. Mid-November to February is a good time to visit if you're a duck or get a family-discount at LL Bean.

what to do

MAGICALLY DELICIOUS

Hearts, stars, and horseshoes. Clovers and blue moons. Pots of gold and rainbows. And ▪Let's Go's red (hot air) balloon!

- **HEARTS:** Head to Dublin's **La Vita** (p. 30) for their **Salad of Hearts** and other vegetarian delights.

- **STARS:** Offering an unbeatable buffet during the day and a raucous pub at night, the **Morning Star** (p. 173) is one of Belfast's gems.

- **HORSESHOES:** If you're looking for a traditional Irish experience, hit up the **Bleeding Horse Tavern** (p. 28) and sidle up to the bar.

- **CLOVERS:** Get a taste of Ireland as you sip down the frothy shamrock the **Reel Inn** (p. 58) draws in the foam of your Guinness.

- **BLUE MOONS: Half Moon Crepes** (p. 26) in Dublin will leave you feeling anything but blue.

- **POTS OF GOLD:** Right off of what was known as Belfast's "Golden Mile," **Bookfinder's Cafe** (p. 169) is rich with classic literature and a comfortable atmosphere.

- **RAINBOWS:** A different kind of tasty, GLBT-friendly **Pantibar** (p. 35) gets pumpin' on the weekends.

green with envy

- **ST. STEPHEN'S GREEN:** Embrace nature right in the heart of Dublin at this palm-tree adorned park (p. 21).

- **FITZGERALD PARK:** A great way to spend your time in Cork, this park has walking paths along the river and a sequined tree (p. 117).

- **KILLARNEY NATIONAL PARK:** A must-see, this park offers lakeside paths, green mountains, and the famous Meeting of the Waters (p. 106).

- **THE PEOPLE'S PARK:** Spend some time among the well-tended gardens in this Limerick park (p. 126).

- **BURREN NATIONAL PARK:** Check out the rocky Ennis countryside and the variety of flowers that dot the landscape (p. 87).

discover ireland

OH, DANNY BOY

What do Pierce Brosnan, Liam Neeson, and Bono all have in common? That's right, they're all hunky Irishmen. What do the following establishments have in common? That's right, they're all places named after what we can only assume are hunky Irishmen.

- **IT MAY NOT BE GOSLING:** But this Ryan is a close second; head to **Ryan's Bar** (p. 137) in Kilkenny for a drink among some slightly racy decor.

- **A STATUE OF AN AUTHOR AS AN OLD MAN:** No one has pulled off round frame eyeglasses like this guy since Harry Potter; gawk at the **James Joyce Statue** (p. 22) in Dublin for a little eye-candy.

- **COOLER THAN THE KRAKEN:** **McCracken's** (p. 179) isn't a legendary sea monster, but this Belfast pub is legendary in its own right, creating a twist on the traditional Irish style.

- **OH, HAPPY DAY:** St. Patrick's Day, that is. Honor Ireland's patron saint (and one handsome devil) at **St. Patrick's Cathedral** (p. 23) in Dublin.

student superlatives

- **BEST PLACE TO FEEL WARM AND FUZZY:** Aran Sweater Market Outlet (p. 110).
- **BEST PLACE TO BUY SOME BLING:** Thomas Dillon's Claddagh Gold (p. 80).
- **BEST PLACE TO SEE PEOPLE DANCE WITHOUT MOVING THEIR ARMS:** The Gaiety Theatre (p. 37).
- **BEST PLACE TO GET WET IF IT'S RAINING:** Sligo Abbey (p. 63).
- **BEST PLACE TO STRUT YOUR STUFF:** The Salthill Promenade (p. 77).
- **BEST PLACE TO NOT BE A KLUTZ:** Waterford Crystal Factory Tour (p. 125)

CASTLE ON A CLOUD (ER, ISLAND)

Some aspects of Ireland are exactly the way you always imagined...except for the leprechauns, of course (they're actually the same size as you and me and look a lot like Colin Farrell). The castles, however, are real and scattered about the island for you to go explore.

- **A MAN'S HOME IS HIS:** The **Bunratty Castle and Folk Park** (p. 92) in Shannon take you back in time, putting you in the shoes of the royalty that once inhabited the castle on the village grounds.

- **AN ENGLISHMAN'S HOME IS HIS:** Admire the small but mighty **Donegal Castle** (p. 56) because small for a castle isn't really very small at all. Storm it: The **Athlone Castle** (p. 148) dominates this picturesque riverfront town.

- **BUILD THEM IN THE AIR:** Kiss the famous Blarney Stone at the top of the **Blarney Castle** (p. 116), and roam around the massive structure tour-guide free.

- **BE KING OF IT:** **Kilkenny Castle** (p. 134) is a must-see, with a lovely, manicured landscape surrounding the massive structure.

- **CASTLES ON CASTLES ON CASTLES:** While it's no longer completely in its original 18th-century state, the **Dublin Castle** (p. 23) is still a sight to behold.

BEYOND TOURISM

Those craving an international adventure that involves more than just sightseeing ought to explore the study, work, and volunteer opportunities available in Ireland. If you have the luck of the Irish, you may come out of the experience with a sexy brogue.

- **STUDY ABROAD:** While you may not be able to study the history of the leprechauns, there are plenty of enticing programs for you to explore at **University College Dublin** (p. 217) or **Queen's University Belfast** (p. 217). If you, like the Irish, have music in your blood, be sure to check out the **Royal Irish Academy of Music, Dublin City University** (p. 218).

- **VOLUNTEER ABROAD:** So you want to help, but you don't know what you want to help? Don't fret, **Volunteers for International Partnership** (p. 221) covers everything from the environment to the arts.

- **WORK ABROAD:** Couldn't find that pot of gold? Consider working as an **au pair** (p. 223) instead of chasing down the end of that rainbow.

suggested itineraries

BEST OF IRELAND (2 WEEKS)

DUBLIN (3 DAYS). Spend your days in Dublin experiencing the many sights, including tours of **Trinity College, Dublin Castle, Jameson Distillery, and the Guinness Storehouse.** If you're looking to spend some time outside, hit **St. Stephen's Green.** Refuel in a classic Irish atmosphere, like the one found at **Mercantile.**

WATERFORD (2 DAYS). Admire all things shiny on the **Waterford Crystal Factory Tour** and then take your curiosity to **Reginald's Tower.** If you're looking for a way to relax after a day of sightseeing, head to **Mint Café** for a specialty latte.

CORK (2 DAYS). Spend some time at **Blarney Castle,** and be sure to kiss the legendary stone. Bring your appetite to **The Fish Hatch** for some traditional Irish fish and chips.

GALWAY (2 DAYS). Walk along the **Salthill Promenade** for the best introduction to this city, then stop by **Ard Bia** for a meal (or just some cake).

DERRY (2 DAYS). Learn about local history at the **Museum of Free Derry** before getting the true local experience at the popular pub, **Peader O'Donnell's.**

BELFAST (3 DAYS). Get a taste for local culture at the **Golden Thread Gallery, Titanic Belfast, and the Ulster Museum.** Grab a bite to eat at **Made in Belfast** and prepare for a a night of raging at **Lavery's.**

HERE COMES (THE) TROUBLE(S) (3 DAYS)

Oh yes, there was trouble, my friends…right here in Ireland. With a capital "T," that rhymes with "P," that stands for…politics.

BELFAST (1 DAY). Get an overview of "the Troubles" and the history of the conflict on a **Black Cab Tour** through the Falls and Shankhill neighborhoods. Then spend an evening chatting with locals about Belfast's history in a pub, like **Whites Tavern.**

DERRY (2 DAYS). Walk through the **Museum of Free Derry** to get a glimpse of the struggles this city has faced in its history and learn about the tragic Bloody Sunday. Then spend some time at the **Tower Museum,** which covers an ambitious amount of Derry's history, including background on the Northern Irish conflict. Finally, hit the **People's Gallery** and admire the commemorative murals.

TO BEERS! CHEERS. (PACE YOURSELF)

DUBLIN. Temple Bar alone is enough to keep even the heaviest of heavyweights busy for a good long time. But, Dublin as a whole offers a plethora (yes, we use fancy words when we're tipsy) of boozin' options (yes, we use the word "boozin'" when we're tipsy). For two Temple Bar options that are sure not to disappoint, try **Mercantile** or **The Temple Bar.** For a more intimate scene, hit "the smallest pub on earth," **The Dawson Lounge. Farrington's** offers a tourist-friendly atmosphere without the tourists. And for an international craft beer, hit the **Porterhouse Brewing Company** and their four floors. If, by the end of your crawl, you're looking to learn a bit about your booze, hit the **Jameson Distillery** or the **Guinness Storehouse** for some learning with a side of alcohol (or vice versa).

CORK. Nightlife in Cork may not offer as many options as Dublin, but has plenty of classic bars that attract tourists and locals alike. **Sin É** is a well-loved bar that offers Irish live music and a tourist-free atmosphere. For a popular bar that welcomes pub-crawlers at both the start and end of their route, hit **John Rearden's.**

KILLARNEY. This city has a number of different nightlife venues. Looking for a nightclub-Irish pub combo? Head to **The Killarney Grand.** For something more on the traditional side, try **O'Connor's Traditional Pub** for live Irish music and hordes of locals.

discover ireland

how to use this book

CHAPTERS

Let's Go Ireland is divided into the Republic of Ireland and Northern Ireland. The Republic of Ireland is further divided into **Dublin** (a stand-alone chapter) and Ireland's historical provinces as an easy way to tackle the diverse country: these chapters include **Ulster and Connacht** (the Republic of Ireland's north and west), **Munster** (the southwest and south-central part of the island), and **Leinster** (the east). **Northern Ireland,** containing coverage of Belfast and Derry, rounds out our coverage of the Emerald Isle.

But that's not all, folks. We also have a few extra chapters for you to peruse:

CHAPTER	DESCRIPTION
Discover Europe	Discover tells you what to do, when to do it, and where to go for it. The absolute coolest things about any destination get highlighted in this chapter at the front of all *Let's Go* books.
Essentials	Essentials contains the practical info you need before, during, and after your trip—visas, regional transportation, health and safety, phrasebooks, and more.
Beyond Tourism	As students ourselves, we at *Let's Go* encourage studying abroad, or going beyond tourism more generally, every chance we get. This chapter lists ideas for how to study, volunteer, or work abroad with other young travelers in Europe to get more out of your trip.

LISTINGS

Listings—a.k.a. reviews of individual establishments—constitute a majority of *Let's Go* coverage. Our Researcher-Writers list establishments in order from **best to worst value**—not necessarily quality. (Obviously a five-star hotel is nicer than a hostel, but it would probably be ranked lower because it's not as good a value.) Listings pack in a lot of information, but it's easy to digest if you know how they're constructed:

ESTABLISHMENT NAME TYPE OF ESTABLISHMENT $$$$

Address ☎phone number website

Editorial review goes here.

🧭 Directions to the establishment. i Other practical information about the establishment, like age restrictions at a club or whether breakfast is included at a hostel. $ Prices for goods or services. ⏰ Hours or schedules.

ICONS

First things first: places and things that we absolutely love, sappily cherish, generally obsess over, and wholeheartedly endorse are denoted by the all-empowering **👍Let's Go thumbs-up.** In addition, the icons scattered at the end of a listing (as you saw in the sample above) can serve as visual cues to help you navigate each listing:

👍	*Let's Go* recommends	☎	Phone numbers	🧭	Directions
i	Other hard info	$	Prices	⏰	Hours

OTHER USEFUL STUFF

Area codes for each destination appear opposite the name of the city and are denoted by the ☎ icon.

PRICE DIVERSITY

A final set of icons corresponds to what we call our "price diversity" scale, which approximates how much money you can expect to spend at a given establishment. For **accommodations,** we base our range on the cheapest price for which a single traveler can stay for one night. For **food,** we estimate the average amount one traveler will spend in one sitting. The table below tells you what you'll *typically* find in Europe at the corresponding price range, but keep in mind that no scale can allow for the quirks of all individual establishments.

ACCOMMODATIONS	WHAT YOU'RE LIKELY TO FIND
$	Campgrounds and dorm rooms, both in hostels and actual universities. Expect bunk beds and a communal bath. You may have to provide or rent towels and sheets.
$$	Upper-end hostels and lower-end hotels. You may have a private bathroom, or a sink in your room with a communal shower in the hall.
$$$	A small room with a private bath. Should have some amenities, such as phone and TV. Breakfast may be included.
$$$$	Large hotels, chains, and fancy boutiques. If it doesn't have the perks you want (and more), you've paid too much.

FOOD	WHAT YOU'RE LIKELY TO FIND
$	Street food, fast-food joints, university cafeterias, and bakeries (yum). Usually takeout, but you may have the option of sitting down.
$$	Sandwiches, pizza, low-priced entrees, ethnic eateries, and bar grub. Either takeout or sit-down service with slightly classier decor.
$$$	A somewhat fancy restaurant. Entrees tend to be heartier or more elaborate, but you're really paying for decor and ambience. Few restaurants in this range have a dress code, but some may look down on T-shirts and sandals.
$$$$	Your meal might cost more than your room, but there's a reason—it's something fabulous, famous, or both. Slacks and dress shirts may be expected.

MAP LEGEND

You'll notice that our maps have lots of crazy symbols. Here's how to decode them.

★	Sight	Castle	Internet Cafe	Police
■	Nightlife/Service	Church	Library	Post Office
●	Accommodation	Consulate/Embassy	Metro Station	Skiing
▼	Food	Convent/Monastery	Mountain	Synagogue
✈	Airport	Ferry Landing	Mosque	Telephone Office
⊓	Arch/Gate	Highway Sign (347)	Museum	Theater
$	Bank	Hospital		Tourist Office
☂	Beach	Park	The Let's Go compass always points NORTH.	Train Station
⊟	Bus Station	Water		Pedestrian Zone
⊕	Capital City	Beach		Stairs

DUBLIN

Grab a pint of Guinness, sit down, and listen up. If you're reading this, chances are you've recently arrived in Dublin, capital of the Republic of Ireland. Now that you're here, however, what's to be done? You can't very well sit around drinking Guinness the whole time you're here. Oh wait—of course you can! Fortunately, Dublin has something for every type of traveler. You can get wasted in Temple Bar with a motley crew of tourists, visit museums of everything from natural history to modern art, tour both the Guinness Storehouse and the Jameson Distillery, while away the day poking your head into luxury clothing stores on Grafton St., see live music, and hit the impressive club scene around Camden, Wexford, and Harcourt Streets—we could go on and on. See as much of it as you can, and don't constrain yourself to specific areas because you're sure that things just couldn't get any better. They can and will.

greatest hits

- **BOTTOMS UP:** Dublin is home to both the Jameson Distillery (p. 23) and the Guinness Storehouse (p. 24); finally, two places where alcohol is permitted on tours.
- **GREEN WITH ENVY:** The beautiful St. Stephen's Green (p. 21) is enough to make all other Irish parks jealous.
- **OKEY DOKEY, POKEY:** Spend some time in the slammer, Kilmainham Gaol (p. 24) that is, and get the nitty gritty details on Ireland's history.

student life

If you're already over all the castles and all that drinking—yeah, we see you hitting up those brewery and distillery tours—head over to Trinity College and mingle with some students. Okay, let's be real: don't try to hang out with Irish students if you're tired of drinking. Even if you're in peak can-crushing form, you will have a hard time matching their pounding pace. If you can keep the drinks down and your head up, though, you will surely be led to the hidden hotspots in Temple Bar and around Grafton St. This is where the Trinity kids (and just about everyone else in Dublin) go to rage. Remember, though, Trinity College is one of Dublin's major attractions, so if you are trying to get in with the local student crowd, avoid being that fanny-pack toting, picture-snapping tourist that the students have to stumble over to get to class. It won't win you any friends.

orientation

Dublin is more of a sprawling metropolis than a concentrated urban center. The **Liffey River** cuts the city in two, making navigation easy even for the direction illiterate. The south side is tightly condensed, home to Dublin's most famous neighborhoods, including **Temple Bar** and **Grafton Street.** Just west of these areas lies the historic and scenic neighborhood known as **Georgian Dublin.** Expect a different scene on the north side of the river, where prices are cheaper and the neighborhoods less touristy, for good reason: they certainly lack the charm that is so abundant on the south side. The **O'Connell Street** neighborhood is the economic center on this side of the river, and serves as a great place for cheap shopping and local pubs. The farther north you go, the less we advise going out at night. The area north of O'Connell Street has some great finds during the day, but is of little interest after dark for those without a taste for heroin.

TEMPLE BAR AND THE QUAYS

Navigating Temple Bar pretty much consists of stumbling from one pub to the next while singing, or—more likely—shouting Irish drinking songs. On a weekend, chances are you'll be so drunk that just making it to the end of the block will seem like a challenge. However, in the clear light of day, when you feel like walking around in a soberer state of mind, take the main east-west drag, **Temple Bar,** and diverge onto any of the multiple lanes that run north-south from there. Heading north will take you up toward the **River Liffey** and **the Quays,** while heading south will take you toward **Dame St., Trinity College,** and neighboring **Grafton Street.**

The Quays (pronounced "keys") are even easier to maneuver. You'll walk either on the north side (**Ormond Quay** and **Bachelors Walk**) or the south side (**Aston** and **Wellington Quay**) of the Liffey. Keep an eye out for the little restaurants lining the Quays; some of the best are easy to miss.

GRAFTON STREET

Ah, **Grafton Street,** pedestrian highway of purchasing pleasure. Taking off from the intersection of **Suffolk** and **Nassau Streets,** Grafton Street climbs on a slight incline up from **Trinity College** to **St. Stephen's Green.** Small pedestrian walkways branch off from either side of the street, leading to more shops and—more importantly—several excellent pubs.

Shopping on Grafton Street is not for the faint of heart…or those strapped for cash. Several top-tier brands have outlets here, but the south side is hardly a penny-pincher's paradise. Cheaper shopping can be found elsewhere if you're looking to

dublin

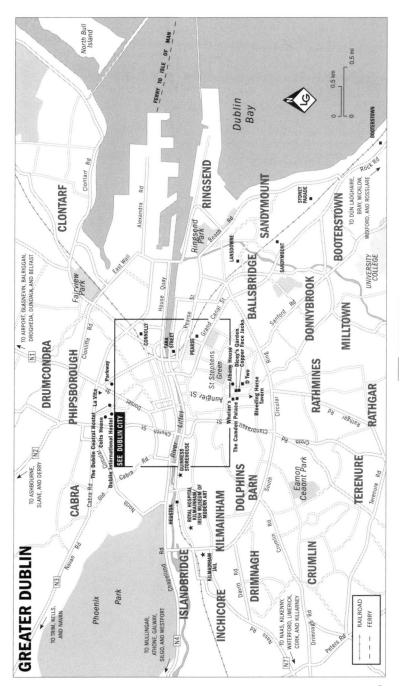

GREATER DUBLIN

orientation

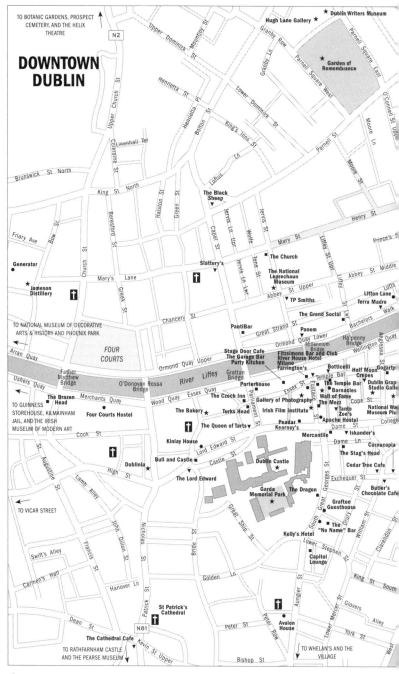

DOWNTOWN DUBLIN

TO BOTANIC GARDENS, PROSPECT CEMETERY, AND THE HELIX THEATRE

N2

TO NATIONAL MUSEUM OF DECORATIVE ARTS & HISTORY AND PHOENIX PARK

TO GUINNESS STOREHOUSE, KILMAINHAM JAIL, AND THE IRISH MUSEUM OF MODERN ART

TO VICAR STREET

TO RATHFARNHAM CASTLE AND THE PEARSE MUSEUM

TO WHELAN'S AND THE VILLAGE

Dublin Writers Museum
Hugh Lane Gallery
Garden of Remembrance

Upper Dominick St
Mountjoy St
Granby Row
Granby Ln
Parnell Square North
Parnell Square West
Parnell Square East
O'Connell St Upper
Henrietta St
Lower Dominick St
Moore Ln
Parnell St
Henrietta Pl
Bolton St
King's Inns St
Loftus Ln
Moore St
Upper Church St
Linenhall Ter
Coleraine St
Brunswick St North
King St North
Beresford St
Halston St
Green St
Jervis St
Jervis Ln Upr
Henry St
Prince's
Friary Ave
Bow St
Church St
Mary's Lane
Greek St
Capel St
Jervis Ln Upr
Wolfe Tone St
Tone St
Jervis Ln Lwr
Mary St
Liffey St Upr
Abbey St Middle
Lotts
Litton Lane
Terra Madre
Walk
Anglesea Quay
Bachelors Walk
Ha'penny Bridge
Wellington Quay
Gogarty
Half Moon
Crepes
Dublin Grap
Studio Galle

The Black Sheep
Slattery's
The Church
The National Leprechaun Museum
Abbey St Upper
TP Smiths
The Grand Social
PantiBar
Panem
Great Strand St
Ormond Quay Lower
Millennium Bridge
Fitzsimons Bar and Club
River House Hotel
Milano
Farrington's
Botticelli
The Temple Bar
Barnacles
Wall of Fame
The Mezz
National Wa
Museum Plu
College

Generator
Jameson Distillery

FOUR COURTS

Stage Door Cafe
The Garage Bar
Purty Kitchen
Chancery St
Ormond Quay Upper
River Liffey
Grattan Bridge
Porterhouse
Essex Quay
Eustace
Temple Bar
Cope St
Tante Zoe's
Apache Hostel

Father Matthew Bridge
O'Donovan Rossa Bridge
The Czech Inn
The Bakery
Turks Head
Gallery of Photography
Irish Film Institute
Arran Quay
Ushers Quay
Merchants Quay
Wood Quay
Essex Quay
Parliament St
Peadar Kearney's
Dame St
Iskander's
Dame Ln
Cornucopia

The Brazen Head
Four Courts Hostel
The Queen of Tarts
Kinlay House
Lord Edward St
Mercantile
The Stag's Head
Cedar Tree Cafe
Cook St
Castle St
Dublin Castle
Great Georges St
Exchequer St
Butler's Chocolate Cafe

Bull and Castle
Dublinia
The Lord Edward
High St
Lamb Alley
St. Augustine St
Garda Memorial Park
The Dragon
Grafton Guesthouse
The "No Name" Bar
Drury St
William St

John Dillon St
Francis St
Nicholas St
Bride St
Great Ship St
Kelly's Hotel
Lower Stephen St
Capitol Lounge
King St South
Glovers Alley
Lower Mercer St
Clarendon St

Swift's Alley
Carmen's Hall
Hanover Ln
Golden Ln
Aungier St
Peter Row

St Patrick's Cathedral
N81
Patrick St
Dean St
The Cathedral Cafe
Kevin St Upper
Peter St
Avalon House
York St

Bishop St

dublin

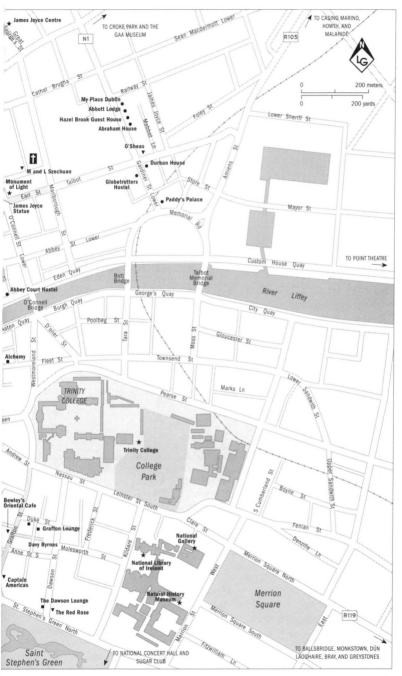

James Joyce Centre

TO CROKE PARK AND THE
GAA MUSEUM

N1

TO CASINO MARINO,
HOWTH, AND
MALAHIDE

R105

Sean Macdermott Lower

Cathal Brugha St

Railway St

James Joyce St

Foley St

Lower Sheriff St

My Place Dublin
Abbott Lodge
Hazel Brook Guest House
Abraham House

Mabbot Ln

O'Sheas

Durban House

M and L Szechuan

Monument
of Light

Earl St

James Joyce
Statue

Talbot St

Gardiner St

Globetrotters
Hostel

Store St

Amens St

Paddy's Palace

Marlborough St

Memorial Rd

Mayor St

Abbey St Lower

O'Connell St Lower

Eden Quay

Custom House Quay

TO POINT THEATRE

Abbey Court Hostel

Butt
Bridge

Talbot
Memorial
Bridge

River   Liffey

O'Connell
Bridge

Burgh Quay

George's Quay

City Quay

Aston Quay

Poolbeg St

Tara St

Moss St

Gloucester St

Alchemy

D'olier St

Fleet St

Westmoreland St

Townsend St

Marks Ln

Lower Sandwith St

TRINITY
COLLEGE

Pearse St

Green

Andrew St

Nassau St

Trinity College

College
Park

S Cumberland St

Boyne St

Upper Sandwith St

Leinster St South

Fenian St

Bewley's
Oriental Cafe

Duke St

Grafton Lounge

Frederick St

Clare St

National
Gallery

Denzille Ln

Davy Byrnes

Grafton St

Anne St S

Molesworth St

Kildare St

National Library
of Ireland

Merrion Square North

Captain
Americas

Dawson St

The Dawson Lounge

The Red Rose

Natural History
Museum

Merrion Square

R119

St. Stephen's Green North

Merrion St West

Merrion Square South

Merrion St East

Saint
Stephen's Green

TO NATIONAL CONCERT HALL AND
SUGAR CLUB

Fitzwilliam Ln

TO BALLSBRIDGE, MONKSTOWN, DÚN
LAOGHAIRE, BRAY, AND GREYSTONES

N

LG

0   200 meters

0   200 yards

orientation

salvage your Guinness fund. Even if you're not buying, though Grafton Street is a place you don't want to miss. Window shopping here is made more enjoyable by the presence of a hodgepodge collection of street performers who busk from dawn until dusk; the best acts come out on weekends.

O'CONNELL STREET

O'Connell Street, the main drag of its namesake neighborhood, runs north-south away from the Liffey. Most hostels are concentrated on **Gardiner Street,** which runs parallel to O'Connell St. and can be found a few blocks to the east. **Henry Street** intersects O'Connell St. about halfway up; follow it west, away from O'Connell, for great shopping. Most of the neighborhood's sights and restaurants (sometimes one and the same; see **The Church,** p. 36) are in the area west of O'Connell St; others can be found around **Parnell Square,** north of **Parnell Street.**

GEORGIAN DUBLIN

When you've had enough of Temple Bar's late-night shenanigans and Grafton Street has lost its charm (read: when your credit card maxes out), head west. Much like Temple Bar, **Georgian Dublin** is compact and raring to go; every corner offers a variety of things to see. This neighborhood is home to some of the city's most famous attractions: **Dublin Castle** and **St. Patrick's Cathedral** are located just south of **Lord Edward St.** Stretched out to the west, Georgian Dublin also includes some of Dublin's best (in our humble, alcohol-loving opinion) attractions: **The Guinness Factory** and **Jameson Distillery.**

NORTH OF O'CONNELL STREET

Something you should know about the area north of O'Connell Street: it's dodgy. As in, not a place you want to take Fluffy for a walk after dark. Located far past the Parnell Monument, this neighborhood has a few hostels and restaurants, but not enough to keep someone happy for more than a day or two. What you will find is an area with smaller and more local shops, and a much lower percentage of tourists on the sidewalk. There are things to see up here—the **Gardens of Remembrance** are worth a look, and the **Hugh Lane Gallery** might just beat out the **Irish Museum of Modern Art** in terms of scale and presentation. And of course, for all the Joyceans in the audience, the **James Joyce Centre** is just up the road on **North Great George's Street.**

accommodations

Expect to pay at least €15 per night for a hostel dorm room, sometimes more. Banking on the heavy party traffic, many establishments in Dublin have adopted weekend rates about 25% higher than weekday prices, so bear that in mind when planning your trip. Hostels on the north side will cost less, but you'll have to sacrifice proximity to Temple Bar and Grafton Street.

TEMPLE BAR AND THE QUAYS

Temple Bar accommodations are usually filled with young travelers—particularly backpackers—who are interested in going out and having a good time. Note that any hostel in the Temple Bar area is bound to be noisy at night, and you might have to deal with people coming into the dorm room at odd hours. Don't expect to sleep well, but do expect to have a roaring good time.

⬛ BARNACLES TEMPLE BAR HOUSE   HOSTEL $
19 Temple Ln. S.   ☎1 671 6277   www.barnacles.ie
The lime-green exterior of Barnacles makes it hard to miss, and you'll be glad for that. This gem of a hostel probably has the best location in Dublin, right in the

heart of Temple Bar. Barnacles attracts quite the crowd of partiers: grab a drink and head to the common room, where you'll have five new friends before you know it. For those bored of Dublin, try their "Coast to Coast Special": a night in Dublin, a bus to Galway (p. 74) and a day there, a night at the Barnacles Hostel in Galway, and a return bus to Dublin (€50).

☇ *Take Dame St. from Trinity College. Turn right onto Temple Ln. S.* **i** *Breakfast included. Free Wi-Fi. Laundry €8 per bag. Towel and lock rental €1.50, plus €5 returnable deposit.* Ⓢ *Dorms €10-33; private rooms €30-44.* Ⓩ *Reception 24hr.*

▨ ABBEY COURT   HOSTEL $
29 Bachelors Walk   ☏1 878 0700 www.abbey-court.com

Even though it's a hostel, the rooms at Abbey Court are not its biggest draw. Don't get us wrong, the rooms get the job done, but colorful, hand-painted signs will point you to the cinema, music room, game room, and smoking room. This hostel has so much to offer you might not even make it outside. Grab a giant beanbag from the hammock room and settle in; this home away from home might be one of the best parts of your trip.

☇ *From the O'Connell St. Bridge, turn onto Bachelors Walk, bordering the River Liffey.* **i** *Breakfast included. Free Wi-Fi.* Ⓢ *20-bed dorms M-Th €12, F-Sa €15, Su €12; 12-bed €15/18/15; 6-bed €18/22/18; 4-bed €23/26/23.*

LITTON LANE HOSTEL (SKY BACKPACKERS)   HOSTEL $$
Litton Ln.   ☏1 872 8389 www.skybackpackers.com

Stay right in the grit and grime of rock 'n' roll with none of the actual grit or grime. Housed in what used to be a recording studio for the likes of U2, Van Morrison, and the Cranberries, this hostel has since been completely remodeled. The rock vibe remains, however, as painted murals of artists and lyrics follow you down the hallways of each floor.

☇ *From O'Connell St. Bridge, take Bachelors Walk; turn right onto Litton Ln.* **i** *Shared bathrooms. Group discounts available.* Ⓢ *10-bed dorms €12-€14; 8-bed €13-€15; 6-bed €14-€16. Private twins €60; doubles €80; 3-bed apartment €75 per night.* Ⓩ *Reception 24hr.*

THE APACHE HOSTEL   HOSTEL $
29 Eustace St.   ☏1 677 1958 www.theapachehostel.com

For those who came to Dublin looking for that Native American touch, Apache is the place to go. Not the most engaging hostel in the Temple Bar area, Apache does boast a rooftop balcony and an attached restaurant with prices reduced 45% for hostel guests.

☇ *Take Dame St. from Trinity College and turn right onto Eustace St.* Ⓢ *Dorms 8-bed M-Th €12, F-Su €17; 6-bed €14/€19. Singles €18/€26. Doubles €22/€30.*

GRAFTON STREET

▨ AVALON HOUSE   HOSTEL $$
55 Aungier St.   ☏1 475 0001 www.avalon-house.ie

You probably won't want a legendary royal burial here, but the rooms are clean and well lit, if not exactly spacious. And those are just the perks. Check out the 12-bed room: that winding staircase in the middle is pretty cool. With bike rentals available and a sign at reception that tells you if it's raining, this hostel will have you ready to take Dublin by storm.

☇ *Follow S. Great Georges St. until it turns into Aungier St; the hostel is on the left.* **i** *Free Wi-Fi. Computers for guest use. Movie projector and DVD rental. Ping-pong. Pool table. Book exchange. ISA 10% student discount for the first night. Towels and lockers available for rent.* Ⓢ *12-bed dorms from €10; singles from €34; doubles from €54; quads from €64; triples from €66. Rates change daily, so check website for more information.* Ⓩ *Reception 24hr.*

THE TIMES HOSTEL HOSTEL $

8-9 Camden Pl. ☎1 475 8588 www.timeshostels.com

Camouflaged nicely and nestled into the surrounding buildings, the Times Hostel won't grab your attention as you pass. Luckily, we found it for you. With rates starting at €11, this place is definitely a sweet deal. Curl up in the blue beds at night where, unlike at noisy and excessively social Temple Bar hostels, you can expect a good night's sleep. Free breakfast, with traditional Irish pancakes on the weekends, will drag you out of bed by your nose, hangover and all.

 # Follow S. Great Georges St. until it turns into Aungier St., then Wexford St., then finally Lower Camden St. Take a left onto Camden Pl. i Breakfast and linens included. Free Wi-Fi. Cable TV. Free luggage storage. $ 6- to 12-bed mixed dorms €11-20; private doubles and quads €20-35. ⏰ Reception 24hr.

KELLYS HOTEL HOTEL $$$

36 S. Great Georges St. ☎1 648 0010 www.kellysdublin.com

Ultra-modern with a sort of farmhouse-chic style, Kelly's Hotel has personality. Antique doors and wine-barrel tables provide the rustic vibe, while the clean, minimalist rooms add some modern flair. The rooms are comfortable, with big beds and modern bathrooms, although doubles are on the smaller side. Free breakfast is provided for guests at Le Gueulenton next door. Both Kelly's Hotel and Grafton Guesthouse get noisy at night from the bars below, so make sure to request a quiet room if you want to sleep through the revelry.

 # From Grafton St., turn right onto Wicklow St., which quickly turns into Exchequer St. Turn left onto S. Great Georges St. and walk 1 block. Kelly's is on the left side of the street. i Breakfast included. No children. $ Doubles from €75. ⏰ Reception 24hr.

ALBANY HOUSE B&B $$$$

84 Harcourt St. ☎1 475 1092 www.albanyhousedublin.com

This one's a bit on the steep side in terms of price, but it's worth it. The Albany House is located in a wonderful Georgian home, with molding more elaborate than month-old bread. You're not likely to find another place this beautiful or full of old-world charm in Dublin (or all of Europe) for anything close to this price, so take advantage of it. This place fills up fast, so book ahead.

 # From the top of Grafton St., head toward and continue past St. Stephen's Green. Continue straight onto Harcourt St. Albany House is on the left. i Continental breakfast included. Free Wi-Fi in common areas. $ Singles from €50; doubles from €65. Check website for specific rates; expect an increase on the weekends and during the summer months. ⏰ Reception 24hr.

THE GRAFTON GUESTHOUSE HOTEL $$$

26-27 S. Great Georges St. ☎1 648 0010 www.graftonguesthouse.com

A less funky cousin of Kellys Hotel, The Grafton Guesthouse offers comfortable, if not very exciting, ensuite rooms. The creaking wooden stairs and high ceilings will only serve to remind you that you're residing in one of the oldest parts of Dublin, and the ruckus from the bars below will remind you that it's also one of the more lively. Try not to get overwhelmed by the massive amount of red accents (the rug, the chairs, the curtains, the brogue) that Grafton throws your way; it's the most stimulating part of the hotel.

 # From Grafton St., turn right onto Wicklow St., which quickly turns into Exchequer St. Turn left onto S. Great Georges St. and walk 1 block. Grafton Guesthouse is on the right. i Continental breakfast included. $ Singles from €59; doubles from €75. ⏰ Reception 24hr., located in Kelly's Hotel across the street.

O'CONNELL STREET

Gardiner Street might as well be called Hostel Row. There are tons of hostels, hotels, guesthouses, lodges, and B&Bs along the entire length of the street. If it's a place to stay in Dublin, chances are it's located here. The quick walk down to the city center and Temple Bar makes this area particularly appealing, although if you're coming back from a late night out, you'll want to be careful—a taxi might be the best bet.

GLOBETROTTERS HOSTEL HOSTEL $$

47-48 Lower Gardiner St. ☎1 873 5893 www.globetrottersdublin.com

There's a reason Hostelworld frequently ranks Globetrotters among its best accommodations—it lives up to its own high standards. An incredible variety of large and eclectically decorated common spaces will make it hard to leave the hostel. In fact, if you're staying in single or double rooms, dial "0" on your phone to order a drink from the bar and have it delivered to your room; you don't even need to leave.

From O'Connell Bridge, turn onto Eden Quay, then left onto Beresford Pl. When you hit Lower Gardiner St., turn left and walk 1 block. The hostel is on the left. ℹ *Free Wi-Fi. Linens included. Kitchen available. Free secure bicycle parking. Free luggage storage. Safety deposit boxes available for small fee. Private rooms ensuite and include breakfast.* $ *Dorms M-F €18, Sa-Su €20; singles €60-70; doubles €80-90.* ⏰ *Reception 24hr.*

ABRAHAM HOUSE HOSTEL $

82-83 Lower Gardiner St. ☎1 855 0600 www.abraham-house.ie

One of the good bargain options on Lower Gardiner St., beds here start out at just €9. There are no lockers—just a luggage storage room, so bring along your own lock or pay the €1 per night for a safety deposit box (plus a €10 deposit). The dorm rooms are small but clean and the common spaces are cheery and modern, if a bit cozy. Expect to meet some fun people over breakfast, as this hostel has a cool vibe.

From O'Connell Bridge, go up O'Connell St. Lower. Turn right onto Earl St. and continue as it turns into Talbot St. Turn left onto Lower Gardiner St.; Abraham House is on the right. ℹ *Breakfast and linens included. Free Wi-Fi in the lobby. Free luggage storage. All rooms ensuite. Bicycle parking available.* $ *20-bed dorms from €9, 10- to 12-bed from €10, 8-bed from €12, 6-bed from €14, 4-bed from €18. Doubles from €48; triples from €60. Expect a price increase for weekend and holiday stays.* ⏰ *Reception 24hr.*

DURBAN HOUSE B&B $$$

69 Lower Gardiner St. ☎1 836 4668 www.durbanresidence.com

A classic bed and breakfast with the occasional funky twist, Durban House will keep you on your toes. Big beds that beg you to fall asleep in them and wavy mirrors (that surprisingly don't make you look like a sideshow act) can be found in each room. The rooms themselves are handsome and modern, and the breakfast area is nothing short of adorable. Welcome to B&B life.

From O'Connell Bridge, turn onto Eden Quay, then left onto Beresford Pl. When you hit Lower Gardiner St., turn left and walk 2 blocks. The hostel is on your right. ℹ *Breakfast included. Private bathrooms. TV in each room. Free Wi-Fi.* $ *Rooms €30-60 during the week, more expensive on weekends.* ⏰ *Reception 24hr.*

MY PLACE DUBLIN HOSTEL, HOTEL $

89-90 Lower Gardiner St. ☎1 707 2894 www.myplacedublin.ie

This place boasts good rates, but little else. Don't come here expecting a social hub with lively common areas: the common room is standard, offering Wi-Fi, couches to lounge on, and a few brochures to peruse, but lacking any sort of fun atmosphere. Don't expect to make fast friends here, but expect a good night's sleep.

From O'Connell Bridge, go up O'Connell St. Lower. Turn right onto Earl St., and continue as it turns into Talbot St. Turn left onto Lower Gardiner St.; My Place Dublin is on the right. ℹ *Breakfast available but not included in the price. Free Wi-Fi in public areas. Linens included. Kitchen, security safes, and lockers available. Free luggage storage on arrival. Free guided walking tours daily.* $ *Hostel: 20-bed dorms €8-10; 10- and 12-bed €9-11; 8-bed €10-12; 4-bed €14-20. Weekly dorms from €60. Hotel: singles from €35, doubles from €49, triples from €69. Prices increase on weekends.* ⏰ *Reception 24hr.*

ABBOTT LODGE
HOTEL $$$

87-88 Lower Gardiner St. ☎1 836 5548 www.abbottlodge.com

Abbott's rooms are a breath of fresh air compared to the rest of the hotels and hostels around. Floral bedspreads and a little extra space place this inviting hotel just a step above its competition. If you book at least two weeks in advance, you can get a room at a decent price.

🍴 *From O'Connell Bridge, go straight up O'Connell St. Lower. Take a right on Earl St., keep going as it turns into Talbot St. Take a left onto Lower Gardiner St. Abbott Lodge will be on your right.* ***i*** *Breakfast included; full Irish 8:30-10am, Continental before 8:30am. Free Wi-Fi.* Ⓢ *Singles from €30; doubles €50.* 🕐 *Reception 24hr.*

HAZEL BROOK GUEST HOUSE
B&B $$$

85-86 Lower Gardiner St. ☎1 836 5003 www.hazelbrookhouse.ie

Don't expect inspiring decor or spacious quarters, but this homey B&B can serve as a comfortable base for exploring Dublin; fuel up on the hearty Irish breakfast and hit the town.

🍴 *From O'Connell Bridge, go up O'Connell St. Lower. Turn right onto Earl St., and continue as it turns into Talbot St. Take a left onto Lower Gardiner St.; Hazel Brook will be on your right.* ***i*** *Breakfast included. Cable TV available. Free Wi-Fi.* Ⓢ *Rooms €40-100+ depending on the day.*

GEORGIAN DUBLIN

Also known as Viking Dublin, this area of the city gets fewer tourists than Temple Bar, so it's a great option if you're looking for a quiet night. For a few extra euro and a 5min. walk, these listings will guarantee you a nearly silent night's sleep.

🏨 FOUR COURTS HOSTEL
HOSTEL $$

15-17 Merchants Quay ☎1 672 5839 www.fourcourtshostel.com

This might just be the best hostel in Dublin; at the very least, it's among the most fun-loving. The staff are determined to keep things lighthearted, evidenced by the tip jar that reads, "Staff Drink fund: We need beer!" Tons of services (DVD, Wii, and guitar rental, to name a few) are all available with the presentation of ID. The dorms themselves are comfortable, with lofty ceilings that reduce stuffiness but amplify snores.

🍴 *From Grattan Bridge, head down Essex Quay as it turns into Wood Quay and then Merchants Quay. Hostel is on the left.* ***i*** *Breakfast included. 24hr. cancellation policy. Free Wi-Fi.* Ⓢ *8- and 10-bed dorms €16-27, 6-bed €18-32, 4-bed €19-34. Family rooms €20-36 per person. Singles €45-55, with bathroom €50-60.* 🕐 *Reception 24hr. Check-out 10:30am.*

🏨 KINLAY HOSTEL
HOSTEL $$

2-12 Lord Edward St. ☎1 679 6644 www.kinlaydublin.ie

A smiling cartoon Viking couple greets you as you walk in: greet them with a kind word or challenge them to grab their tankards and have a drinking match. Kinlay escapes the noise of Temple Bar but certainly not the fun. Standard rooms are nothing to call home about, but there is free dinner. That's right—Monday through Thursday, go crazy on the included meal, which fills you up while you get to know that cute fellow traveler you've been eyeing.

🍴 *From Trinity College, take Dame St. and continue as it turns into Lord Edward St.* ***i*** *Breakfast included. Free Wi-Fi. Kitchen available.* Ⓢ *12-, 16-, and 20-bed dorms €15; 4-, 5-, 6-, and 8-bed dorms €16; private doubles €50.* 🕐 *Reception 24hr.*

GENERATOR HOSTEL DUBLIN
HOSTEL $$

Smithfield Sq. ☎1 901 0222 www.generatorhostels.com/dublin

Located in one of Dublin's newer neighborhoods, Generator's wine-bottle lights and book-supported tables give this hostel a high-tech-meets-hipster-meets-creative juices vibe. The clean-cut rooms are truly the only part of the hostel that is really simple, but travelers will find comfort here nonetheless.

From O'Connell Bridge, take Bachelors Walk and continue until it becomes Arran Quay. Turn right onto Lincoln Ln. and follow it as it turns into Bow St. Turn left onto New Church St. and then right onto Smithfield Sq. ***i*** *Free Wi-Fi. Kitchen available. Becomes a public bar on weekend nights.* [$] *Dorms from €15; doubles from €60.* ⏰ *Reception 24hr.*

NORTH OF O'CONNELL STREET

As you head north of O'Connell Street and start to get into the outskirts of Dublin's city center, you're looking at a long walk or a bus ride into town. That said, it can be a nice escape. Nevertheless, be careful and plan your return if you plan on staying out late at night. Walking is not recommended, and the buses stop running at 11:30pm, so make sure to set aside some cash for a taxi home.

ASHLING HOUSE/AZALEA LODGE — B&B $$$$

Ashling: 168 Upper Drumcondra Rd. ☎1 837 0300 www.ashlinghouse.ie
Azalea: 67 Upper Drumcondra Rd. www.azalealodge.com

Owned by the same couple, these two B&Bs might just be the greatest thing since sliced bread. Or, maybe since scones, which you'll receive upon entering the Azalea Lodge. Breakfast at the Ashling is Continental, which is reflected in the slightly cheaper prices. But if you're willing to splurge, everything in the full Irish breakfast at Azalea is fresh and cooked to order. Amazing.

From O'Connell St., continue past the Rotunda Hospital onto Frederick St. N. Turn right onto Dorset St. and continue as it becomes Drumcondra Rd. The hostel is about a mile up the road. ***i*** *Breakfast included. All rooms ensuite.* [$] *Ashling House singles from €40; doubles from €48; family rooms from €20 per person. Azalea Lodge singles from €55; twins and doubles from €90; family rooms from €35 per person.*

THE DUBLIN CENTRAL HOSTEL — HOSTEL $

5 Blessington St. ☎86 104 3490 www.thedublincentralhostel.com

With bright colors in the hallways and a cheerily furnished common room that really lifts your mood, this hostel has some personality. The bedrooms are quieter, which should help you sleep after a long day of exploring. Not a lot of room options means you should either book far ahead of time or travel in groups of four so you can rent out an entire quad.

From the top of Parnell Sq., head up Frederick St. N.; cross Dorset St. and continue onto Blessington St. ***i*** *Breakfast included. Free Wi-Fi. Lockers included for those staying under 1 week. All rooms ensuite.* [$] *8-bed dorms €10-14; 4-bed €12-16. Private doubles €40-50.*

DUBLIN INTERNATIONAL — HOSTEL $

61 Mountjoy St. ☎1 830 1766 www.anoige.ie

It may feel like you're entering a high-security area as you walk inside, but don't worry—it's just the hostel's safety precautions. This place has clean rooms, and lots of 'em. With just a few couches and a pool table, the common room is not noteworthy, but the staff is fantastic and will provide the entertainment you need. Sit back and watch them fling good-hearted insults at each other, or join in if you think you can handle it.

From O'Connell St., turn left onto Parnell St. and right onto Parnell Sq. Continue as it becomes Granby Row, then St. Mary's Pl. Turn right onto Mountjoy St. [$] *10-bed dorms €15, 8-bed €22, €6-bed €24.* ***i*** *Breakfast and lockers included. Free Wi-Fi. Free parking.* ⏰ *Reception 24hr.*

CELTS HOUSE — HOSTEL $

32 Blessington St. ☎1 260 9280

With no frills and no hidden fees (and hardly any visible fees), Celts is the bare minimum. It's clean enough, meaning there is no visible dirt, but the place isn't terribly inspiring. You'd better bring your own character here; the place is literally a blank canvas of white walls and brown chairs.

‡ Take O'Connell St. until it turns into Frederick St. N. Continue straight and then make a slight left onto Blessington St. $ 10- and 12-bed dorms €15; 6- and 8-bed €22; twins €25 per person.

PARKWAY B&B $$$

5 Gardiner Pl. ☎1 874 0469 www.parkwaydublin.com

Don't let the flickering gas station-like sign out front deter you—this is actually a pretty nice place to stay. Leather couches and wooden tables class up both the common room and dining area. The rooms are more interesting than the typical white shoebox found in most budget accommodations, and some beds can be found in their own little nook. If you're looking for a quiet place outside of the city center, this is a good find.

‡ Take Lower Gardiner St. away from the river, then turn left onto Gardiner Pl. Parkway is on the right.
i Breakfast included. Free Wi-Fi. All rooms ensuite. $ €40 per person, per night. ⏰ Reception 24hr.

sights

Dublin is not a huge city. For the rushed traveler, the city's hotspot sights can be hit in less than a day, and the dedicated might find that a 3hr. walking tour is enough. Those who can, however, should dig a little deeper. Dublin is a city rich with history, and its sights won't let you forget it. From the city's early roots and its Viking period to the War of Independence, Dublin—like rock 'n' roll—never forgets.

TEMPLE BAR AND THE QUAYS

Sights in the Temple Bar area are packed close together, making tourist life a breeze. And the Quays? Hit the river and run in either direction.

WALL OF FAME WALL

Temple Lane, Temple Bar ☎1 602 9202 www.visitdublin.com

See Sinéad O'Connor staring down at you? A young U2 doing their best to look cool? You're probably at the Wall of Fame. We don't recommend standing right in front of the wall and craning your neck to see; it's pretty uncomfortable and makes you a nice target for any nearby pickpockets. Grab a seat on the outdoor patio of one of the cafes across the street, and get an eyeful of Ireland's top 12.

‡ From Trinity College, head down College Green and continue as it turns into Dame St.; turn right onto Temple Ln. and go 2 blocks. $ Free.

GALLERY OF PHOTOGRAPHY GALLERY

Meeting House Sq., Temple Bar ☎1 671 4654 www.galleryofphotography.ie

Showcasing the work of students and professionals alike, the Gallery of Photography makes good use of its two stories of winding space. The exhibits, which change every two months or so, have included everything from "Creativity in Older Age" to "Under a Grey Sky." An hour or two spent perusing the photos makes for a wonderful—and free, free is always good—activity. Check out the large selection of photography books or pick up a postcard in the lobby.

‡ From Dame St., turn onto Eustace St., walk ½ block, and turn left into Meeting House Sq. $ Free. ⏰ Open Tu-Sa 11am-6pm, Su 1-6pm.

IRISH FILM INSTITUTE CINEMA

6 Eustace St. ☎1 679 5744 www.irishfilm.ie

Walking down a long hallway paved in movie reels and plastered with classic movie posters, this refurbished Quaker building is a movie junkie's dream come true. Skylights let the natural light filter in as you enjoy a drink from the bar or a bite to eat from the restaurant. Check out the in-house DVD store, then hit up the cinema; be sure to see the indie and Irish flicks. Also look for the monthly director's retrospectives; if the director is Irish, you might just get to attend a Q-and-A session.

From Dame St., turn onto Eustace St. The Irish Film Institute is halfway down the block on the left. $ Movie tickets €7.50 until 6pm, €8.90 after 6pm. ⏰ Film institute open M-F 10am-6pm; cinema open M-F 10am-9:30pm.

THE NATIONAL WAX MUSEUM PLUS MUSEUM, TOURIST TRAP

4 Foster Pl. ☎1 671 8373 www.waxmuseumplus.ie

This is how wax museums should be: the wax statues are so realistic, you could swear you saw them move. Oh wait, some of them do move. Get your educational quota out of the way early (start with the "Writers' Room" and "History Vaults") and then move on to the fun stuff (Hannibal horror rooms and waxen celebrities). Get closer to Pierce Brosnan's ruggedly strong chin than you ever thought possible, but watch out for Frankenstein (people run screaming from that room for a reason).

From Trinity College, head down College Green and turn right onto Foster Pl.; the museum is on the left. i Horror Room has a parental advisory for those 16 and under. $ €12, students and seniors €10, children €8, family €35. ⏰ Open daily 10am-7pm.

DUBLIN GRAPHIC STUDIO GALLERY GALLERY

"Through the arch" off Cope St. ☎1 679 8021 www.graphicstudiodublin.com

White walls and light wood floors give this gallery an ethereal look. In this artist-owned gallery where 99% percent of the works on display are up for sale, any purchase you make will help fund both artist workshops and the awards given to local art students. But even if you're not buying, the gallery is a great stop. Free postcards of the prints are available: be creative and send home some artwork to Mom and Dad.

From Dame St., turn onto Anglesea St., then take 1st left onto Cope St. Head through the archway on the right. $ Prices vary. ⏰ Open M-F 10am-5:30pm, Sa 11am-5pm.

GRAFTON STREET

TRINITY COLLEGE UNIVERSITY

College Green ☎1 896 1000 www.tcd.ie

Jump on a tour of Trinity College and follow in the footsteps of greats like Joyce, Swift, and oh, yes, your ever-sassy student tour guide. Ghosts and deadly student feuds await you, as do stories told with all the college sarcasm money can buy. Your guide leaves you at what seems like too long of a line to the Old Library; be patient, and you will be rewarded with the famous **Book of Kells.** The book itself is housed in a dark and crowded room, so you have to squint and jostle around to get a good look. More easily enjoyed is the Long Room, a wonderful, wood-paneled room that stretches the length of the building and houses shelves upon shelves of some of the university's oldest and rarest books. A rotating themed exhibit is available for perusal in the glass display cases that run the length of the room.

From O'Connell Bridge, follow Westmoreland St. for 5min.; Trinity College is on the left. $ Tour plus admission to the Old Library and Book of Kells €10, tour without admission to library €5, admission to library without tour €9. ⏰ Tours M-Sa roughly every 30min. 10:15am-12:45pm and every 45min. 2:15-3:40pm.

ST. STEPHEN'S GREEN PARK

St. Stephen's Green ☎1 475 1816 www.heritageireland.ie

If you're looking for the best place to chase pigeons in Ireland, this might be it. If you're looking for a little peace and woodsy quiet, St. Stephen's Green does that well, too. At the man-made pond in the middle, you will find groomed gardens and palm trees (yes, palm trees) swaying casually in the center of Dublin. Take a break from the shopping and soak up the sun (or the slightly cool, most likely rainy weather). At least there are palm trees.

From Trinity College, take Grafton St. until the end. $ Free. ⏰ Open daily 7:30am-dusk.

NATIONAL LIBRARY OF IRELAND LIBRARY

2-3 Kildare St. ☎1 603 0200 www.nli.ie

The main show, so to speak, is the exhibit detailing the life and works of **William Butler Yeats,** whose poems are read aloud in a lilting Irish accent as you wander through the exhibit. It's more Yeats than you ever thought possible; intellectuals discussing him, old journals of his on display, and—wait, is that a lock of his hair? Yes. Yes, it is. The Irish love their Yeats, and if you do, too, then this is a must-see.

🪧 Follow Nassau St. along Trinity College; turn right onto Kildare St. The library is on the left. $ Free. ⏰ Open M-W 9:30am-7:30pm, Th-F 9:30am-4:45pm, Sa 9:30am-4:30pm. Guided tours W 1pm and Sa 3pm.

NATIONAL GALLERY OF IRELAND MUSEUM

Merrion Sq. W. ☎1 661 5133 www.nationalgallery.ie

While you're on the museum kick, head to the National Gallery, home of the Irish Masterpieces Collection. Get an eyeful of Ireland's other Yeats (Jack B.) and his dark, slightly abstract works, or head to the ever-so-Irish *Dubliners* display. Don't like art? (Or just don't appreciate the less-than-renowned work of Irish painters?) It's still worth the trip. The cafe has all-organic, all-delicious selections. Get some work done with the free Wi-Fi while simultaneously stuffing your face with some ham and white cheddar quiche (€8.95).

🪧 From Trinity College, take Nassau St. Continue as it turns into Leinster St. S. and then Clare St. Take a right onto Merrion Sq. W. $ Free. ⏰ Open M-W 9:30am-5:30pm, Th 9:30am-8:30pm, F-Sa 9:30am-5:30pm, Su noon-5:30pm, public holidays 10am-5:30pm.

NATURAL HISTORY MUSEUM MUSEUM

Merrion St. ☎1 677 7444 ext. 361 www.museum.ie

The ground floor of this museum houses fauna from all over the island, including skeletons of the Ancient Irish Elk (it's like Bambi from Hell), as well as tons of other birds, bugs, and fish. If you haven't gotten your preserved dead-animal fix for the day, head to the Kingship and Sacrifice exhibition, home to bodies found preserved in Irish bogs. Hair, skin, and fingernails are all still intact: this display is not for those with a weak stomach.

🪧 Follow Nassau St. as it turns into Leinster St. and then Clare St.; turn right onto Merrion Sq. W. The museum is on the right. $ Free. ⏰ Open Tu-Sa 10am-5pm, Su 2-5pm.

O'CONNELL STREET

👍 **JAMES JOYCE STATUE** STATUE

Grab a photo with one of Ireland's biggest names ever. Jauntily leaning into everyone who puts their arm around him, the Joyce statue provides a photo-op for an oh-so-Irish souvenir from Dublin.

🪧 From O'Connell Bridge, take O'Connell St. Lower; statue will be at the intersection with Earl St.

THE NATIONAL LEPRECHAUN MUSEUM MUSEUM

1 Jervis St. ☎1 873 3899 www.leprechaunmuseum.ie

If you're really feeling your inner child, this is a fun way to spend the afternoon. Be warned, though: your inner adult might not have a blast. A mix of folklore, mythology, and pure childish fun, the tour attempts to simulate what it would be like to be a leprechaun. Bring a lot of imagination, and get ready for the mandatory coloring at the end.

🪧 From O'Connell Bridge, take Bachelors Walk. Continue onto Lower Ormond Quay, then take a right onto Jervis St. $ €10, students and children €8.50, families €30. ⏰ Open daily 10am-6:30pm.

MONUMENT OF LIGHT MONUMENT

More colloquially known as the Spire, this 393ft. phallic wonder makes it hard to ever get truly lost north of the River Liffey. Follow the Spire to hit Henry St., the jackpot of cheap shopping options.

From O'Connell Bridge, take O'Connell St. Lower. The Spire is at the intersection of O'Connell St. and Henry St. $ Free.

GEORGIAN DUBLIN

DUBLIN CASTLE CASTLE, GOVERNMENT BUILDING

Off Dame St. ☎1 645 8813 www.dublincastle.ie

The original Dublin Castle, built by the English in the 13th century, burned down in an accidental fire (ouch). The castle was rebuilt in the 18th century and was the headquarters of British rule in Ireland until the Irish Revolution in 1920. Today, it's a series of government buildings, which doesn't sound nearly as cool as a burned-out castle. The tour will take you through several impressive state rooms, including the blue-carpeted ballroom where the President of Ireland's inauguration takes place. The tour ends in the bowels of one of the castle's original towers. You can see the darkly colored waters that once formed a pool in the castle gardens, giving the city its name—*Dubh* (black) and *Linn* (pool).

Walk over the O'Connell Bridge past Temple Bar and turn right onto Dame St. Follow Dame St. for 10min.; Dublin Castle is on the left. $ €5.50, students and seniors €4.50, under 12 €2. ⏰ Open M-F 10am-4:45pm, Sa-Su and public holidays 2-4:45pm.

JAMESON DISTILLERY MUSEUM

7 Bow St. ☎1 807 2355 www.jamesonwhiskey.com

Hurray! A tour that rewards you with free drinks! Volunteer at the beginning of the tour for an opportunity to become an official whiskey taster, certificate and all. Not up to the task? Don't worry, everyone gets a taste of the famous Irish whiskey at the end of the hour-long tour. Spend some time in the cask room; the evaporating whiskey gives the air a sweet vanilla scent. Because even angels drink Jameson. Especially angels.

From the O'Connell Bridge, take Bachelors Walk and continue as it becomes Ormond Quay, Inns Quay, and finally Arran Quay. Turn right onto Church St., then turn left onto May Ln. $ €12.50, students €10.50. ⏰ Open M-Sa 9am-6pm. Tours every 15min.

ST. PATRICK'S CATHEDRAL CATHEDRAL

Patrick St. ☎1 453 9472 www.stpatrickscathedral.ie

It should come as no surprise that a church named for St. Patrick is one of Dublin's must-see sights. The sky-high archways house exhibits of Ireland's holy history and the legends that go with it. Come pay tribute to Ireland's favorite saint or just to the amazing architects of year 1191 CE. Be sure to leave some time to lounge in the gardens out front—the views of the cathedral's exterior are quite a backdrop for a lazy afternoon.

Follow Dame St. until it turns into Lord Edward St, then Christ Church Pl. Turn left onto Nicholas St., which turns into Patrick St. The Cathedral is on the left. $ €5.50, students and seniors €4.50. ⏰ Open M-F 9am-5pm, Sa 9am-6pm, Su 12:30-2:30pm and 4:30-6pm.

DUBLINIA MUSEUM

St. Michael's Hill ☎1 679 4611 www.dublinia.ie

Ah, yes, those terribly misunderstood creatures of the past—the Vikings. At least that's what this museum would have you believe. Giving rare insight into the non-pillaging, non-raping side of these Scandinavian terrors, Dublinia is an eye-opening look into the other side of Viking life—and we mean all aspects of Viking life. (Was the outhouse exposé necessary?)

Follow Dame St. until it turns into Lord Edward St. and then Christchurch Pl. Dublinia is across from Christ Church Cathedral. $ €7.50, students €6.50, children €5. ⏰ Open daily 9:30am-5pm.

GARDA MEMORIAL GARDEN PARK

Santry Business Park

If you're starting to get weary from all the sightseeing, head to this park. Great views of Dublin Castle, Chester Beatty Library, and the Coach House wait you. *Let's Go* enjoys lying in the grass and listening to the trickling waterfall—not a bad way to spend an afternoon.

From Dame St., turn left onto Castle St.; the park is across from the Dublin Castle. [$] Free. Open daily 9:30am-5:30pm.

WEST OF TEMPLE BAR

GUINNESS STOREHOUSE BREWERY

St. James's Gate ☎1 408 4800 www.guinness-storehouse.com

This isn't a tour. It's an ambush (albeit a welcome one) of everything Guinness. The old brewery has been transformed into an overload of information that requires every one of your senses to take it in. At the Guinness Storehouse, you can examine old Guinness ads, learn how to drink a pint properly (free samples!), and even enjoy a free mug of Guinness at the Gravity Bar, a circular glass bar that overlooks all of Dublin. **Tl;dr:** great tour, great views, free beer. Sound good? You betcha.

Follow Dame St. as it turns into High St., then Cornmarket, and then Thomas St. Turn left onto Crane St. i Tour brochures available in multiple languages. [$] €15, students and seniors €11, students under 18 €9, children 6-12 €5. Open daily July-Aug 9:30am-7pm; Sept-June 9:30am-5pm.

KILMAINHAM GAOL MUSEUM, JAIL

Inchicore Rd. ☎1 453 5984 www.heritageireland.ie/en/dublin/kilmainhamgaol

This former prison holds the secrets to nearly every street name, monument, and government building in Dublin. The 45min. required tour digs into the gritty details of Ireland's fight for independence. Why here? First built by the British, most of the major Irish leaders were at one point jailed or put to death here. Take our word for it:, history becomes a little too real when you stand in the same place as firing-squad victims.

From Christ Church Cathedral, take Thomas St.; continue as it turns into James's St. Stick to the right of the fork to continue onto Bow Ln., and continue as it turns into Kilmainham Ln. Take a right onto S. Circular Rd., then the 1st left onto Inchicore Rd. i Guided tour mandatory. [$] €6, students and children €2, families €14. Open daily Apr-Sept 9:30am-6pm; Oct-Mar M-Sa 9:30am-5:30pm, Su 10am-6pm.

PHOENIX PARK PARK

Parkgate St. www.phoenixpark.ie

It's a bit of a hike from the city center, but this park is bursting with a full day's worth of activities. Come with a picnic lunch; any spot in the 1752-acre grounds makes for a good place to sit and relax a while. The visitor's center is itself a sight: it's located in the **Ashtown Castle,** which dates back to the 15th century. You also probably noticed the **Wellington Testimonial,** the tallest obelisk in Europe (62m). A tribute to the Duke of Wellington, the bronze plaques at the base are cast from cannons. The **Magazine Fort** is closed to the public, but a climb to the hilltop where it's located gives good views of the city. The giant white cross commemorates the Pope's visit in 1979, a day that any Irish citizen over 40 still remembers. Phoenix Park is also home to many recreational facilities, including camogie fields, football fields, polo grounds, and a model airplane arena, to name a few.

Take bus #37, 38, 39, or 70. i Concerts held in summer; check website for details. [$] Free. Open 24hr., but Let's Go does not recommend visiting after dark.

NATIONAL MUSEUM OF IRELAND: DECORATIVE ARTS AND HISTORY MUSEUM

Collins Barracks, Benburb St. ☎1 677 7444 www.museum.ie

One would think that housing both an Irish military history museum and a decorative arts museum under the same roof would cause some confusion and painfully little overlap of interests. And one would be right in so thinking. Fortunately, this gigantic former military barracks that is now home to both is big enough that it's not really an issue. Even if neither museum appeals to you, the impressively huge courtyard bordered on all sides by the historic building is well worth the trip.

🚶 From the O'Connell Bridge, take Bachelors Walk and continue as it becomes Ormond Quay, Inns Quay, and finally Arran Quay. Turn right onto Queen St., then left onto Benburb St. ℹ No photos of the exhibits allowed. $ Free. ⏰ Open Tu-Sa 10am-5pm, Su 2-5pm.

IRELAND MUSEUM OF MODERN ART (IMMA) MUSEUM

Royal Hospital, Military Rd., Kilmainham ☎1 612 9900 www.imma.ie

A long walk through the immaculately tended park gets you to the IMMA. Usually housing three or four separate exhibits, the long halls and quiet atmosphere of the IMMA are perfect for contemplating whether the artist you're seeing was actually influenced by Jackson Pollock or just spilled some extra paint on the canvas.

🚶 From Christ Church Cathedral, take Thomas St. and continue as it turns into James's St. Stay to the right at the fork and head onto Bow Ln.; continue as it turns into Kilmainham Ln. Turn right onto S. Cicular Rd. The museum is immediately on the right. ℹ Free guided tours every W, F, and Su at 2:30pm. $ Free. ⏰ Open Tu 10am-5:30pm, W 10:30am-5:30pm, Th-Sa 10am-5:30pm, Su noon-5:30pm.

NORTH OF O'CONNELL STREET

For the **Hugh Lane Gallery** and the **Garden of Remembrance,** head behind the Parnell Monument to the northern end of Parnell Square. Leaving the Hugh Lane Gallery, turn left to get to the **Writers Museum;** the **James Joyce Centre** is just a few blocks down in the same direction.

sights

👍 **GARDEN OF REMEMBRANCE** PUBLIC PARK

1 Parnell Sq. E. ☎1 821 3021 superintendent.park@opw.ie

This garden is a true delight for the senses. Seriously: the cruciform pool sparkles with vibrant blue mosaics, the city noises recede, and something—probably either the flowers or the happiness—smells really, really good. The twisting statue of falling Irishmen and flying geese is a bit too symbolic to handle; sit for a minute or two and take it all in. Keep off the grass, though—the Irish like to keep their lawns green.

🚶 Take O'Connell St. Upper, continue as it becomes Parnell St., then turn left onto Parnell Sq. N. $ Free. ⏰ Open daily Apr-Sept 8:30am-6pm; Oct-Mar 9:30am-4pm.

JAMES JOYCE CENTRE MUSEUM

35 N. Great George's St. ☎1 878 8547 www.jamesjoyce.ie

You can find those that claim to understand *Ulysses*, but we know better. The James Joyce Centre is part museum, part headquarters for Joyce fanatics in Dublin and, mecca for Joyce fanatics from around the globe. And trust us, there are plenty. Pieces to note include a copy of Joyce's deathmask, a table at which part of *Ulysses* was written, and the door to 7 Eccles St., the fictional residence of Leopold Bloom.

🚶 From the O'Connell Bridge, walk up O'Connell St. to the Parnell Statue; turn right onto Parnell St. and then left onto N. Great Georges St. ℹ Group discounts available. $ €5, students and seniors €4. ⏰ Open Tu-Sa 10am-5pm, Su noon-5pm.

DUBLIN WRITERS MUSEUM MUSEUM

18 Parnell Sq. ☎1 872 2077 www.writersmuseum.com

James Joyce may have his own digs just up the road, but Ireland's other literary greats are surely not forgotten. The Dublin Writers Museum showcases old manuscripts, first editions, and tons of memorabilia and journals galore. You don't need to like Irish literature to enjoy a visit here: the building itself, former home of John Jameson, is worth the trip. Stained-glass windows and marble archways? Looks like whiskey's not a bad business in Ireland.

⇆ From the O'Connell Bridge, head up O'Connell St. Continue onto Parnell St., then turn left onto Parnell Sq. N.; the museum is on the right. $ €7.50, students and seniors €6.30, children €4.70, families €18.70. ⏰ Open M-Sa 10am-5pm, Su 11am-5pm. Last entry 45min. before close.

HUGH LANE GALLERY GALLERY

22 Parnell Sq. N. ☎1 222 5550 www.hughlane.ie

An exact replica of one of Francis Bacon's studios has been brought in and assembled right in the gallery, so now you can see just how much disorder it takes to create the art that adorns its walls. Work up an appetite as you wander; the cafe is waiting in the basement. (Isn't that always everyone's favorite part?)

⇆ At the northern end of Parnell Sq., across the street from the Gardens of Remembrance. From the O'Connell St. Bridge, head up O'Connell St. Continue onto Parnell St., then turn left onto Parnell Sq. N.; the gallery is on the right. ℹ Cafe and bookstore downstairs. $ Free. Suggested donation €2. ⏰ Open Tu-Th 10am-6pm, F-Sa 10am-5pm, Su 11am-5pm.

food

Contrary to popular belief, Dublin's food is quite good. Sure, there are a lot of boiled and fried foods liberally doused in salt, but time and practice have honed those dishes down to their delicious cores. Potato haters need not worry, though—a huge variety of ethnic restaurants can be found all over the city too. Unfortunately, it's easy to find a bad fast-food chain as well. As a rule of thumb, just remember: if it smells the same back home as it does in Dublin, shy away.

TEMPLE BAR AND THE QUAYS

If there's a place to escape Ireland's infamy as a country with "bad" or "dull" food options, that place is Temple Bar. It's got traditional Irish fare, but it's also become quite the cosmopolitan neighborhood, so you won't have far to go to find several international options.

★ **PANEM** CAFE $

21 Lower Ormond Quay ☎1 872 8510

Run by a Sicilian man and his Irish wife, Panem has got your coffee and pastry fix covered. It's a tight squeeze into the tiny cafe, where you will be surrounded by Irish regulars and curious travelers all eyeing up the quiche and hot ham sandwiches on display. With imported Italian coffee (€2.50-3) and mind-meltingly delicious Sicilian almond biscuits (just €1 each), don't be surprised if Panem becomes your morning, afternoon, and evening ritual.

⇆ Cross the Millennium Bridge from Temple Bar. $ Sweets from €0.90. Sandwiches as much as €6.50. Cash only. ⏰ Open M-Sa 9am-5:30pm.

★ **HALF MOON CREPES** CAFE $

5 Crown Alley ☎1 649 3748 www.halfmoon.ie

Hand made crepes—check. Nutella—check. An option for bacon on anything—check! If you're looking for a deal, Half Moon offers giant, (we're talking 2ft. in diameter) crepes from €3.50. Go for a meal (we recommend the Traditional Irish) or stop by for something sweet (ice cream and Nutella, anyone?). Open early, with a good coffee selection, this cafe has got your day covered from start to finish.

⇆ From Dame St., turn onto Anglesea St., then left onto Cope St., and finally right onto Crown Alley. ℹ Free Wi-Fi. $ Crepes start at €3.50. Wine €3.50. ⏰ Open M-Th 10am-8:30pm, F-Sa 10am-12:30am, Su 10am-8:30pm.

TERRA MADRE ITALIAN $$

13A Bachelors Walk ☎1 873 5300

Escape the clamor of the Quays and dip into Terra Madre's basement restaurant. Mismatched chairs give a casual, eclectic vibe, but it's not the chairs you're there for. It's the oh-so-mouth-watering pasta and panini that make this place hard to beat. Try the Gricia, made with pig's cheek, if you're feeling adventurous.

From the O'Connell Bridge, turn left onto Bachelors Walk. i Stop by early in the day to make a reservation. $ Entrees €6.50-13. Open M-Sa 12:20-3pm and 5-10pm.

GALLAGHER'S BOXTY HOUSE TRADITIONAL $$$

20-21 Temple Bar ☎1 677 2762 www.boxtyhouse.ie

Nearly all of the pubs in the Temple Bar area serve some kind of Irish food, but Gallagher's takes it a step further than the rest. An interior most reminiscent of a 19th-century Irish household gives off a welcoming, comforting vibe—it's as though you're eating in a home in the Irish countryside. Try some Boxty (a potato dish offered in ten different variations), and be sure to pair it with a Beamish stout if you want to fit in with the rest of the diners.

On Temple Bar, just off Anglesea St. $ Appetizers €4-11. Entrees €19-23. Open daily 11am-11pm.

BOTTICELLI ICE CREAM $

3 Temple Bar ☎1 672 7289 www.botticelli.ie

Providing Temple Bar's ice cream fix, Botticelli serves Italian gelato in cups or cones (€2.50-5). If you happen to think cones are too mainstream, liven things up with the spaghetti ice (a bowl of vanilla gelato, slathered with strawberry sauce and sprinkled with some shaved white chocolate as a "cheesy" topping; €6.50). Not a spaghetti fan? Maybe the gelato pizza (€7.50) will do it.

From Dame St., turn onto Temple Ln. S. and follow it to the intersection of Temple Bar. i Cash only. Open daily 11am-midnight.

ISKANDER'S LATE NIGHT $

30 Dame St. ☎1 670 4013

After a long night of drinking, you'll swear the food here is the greatest thing you've ever eaten. And it's good sober, too. Iskander's is a Dublin institution and its massive shawarma with fries and a Coke (€10) should not be missed. They do deem themselves "shawarma specialists," after all.

From Trinity College, go down College Green onto Dame St. Continue 1 block and Iskander's is on the left. i Cash only. Open daily 11am-4:30am.

MILANO ITALIAN $$

19 E. Essex St. ☎1 670 3384 www.milano.ie

This joint serves fresh, made-in-front-of-you pizzas in both "classic" or "romana" style (i.e., with a thinner, crispier crust), as designed by star BBC chef Valentine Warner. The modern interior, with sweeping lines and tiny table lamps, ensures a pleasant evening for both families and students, even in the rowdy Temple Bar area. For a more intimate setting, head down the winding staircase to the basement.

From Dame St., turn onto Eustace St. and walk 1 block to the intersection with Temple Bar. $ Pizza €7-15. Open M-Sa noon-10:30pm, Su noon-10pm.

TANTE ZOE'S CREOLE $$$

1 Crow St. ☎1 679 4407

The food is all Creole, all the time (jambalayas and gumbos are the *plats du jour, toujours*), but the ambience is divided—sit upstairs for the feel of a French bistro or head downstairs for a close-quartered jazz club. Come on Saturday nights with hopes to hear the singing waitress.

From Dame St., make a right onto Crow St. (1 block over from the Central Bank plaza). $ Entrees €7-30. Open Tu-Th noon-10pm, F-Sa noon-11pm, Su noon-10pm.

STAGE DOOR CAFÉ CAFE $

11-12 E. Essex St. ☎1 677 6297

Although a bit cramped inside, this cafe has an atmosphere as fun and eclectic as the food and drinks are tasty. If none of the Irish or Italian menu items appeal to you, there's also a "create your own" sandwich or wrap option available (€7). We recommend the ciabatta with brie, bacon, and tomato. After all, can you ever go wrong with bacon?

 # From Dame St., head up Eustace St. and make a left at E. Essex St. [$] Coffee €2-6. Meal €3-9. ⏰ Open M-Sa 8am-8pm, Su 9am-9pm.

GRAFTON STREET

👍 **CORNUCOPIA** VEGAN, VEGETARIAN $$$

19-20 Wicklow St. ☎1 677 7583 www.cornucopia.ie

Prepare to get your health on. Cornucopia serves meals that are vegan, gluten-free, wheat-free, yeast-free, dairy-free, egg-free and low-fat. While meals here don't quite compare to the food coma-inducing splendor of a double bacon cheeseburger, it is worth waiting in line with the well-to-do granola babies for a surprisingly sweet wheat grass shot (€3.50). Come Thursday through Saturday nights to enjoy some organic wine (€5.35 per glass, €21.50 per bottle) and live harp and guitar music.

 # From Trinity College, head down Grafton St., then take a right onto Wicklow St. i Upcoming bands post flyers for upcoming shows in the entrance. ⏰ Open M-Tu 8:30am-9pm, W-Sa 8:30am-10:15pm, Su noon-9pm.

👍 **THE BLEEDING HORSE TAVERN** TRADITIONAL $$

24 Upper Camden St. ☎1 475 2705

Established in 1649, this bar boasts the exposed brick, wooden tables, and leather that make it feel like it hasn't changed a bit since its founding; the four flatscreens and riled up Irish rugby fans, however, will quickly remind you that this is the 21st century. Stick by the bar if you're keeping an eye on the game, or hole up in one of the many nooks with a pint of Guinness (€3.80) and some bangers and mash (€10) for a quieter night.

 # From Trinity College, take Dame St. Turn left onto S. Great Georges St. and follow it as it turns into Aungier, Wexford, and then Camden. The bar is on the left. i DJ Th-Sa. [$] Entrees €8-13. Pints €3.80. ⏰ Open M-W 10am-11:30pm, Th-Sa 10-2:30am, Su 10am-11pm.

CAPTAIN AMERICAS STEAKHOUSE $$$

44 Grafton St. ☎1 671 5266 www.captainamericas.com

Captain Americas is an Ireland-themed rock memorabilia restaurant, which means it is heavy on the U2. Plates here are pricey, but where else can you dig into some fries underneath a framed pair of underwear signed by the Boyz?

 # From Trinity College, head down Grafton St. Captain Americas is on the left. i Check out the website for student deals. [$] Entrees €10-17. ⏰ Open M-Th noon-10:30pm, F-Sa noon-11pm, Su noon-9pm.

THE RED ROSE CAFE $

23 Dawson St. ☎086 370 4873

All right, this is no gourmet meal, but it is a good sandwich for a good price. Breakfast is sold all day (Nutella pancakes for €5, anyone?), but it's the lunch deals that are worth stopping by for. At €5.50 for a giant sandwich and a Coke, make it the BLT and you'll be a happy traveler.

 # From Nassau St. (borders Trinity College), turn onto Dawson St. Walk all the way to the end of the street. [$] Lunch €4-7. ⏰ Open M-Sa 8:30am-5pm.

BEWLEY'S ORIENTAL CAFÉ CAFE $$

78-79 Grafton St. ☎1 672 7720 www.bewleys.com

A Grafton Street institution, Bewley's is something to see in and of itself. Beautiful stained glass windows by Dublin's own Harry Clark line the downstairs walls, making the place look more like a cathedral than a cafe. If you're looking for a "cafe's cafe," then head upstairs, where you can sit out on a tiny balcony overlooking the street. Enjoy some delicious coffee made from beans roasted inhouse, as you ponder the extensive dessert menu.

🧭 From Trinity College, go down Grafton St. The cafe is on the right about 2 blocks down. $ Coffee €2-4.50. Lunch €6-16. ⏰ Open M-W 8am-10pm, Th-Sa 8am-11pm, Su 9am-10pm.

BUTLERS CHOCOLATE CAFÉ CAFE $$

24 Wicklow St. ☎1 671 0591 www.butlerschocolates.com

This is the cafe where diets come to die. "No," you tell yourself as you approach the counter, but, "Gasp! They have all of their delicious truffles on display under a glass counter at the register! In every flavor! At only €0.30 a truffle!" You may tell yourself just one, but we're warning you—someone will have to drag you out of there kicking, screaming, and covered in chocolate.

🧭 From Trinity College, walk down Grafton St. and take a right onto Wicklow St. It is right across the street from Munchies Cafe. $ Coffee €2-3.50. Boxes of chocolate €2-50, depending on size. ⏰ Open M-W 7:45am-7pm, Th 7:45am-9pm, F 7:45am-7pm, Sa 8:45am-7pm, Su 10:45am-7pm.

CEDAR TREE LEBANESE RESTAURANT LEBANESE $$

11A St. Andrew's St. ☎1 677 2121

If you're looking for a good lunchtime spot, Cedar Tree is cheap and delicious. We're talking spicy *kafta* and falafel that crumbles in your mouth. While you're there, we recommend trying some Almaza, a Lebanese beer. You can't get it just anywhere. Get an eyeful of the Lebanese landscape mosaics while soaking up the fact that you just got so much food for so few euro.

🧭 From Trinity College, go down Grafton St. Take a right onto Wicklow St. and then another right onto St. Andrew's St. $ Wraps €5. Platters €12. ⏰ Open M-W 5:30-11:30pm, Th-Sa 5:30pm-midnight, Su 5:30-10:45pm.

O'CONNELL STREET

👍 **THE BLACK SHEEP** CAFE $$

61 Capel St. ☎1 878 2157

The wooden tables and bookshelves will make you feel as though you've walked into an Irish country home, and your first bite of the lamb stew will make you sure of it. Offering simple food, Black Sheep delivers in the tastiest ways possible. Make sure to grab a drink from their selection of over 110 craft beers.

🧭 From O'Connell Bridge, take Bachelors Walk and follow it until the end of Lower Ormond Quay. Take a right onto Capel St. $ Entrees €4.50-20. ⏰ M-Th 10:30am-11:30pm, F-Sa 10:30am-12:30am, Su noon-11pm.

👍 **TP SMITHS** PUB $$

9-10 Jervis St. ☎1 878 2067 www.thesmithgroup.ie

If you're ever in the mood for a Thai/Mexican/Middle Eastern/Irish place, this place has got you covered. After catching a glimpse of the classic Irish pub exterior (read: Guinness signs and Jameson casks), the menu at TP Smiths may come as a surprise. Paninis, wraps, couscous, burritos, curry—looks like someone couldn't make up their mind on a genre. Sit downstairs near the giant landscape mosaic or head up the winding copper staircase to the balcony seats above.

🧭 From O'Connell Bridge, take O'Connell St. Turn left onto Middle Abbey St., continue onto Upper Abbey St., then take a right onto Jervis St. $ Entrees €5-13. Pitchers €12.30. ⏰ M-Th 10:30am-11:30pm, F-Sa 10:30am-1:30am, Su 12:30-11:30pm.

SLATTERY'S
CARVERY $$$

129 Capel St.   ☎1 874 6844 www.slatterysbar.com

Once the smell of roasting meat hits you, there's no turning back from this carvery popular with both tourists and locals. Although there's not a large selection at the bar, the essentials are available. This place isn't trendy, so don't expect its drinks to be. The meat, however, will leave you smiling.

⚑ From O'Connell Bridge, take Bachelors Walk and follow it to the end of Lower Ormond Quay. Take a right onto Capel St. *i* Free Wi-Fi. ⑤ Lunch €4-12. Dinner €7-15. ⌚ Kitchen open M-Sa 8am-9:30pm, Su 10:30am-9:30pm.

O'SHEAS
TRADITIONAL $$

19 Talbot St   ☎1 836 5670 www.osheashotel.com

All Irish, all the time. Grab a Guinness, order some fish 'n' chips, and enjoy the soccer (excuse us, football) game. The food comes out so fast, you will think that they had it waiting for you. Eat in the restaurant section for more of a family vibe, or head over to the bar to sit with all the old Irish men quietly drowning their sorrows.

⚑ From O'Connell Bridge, head up O'Connell St. Take a right onto Earl St. N., which will turn into Talbot St. *i* Free Wi-Fi. ⑤ Meals €3-15. ⌚ Open daily 7:30am-10pm.

M&L SZECHUAN
CHINESE $$$

13 Cathedral St.   ☎1 874 8038

You won't find any buffet tables here. This is the real deal. So real, in fact, that, unless you dine with someone who speaks Chinese, you can expect an adventurous meal. Either way, the food will be worth it.

⚑ From O'Connell Bridge, head up O'Connell St. Take a right onto Cathedral St. ⑤ Entrees €10-30. ⌚ Open M-Sa 11:30am-10:30pm, Su noon-10:30pm.

NORTH OF O'CONNELL STREET

🏠 LA VITA
CAFE $

77A Dorset St. Upper   ☎1 860 2541

If you're looking for something other than pub grub, La Vita offers a nice change. Mostly vegetarian options make it a good lunch place for the non-meat eaters, and the fresh fruit smoothies (€4.50) appeal to all types. We suggest the Salad of Hearts (€5), partly because of the gruesome name, but mostly because those artichoke hearts are pretty darn good.

⚑ From O'Connell Bridge, take O'Connell St toward the spire. Turn left onto Parnell St. and follow as it becomes Cavendish Row. Continue onto Parnell Sq. E. then Frederick St. N. Turn right onto Dorset St. Upper. The cafe is on the left. ⑤ Meals €4-€9. *i* Free Wi-Fi. ⌚ Open M-F 8am-5pm Sa 11am-4:30pm.

TESCO
SUPERMARKET $

Moland House, Talbot St.   ☎1 890 928 451

Don't feel like going out to eat? Pick up some goods to go at Tesco. There's also a 24hr. ATM outside that accepts just about any kind of credit card.

⚑ Across from the Irish Life shopping mall. ⌚ Open M-Sa 7am-11pm, Su 8am-10pm.

GEORGIAN DUBLIN

🏠 THE LORD EDWARD
RESTAURANT, LOUNGE $$$$

23 Christchurch Pl.   ☎1 454 2420 www.lordedward.ie

This is where young people come to get fancy for an evening and where old people come to be around their peers. Yes, you might be the only one under 65 in the building, but once that Morhay lobster with cheese sauce is sitting in front of you, you probably won't care. Strike up a conversation with the aging barman for a not-so-brief history of the oldest seafood restaurant in Dublin.

⚑ From Trinity College, take Dame St. Continue as it turns into Lord Edward St., then Christchuch Pl. Across from Christchurch Cathedral. ⑤ Appetizers from €10. Entrees €25-30. ⌚ Open M-F 12:30-2:30pm and 6-10:45pm, Sa 6-10:45pm.

THE BAKERY CAFE $

3 Essex St. W. ☎1 672 9822

The name really doesn't lie—this is just a bakery. Wait, no, that's not right, it's not "just" a bakery. This is a "we will make everything right in front of you" bakery. With the kitchen taking up most of the establishment, it's worth grabbing a coffee (€1.70), digging into that oh-so-savory lemon tart (€1.50), and watching those bakers do work.

⇟ From Trinity College, take Dame St. Turn right onto Upper Exchange St., then a left onto Essex St. W. ℹ Free Wi-Fi. $ Baked goods €3-6. ⏰ Open M-F 7am-5pm, Sa 8am-4pm.

THE QUEEN OF TARTS CAFE $$

Cork Hill, Dame St. ☎1 670 7499 www.queenoftarts.ie

The little window peeking into the kitchen makes you want to grab a pie right off the windowsill and run. We advise grabbing one of the Irish country wooden tables, instead, and ordering the spinach, Brie, and pecan salad (€10). It's so good, you won't even mind paying for it.

⇟ From Trinity College, take Dame St.; continue as it turns into Cork Hill. The cafe is on the corner. ℹ Free Wi-Fi. $ Meals €4.50-13. ⏰ Open daily 8am-5pm.

THE CATHEDRAL CAFÉ CAFE $

Dean St. ☎1 379 0680

Grab the Last Supper (don't worry, it's only lunch!) at Cathedral Café. Owned by a family of fiery Italians, it's easy to feel right at home here. Come in for the early morning service (breakfast) and grab something from the "Forgive Me, Father" part of the menu. A scone with freshly made cream might be just the thing that gets you through the day.

⇟ From Trinity College, take Dame St. Continue as it turns left into Nicholas St. Continue as it becomes Patrick St., take a right onto Dean St. Across the street from St. Patrick's Cathedral. ℹ Free Wi-Fi. $ Meals €4.50-7.50. ⏰ Open daily 8am-5pm.

nightlife

Janey Mack! Dublin really knows how to party. Temple Bar sees crazy parties every night, but weekends in this city can hardly be topped. Thursday is payday for the locals, so expect more of them out and about before you can say TGIF. Sunday nights are quiet, but on Mondays, things start right back up again. The best cluster of real, honest-to-goodness house-pumpin', beat-layin' clubs can be found on **Harcourt Street** and **Harcourt Road,** up near **St. Stephen's Green.** An area with several excellent clubs, **Camden** and **Wexford Streets** (referred to as the "Village") are nearby. **South William Street** has some great bars and pub options as well.

TEMPLE BAR AND THE QUAYS

There's one neighborhood in Dublin where you're nearly guaranteed a combination (if not all of) of the following: public drunkenness, public vomiting, public nudity, a stag party, a hen party, women in high heels and halter tops, men in high heels and halter tops, beer, beer, and more beer. If you're staying at a hostel here, chances are you're not planning on making the most of their foosball table. On any given night, Temple Bar's streets fill with tourists walking about in various stages of inebriation. It might not be the thing you want to do every night, but it's certainly something you shouldn't miss.

MERCANTILE PUB

28 Dame St. ☎1 670 7100 www.mercantilehotel.ie

A favorite among hostelgoers, Mercantile is the start to the ever-so-famous hostel pub crawl. Expect a pretty rowdy, foreign crowd around 9pm and a bit of debauchery after that. No live music, but this bar doesn't need it to keep the 20-something crowd coming back.

➜ From Trinity College, head down Dame St.; the pub is on the left. ℹ Free Wi-Fi. $ Pints €5. ⏰ Open daily 10:30am-midnight.

★ GOGARTY'S BAR, LIVE MUSIC

58 Fleet St. ☎1 671 1822 www.gogartys.ie

Okay, you'll be hard-pressed to find a local here, and it's basically a tourist trap, but it's a pretty cool tourist trap: three floors, two bars, a beer garden, and a very posh à la carte restaurant on the top. Live music starts as early as 1:30pm, moves upstairs at 8pm, and continues all night long. Grab a few extra euro and those dancing shoes; you won't want to leave this bar.

➜ From Dame St., turn onto Anglesea St. Turn right onto Fleet St. It is the big yellow building. $ Bar food €5-15, prices increase upstairs. ⏰ Open M-Sa 10:30am-2:30am, Su noon-1am.

THE TEMPLE BAR BAR

47-48 Temple Bar St. ☎1 672 5287 www.thetemplebarpub.com

With possibly the best beer garden in the area, The Temple Bar is a pun-merited hotspot on a sunny day. Expect to pay the TB standard: €5 for a pint and slightly more for a mixed drink. Music starts with traditional Irish tunes at 2pm and changes to U2 at night. You'd be hard pressed to find a local here, but you'll also be hard-pressed to care.

➜ From Dame St., turn onto Temple Ln. S. and continue to the intersection with Temple Bar St. ℹ No cover. $ Guinness €5, lager €5.50. ⏰ Open M-W 10:30am-12:30am, Th 10:30am-2am, F-Sa 10:30am-2:30am, Su noon-1am.

PEADAR KEARNEY'S PUB, LIVE MUSIC

64 Dame St. ☎1 707 9701 www.peadarkearneys.com

Named for the composer of the Irish National Anthem who was raised upstairs, it's only fitting that this pub has great live music seven nights a week. Come in early and score a cheap drink (€3.50) or wait until the band starts up at 9pm. Brian Brody is a one-man musical powerhouse on Saturday nights, playing traditional Irish tunes intermixed with several classic American requests. He's also quite the cutie. Don't miss it.

➜ From Trinity College, head down Dame St. The pub is on the right. ℹ Cash only. $ When daily specials end, drinks start around €5. ⏰ Open daily noon-1am. Happy hour M-F noon-7pm, Sa-Su noon-5pm.

ALCHEMY CLUB

13 Fleet St. ☎866 629 575 www.alchemyclub.ie

While the two flights of stairs to get down to this club may be unfortunate for drunks and those in heels (especially if you're both), the NYC-inspired interior is worth the perilous venture down. Top-40 hits blare all night long, while upturned liquor bottles behind the bar get constant use. Students should come late on Wednesdays for discounted drinks or late on Sundays for free admission. Things don't heat up until after 1am.

➜ From Trinity College, head up Westmoreland St. towards the Liffey. Turn left onto Fleet St. $ Cover F-Sa €9. Guinness and lager €5. ⏰ Open W-Su 10:30pm-3am.

FITZSIMONS BAR AND CLUB BAR, CLUB

21-22 Wellington Quay ☎1 677 9315 www.fitzsimonshotel.com

Located in the heart of Temple Bar, Fitzsimons has five different floors, including a nightclub, a cocktail bar, and an open-air rooftop terrace. Hugely popular on the weekends, this emporium of nightlife entertainment is open until 2:30am daily. Be forewarned, there's no A/C in the club downstairs, so it can turn into a sweatbox; but it's a fun sweatbox, nonetheless. The multiplicity of tourists in this bar do make it a prime place to get scammed, though, so keep a sharp eye.

➜ From Dame St., turn onto Eustace St. It's on the corner of Eustace and E. Essex St. ℹ Fitzsimons also has a hotel and restaurant. $ Stout €4.85, lager €5.35. ⏰ Open daily noon-2:30am.

GRAFTON STREET

WHELAN'S BAR, MUSIC VENUE

25 Wexford St. ☎1 478 0766 www.whelanslive.com

The place for Dublin's alternative music, Whelan's boasts a large interior with several bars, an excellent balcony area, and two stages. The main stage hosts the biggest names in up-and-coming music (ever heard of John Mayer? Franz Ferdinand?), while the smaller upstairs stage handles local and acoustic acts. Featured in the blockbuster hit *PS I Love You*, don't be surprised if you find love here yourself—either with the overly talkative old man at the bar or the brooding German smoking in the beer garden. Whelan's is a must for music lovers and curious travelers alike.

From Dame St., turn onto S. Great Georges St. and continue as it turns into Aungier and then Wexford. Whelan's is on the right. ℹ €5-10 cover for the club after 10:30pm on weekends. $ Guinness €4.40. Lagers €4.90. ⏰ Open M-F 2:30pm-2:30am, Sa 5pm-2:30am, Su 5pm-1:30am.

THE DRAGON BAR, CLUB, GLBT

64-65 S. Great Georges St. ☎1 478 1590 thedragon@capitalbars.com

A heady combination of Paris chic, Vegas neon, and Addams macabre, **The Dragon** is a popular gay bar whose younger crowd gets hopping around midnight. Check out the wildly believable drag shows on Monday, Thursday, or Saturday, and throw your sexual orientation out the window.

From Dame St., turn onto S. Great Georges St. The club is a few blocks down, on the right. ℹ Mezzanine and 2nd dance floor upstairs. $ Pints €3-6. ⏰ Open M 8pm-3am, W-Sa 8pm-3am.

THE DAWSON LOUNGE PUB

25 Dawson St. ☎1 671 0311

Protect yourself from nuclear fallout by climbing down the stairs into "the smallest pub on earth" (or in Dublin, at least). A bit of a novelty, it's a fun place to stop during the afternoons when you can benefit from its dimly lit, cool ambience. Let it get crowded, however, and you'll come to the uncomfortable realization that it's really just a walk-in closet with a Guinness tap. For stout lovers, it's worth the trip. Claustrophobics might want to stay above ground.

From Trinity College, head down Grafton St., then around the bend onto Nassau St. Turn right onto Dawson St. and head to the end. The pub is on the right. ℹ Tiny packages of peanuts available for purchase. ⏰ Open M-Th 12:30-11:30pm, F-Sa 12:30pm-12:30am, Su 3-11pm.

a whole new ball game

There's probably already enough football confusion when you're traveling through Europe—are people talking about American football with field goals and helmets, or European football, better known in the US as soccer? Well, Ireland adds another game to the mix: Gaelic football, the most popular spectator sport in the country. The game resembles other sports than just the two suggested by its name: the field and tackling rules are similar to rugby, the ball resembles a volleyball, and you can both kick and hold the ball during play. The biggest event of the Gaelic football season is the All-Ireland Final in late September. Regularly drawing over 80,000 spectators, this historic tournament and final match has been around since 1887, and the winner gets the ultimate bragging rights in Ireland's athletic world. Dublin has the second-highest win total under its belt, holding 22 All-Ireland titles, though they still have a bit to go before they catch up to Kerry's 32 wins.

THE STAG'S HEAD PUB

1 Dame Ct. ☎1 679 3687 www.louisfitzgerald.com/stagshead

Established in 1895, the Stag's Head is the everyman pub of Dublin. Everybody drinks here—businessmen drink next to soccer hooligans, next to punk rockers. When we say next to, we truly mean elbow to elbow; this place gets packed weekend nights. Oh yeah, and there's a giant stag head inside.

🚶 From Dame St., turn onto Trinity St, then a quick right onto Dame Ln. Continue to the intersection with Dame Ct. $ Guinness €4.55, lager €4.90. ⏰ Open M-Sa 10:30am-1am, Su 10:30am-midnight.

DAVY BYRNES PUB

21 Duke St. ☎1 677 5217 www.davybyrnes.com

Getting a famous mention in James Joyce's *Ulysses*, this literary pub fills up on Bloomsday with patrons looking for gorgonzola sandwiches and glasses of "burgundy" (the same meal consumed by the novel's main character). If impossible-to-read novels aren't your thing, it's still worth making a stop. Mingle with happily inebriated locals and young travelers in one of Ireland's most famous landmarks.

🚶 From Trinity College, head down Grafton St., then turn left onto Duke St. $ Entrees €6-20. Extensive wine selection at €5-7.50 per glass. ⏰ Open M-Th 11am-11:30pm, F-Sa 11am-12:30am, Su 11am-11pm.

D TWO CLUB

60 Harcourt St. ☎1 476 4603 www.dtwonightclub.com

This is where George of the Dublin jungle comes to get his pint. A popular club, its enormous jungle-themed beer garden is packed on the weekends, especially during the summer. The music pulses at an aggressively loud volume, so this isn't the place for you to engage in some quiet conversation. Come before 8pm and all drinks are €3.50.

🚶 From Dame St., turn onto S. Great Georges St.; continue as it becomes Aungier, then Wexford. Turn left onto Montague St. and right onto Harcourt St. $ Lagers €5. Guinness €4.90 after 11pm. ⏰ Open M-W 11am-2am, Th-Sa 11am-2:30am, Su 11am-1:30am.

THE CAMDEN PALACE CLUB

84-87 Lower Camden St. ☎1 478 0808 www.thecamdenpalace.com

Dear. God. Somebody let out the crazy. The Camden Palace takes everything over the top and then throws it overboard. In a huge amphitheater of a club, people get freaky on the light-up go-go platforms (and with each other). Can't seem to find it? Look for the guys swinging fire-tipped chains outside the entrance on weekend nights.

🚶 Follow S. Great Georges St. as it turns into Aungier, and then into Camden. The club is on the right. ℹ IDs are a must. $ Guinness €4.70, lagers €5. Mixed drinks €8. Cover €10 on weekends. ⏰ Pool hall and bar open noon-3am. Nightclub open Th-Sa 10pm-late.

COPPER FACE JACKS CLUB

29-30 Harcourt St. ☎1 475 8777 www.jackson-court.ie

Rumor has it that the longstanding Copper Face Jacks is a good place for those looking for love. Without saying anything about whether or not that's true (here at Let's Go we don't kiss and tell), Copper's—as it's affectionately called—makes for a hair-tossing, muscle-flexing sort of night. With two stories, two dance floors, and two big bars, you'll have a great time. Be prepared for a younger crowd; Copper's is for the freewheeling and fun-loving.

🚶 From Dame St., turn onto S. Great Georges St.; continue as it becomes Aungier, then Wexford. Take a left on Montague St. and then a right on Harcourt St. ℹ 20+. Cover €5+. $ Guinness €4.50, lager €4.80. ⏰ Open daily 4pm-3am.

CAPITOL LOUNGE CLUB, LOUNGE

1-2 Aungier St. ☎1 475 7166 www.capitol.ie

Cocktails are the thing at the Capitol lounge—€5, all day, every day. With over 100 varieties on the menu, you're going to have watch yourself to make sure you don't get too sloppy. Head upstairs, where the music is slightly quieter, to chat with friends, or wade through the crowd downstairs as the DJs bang out that house music pulse. Regardless, spiffiness is welcome; heels or a button-down are not uncommon.

⇞ From Dame St., turn onto S. Great Georges St. When the street becomes Aungier, the club will be immediately on the left. ℹ 21+. ⏰ Open daily 3pm-3am.

THE "NO NAME" BAR BAR

3 Fade St. ☎1 764 5681

Dancing on tables your aim? Not at "No Name." With a soft atmosphere, this is more like a flat party in New York than a frat party in Texas. The brick walls and sparse furniture in this bar give the late 20-something crowd a chance to mingle. And mingle they do, over much-craved mojitos and homemade Bloody Marys. Get your weeknight groove on as the DJs take over from 8pm until closing.

⇞ From Dame St., turn onto S. Great Georges St. and then turn left onto Fade St. $ Guinness €4.50. Lager €5. Bar food on weekdays €10 or less. ⏰ Open M-W 1-11:30pm, Th 1pm-1am, F-Sa 1pm-2:30am, Su 1pm-1am.

GRAFTON LOUNGE CLUB

Unit 2, Royal Hibernian Way, Dawson St. ☎1 679 6260 www.thegraftonlounge.ie

White leather couches and smooth wooden bar chairs host the beautiful women and the slightly-too-old-for-them businessmen. House music is pumped in quietly at first, but it gets louder as the night goes on. Go early if you're looking to talk; go late if you're looking to dance. But whatever you do, don't show up looking scruffy.

⇞ From Trinity College, head down Grafton St., then around the bend onto Nassau St. Turn right onto Dawson St., right onto Duke St., and left onto Upper Duke Ln. It's on the left. $ Guinness €5. Mixed drinks from €10. ⏰ Open M-W 11am-11:30pm, Th-Sa 11am-2:30am, Su 4:30pm-1:30am.

O'CONNELL STREET

★ PANTIBAR BAR, CLUB, GLBT

7-8 Capel St. ☎1 874 0710 www.pantibar.com

Probably the friendliest nightclub in town, PantiBar is a GLBT playground. Bright neon lights give a good view of the tight T-shirt wearing men serving €5 cocktails all night, but the drinks are hardly the best part. Thursday night is craft night, affectionately referred to as "Let's make a do-do." Come early for a chance to meet Panti and play with her ever-so-adorable terrier. Yes, the club is dog-friendly. How often do you find that?

⇞ From Parliament St. and Temple Bar, take the Grattan Bridge over the Liffey to Capel St. The bar is on the right. $ Pints €4. Cocktails €5. Drinks ½ price on Su. ⏰ Open M-F 5-11:30pm, Sa 5pm-2:30am, Su 5-11:30pm.

THE GRAND SOCIAL CLUB

35 Lower Liffey St. ☎1 874 0076 www.thegrandsocial.ie

Meet the guitar-strumming, slouchy-hat wearing man/woman of your dreams at The Grand Social. Old records cover the walls, and obscure Irish indie songs hum in the background. With candlelit tables, this is not the place to get crazy. Lean up against the vending machine selling guitar strings and get ready to discuss your favorite bands that no one else knows about yet.

⇞ From O'Connell Bridge, facing the spire, turn a left onto Bachelors Walk, then right onto Liffey St. $ Pints from €5. Cocktails €6. ⏰ Open M-Th 4-11:30pm, F-Sa 3pm-2:30am, Su 3-11:30pm.

THE CHURCH CLUB

3A Jervis St. ☎1 828 0102 www.thechurch.ie

Also a restaurant and a Dublin landmark, this bar is not the place for cash-strapped travelers. For those with a little extra to spend, worship in the Irish way in this bar and Dublin landmark. This church-turned-bar is nearly sinful. Head through the late-night restaurant and down to the basement to find the high-class tourists and well-to-do Irish businessmen sipping on specialty cocktails.

 # From O'Connell Bridge, turn left onto Bachelors Walk. Continue along the river and turn right onto Jervis St. $ Pints and cocktails €5. ⏰ Open M-Th 4pm-midnight, F-Sa 4pm-2am.

GEORGIAN DUBLIN

PORTERHOUSE BREWING COMPANY BAR

16 Parliament St. ☎1 679 8847 www.porterhousebrewco.com

Beer bottles line the four different floors, back-lit by an orange glow. There is nothing a beer drinker could desire that isn't in this bar. Brewing ten different types of beers, the Porterhouse still manages to diversify its drink menu by serving craft beers from all over the world. Grab a beer from any one of the four levels; there is a bar on each one.

 # From Trinity College, head down Dame St. Turn right onto Parliament St. i Free Wi-Fi. $ Meals €7-13. Pints €3.50-7. ⏰ Open M-Th 10:30am-11:30pm, F-Sa 10:30am-12:30am, Su noon-11pm.

FARRINGTON'S BAR

29 E. Essex St. ☎1 671 5135 www.thesmithgroup.ie

On the border of Temple Bar and the Georgian District, this bar embodies the best of both. It's got the "we're Irish and we know it" feel of Temple Bar, minus the masses of tourists. Come early to order the whiskey tasting platter (€10) or later for the Irish music.

 # From Trinity College, take Dame St. Turn right onto Eustace St. The bar is at the corner of Eustace and Essex St. i Free Wi-Fi. $ Pints €5. Cocktails €6. ⏰ Open M-Th 10:30am-11:30pm, F-Sa 10:30am-2:30am, Su 12:30-11:30pm.

PURTY KITCHEN CLUB

34-35 E. Essex St. ☎1 677 0945 www.purtykitchen.com

Girls, get out the high heels and short skirts. Boys, get ready to buy some drinks. Top-40 hits pumping, walls that look like disco balls, and three levels of dance floors? This is your standard, hoppin' nightclub. Though it doesn't have much to make it stand out, the Purty Kitchen does a great job at good, ol' fashioned clubbin'.

 # From Trinity College, take Dame St. Turn right onto Sycamore St., then left onto E. Essex St. i €3.50 pints on Th. $ Pints €5. Cocktails €6. ⏰ Open Tu-Sa 10pm-3am, Su 10pm-1am.

THE GARAGE BAR BAR

E. Essex St.

Across from the Purty Kitchen, this bar is worlds away inside. Red light illuminates the grungy rock poster-decorated walls, and a slightly-unshowered-but-in-a-cool-way crowd populates the small bar. Expect some Zep to play while you drink your beer at the giant spool tables.

 # From Trinity College, head down Dame St. Turn right onto Sycamore St., then left onto E. Essex St. $ Pints €5. Pitchers €12.50. ⏰ Open M-Tu 5pm-12am, W-Sa 5pm-2:30am.

THE CZECH INN CLUB

Essex Gate ☎1 671 1535 www.czech-inn.org

A large central hallway leads to the dance floor at the back, past all the almost see-through windows to the tiny rooms that line the place. Posters of grinding models smile down on you as you get crazy to Top-40 hits under the laser lights. This is the sort of place you don't tell your mother about.

 # From Trinity College, take Dame St. Turn right onto Parliament St., then a left onto Essex St. i Don't come before 1am; it will be dead. $ Pints €5. Cocktails €6-8. ⏰ Open M-Sa noon-3am.

BULL AND CASTLE BEER HALL

2 Lord Edward St. ☎1 475 1122 www.bullandcastle.ie

You might think you've stepped out of Dublin and into Germany during Oktoberfest. Giant wooden tables fill the open room, with equally giant liters (yes, liters) of Irish craft beer being guzzled down. A good mix of travelers and locals makes this a fun place for drinking songs.

⇄ From Trinity College, take Dame St. until it turns into Lord Edward St. Look left as the street curves left. ℹ Outdoor beer garden. $ Pints €4-5. Liters €8. ⏰ Open M-W 11:30am-11:30pm, Th 11:30am-12:30am, F 11:30am-1am, Sa 11:30am-2:30am, Su 11:30am-11:30pm.

TURKS HEAD BAR, CLUB

27 Parliament St. ☎1 679 9701

Half nightclub, half bar, and with a restaurant in the back, this is your one-stop shop for that Turkish fix in Dublin. Glittering mosaics cover the supports like shiny trees holding the building up. The young people dance while the older part of the crowd nurses their beer next to the dancing Shiva statue.

⇄ From Trinity College, take Dame St. Take a right onto Parliament St. $ Pints €4. ⏰ Open M 10am-2:30am, Tu-Sa 9am-2am.

arts and culture

Traditional Irish music wafts from every pub you walk by in Temple Bar and there is a wealth of traditional Irish dance shows. If you're looking for something more modern, head to one of the many rock venues, which showcase Irish talent as well as a few big international names. Ireland is buzzing with a little something for everyone, so stop reading and get out there.

THEATER

👍 **THE GAIETY THEATRE** GRAFTON ST.

S. King St. ☎1 677 1717 www.gaietytheatre.ie

A beautiful old house theater with three levels of red velvet seating showcases Irish drama at its finest. Student discounts are offered up to 15%, but another good money-saving tip (regular prices run anywhere from €25-55) is to go for the "restricted view" seats. Rumor has it that the large drop in price is coupled with a minimal loss in stage visibility. Check the website for a complete show schedule. *Riverdance* comes for two months every summer.

⇄ From Trinity College, take Grafton St. to the end and turn right onto S. King St. ℹ No exchanges or refunds. Doors close promptly when the show begins. Concessions available. $ Tickets €19-55. ⏰ Box office open M-Sa 10am-7pm.

ABBEY THEATRE O'CONNELL ST.

26-27 Lower Abbey St. ☎1 878 7222 www.abbeytheatre.ie

First opened in 1904 through the efforts of a certain Mr. William Butler Yeats, the Abbey Theatre has burned down, moved away, moved back, and rebuilt on its original location. Apparently the physical space is doing its best to mimic the creative atmosphere, which has promotes an ever-changing landscape of new Irish writers. Some say it falls short; we think that it's still Ireland's National Theater, so it's worth a visit.

⇄ From O'Connell St., turn onto Lower Abbey St. $ Tickets €18-40. ⏰ Box office open M-Sa 10:30am-7pm.

BEWLEY'S CAFÉ THEATRE GRAFTON ST.

78-79 Grafton St. ☎86 878 4001 www.bewleyscafetheatre.com

Soak up some of the best of Irish culture at Bewley's Café Theater. Famous for being one of James Joyce's writing spots, this Dublin landmark is a good place for lunchtime entertainment as well as jazz or cabaret in the evenings. Don't expect too many locals here—they already have enough of that good ol' Irish culture.

➹ From Trinity College, take Grafton St. Look for the theater on the right. $ Tickets €10. ⏰ Doors open at 12:50pm for lunchtime performances and 8pm for evening performances.

PROJECT ARTS CENTRE GEORGIAN DUBLIN

39 E. Essex St. ☎1 881 9613 www.projectartscentre.ie

The Project Arts Centre divides itself between modern gallery exhibitions (read: hard to understand) and plays that, at first blush, appear to have no plot. Avant-garde is this place's bread and butter. Stop in to check out upcoming shows and take advantage of the free coffee and W-Fi. Check the website for show schedules.

➹ From Trinity College, take Dame St. Turn right onto Sycamore St., and turn left onto E. Essex St. $ Tickets €15-25. ⏰ Box office open M-Sa 11am-7pm. Gallery open M-Sa 11am-8pm.

JAZZ

JJ SMYTHS GEORGIAN DUBLIN

12 Aungier St. ☎1 475 2565 www.jjsmyths.com

Serving as just another pub during the day, JJ Smyths defines itself with some smooth jazz at night. With few jazz clubs in Dublin, a good mix of tourists and locals will fill the place up.

➹ From Dame St., follow S. Great Georges St. as it turns into Aungier St. i Live music every Sa, plus weekly events. Check the website for specifics. $ Pints from €4. Spirits from €3.90. ⏰ Open M-F 10:30am-11:30pm, Sa-Su 10:30am-12:30am.

27 CLUB TEMPLE BAR AND THE QUAYS

27 Westmoreland St. ☎1 670 8604 www.the27club.com

Downstairs in the Cassidy Pub, this little jazz club attracts some cool, jazz-loving cats. Come here for those sultry sounds, and grab a bite at the upstairs bar before heading to the basement to groove to the smooth beats.

➹ On the Temple Bar side of the river, just past O'Connell Bridge. $ Drinks from €4. ⏰ Open F-Su 8pm-1:30am.

ROCK AND ROLL

🏆 GYPSY ROSE ROCK AND BLUES CLUB TEMPLE BAR AND THE QUAYS

5 Aston Quay www.gypsyroseclub.com

A skull, cross, and rose painted on the windows out front invite every Deadhead and Springsteen lover alike. Old rock posters cover the ceiling of the small bar entrance, but don't be fooled: this club has three different venues inside. Stay upstairs for live music at the acoustic bar or take the stairs covered in drug-fueled wall murals to the downstairs lounge. Hang a sharp right to check out the club venue, perfect for rocking out to some Guns N' Roses (yeah, they play here).

➹ From O'Connell Bridge, walk down Aston Quay on the Temple Bar side of the Liffey. $ Before 11pm all drinks €4. After 11pm all drinks €5. ⏰ Open M 5pm-1am, Tu 5-9:30pm, W 5pm-1am, Th-Sa 5pm-3am, Su 6pm-1am.

THE ACADEMY O'CONNELL ST.

57 Middle Abbey St. ☎1 877 9999 www.theacademydublin.com

It's new, it's hot, and it has all the…well, medium names anyone in Dublin could want to see. Sticking to the rock genre, The Academy varies from punk to indie, so make sure you know what's playing before you go. With two stages and a whole lot of buzz, this is one of the top rock venues in Dublin.

➹ From O'Connell Bridge, take O'Connell St., then turn left onto Middle Abbey St. i Outdoor smoking patio and full bar. $ Tickets €5-25. ⏰ Open daily 10am-5:30pm.

FIBBERS ROCK BAR

O'CONNELL ST.

80 Parnell St. ☎87 914 1249 www.fibbermagees.ie

Get your party shirt on, and we mean the all-black Korn party shirt—we found the best metal venue in Dublin. The music is loud and it is angry (although the people are really quite pleasant). Check the website to hit up a live show, or just stop by for some pool and like-minded people.

✠ *From O'Connell Bridge, take O'Connell St, and turn right onto Parnell St.* ✢ *Outdoor smoking patio.* ⑨ *Pints start at €3.50.* ⌚ *Open daily noon-3am.*

DANCE

Yes, you're in Dublin, and yes, there is plent of traditional Irish dancing to be seen. We picked out the best ones for you.

🎖 ARLINGTON HOTEL TEMPLE BAR

GEORGIAN DUBLIN

16-18 Lord Edward St. ☎1 670 8777 www.arlingtonhoteltemplebar.com

With some of the best river dancing we've seen in Ireland, the Arlington Hotel knows they've got quite a show. Spring for the three-course dinner plus a show (€30), and you'll get set up at a table front and center. If you don't feel like eating, however, you're still welcome to enjoy the performance from the bar. Just make sure you grab a drink or a light snack.

✠ *From Trinity College, follow Dame St. Look for Arlington Hotel on the right.* ⑨ *Free with drink or food purchase.* ⌚ *Shows daily 8:30-11pm.*

🎖 GOGARTY'S

TEMPLE BAR AND THE QUAYS

58 Fleet St. ☎1 671 1822 www.gogartys.ie

How do you make a skinny redhead attractive and cool? River dancing. No, we swear it's true. Never has the traditional Irish dance been so cheeky. Set down your drink and get ready to clap, cheer, and get hustled by the sassiest river dancers in town.

✠ *From Trinity College, take College Green and then turn right onto Anglesea St.* ⑨ *Free.* ⌚ *Dancing nightly 11-11:30pm.*

BLARNEY INN PUB

GRAFTON ST.

47-49 Kildare St. ☎1 679 4388

This place will be chock-full of tourists, but you might not care. The live Irish band accompanied by a dancing team makes for an enjoyable night. The show begins at 8pm, but the dancers don't usually come on until 9pm. Performers are either co-ed or all-female, depending on the day.

✠ *From Trinity college, follow Nassau St. with the College on your left. The Blarney Inn Pub is on the right on the corner with Kildare St.* ⑨ *Pints €5-6. Entrees from €15.* ⌚ *Open M-F 10:30am-11pm, Sa-Su 9am-11pm.*

shopping

CLOTHING

🎖 THE HARLEQUIN

GEORGIAN DUBLIN

13 Castle Market ☎1 671 0202 susannaharlequin@hotmail.com

The Harlequin is a great little vintage shop where you'll have trouble finding something that doesn't totally match your new retro ensemble. With three floors, costume jewelry, and the sexiest collection of men's velvet jackets this side of the Channel, it's a must-hit for any clothing shopper.

✠ *From Dame St., take S. Great Georges St., then turn left onto Exchequer St. Turn right onto Drury St. and left onto Castle Market.* ⌚ *Open M-W 10am-6pm, Th 10am-8pm, F 10am-6pm, Sa 9:30am-6pm, Su 12:30-5:30pm.*

GENIUS GRAFTON ST.

6A Powerscourt Townhouse Centre, Clarendon St. ☎1 679 7851 www.genius.ie

Mm, what's that smell? Oh yeah, testosterone. Or maybe leather, we can't be sure. Genius offers a pure man-fueled assortment of name brand jackets and men's accessories, as well as a large selection of stylish leather boots. It's up to you to decide if throwing down €100 or more for boots is a smart move or not.

🚶 From Grafton St., take a right onto Wicklow St., then a left onto Clarendon St. ℹ Annual sales in June and Jan. ⏰ Open M-W 10am-6pm, Th 10am-8pm, F-Su 10am-6pm.

AVOCA GRAFTON ST.

11-13 Suffolk St. ☎1 677 4215 www.avoca.ie

This store is one of the many that originated in the 1723 weaving mill (still in service). You'll come for the oh-so-soft cashmere throws, but we're warning you: you might get distracted by the gourmet jam selection, homemade scones, and selection of impossibly hard-to-put-down coffee table books.

🚶 Down the street from Dublin Tourism on Suffolk St. From Grafton St., turn onto Suffolk St. ⏰ Open M-W 10am-6pm, Th 10am-7pm, F-Sa 10am-6pm, Su 11am-6pm.

INDIGO & CLOTH GRAFTON ST.

27B, S. William St. ☎1 670 6403 www.indigoandcloth.com

Down in a little basement shop on S. Williams St. lies God's own collection of simple yet trendy clothing. Carrying an ever-changing variety of top-tier brands, this place does essentials like no other. Unfortunately, God's closet is not cheap; basic tops or T-shirts here can run up to €60, and jackets or dresses up to €350. If you can spring the dough, you'll be one impeccably dressed individual walking the streets of Dublin.

🚶 From Grafton St., take Wicklow St., then turn left onto S. William St. ⏰ Open M-W noon-6pm, Th noon-7pm, F noon-6pm, Sa 10am-6pm, Su 1-5pm.

FLIP TEMPLE BAR AND THE QUAYS

3-4 Fownes St. ☎1 671 4299 www.flipclothing.com

Open since the mid-80s when Temple Bar had none of its present day veneer, Flip is a combination of vintage and not, with leather and military jackets, funky Hawaiian prints, and a liberal price negotiation policy. Getting that great deal might just depend on how willing you are to beg.

🚶 From Dame St., turn right onto Anglesea St., then left onto Temple Bar, then right onto Fownes St. $ T-shirts from €15. Jeans from €20. ⏰ Open M-W 10am-6pm, Th 11am-7pm, F-Sa 10am-6pm, Su 1-6pm.

GREAT OUTDOORS LIMITED GRAFTON ST.

2 Chatham St. ☎1 679 4293 www.greatoutdoors.ie

Planning an epic camping trip to the Wicklow Mountains? Maybe you are just sick of getting drenched to the bone every time you walk outside. Either way, this store is ready for any outdoor adventure that you need to gear up for. Ask the very knowledgeable staff for help finding a good fit or a good trip. Those guys know their Dublin outdoors.

🚶 From Grafton St., near St. Stephen's Green, turn right onto Chatham St. ℹ Some outdoor clubs' discounts honored. ⏰ Open M-W 10am-6pm, Th 10am-8pm, F 10am-6pm, Sa 9:30am-6pm, Su 12:30-5:30pm.

BOOKS

💰 **BARGAIN BOOKS** O'CONNELL ST.

ilac Shopping Center, Henry St.

Damn—you've just finished that new Dan Brown novel and the hostel's book exchange is looking a little weak. Head over to Bargain Books, where factory outlet prices are the thing. Copies of *Ulysses* can be purchased for just €3. Do you dare?

🚶 Inside the ilac Shopping Center on Henry St., just off O'Connell St Upper. $ Cash only. ⏰ M-W 9am-6:30pm, Th 9am-8pm, F-Sa 9am-6:30pm, Su 11am-6:30pm.

TEMPLE BAR BOOK MARKET TEMPLE BAR AND THE QUAYS

Temple Bar www.templebar.ie/markets/book_market

Every Saturday and Sunday, local booksellers set up tents and deal new, used, and antique books here at good prices. Have a few afternoon pints in Dublin's most popular bar district and then go browse for a good read. Books and beer—this is the life.

Just through Merchant's Arch on Temple Bar [$] *Books from €3.* ⏰ *Sa-Su 11am-6pm.*

DUBRAY BOOKS GRAFTON ST.

36 Grafton St. ☎677 5568 www.dubraybooks.ie

Dubray Books is a multi-level bookstore offering new titles. Check out either the sale section or the staff recommendations, available in a handy pamphlet at the counter. Don't let your book choices be influenced by wildly good street music wafting in from Grafton. Or do. We don't control you.

Almost to the top of Grafton street on the left. ⏰ *Open M-F 9am-9pm, Sa 9am-7pm, Su 9am-6pm.*

BOOKWORMS O'CONNELL ST.

75 Middle Abbey St. ☎873 5772 booba@eircom.net

A long-standing discount and secondhand bookstore, the emphasis here is on prices. Cheap prices. Books lie scattered on shelves, boxes, and the cat in the corner (we're kidding about that last one), yet they still manage to be organized alphabetically and by genre.

From O'Connell St., facing away from the river, turn left onto Middle Abbey St. **i** *Children and young readers sections available.* ⏰ *Open M-F 9:30am-7:30pm, Sa 9:30am-7pm, Su 1-6pm.*

THE WINDING STAIR BOOKSTORE TEMPLE BAR AND THE QUAYS

40 Lower Ormond Quay ☎872 6576 www.winding-stair.com

This bookstore is on the smaller end, considering Dublin's plethora of them. They don't have a huge selection, but on the plus side, they do sell refreshments. You know, in case all that book browsing gets exhausting.

Across the Millennium Bridge from Temple Bar. ⏰ *Open M-W 10am-7pm, Th-Sa 10am-8pm, Su noon-7pm.*

OUTDOOR MARKETS

THE HA'PENNY FLEA MARKET TEMPLE BAR AND THE QUAYS

35 Lower Liffey St.

While it claims to have vintage items, this market is more of a high-end arts and crafts show. So though you shouldn't expect to find the 1950s vase of your dreams, focus on the individual stalls' goods and the stories behind them. That's where this market comes alive.

On the north side of the Ha'Penny Bridge—the white pedestrian bridge just down from O'Connell Bridge. **i** *In the Grand Social.* ⏰ *Open Sa 11am-5pm.*

SOUTH CITY MARKET OR ST. GEORGE'S ARCADE GEORGIAN DUBLIN

S. Great Georges St.

This open-air market is a good place to find vintage wear, old LPs, used DVDs, Asian treasures ("Hello Kitty" bra, anyone?), coffee, flowers, jewelry, used books and more. More of an off-beat crowd lingers here. Great for one-of-a-kind gifts!

From Trinity College, take Grafton St. toward St. Stephen's Green, turn right onto Johnson's Ct., and follow it to the South City Market. ⏰ *Open M-F 10:30am-6pm, Sa 10:30am-6:30pm, Su noon-6pm.*

LIQUOR STORES

Ah, the fine art of boozin'. The establishments below have been chosen for their selection and for the personable, welcoming nature of their staff. If you're interested in become a professional whiskey drinker, or at least maintaining the claim when you're sober, head to the bottle shops below. If you're just interested in finding a cheap bottle of wine to take to the party, there are liquor stores located all over Dublin, handily marked with the vaguely black-market sounding "off license." Cheers.

⬛ PROBUS WINES AND SPIRITS   GRAFTON ST.

26 Fenian St.   ☎1 662 9649 www.probuswines.ie

Beer drinkers rejoice: we found your liquor store. The knowledgeable owner is more than willing to give you the rundown on his selection of craft beers. Wines, spirits, and some food products also available.

⚑ *On the other side of Trinity College from Dame St.; off of Lincoln Pl.* ⏰ *Open M-Sa 9:30am-6pm.*

⬛ CELTIC WHISKEY SHOP   GRAFTON ST.

27-28 Dawson St.   ☎1 675 9744 www.celticwhiskeyshop.com

With everything from tiny bottles as found in hotel minibars to bottles at €3000 a pop, you can find all your inebriating needs at Celtic Whiskey Shop. Wine, whiskey, and microbrews are all available. Daily whiskey tastings make even the shopping experience smooth.

⚑ *From Trinity College, take Grafton St. and follow the bend to the left onto Nassau St. Turn right onto Dawson St.* Ⓢ *Prices vary. Whiskey from €25.* ⏰ *Open M-Sa 9:30am-5:30pm.*

TESCO   TEMPLE BAR AND QUAYS

Omni Centre   ☎1 842 9122 www.tesco.ie

Though a grocery store, Tesco should not be overlooked by those travelers looking for a good time and the best deals. Two liters of cider for €3? A ten-pack of Carlsberg for €10? Yes, the selection may not be high-class, but boy is it cheap.

⚑ *On Temple Ln. S., just off of Wellington Quay.* ⏰ *Open daily 8am-8pm.*

JAMES FOX   GRAFTON ST.

119 Grafton St.   ☎1 677 0533 www.jamesfox.ie

This, my friends, is a gentlemen's store. Need a fine cigar and that hard-to-find Jameson 12-year? Check. An old-time shaving kit and a new pipe? Check. Swiss Army Knives? Check. Seriously, they should rename this store The Gentleman's Starter Kit. Enjoy the free mead tasting as you walk in.

⚑ *At the intersection of College Green and Grafton St., just in front of Trinity College.* ⏰ *Open M-Sa 9:30am-6pm, Su 12:30-5:30pm.*

ELECTRONICS

COMPU B AND MAC EXCHANGE   GRAFTON ST.

111 Grafton St.   ☎1 507 9101 www.compub.com

Apple users, you didn't think we were going to leave you out in the cold, did you? Compu B offers a wide selection of Mac products, including iPods and Macbooks. They also have a tech support group for those of you who come in sobbing because you dropped your iPod in a pitcher of beer. If you've got a warranty, they'll gladly accept it. If not, however, it's €75 for a diagnostic test plus the cost of your repair.

⚑ *Just down Grafton St. from the Molly Malone statue.* ⏰ *Open M-W 9am-7pm, Th 9am-9pm, F-Sa 9am-7pm, Su 11am-6pm.*

FURNITURE

BEDROOM ELEGANCE   NORTH OF O'CONNELL

55-56 Upper Dorset St.   ☎1 872 8210 www.bedroomelegance.ie

Get ready to see some wood. Offering made-to-measure furniture, this stuff is custom-made, so go in with an idea of what you are looking for. That wraparound couch with the ten cupholders can be done; just say the word.

⚑ *Follow O'Connell St. as it turns into Parnell St. and then Frederick St. N.; turn right onto Upper Dorset St.* ⏰ *Open M-F 9:20am-5:30pm, Sa 9:30am-4pm.*

ANTIQUES

COURTVILLE ANTIQUES GRAFTON ST.

Powerscourt Townhouse, S. William St. ☎1 679 4042 www.courtvilleantiques.com

Sick of people telling you that their oversized Aerosmith tour '99 T-shirt is an "antique?" Come to Courtville Antiques, where almost all of the items are certified as being at least 100 years old. A fine selection of women's jewelry, old paintings, and some beautiful glassware from County Cork makes this a fine place for lovers of fine things.

➡ From Grafton St., turn onto Johnson's Ct., then turn right onto Clarendon St. Go into the Powerscourt Townhouse. $ Prices vary; jewelry generally a few hundred euro. ⏰ Open Tu-Sa 10am-5:30pm.

MICHAEL DUFFY O'CONNELL ST.

10 Parnell St. ☎1 872 6928

With more of a furniture focus, Michael Duffy is a fun place to plan your dream house. That is, if your dream house includes giant crystal chandeliers and a stone fireplace. Smaller trinkets are available to look at, too, but are definitely not this store's biggest draw.

➡ From O'Connell Bridge, take Bachelors Walk and follow it until the end of Lower Ormond Quay. Turn right onto Capel St., then right onto Parnell St. ⏰ Open M-Sa 9:30am-5pm.

JOHNSON'S COURT VINTAGE EMPORIUM GRAFTON ST.

12A Johnson's Ct. ☎1 670 6825

A store full of so many knickknacks and interesting pieces you'll wonder how you're ever going to leave. The owner has a large selection of items from Ireland as well as a significant collection brought in from the rest of Europe. Prices hang steady around €35; sometimes it's a steal and sometimes it's not.

➡ From Grafton St., turn onto Johnson's Ct. ⏰ Open M-Sa 10:30am-5:30pm.

DEPARTMENT STORES

★ **PENNEYS DEPARTMENT STORE** O'CONNELL ST.

O'Connell St. ☎1 656 6666 www.primark.ie

Imagine if Walmart were Irish. Now imagine that it's high-quality and dirt-cheap. Now you've got Penneys. This department-store chain is beloved in Ireland, and with T-shirts or sneakers from €5, the love is well-deserved. Low on underwear? (What? Where did you leave yours last night?) Treat yourself to a new pair stat (€2-3).

➡ On O'Connell St. Lower, just below the post office. ⏰ Open M-W 8:30am-8pm, Th-F 8:30am-9pm, Sa 8:30am-7pm, Su 11am-7pm.

ST. STEPHEN'S GREEN SHOPPING CENTRE GRAFTON ST.

Stephen's Green West ☎1 478 0888 www.stephensgreen.com

A mall offering your usual collection of retail chains (Quiksilver, GameStop, etc.), there's no real reason to go in here if you're not shopping, except perhaps to observe the incredibly large clock that hangs from the ceiling.

➡ At the top of Grafton St., across from St. Stephen's Green. ℹ Toilet use €0.20. ⏰ Open M-W 9am-7pm, Th 9am-9pm, F-Sa 9am-7pm, Su 11am-6pm.

CLERYS DEPARTMENT STORE O'CONNELL ST.

18-27 O'Connell St. ☎1 878 6000 www.clerys.com

Classy (read: expensive) lingerie, limited (read: even more expensive) make-up collections, and some (you guessed it) pricey perfume selections, this is where you wish your parents' credit card weren't just for emergencies. Smelling bad is an emergency, right?

➡ From O'Connell Bridge, head up O'Connell St. It is across the street from Penneys. ℹ Customer service desk located on the 2nd fl. ⏰ Open M-W 10am-6:30pm, Th 10am-9pm, F 10am-6:30pm, Sa 9am-7pm.

excursions

MALAHIDE

Malahide's main sight is the impressive **Malahide Castle,** which looks exactly the way you picture the definition of "castle." (☎1 890 5000 www.malahidecastle.com ⚔ From the DART station, head right on Main St. for 5min. Ⓢ €7.50, under 12 €4.70; concessions €6.30. Combined ticket for Malahide Castle and either Dublin Writers' Museum, James Joyce Museum, or George Bernard Shaw Birthplace €11.50, under 12 €7.50; concessions €9.50. ⛱ Open Apr-Sept daily 10am-5pm; Oct-Mar M-Sa 10am-5pm, Su 11am-5pm.) The 800-year-old fortress, located on 250 acres of parkland, is a sight to behold and a pain to besiege. Go inside for a tour of the castle and its history (watch out for ghosts!) or wander the estate for some fresh air and darn good photo opportunities. When you've finished pretending to be royalty, be sure to check out Malahide's **beaches** (⚔ Follow Main St. to the end). A short walk from the city center, the beaches offer great views of the city no matter the weather. On the walk back to the city, check out the **Seabank Bistro** (Coast Rd. ☎1 845 1988 www.seabankbistro.ie ⚔ Main St. becomes Coast Rd. Ⓢ Meals €18-€25 ⛱ Open M-Sa 5:30-10pm, Su 2:30-9pm), where the day's catch greets you as you walk in. Don't get too attached, though—they're your dinner. If you're looking for a cheaper option, find **James Gibney's** in the city center. (6 New St. ☎1 845 0606 www.gibneys.com ⚔ From Main St. as you head toward the water, turn left onto New St. Ⓢ Meals €4-€13.) On sunny days, grab some bangers and mash (€5.50) in their outdoor beer garden, with your own bottle of wine (€6 corking fee). If the beaches are too hard to drag yourself away from, get a room in the **Grand Hotel.** (Grove Rd. ☎1 845 0000 www.thegrand.ie ⚔ At the end of Main St., by the water. Ⓢ Rooms from €75.) Ask for a beach view room to complete the royal experience. If you don't have too much cash to spare, try the **Beechwood Country House.** (Blackwood Ln. ☎1 846 1738 www.beechwood.ie ⚔ From Main St. heading toward the water, right onto Church St., which becomes The Hill and Malahide Rd., then left on Blackwood Ln. Ⓢ Rooms from €50.) No beach views, but the O'Reilleys will do their best to meet your every need.

Getting There

Take the **DART** northbound to Malahide (€8.70 round-trip).

BRAY

There's a lot to do in and around Bray, so plan accordingly (www.braytourism.ie). If you're lucky enough to enjoy a sunny day, the **Bray Bay,** with its only slightly rocky beaches, is a must. (⇄ From the DART Station, turn right and then right again on Seapoint Rd.) Join the hundreds of way-too-pale Irish in trying to toe the fine line between golden brown and lobster red. After your beach time, haul that sunburned bum of yours up to **Bray Head** for views that rival those of Killiney Hill. (⇄ From Bray Bay, follow the pedestrian walking path toward Bray Head; the bay should be on the left. Where the pavement ends, take the hiking path to reach the top.) The giant cross at the top will keep you headed toward great views or God—whichever motivates you more. End the day with a tour of **Sea Life,** an aquarium with a conservationist agenda. (Strand Rd. ☎1 286 6939 www.visitsealife.com/bray ⇄ From Seapoint Rd., follow the bend. As you turn right, it becomes Strand Rd. Sea Life is a few blocks down. [$] €12, students €11, children €9.) It's fun to watch the sharks fight over the daily catch: check the website for feeding times. After all the sun and sea—or at least all the sea—head to one of the many pubs and restaurants in town. **Barracuda** offers great views of the Irish boiling on the beach as well as great tastes of the already boiled lobster. (Strand Rd. ☎1 276 5686 www.barracuda.ie ⇄ From Seapoint Rd., head down Strand Rd. with the Bay on your left. [$] Appetizers €6-12. Entrees €14-25. ⏰ Open M-Th 10am-9:30pm, F-Sa 10am-10pm, Su 10am-9:30pm.) If you're looking for more of a snack, **Finnbees** will do the trick, with offerings like sandwiches (€5), smoothies (€4), and sweets (€2-€3). (Strand Rd. ☎1 286 3456 www.finnbees.com) For a drink, head to **The Hibernia Inn.** (1 Royal Marine Terr. ☎286 2183 ⇄ From Main St., take Quinsborough Rd.; the restaurant is at the intersection with Strand Rd. [$] Meals €8-€13.) Two outdoor garden patios make this a Bray favorite on sunny days. For the other 360 days of the year, the beer is enough to keep the customers coming back. **Pizza'n' Cream** offers homemade pizzas and even better creamy and oh-so-sweet homemade gelato. (9 Albert Ave. ☎1 286 1606 ⇄ From Strand Rd., turn onto Albert Ave. [$] Pizza €11.95. Gelato €4.) If it's nightlife you're looking for, be a bit careful. Bray isn't known for being the safest after hours. **Dicey Reilly's** provides a traditional pub atmosphere popular with the locals. (Quinsborough Rd. ⇄ Can get to Quinsborough by turning off of either Main St. or Strand Rd. [$] Pints €3-€5.) Warm up by one of the three fireplaces while clapping along to some traditional Irish music.

Great Outdoors

POWERSCOURT GARDENS AND WATERFALL

Powerscourt Estate ☎1 204 6000 www.powerscourt.ie

About a 15min. bus ride outside of Bray, this estate is worth every second spent stuck in the middle of that over-excited German couple. Dodge the serious cyclists and the over-eager Nordic hikers on the walk up Eagle Valley Rd. from Enniskerry; it's all worth it when you stroll through those gates. Take the hour-long self-guided tour through the seven gardens, taking in the smells of the Japanese garden and the less appetizing algae stench of the Titan Pond. If you have the energy, take the 6km trip to the waterfalls. Late spring or any time after a heavy a rain is the best time to go, although a spectacular view can really be had at any time.

⇄ From Bray city center, take bus #185 (€2.15). [$] Garden admission €8.50, students €7.50, children ages 5-11 €5, children under age 5 free, families €25. Waterfall admission €5.50, students €5, children ages 2-11 €3.50, children under age 2 free, families €16. ⏰ Gardens open daily 9:30am-5:30pm. Waterfall open May-Aug 9:30am-7pm; Mar-Apr and Sept-Oct 10:30am-5:30pm; Nov-Feb 10:30am-4pm.

KILLRUDDERY

Southern Cross ☎1 286 3405 www.killruddery.com

The gardens are not quite as impressive as those at Powerscourt, but Killruddery's proximity to Bray gives it an extra edge. The oldest gardens in Ireland, these are less groomed and more aimed at long walks with some furry friends. The house itself stars in many a medieval-themed television show, including *The Tudors*. Head to the farm if you're the animal type—you might be lucky enough to see some newborn lambs.

⇞ From Bray, take bus #184 to Lord Meaths Gate (€1.85). Walk 500m uphill. $ Free. ⏰ Garden open May-Sept 9:30am-5pm. House open July-Sept 1-5pm.

Getting There

From Dublin, take the **DART** southbound to Bray (fares as low as €6 round-trip). A one-way trip will take approx. 40min.

SKERRIES

Start your daytrip out at the **Skerries Mills,** the town's main tourist attraction. (Mill St. ☎1 849 5208 www.skerriesmills.org ⇞ From the DART Station, take a left off Station St. onto Dublin Rd; then take a right onto Millhill Park and follow the windmills. ⏰ Open daily from 10am. Last guided tour at 4:30pm in summer; 3:30pm in winter.) Part museum and part tour, the Skerries Mills provide an inside look at early Irish life. A view of a running mill is an uncommon but fun way to start your day. Guided tours through the dusty cellars run daily and last for the better part of an hour (€6.25, students €4.80). From the mills, take Holmpatrick Rd. to the city center. Continue on Harbour Rd. to reach **The Strand** and the 5km walking tour of the best Skerries has to offer. Watch for seals on the pier, gaze off at the Skerries Islands, and end up on the beach for a relaxing afternoon. If you are hungry while on the pier, stop for some sweets at, **Storm in a Teacup.** (19 Harbour Rd. $ Sweets €1-5. ⏰ Tu-F 2-8pm, Sa-Su 11am-8pm.) The bright green and pink may seem contrary to the pier's dark, storm-washed colors, but the delicious ice cream or crepe you get will be just the thing to compete your seal-watching experience. For drinks with views of the ocean, head to **Stoop Your Head,** and be sure to grab a bite to eat, too. (Harbour Rd. ☎1 849 2085 www.stoopyourhead.ie ⇞ Take Strand St. to Harbour Rd.; walk out toward the pier. $ Entrees €15-20. ⏰ Open daily noon-3pm, 5:30-10pm.) Afternoon coffee is best at the main street **Olive Deli and Café.** (86A Strand St. ☎849 0310 www.olive.ie $ Meals €4-6. Coffee €2-3. ⏰ Open M-Sa 8:30am-6pm, Su 9am-6pm.) A patio out front and a back garden make this the place to be on a sunny day. The artisan cheese plates make it worth it on a rainy day, too. To mingle with locals, head to **The Black Raven.** (3 Church St. ☎1 849 1242 ⇞ From Strand St., turn onto Convent Ln., then take a right onto Church St. $ Pints €3. ⏰ Open daily 10:30am-12:30am.) Be careful where you sit, or you might just find yourself in the middle of a cross-bar rugby argument. If you're looking for a more substantial dinner than a Guinness and some peanuts, the award-winning **Red Bank** restaurant (5-7 Church St. ☎1 849 1005 www.redbank.ie ⇞ From Strand St., turn onto Convent Ln., then take a right onto Church St. $ Entrees €18-40 ⏰ Open daily 7:30am-9pm) is just down the street. There are not many places to stay in the Skerries; it's much more of a daytrip than a week-long stay. If the beaches and seals are too hard to leave, check out the **Hamilton House** in the city center. (32 Thomas Hand St. ☎1 849 4380 www.hamiltonhouseskerries.com ⇞ From Strand St., turn onto Thomas Hand St. $ €40-€45 per person.) Family-owned, this is the closest B&B to the city's sights. The **Jantol House B&B** (32 Balbriggan St. ☎1 849 0143 www.jantolhouse.com ⇞ From the DART Station, take a left off of Station St. onto Dublin Rd.; continue as it becomes Thomas Hand St., then take a left onto Balbriggan St. $ Rooms from €60) might suit you as well, with its great views of the city and owners who are eager to share their city with you.

Getting There

From Dublin, take the **DART** northbound toward Howth (€5.40 round-trip). A one-way trip will take approx. 40 min.

HOWTH *binn éadair*

Accommodations

The no-nonsense **Ann's Guesthouse** (East Pier ☎1 832 3197 www.annsofhowth.com $ Rooms €80 ⏰ Reception 24hr.) has rooms overlooking the water. Situated right where the East Pier meets Harbour Rd., this is also the easiest (read: the least of a hill climb) of the accommodations to get to. A little ways up the hill will bring you to **Gleann na Smól B&B,** (Nashville Rd. ☎1 832 2936 ⇆ From Thormanby Rd., turn left onto Nashville Rd. $ Singles €35; doubles €40. 10% discount for students, 50% discount for children under 12 ⏰ Call ahead if arriving after 10pm) where the owners will make you feel like part of the family. Grab some of Kitty's fresh soda bread, while Sean gives you inside tips on the best restaurants in town. Keep going up the hill to find the winding driveway that leads you to **Highfield B&B.** (Thormanby Rd. ☎1 832 3936 ⇆ Hike a ways up Thormanby Rd., and look for the B&B sign on the left. ℹ Full Irish breakfast made daily. $ Singles €45; doubles €70. ⏰ Call ahead if arriving after 10pm.) Less homey and more professional, Highfield still does an excellent job of making its guests feel welcome.

Sights

The **cliff walk** is Howth's biggest tourist attraction. Offering 2- to 4hr. hikes, the rocky crags and old lighthouses make it a walk like no other. Pick up maps for the trails at the tourist center. To get to the trailhead, follow Harbour Rd. until it turns into Balscadden Rd.; the trailhead is at the end of the road. The **Martello Tower,** just behind East Pier, is home to **Ye Old Hurdy-Gurdy Museum of Vintage Radio.** (☎86 815 4189 $ €5. ⏰ Open May-Oct daily 11am-5pm.) The music and radio paraphernalia might be exciting (for some), but be sure to check out the views too. The tower overlooks Howth Harbour and **Ireland's Eye,** the nearby island bird sanctuary. Boat tours are available every hour on the hour from 11am-6pm (€15). Check out the island's own Martello Tower or see the ruins of 8th-century **St. Nessan's Church.** For the biggest cluster of Howth's sights, turn right out of the DART station, then left at the castle gates. **Howth Castle** itself is closed to the public, but the gates to the grounds are always open. Get a few photos of the somewhat deteriorating outer structure, then keep heading up the road. Past the castle is the **Deer Park Golf Club.** Four courses overlook the city and harbor, so don't get too distracted while swinging. (☎1 832 3487 www.deerpark-hotel.ie $ €18 for 18 holes. ⏰ Open M-F 8am-dusk, Sa-Su 6:30am-dusk.) If you're not a golfer, go right around the club to the **Rhodendron Garden** path ($ Free ⏰ Open 24hr). Best known for starring in the last chapter of James Joyce's *Ulysses*, these gardens are quite literally breathtaking. Yes, the vibrant colors are part of it, but so are the steep, mossy paths up the side of the hill. Keep taking right turns to get to **Aideen's Grave,** a collapsed portal dolmen believed to be the grave of an old Irish hero's daughter. On your way out, stop by the **National Transport Museum** for a tour of trains, cars, and tanks past. (☎1 832 0427 www.nationaltransportmuseum.org $ €3. ⏰ Open Sa-Su 10am-5pm.)

Food

With four fireplaces warming up its three rooms, **Abbey Tavern** lives up to its self-proclaimed "Warmest Welcome in Howth." The smell of roasting meat permeates the interior; if you weren't hungry when you walked in, you will be once you sit down. (28 Abbey St. ☎1 839 0307 www.abbeytavern.ie ⇆ From Harbour Rd., take Abbey St. and look on the left. $ Pints from €4, entrees from €10. ⏰ Open M-F 12:30-7pm, Sa-Su 12:30-9pm.) **Ella Jazz and Wine** (☎1 839 6264 www.ellawinebar.com ⇆ From Harbour

Rd. and East Pier, take a right onto Main St. $ Starters €4-5. Entrees €6-14. ⏰ Open M-Sa noon-3pm and 5:30pm-late) is the perfect place for a girls day, lunch date, or any sort of date for that matter. The funky purple storefront and engaging staff are hard to miss. **The Country Market,** a part deli, part organic grocery store will pack fresh sandwiches with gourmet ingredients for hungry hikers. (15 Main St. ☎1 832 2033 ➡ To the right of the church. $ Sandwiches from €5. ⏰ Open M-Sa 8:30am-6pm, Su 9am-1pm.) **Kruger's** has your Irish bar food craving covered. Grab a seat in one of the leather chairs in front of the fireplace to warm up on a rainy day. (☎1 832 2229 ➡ On Main St across from the church. $ Pints from €5, food €3.50-10. ⏰ Open daily 12:30-8pm.) If you have somehow managed to make it to the top of Thormanby Rd. (and thus the top of all Howth), you deserve a drink at the **Summit Inn.** (☎1 832 4615 ⏰ Open M-Th 11am-11:30pm, F-Sa 11am-12:30am. $ Pints €5, bar food €4.50-12.) Located halfway down West Pier, the **Oar House** (☎1 839 4568 $ Starters €4-12, mains €12-23 ⏰ Open daily 12:30pm-late) serves seafood that you may have actually seen in the harbor earlier. Yep, that fresh. **The Bloody Stream Pub** (☎1 839 5076 $ Pints €5-6. Starters €4-9. Entrees €8-17 ⏰ Open daily noon-late) is located at the DART station; don't think that deters the traditional Irish fun at all. Pub songs play, locals and tourists sing along, and that good ol' Irish food keeps coming. If you're looking for something a bit fancier, try **The House.** A blend of seafood and traditional Irish menu items appeal to all sorts, and the live jazz Wednesdays at 8pm makes this a great place to class up your night. (☎1 839 6388 ➡ Take Harbour St. to East Pier, then left on Main St. $ Starters €6-8, mains €12-22.50. ⏰ Open M-F 8:45am-9:30pm, Sa-Su 10am-10pm.)

Essentials

PRACTICALITIES

- **TOURIST INFORMATION:** The **tourist information center** is at the end of West Pier. (1 West Pier ☎1 839 6955 www.howthismagic.com) A general map of the peninsula is located at the start of each pier.
- **ATMS:** ATMs are located just outside the SPAR on Main St. (across from the church) and at the Texaco across from West Pier.
- **INTERNET:** There is free internet access at the **public library** on Main St. across from the church. (☎1 832 2130 ⏰ Open M 2pm-8:30pm, Tu 10am-1pm, W 2pm-8:30pm, Th 10am-1pm, F-Sa 10am-5pm.)

- **POST OFFICE:** The post office is located just off Harbour Rd. on Abbey St. (☎1 832 0899 ⏰ Open M-F 9am-1pm and 2:15-5:30pm, Sa 9am-1pm.)

EMERGENCY

- **POLICE:** The **Garda** station is at the intersection of Howth Terr. and Church Rd. (☎1 666 4900 ⏰ Open 24hr.)
- **PHARMACY:** **McDermott's Pharmacy** is on Main St. across from the church. (☎1 832 2130 ⏰ Open M-Sa 9am-6pm, Su 9am-1pm.)

GETTING THERE

The easiest and most picturesque way to reach Howth is by **DART,** taking the northbound train to Howth (€2.50, €4.70 round-trip.) Or, take bus #31 or 31B from Dublin city centre (€2, €3.50 round-trip). To get into town from the DART station, take a left on Harbour Rd. Take another left onto West Pier to get to the tourist information center at the end of it.

KILLINEY

Definitely Dublin's poshest suburb, Killiney has more than its namesake hill to offer. Spend the day tanning on what may be the best beaches in Ireland, or take a stroll in the neighborhood of Ireland's rich and famous. (What's that, you want to check out Bono's house?) Follow Vico St., and look for the U2 quotes covering the walls. Or from the beach, make the hike to the top of Killiney Hill. The views of the Wicklow Mountains will make you believe in life again, and the hike itself will make you believe in exercising again. If you're looking for a place to stay, though, you won't find much. **The Druid Lodge** (Killiney Hill Rd. ☎1 285 1632 www.druidlodge.com ⇞ From the DART station, take a right turn and follow the coast road for about 300m, turning left turn up Saintbury Ave., also known as Kilmore Ave., to the intersection with Killiney Hill Rd. [$] Rooms from €40 per person) is a little ways outside of the city but has great views of the beach and hill. If you have a couple hundred extra euro to throw around, spend it on **Fitzpatrick Castle Hotel** (yes, it's an actual castle). Just up the street from Bono's digs, this place will make you feel like royalty. (☎1 230 5400 www.fitzpatrickcastle.com ⇞ From the DART station, take a right onto Vico Rd. and follow it for a while. Turn left onto Victoria Rd., then right onto Killiney Hill Rd. [$] Rooms from €150.)

Getting There

Take the DART southbound toward Bray (€3, €5.40 round-trip), or bus #7 or 7B from Mountjoy St. (€2.50, €4.60 round-trip). From the DART Station, go right on Vico Rd. Take another immediate right for the beach, or follow Vico Rd. uphill for a look at Bono's house. To climb the hill, take Vico Rd. past the beach, then turn left onto the labeled path.

essentials

PRACTICALITIES

- **TOURIST OFFICES:** **College Green Tourism Office,** Dublin's only independent tourist agency, will help you get a jump on any tour you have in mind. From booking tickets for the Guinness Storehouse to reserving your stay for the night, they do it all. (37 College Green ☎1 410 0700 info@daytours.ie ⏰ Open daily 8:30am-10pm.) However, it's worth stating that they are a booking service, and while they can answer most of your questions, if you're looking for information, take the short walk over to **Dublin Tourism** on Suffolk St. Located in a converted church with beautiful arched ceilings and stained glass windows, this may be the only tourist office that's a sight in itself. The staff are knowledgeable and friendly. Head to the general information desk with general questions or head over to one of the many tour companies that have desks in the office. (The former St. Andrew's Church, Suffolk St. ☎1 605 7700 www.visitdublin.com ✈ From College Green, walk up Suffolk St. Dublin Tourism is on the right. 🕐 Open daily 8:30am-9pm.) To get to the **O'Connell St. branch** from the river, walk up O'Connell St. An off-shoot of the Dublin Tourism head offices in the converted St. Andrew's cathedral, this office offers many of the same services (e.g., tour bookings, room reservations, and general tourist information), just in a slightly more boring building. (14 O'Connell St. ☎1 874 6064 www.visitdublin.com 🕐 Open M-Sa 9am-5pm.) The **Northern Ireland Tourist Board** is the place to go for information on Belfast and Northern Ireland, they're also a booking service and will make any reservations you require, free of charge. (Inside Dublin Tourism, Suffolk St. ☎1 605 7732 www.discovernorthernireland.com 🕐 Open Sept-June M-Sa 9am-5:30pm, Su 10:30am-3pm; July-Aug M-Sa 9am-7pm.)

- **GENERAL POST OFFICE:** From the O'Connell St. bridge, it is a few blocks away from the river along O'Connell St. on the left. Look for a new museum detailing the role of the post office in Irish society over the years. (O'Connell St. ☎1 705 7000 www.anpost.ie *i* Cash only. 🕐 Open M-Sa 8:30am-6pm.)

- **LUGGAGE STORAGE: Global Internet Café.** As a nice internet cafe (and they actually do serve coffee), possibly the best thing about this place is their luggage storage rates. A lot of hassle averted for a little money. (8 Lower O'Connell St. ✈ Head over the bridge and onto O'Connell St.; the cafe is on the right. ☎878 0295 www.globalcafe.ie *i* Wi-Fi: 20min. €1.85, students €1.70; 40min. €2.25/2; 1hr. €2.95/2.65. Luggage storage: 1st day €4.50, each additional day €2.15. 🕐 Open M-F 8am-10pm, Sa 9am-9pm, Su 10am-9pm.)

- **CURRENCY EXCHANGE:** €6,000 limit. (1 Westmoreland St. ☎670 6724 🕐 Open M-Th 9am-6pm, F-Sa 9am-8pm, Su 10am-6pm.)

- **ATMS:** A 24hr. ATM can be found at the bottom of Grafton St., across Nassau St. from the Molly Malone statue. There are also two 24hr. ATMs at the **Ulster Bank** on Dame St. across from the Wax Museum Plus. ATMs are also located in every **SPAR.**

EMERGENCY

- **EMERGENCY NUMBER:** ☎999 or 112. Ask for the service (ambulance, fire, or police) you require.

- **POLICE:** There are several **Garda** (police) stations located around Dublin. To get to the Harcourt station, follow Harcourt St. away from the city center and away from St. Stephen's Green (Harcourt Sq. ☎01 666 666 www.garda.ie 🕐 Open 24hr.). On the north side, follow the Quays from O'Connell Bridge, taking Bachelors Walk as it becomes Lower Ormond Quay then Upper Ormond Quay. Take a right onto Chancery Pl. then a right onto Chancery St. (Chancery St. ☎1 666 8200 www.garda.ie 🕐 Open 24hr.)

- **PHARMACIES: Hickey's Pharmacy** is up Grafton St. on the left. (21 Grafton St. ☎1 679 0467 🕐 Open M-Th 8:30am-8:30pm, F 8:30am-8pm, Sa-Su 10:30am-6pm.) Another Hickey's Pharmacy is located on O'Connell St., right after the bridge (55 Lower O'Connell St. ☎1 873 0427 www.hickeyspharmacy.ie 🕐 Open M-F 7:30am-10pm, Sa 8am-10pm, Su 10am-10pm.) Or try **Temple Bar Pharmacy.** (21 Essex St. ☎1 670 9751 www.templebarpharmacy.ie 🕐 Open M-W 9:30am-7pm, Th-Sa 9:30am-8pm, Su 1pm-5pm.)

- **SEXUAL ASSAULT: Dublin Rape Crisis Center** provides a 24hr. hotline, free counseling, advocacy, and legal advice for victims of recent rape or sexual abuse. (70 Lower Leeson St. 24hr. toll-free national hotline ☎1 800 77 8888; office number ☎1 661 4911 www.drcc.ie Ⓢ Free. 🕐 Open M-F 8am-7pm, Sa 9am-4pm.)

GETTING THERE
BY PLANE

Flights go through **Dublin International Airport** (DIA; www.dublinairport.com). The DIA houses desks for several different flight companies, some of which do flight bookings at the desk.

- **RYANAIR:** Available for last-minute changes to your tickets, no phone or booking done here. Do that at www.ryanair.com. Be careful of last-minute charges here. Print your ticket beforehand and arrive with plenty of time to spare.

- **LUFTHANSA:** ☎1 844 5544 🕐 Open daily 5-7am, 8:15am-12:30pm, 3:30-5:30pm.

- **AER ARANN:** For domestic flights in Ireland. Book online or reserve at the desk. (☎081 821 0210 www.aerarann.com 🕐 Open daily 5:30am-10pm.)

- **AER LINGUS:** Book flights, change flights, collect excess baggage (there's a 20kg weight limit), and rebook (www.aerlingus.com).

- **US AIRWAYS:** ☎809 092 5065 www.usairways.com 🕐 Open daily 7:30am-noon.

- **CONTINENTAL AIRLINES:** ☎189 092 5252 www.continental.com.

- **AIR FRANCE:** ☎01 605 0383 www.airfrance.ie 🕐 Open M-F 4am-7:50pm, Sa 4am-5:45pm, Su 4am-7:50pm.

- **DELTA:** ☎1 850 088 2031 www.delta.com 🕐 Open 6am-1pm. May change according to day's flight schedule.

BY CAR

- **BUDGET:** ☎9066 27711 www.budget.ie 🕐 Open daily 5am-midnight.

- **HERTZ:** ☎01 844 5466 www.hertz.ie 🕐 Open daily 5am-1am.

- **EUROPCAR:** ☎1 812 2800 www.europcar.ie 🕐 Open daily 6am-11pm.

- **SIXT RENT-A-CAR:** ☎018 1204 www.sixt.ie 🕐 Open daily 6am-midnight.

- **AVIS:** ☎31 605 7500 www.avis.ie 🕐 Open M-F 5am-11:30pm, Sa 5am-11pm, Su 5am-11:30pm.

GETTING AROUND
BY BUS

Dublin Bus runs using a system of stages. The price of your bus fare in Dublin depends on how far you're traveling: 1-3 stages €1.40, 4-7 €1.90, 8-13 €2.15 and over 13 stages is €2.65. The "Rambler Pass" is advertised for tourists, but though it lets you travel on any bus for a set amount of time, it is priced pretty steeply, so only buy it if you're sure to be moving around quite a bit (1-day pass €7, 3-day €14, 5-day €23). Bus times vary, but can usually be caught every 8-20min. 6am-8pm and every 30min. 8pm-midnight. (☎1 873 4222 www.dublinbus.ie.)

BY TRAIN

Luas, Dublin's light rail tram system, traverses the city, making its way to several of Dublin's suburbs. One-way tickets are €2-3, depending on the distance traveled and time, while round-trip tickets are €3-6. The fares are divided into zones, much like the bus system. Maps at each station let you know which zone you need to get to. For longer stays, a 7-day (€13-30) or 30-day (€50-89) bargain pass is available. Use it to get from one end of the city to the other or to hit up Dublin's suburbs quickly and for cheap. (☎800 300 604 www.luas.ie 🕐 Operates M-F 7am-7pm and Sa 10am-2pm.) Dublin Area Rapid Transit (DART) runs along Dublin's coast south-

essentials

ward from Malahide and Howth to Greystones. One-way tickets are €2-5, depending on the destination, and round-trip tickets are €4-10. Student discount tickets and special offers for tourists are often available, so check for availability. (☎1 703 3504 www.irishrail.ie.)

BY TAXI

Taxis in Dublin are, much like everything else, expensive. Expect to pay anywhere from €7-10 to get from one destination to another, and more if you're heading across town. Obey the general rules of foreign taxi travel—ask ahead to find the shortest route to your destination, and then make sure the cabbie follows it. **Blue Cabs** is the most popular taxi company in Dublin. They offer wheelchair-accessible cabs. Call ahead of time to book. It's an extra €2 to order a cab ahead by phone and an extra €1 for each passenger. (☎1 802 2222 www.bluecabs.ie.) There are taxi stands (or "ranks") at the following places:

- **TEMPLE BAR:** On the **Aston Quay** and on **College Green** in front of the Wax Museum and Bank of Ireland.

- **GRAFTON STREET AREA:** Near the intersection of **Dawson St.** and **Duke St.** On **Harry St.,** off the top of Grafton St. and to the right.

- **VIKING/GEORGIAN AREA:** On **Christchurch Pl.** across the street from the Christchurch Cathedral.

- **NORTH OF O'CONNELL ST.:** On **Eden Quay,** just to the right of the O'Connell Monument. In the median of **O'Connell St.,** just south of the Parnell Monument. On **Sackville Pl.,** walk ¼ of the way up O'Connell St. and turn right.

BY BIKE

Dublin is a bikable city. It's not common for bike shops to do rentals; get ready to bargain if you're going that route. We suggest **Dublin Bikes.** Rent a bike at any of the 44 stations and return it to any as well. Get an account online and use it for as long as you are in Dublin. It's €10 for a year-long subscription or €2 for the first half hour then €0.50 per hour after that. (www.dublinbikes.ie.)

ULSTER AND CONNACHT

Toto, I have a feeling we're not in Dublin anymore. The island's less traveled northwest sector is a far cry from touristy Temple Bar, and there's a little bit more open green space than you'll find in Phoenix Park. The urban alleyways and heavily trafficked thoroughfares are exchanged for perhaps a more stereotypically Irish landscape: contains crumbling castles and abbeys, picture-perfect towns, rolling green countryside, and a vibrant artistic and cultural scene. Miss the feel of Publin? You'll find a watering hole or two in this chapter (a Guinness-ing hole?), but you may soon find yourself drawn away from the taps and toward the magnificent outdoors, from the region's rocky bays and windswept islands to the peak of Croagh Patrick, with the whole domain extending before you. You won't find the Emerald City here, but this is certainly the Emerald Isle at its best.

greatest hits

- **▢DRAGON CROSSING:** There may not be any fantastical creatures protecting locked-away princesses at Donegal Castle (p. 56), but it is still a must-see while you are in Donegal.

- **ABBEY CAT:** Head to Sligo Abby (p. 63) to check out these roofless ruins and make some feline friends.

- **HOLY HIKE:** Climb up Croagh Patrick (p. 70) outside Westport for a breathtaking view (the trek itself may take your breath away as well).

student life

The National University of Ireland, Galway has a significant presence in the city of Galway and in its region; St. Angela's College in Sligo is also an affiliate. Ireland's President, Taoiseach (Prime Minister), Tánaiste (Deputy Prime Minister), and Attorney General all attended NUI Galway (then known as University College, Galway), and with 17,000 current students, the university certainly makes Galway a student town.

donegal ☎73

A little town surrounded by rolling fields, Donegal lives up to all the postcards you've ever seen of Ireland. While sleepy most of the time, every place you come to will be better than the last. You can stare out to sea from the ruins of a Franciscan friary, sit by the ancient stone obelisk in the town center, or go browse through Craft Village. Sniff the air, laden with scents of cow, or feel the coolness after the frequent drizzling rain. On the weekends, take a turn at Riverdancing in one of the bright pubs. Whatever you wanted when you decided on Ireland, Donegal has it.

ORIENTATION

Most everything in this town is either directly adjacent or very close to the town center, **the Diamond.** Walking from here up **Main Street,** you will find a few more shops, restaurants, and pubs, but they end fairly quickly. Heading down **Quay Street,** meanwhile, will lead you toward **Donegal Bay** and **Craft Village.** Going over the river by **Bridge Street** will take you toward the majority of the local accommodations, including the wonderful **Donegal Town Independent Hostel.**

ACCOMMODATIONS

There is an almost limitless number of B&Bs surrounding the town, as every family with a couple spare rooms is happy to welcome in world-weary travelers looking for some Irish-style R and R.

DONEGAL TOWN INDEPENDENT HOSTEL HOSTEL $

Killybegs Rd. ☎74 972 2805 www.donegaltownhostel.com

This is without question one of the finest hostels in Ireland. While the facilities are simple, with a kitchen and a cozy sitting area, the real prize here is the warmth of the welcome from hosts Linda and Andy. They do their absolute best to make sure that your visit is as enjoyable as it could possibly be. Always free for a chat and a smile, Linda and Andy ensure that you will find yourself at home here. The rooms themselves are comfortable and well-furnished, but if you can, spend the extra bit of money on one of the private rooms, whose large comfortable mattresses, soft lamp lighting, and thick duvet covers will make you never want to leave.

From the Diamond, walk down Castle St. Continue onto Killybegs Rd. At the roundabout, take the 1st exit towards Doonan. The hostel is on the right. ℹ *Free Wi-Fi. Laundry available. Kitchen available.* $ *4- to 6-bed dorms €17; singles €19; doubles €18, ensuite €22.* ⏰ *Check-in from noon. Check-out 11am.*

DRUMHOLM B&B B&B $$$

Drumcliff Terr. ☎074 972 3126

This simple B&B has some perks that make it a cut above the many others scattered around the area. Not least is their extreme proximity to the town center.

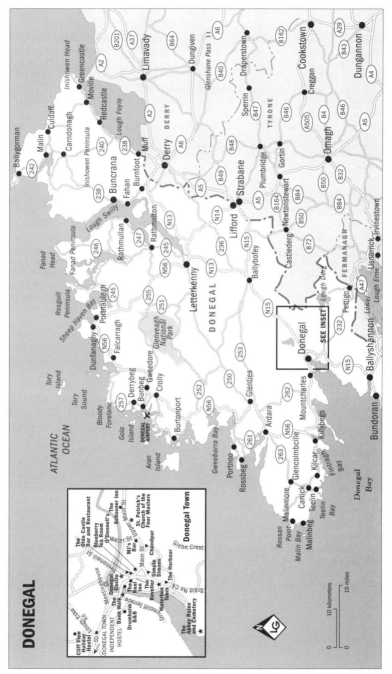

DONEGAL

Donegal Town

Cliff View Holiday Hostel
DONEGAL TOWN INDEPENDENT HOSTEL
Drumholm B&B
The Waterbus
Bank Walk
The Reveller
The Donegal Castle
The Reel Inn
MJ's Bar
O'Donnell's The Schooner Inn
The Blueberry Tea Room
The Olde Castle Bar and Restaurant
St. Patrick's Church of the Four Masters
Main St.
Water St.
The Diamond
The Meetinghouse
Tirconaill Terrace
The Harbour
Simple Simons
Chandpur
The Mall East
Glebe Crest
Sráid Na Cé
Sligo Rd.
The Abbey Ruins and Cemetery

DONEGAL AIRPORT

Glenveagh National Park

ATLANTIC OCEAN

Donegal Bay

SEE INSET

donegal

Otherwise, their delicious breakfast served every morning and well-appointed comforts in every room ensure that you can unwind in the Irish countryside.

 # From the Diamond, walk down Castle St. After crossing the bridge, turn left onto Drumcliff Terr. The B&B is on the right. i Breakfast included. $ Singles €30-45; doubles €45-60.

CLIFF VIEW HOLIDAY HOSTEL HOSTEL $$

Coast Rd. ☎074 972 1684

While Cliff View Holiday Hostel is only a short walk from town and its prices are right, it isn't entirely surprising that many people would rather make the trek out to the Independent Hostel. The high metal fences and battered exterior might feel somewhat less than inviting, while the rooms themselves are in a livable condition, although you will probably want to spend a little more time in town than you might otherwise.

 # From the Diamond, walk down Castle St. Continue onto Killybegs Rd. Turn right onto Coast Rd. The hostel is ahead. i Kitchen available. $ Dorms €15-25. ⏰ Reception 24hr.

SIGHTS

★ DONEGAL CASTLE CASTLE

Tirchonaill St. ☎74 972 2405 www.heritageireland.ie/en/north-west/donegalcastle

This small keep was a holdfast of the powerful O'Donnell clan for centuries, including the famous Red Hugh himself. Maybe you don't know these heroes now, but spend long enough sitting at the local pubs and the old Gaelic legends are sure to start creeping in from the shadows. Donegal Castle is no exception. The manor house, constructed by a conquering English soldier, is almost an insult to the otherwise Irish fortress. The interior is more comfortable now, swaddled as it is in Persian rugs and heavy-hanging tapestries.

 # From the Diamond, walk down Castle St. Bear right onto Tirchonaill St. The castle entrance is on the left. i 30min. guided tours are available every hr. $ €4, students €2. ⏰ Open Apr-Sept daily 10am-6pm; Oct-Mar Th-Su 9:30am-4:30pm.

THE ABBEY RUINS AND CEMETERY RUINS

The Pier

You can stare out to sea from under the ruinous arches in this once-great monastery on the shores of Donegal. True, the roof, floor, and most of the walls are gone, but somehow the feeling of the place is intensely powerful and quiet. This is undoubtedly due in part to that restful quality of cemeteries, but there is also history here. You can easily imagine the wizened Four Masters crouched in this stone monastery on the edge of the sea. They wrote the first real "Irish history," or, in other words, the first record of Gaelic mythology, in the epic "Annals of the Four Masters."

 # From the Diamond, walk down Quay St. Turn right onto the quay itself. Walk down the pier to the headland.

THE BANK WALK FOOTPATH

Castle St.

For such a small town, it can sometimes be difficult to actually get away from all the hustle and bustle of the Diamond and Main St. Those hills in the distance can start to look pretty appealing. Well, if you only have a little time, stroll this tiny tree-lined track along the river. The woody smells and golden rays shining between the leaves overhead will remind you of the countryside which is apparently all around you. At the end of the walk, there is a perfect bench for sitting and meditating on the abbey on the opposite headland or just out to the sea.

 # From the Diamond, walk along Castle St. Immediately after crossing the bridge, turn left onto the footpath.

ST. PATRICK'S CHURCH OF THE FOUR MASTERS
Main St.

CHURCH

☎74 972 1026

Dedicated to the Four Masters, this church is the heart of the predominantly Catholic local church-goers. The impressive Romanesque façade belies the delicate artistry of the interior. This place offers a part of the local history suitable for a short visit.

☂ *From the Diamond, walk up Main St. The church is on a small hill on the right.* Ⓢ *Donations welcome.* ⓐ *Open M-Sa 9am-5pm. Mass Su 9am and 11:30am.*

WATERBUS TOURS
The Quay

BOAT TOUR

☎74 972 3666 www.donegalbaywaterbus.com

Offering wind-swept tours of Donegal harbor, these tours will provide you all the information you want on the local attractions. Get off your feet for a little bit and enjoy this waterbus. Most fun is a visit to the nearby seal colony, where you can grow increasingly jealous of the creatures' lolling, blubber-cushioned existence.

☂ *From the Diamond, walk down Quay St. The ticket office is on the right.* ⓘ *Tickets must be purchased 30min. before scheduled departure.* Ⓢ *€15, students €10.* ⓐ *Tours daily. Sailing times depend on tides, but last trip typically leaves at 4:30pm.*

FOOD

Without anything in the way of chains or the usual budget staples, finding a budget meal can be a little tricky. But, surprisingly for such a small town, there is a wide selection of traditional cafes, more upper-crust restaurants, and well-priced take-out joints to choose from. So while it might not be the cheapest, you can rest assured you will get your money's worth.

⬛ THE BLUEBERRY TEA ROOM
The Diamond

TEA ROOM $$

☎74 972 2933

The floury smell of freshly baked scones wafts over the hubbub at this heart of local life. If you are lucky enough to get a table, relax under the twinkling lights in the branches of painted silver trees overhead while wondering what the real time is between the dozen or so clocks on the wall. The Blueberry Tea Room merrily mixes the traditional local cafe image with a spark of something new and creative. After ordering your gourmet-quality main course, don't miss one of their freshly baked and decadently delicious desserts, like the steamed chocolate pudding, swimming in chocolate sauce and garnished with a thick dollop of fresh cream (€4.50). You can't go to Donegal without going here.

☂ *From the Diamond, walk toward Donegal Castle. The tea room is on the right.* ⓘ *Cash only. Internet cafe upstairs.* Ⓢ *Entrees €5-13.* ⓐ *Open M-Sa 9am-7pm.*

SIMPLE SIMONS
The Diamond

DELI $

☎74 972 3690

With a huge range of local goods, including homemade spreads, cheeses from the goats you saw on the way into town, and generously proportioned sandwiches, Simple Simons is a great deal. Now that there are some metal chairs scattered around and free Wi-Fi, you can tuck into your choice of the many delights in the comfort of the shop with those classic deli smells drifting around. Otherwise, take your sandwich out to the Diamond and watch everyone go about their day.

☂ *Directly adjacent to the Diamond.* ⓘ *Free Wi-Fi.* Ⓢ *Sandwiches €2.75-5.15.* ⓐ *Open M-Sa 9:30am-6pm.*

THE HARBOUR
Quay St.

SEAFOOD $$$$

☎74 972 1702 www.theharbour.ie

One of the fancier restaurants in the area, this is the place to come for some seriously fresh seafood or one of the most savory pizzas ever. If you are willing to splash out, you won't regret trying the herb-crusted cod with caramelized balsamic red onion and roasted cherry tomato (€18). Yes, it is expensive, but you

donegal

can just smell the sea coming off it. What better way to enjoy the pleasures of a coastal village in Ireland?

🚶 *From the Diamond, walk down Quay St. toward the bay. The restaurant is on the left.* ℹ️ *Reservation recommended on weekends.* 💲 *Entrees €12.25-21.75. Pizzas €8.75-14.* 🕐 *Open M-Th 5-9:30pm, F-Sa 5-10pm, Su 3-9pm.*

THE OLDE CASTLE BAR AND RESTAURANT   PUB $$$

Castle St.   ☎74 972 21062 www.oldecastlebar.com

Tuck into some spectacular pub food while surrounded by the softly flickering lights in this subterranean-feeling restaurant. The flagstone floor and curved ceilings will make you almost want to huddle for warmth, which is completely unnecessary considering the piping hot dishes turned out daily. If you are in the mood, there is also a fully-stocked bar, so you can enjoy your frosty pint with your food. Try their famous seafood pie, crammed with all kinds of fresh local seafood and topped with cheddar cheese and potato (€14).

🚶 *From the Diamond, walk down Castle St. The restaurant is on the right.* ℹ️ *Some prices vary depending on seafood market prices.* 💲 *Entrees €12.50-22.50.* 🕐 *Open daily noon-late.*

CHANDPUR   INDIAN $$$

Unit 4, Main St.   ☎74 972 5452 www.facebook.com/chandpurindianrestaurant

While it would be understandable to balk a little bit at eating Indian food while in the heart of the old-school Irish countryside, sometimes that chicken tikka masala (€11), steaming and creamy, along with a healthy portion of naan or rice to match, is just what the doctor ordered. When that Irish countryside starts to live up to its reputation for gray drizzle rather than sun-drenched green fields, the hot, tangy dishes here are exactly what you want to be savoring.

🚶 *From the Diamond, walk up Main St. Turn right toward the Main St. parking area. The restaurant is on the left.* ℹ️ *Take-out available.* 💲 *Entrees €10-22.* 🕐 *Open daily noon-midnight.*

NIGHTLIFE

When things are as concentrated as it is here, everywhere is a local spot. Don't bother looking for rowdy clubs—you won't find them. Instead, settle in for some good, old-fashioned Irish pubs, most with live music, and all with plenty of Guinness.

☒ THE REEL INN   PUB, LIVE MUSIC

Castle St.

The most respected of the local pubs, sitting on a barstool in here is the thing to do as many nights as you can. Take your Guinness with its frothy shamrock and listen to all the Irish classics, from local trios to solo artists just starting out, on everything from accordions to the electric guitar. Chant out the names of the classics you want to hear or maybe just sit and mutter the words along with everyone else. The warmth of both the people will make you reluctant to eventually troop out into the cool night air.

🚶 *From the Diamond, walk down Bridge St. The pub is on the left.* ℹ️ *Irish dancing nightly at 9pm. Live music every night* 💲 *Pints €3.10-4.40.* 🕐 *Open daily noon-late.*

O'DONNELL'S   PUB

The Diamond   ☎74 972 1049

The biggest and rowdiest of the pubs on the central Diamond, O'Donnell's lives up to all expectations of a local Irish pub. With some bric-a-brac scattered around, this place is mostly filled with plenty of groups of a younger variety, along with some more weathered patrons. You've probably been to one or two Irish pubs before, and this is probably pretty similar to most of them—the crucial difference being that this one is actually in Ireland.

🚶 *Directly adjacent to the Diamond.* ℹ️ *Live music on weekends.* 💲 *Pints €3-4.20.* 🕐 *Open M-Sa 11am-late.*

THE SCHOONER INN
PUB

Upper Main St.　　　　　　　　　　　　　　　　　　　☎074 972 1671

Living up to its seafaring name, it is no surprise that this place is filled with model ships and other memorabilia of a nautical variety. The lantern lighting casts long shadows all over the wooden walls, making you feel like you might be sitting in the belly of some voyaging galleon. By the time your last Guinness is finished, the floor will be heaving and hauling, just as if you were.

☞ *From the Diamond, walk up Main St. The bar is on the left.* **i** *Live music often.* Ⓢ *Pints €3-4.20.* 🕓 *Open daily noon-midnight.*

MJ'S BAR
BAR, LIVE MUSIC

Upper Main St.

Crammed into a small unit on Main St., the loud red and black exterior of this live music bar might seem a little more rock 'n' roll than you might expect or want in quiet Donegal. But give it a chance. Go through the darkened bar area into the cool beer garden and enjoy the night air, while some musician rouses the cheering locals. And hey, if you happen to be even slightly musically talented, get up there and give it a go.

☞ *From the Diamond, walk up Main St. The bar is on the left.* **i** *Live music most nights.* Ⓢ *Pints €3.10-4.40.* 🕓 *Open M-Sa noon-late.*

THE REVELLER
PUB

The Diamond　　　　　　　　　　　　　　　　　　　☎74 972 1201

The Reveller is a local sports pub, so if Donegal happens to be playing in a GAA match, get over here quick. The widescreen TVs broadcast Gaelic Football most of the time, though daring souls occasionally switch it over to something else. The low ceilings and dark wood furnishings make those barstool starers notice anyone who walks in, but be bold, neck some Guinness, and you'll be welcomed in. Join in the cheering and chanting—just make sure it is for the right team.

☞ *The corner of the Diamond toward Bridge St.* **i** *Live music most nights.* Ⓢ *Pints €3-4.20.* 🕓 *Open daily 11am-late.*

ARTS AND CULTURE

▨ CRAFT VILLAGE
ARTS CENTER

Ballyshannon Rd.　　　　　　　　　　☎74 972 2225 www.donegalcraftvillage.com

A collection of local artists all sharing close quarters lends this place an air of authenticity that is lost in the millions of plastic leprechauns that most visitors are seduced by. Watch glass get hand blown or a gorgeous new scarf get woven, both right in front of you by master craftsmen. Once you have realized that you would have to sleep outside for the rest of your trip to afford all the gorgeous ornaments, go to the ▨**Aroma Cafe,** where the art created from food is just as impressive and more satisfying.

☞ *From the Diamond, walk down Quay St. Continue on this road. The center is on the left.* Ⓢ *Prices vary.* 🕓 *Open June-Aug M-Sa 9:30am-6pm, Su noon-5:30pm. Cafe open M-Sa 9:30am-5:30pm.*

SHOPPING

FOUR MASTERS BOOKSHOP
BOOKSHOP

The Diamond　　　　　　　　　　　　　　　　　　　☎074 972 1526

Creating a white and blue contrast to the black front of O'Donnell's next door, this local bookshop is the perfect place to pick up a book of the local history. Or, if you are more fantastically minded, get a tome of Irish mythology to read by the fire at night. You probably will be more likely to read about giant boars than ▨**dragons,** or about the maiden saving the hero for a change, but that is what makes them great.

☞ *Directly adjacent to The Diamond.* **i** *Check for book readings.* 🕓 *Open M-Sa 10am-5:30pm.*

ESSENTIALS

Practicalities

- **TOURIST OFFICE: Discover Ireland Centre.** (The Quay ☎74 972 1148 www.discoverireland.ie ➜ From The Diamond, walk down Quay St. The center is on the right on the Quay itself. *i* Free travel literature. Accommodation bookings system. ⏰ Open June-Aug M-Sa 9am-5:30pm, Su 11am-3pm; Sept-May M-Sa 9am-5pm.)
- **CURRENCY EXCHANGE:** The reception at the **Abbey Hotel** can help you change cash. (The Diamond ☎74 972 1148 ⏰ Open 24hr.)
- **INTERNET ACCESS:** The **Blueberry Tea Room** maintains a small cyber cafe above the main cafe. (Castle St. ☎74 972 2933 ➜ From the Diamond, walk toward Castle St. The cafe is on the right. [$] €2 for 30min. ⏰ Open M-Sa 9am-7pm.)
- **POST OFFICE:** Tirconaill St. ☎74 972 1024 ➜ From the Diamond, walk toward Castle St. The cafe is on the right. ⏰ Open M-Sa 9am-5:30pm.

Emergency

- **POLICE: Garda Station.** (Quay St. ☎74 974 0190, ☎999 for emergencies www.garda.ie ⏰ 24hr. assistance.)
- **DOCTOR: Millrow Family Practice.** (New Row ☎74 9721545, ☎999 for emergencies. ⏰ Open M-Sa 10am-7pm.)
- **PHARMACY: Cara Pharmacy.** (3 Glebe Shopping Centre ☎74 9721112 www.lifepharmacy.ie ⏰ Open M-Sa 9am-7pm.)

Getting There

BY BUS

Bus Éireann stops at the Diamond in front of the Abbey Hotel daily. Routes come from anywhere between Derry, Dublin, Galway, and Sligo bus stations. (☎74 912 1309 www.buseireann.ie [$]€8-15, students €2 off.)

BY PLANE

City of Derry Airport (LDY; ☎28 7181 0784 www.cityofderryairport.com) receives flights from Tyrone and Donegal in the Republic of Ireland. **Flybe** delivers flights from Manchester. **Ryanair** flies from Birmingham, Faro, Glasgow, Liverpool, London Stansted, and Tenerife. From Derry, you will need to take a bus from the **Derry Bus Station.**

BY TRAIN

Mac Diarmada Railway Station in Sligo is the only way to get to Donegal Town by train. (☎71 916 9888 www.irishrail.ie.) From the station, you will again have to take a bus to Donegal.

Getting Around

All you need are your own two feet to get anywhere in this little town. Should you need to venture a little farther, however there are some options.

BY BUS

Local bus services to Letterkenny and Ballybofey are operated by **Donegal-Link.** (☎86 248 0794 www.donegallink.ie [$] €4-9, students €3-8.) For going farther afield, **Bus Éireann** operates between Sligo, Derry, Dublin, and Galway bus stations, most of which stop in the Diamond. (☎74 912 1309 www.buseireann.ie [$] €8-15, students €6-13.)

BY TAXI

Metered taxis run through the town; call **Gallagher Cabs** to book. (☎87 417 6600.)

Bicycle rentals are available from **The Bike Shop.** (Waterloo Pl. ☎74 972 2515 Ⓢ €10 per day, €60 per week. ☒ Open M-Sa 10am-6pm.)

sligo ☎71

A strange blend of town and city, Sligo can seem a bit intimidating and unpleasant at first sight—particularly if it is plagued by one of its frequent rain spells. But once you have settled in and gotten to know the city a little better, it becomes very clear that it has some excellent spots. There are crumbling abbey ruins, soaring cathedrals, and a throbbing nightlife scene that will shock the system after a diet of quiet, traditional Irish pub food. And we can't forget the truly excellent dining options that await. Walk

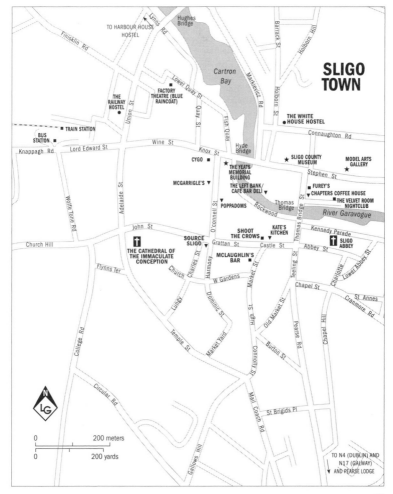

SLIGO TOWN

sligo

down the banks of the dark river **Garavogue** and enjoy the bustling but intimate feel of this Irish coastal city.

ORIENTATION

You will most likely arrive by bus or train into **Mac Diarmada Station** on **Lord Edward Street.** To reach the town center, turn left and walk up Lord Edward St., which will eventually become **Wine Street** before you reach **Hyde Bridge,** the geographical center of town. Turning right along Wine St. will take you down **O'Connell Street,** one of the major thoroughfares of the town, which will itself branch off toward more pubs, restaurants, and shops. Should you cross the river, though, you will head to a more residential area, still interspersed with some good pubs and shops, along with **The Model,** a celebrated contemporary art gallery.

ACCOMMODATIONS

👍 **HARBOUR HOUSE HOSTEL** — HOSTEL $$

Finisklin Rd. — ☎71 917 1547 www.harbourhousehostel.com

Cheap and cheerful is an apt description of Harbour House Hostel. The stone building is not exactly palatial inside, with most of the space in the bedroom taken up by the bed. The atmosphere is relaxed, however, and the sitting area, with a somewhat out-of-place ornate fireplace, is a good place to envelop yourself in a comfortable couch.

☞ From Hyde Bridge, walk down Wine St. Turn right onto Fish Quay, which turns into Lower New St. Turn right onto Custom House Quay. Follow the river onto Ballast Quay. Follow the bend to the left onto Finisklin Rd. The hostel is on the right. ℹ Free Wi-Fi in reception. Laundry available. Free luggage storage. $ Dorms €20; doubles €22, ensuite €25. ⏰ Check-in M-F 2-10pm, Sa-Su 2-9pm.

RAILWAY HOSTEL — HOSTEL $

1 Union Pl. — ☎83 421 8649 www.therailway.ie

On the outside, Railway Hostel definitely seems to be a battered station hostel, with little in the way of comfort or character. It even has "railway" in the name. But on the inside, Railway offers spacious common areas with light wood flooring, bookshelves crammed with discarded novels, and armchairs that beg to sat upon. The rooms themselves are simple, so don't expect to be blown away.

☞ From Mac Diarmada Station, turn left onto Lord Edward St. Take the 1st left onto Union St. The hostel is on the left. ℹ Free Wi-Fi. Microwaves available. $ Dorms €16-18; singles €25; doubles €20. ⏰ Reception 11am-midnight.

PEARSE LODGE — B&B $$$$

Pearse Rd. — ☎71 916 1090 www.pearselodge.com

Should you feel like splurging and should you happen to be traveling with a partner, spring for this luxuriously comfortable B&B just a few minutes' walk from the center of Sligo. The rooms are cozy, with beds that make you want to curl up, and nap, and nap, and nap. The downstairs sitting area, meanwhile, offers a stylish way to enjoy the extensive breakfast that includes french toast, smoked salmon with cream cheese, and, of course, a full Irish breakfast. True, this is a seriously pricey option, but sometimes you just have to treat yourself.

☞ From Hyde Bridge, walk down Wine St. Turn left onto O'Connell St. Turn left onto Grattan St. Continue onto Castle St. Turn right onto Teeling St., then continue onto Pearse Rd. The B&B is on left. ℹ Breakfast included. Free Wi-Fi. $ Doubles €70-76. ⏰ Reception 8am-9pm.

SIGHTS

👍 **THE MODEL** — ART GALLERY

The Mall — ☎71 914 1405 www.themodel.ie

The central creative hub of the county, The Model is not limited to galleries. It also hosts concerts, independent film screenings, and poetry presentations, all of which represent the absolute pinnacle of what Sligo has to offer. While the architectural critic in you might be horrified and outraged by the unsuccessful blend of old and new on the exterior, don't let it discourage you from following the multitude of signs leading here from every street corner.

✦ *From Hyde Bridge, walk up Stephen St. Continue onto The Mall. The gallery is on the left.* ℹ *Check online for current listings.* ⓢ *Free.* ⌚ *Open Tu-Sa 10am-5:30pm, Su noon-5pm.*

🖼 SLIGO ABBEY   RUINS

Abbey St.   71 914 6406 www.heritageireland.ie/en/North-West/SligoAbbey

Enjoy a stroll through this roofless temple and its grounds, marveling at how something once so grand is now mostly infested with tourists and cats. The old stone altar still conjures some of the once-magisterial presence of the place. Sit in the grassy graveyard for a while and sink deep into thought—or maybe just play with one of the older cats basking in the sun.

✦ *From Hyde Bridge, walk down Rockwood Parade. Turn right onto Thomas St. Turn left onto Abbey St. The entrance is on the left.* ℹ *30min. guided tours available.* ⓢ *€3, students €1.* ⌚ *Open Apr-Sept daily 10am-6pm; Oct-Nov F-Su 9:30am-4:30pm.*

YEATS MEMORIAL BUILDING   MUSEUM

Hyde Bridge   71 914 2693 www.yeats-sligo.com

Home to the Sligo Yeats Society, this small exhibit displays letters, snippets, and collections of the famous poet's work. As much a shrine as anything else, you can read drafts in Yeats's own hand. Should you be feeling peckish after all that talk of silver apples of the moon and golden apples of the sun, there is also a small cafe with spacious outdoor seating where you can sit by the edge of the river and enjoy a poetic moment of peace and quiet.

✦ *From Hyde Bridge, walk toward Wine St. The museum is on the left.* ⓢ *€2.* ⌚ *Open M-F 10am-5pm.*

Sligo

CATHEDRAL OF THE IMMACULATE CONCEPTION CATHEDRAL

Temple St. ☎71 916 2670 www.sligocathedral.ie

It is certainly true that you cannot understand Ireland without attending a church service. Come here and appreciate the relative simplicity of the pale painted walls, the blue ceiling, the stained glass, and the ostentatiously huge golden shrine behind the high altar.

 # From Hyde Bridge, walk down Wine St. Turn left onto Adelaide St., which becomes Temple St. The cathedral is on the left. $ Donations welcome. ⏰ Open M-Sa 8am-6pm.

SLIGO COUNTY MUSEUM MUSEUM

Stephen St. ☎71 914 1623

Detailing facts about the county's varied and sometimes bizarre history, this museum features the notable families of the region, while also devoting some time to industry and conflict. While it lacks the history of ancient mythology which you might like, it does its job in outlining some key events in moderately modern times.

 # From Hyde Bridge, walk up Stephen St. The museum is on the left. $ Free. ⏰ Open June-Sept Tu-Sa 10am-5pm; Oct-May Tu-Sa 2-5pm.

FOOD

With plenty of great restaurants, Sligo will easily tempt you to break your budget. If you're looking to save money, try **Tesco** on O'Connell St., open 24hr.

KATE'S KITCHEN DELI $$

3 Castle St. ☎71 914 3022 www.facebook.com/KatesKitchen

The mixed aromas of cinnamon, fresh pastries, and a dash of cardamom or ginger hit you immediately upon walking into this "fine foods deli." This place specializes in giving you the gourmet option and helping to purge your taste buds of all that junk food you've had on the road. Try one of their fresh gourmet pizzas, with buffalo mozzarella, sundried tomatoes, and succulent black olives—all for only €4.

 # From Hyde Bridge, walk down Rockwood Parade. Turn right onto Water Ln. Turn left onto Castle St. The deli is on the left. i Free Wi-Fi. $ Prepared food €3-15. ⏰ Open M-Sa 8:45am-6:15pm.

CHAPTERS COFFEE HOUSE CAFE $$

Bridge St. ☎87 774 9234

This small independent coffee house is a delightful change from Starbucks, with clean walls, book-crammed shelves, and an eclectic soundtrack that is sure to distract you from your reading. Sit around on the comfy, cushion-covered couches and take a moment in the upstairs seating to watch people cross the bridge over the cauldron-black waters of the river below.

 # From Hyde Bridge, walk along Rockwood Parade until you reach Thomas St. Turn left and cross the bridge. The cafe is ahead. i Free Wi-Fi. $ Sandwiches €4. Coffee €1.50-2. ⏰ Open M-Sa 9am-5:30pm.

SOURCE SLIGO IRISH $$$

1 John St. ☎71 914 7605 www.sourcesligo.ie

When they say local ingredients, they mean it. Source Sligo knows every single one of their suppliers who comes in each day to bring them what was on the farm or in the sea just a few days earlier. The clean, homey feel of the place will make you half expect Mom to come breezing out of the kitchen at any moment. Should you have a bit of time on your hands, sign up for one of their daily cooking courses to learn basic or advanced skills for a reasonable price.

 # From Hyde Bridge, walk down Wine St. Turn left onto O'Connell St. The restaurant is ahead on the corner with John St. i Reservations recommended on weekends. Check online for available cooking courses. Free Wi-Fi. $ Entrees €7.50-19. ⏰ Open M-Sa 9:30am-9pm, Su 1-9pm.

POPPADOM RESTAURANT INDIAN $$$

34 O'Connell St. ☎71 914 7171 www.poppadom.ie

A local favorite, head here for some of the best Indian food you will find anywhere in Ireland, along with great early-bird deals for two- or three-course meals every night. The barbecued chicken tikka swimming in the creamy, buttery sauce will make you wonder whether your travel budget would have been better spent going to India.

⇞ From Hyde Bridge, walk down Wine St. Turn left onto O'Connell St. The restaurant is on the left.

ℹ "Early Menu" deal available 5-7pm. Make reservations online. $ Appetizers €6-12. Entrees €16-17.50. ⏰ Open daily 5pm-midnight.

NIGHTLIFE

As in most of Ireland, the nightlife scene here is dominated by excellent pubs. Somewhat surprisingly, though, there are also some decent clubs, if you're into that sort of thing.

FUREY'S PUB PUB

1 Bridge St. ☎87 958 3080 www.facebook.com/fureyspub

This local favorite is the perfect place to kick back after a long day on the road. There will probably be someone plucking at a guitar in the corner, but this isn't a music venue. Best of all, the completely traditional interior, from the dark wood bar to the glittering bottles all over the place, doesn't feel like it was bought out of the latest DIY pub catalogue. The authenticity and relaxed atmosphere hits all the right notes.

⇞ From Hyde Bridge, walk along Rockwood Parade until you reach Thomas St. Turn left over the bridge. The pub is on the right. ℹ Live music most nights. $ Pints €2.50-3.20. ⏰ Open M-Th 2-11:30pm, F-Sa 2pm-12:30am, Su 4-11pm.

MCLAUGHLIN PUB, LIVE MUSIC

9 Market St. ☎071 914 4209

A true live music venue, this is where the musicians come to listen to their peers and hone their skills in a cool and hip spot. The traditional decor, with low doors and plenty of memorabilia hanging on the walls, only makes the joys of every new act all the better.

⇞ From Hyde Bridge, walk down Wine St. Turn left onto O'Connell St. Turn left onto Grattan St. Turn right onto Market St. The pub is on the left. $ Pints €2.50-3.20. ⏰ Open M-Th 5pm-midnight, F-Sa 5pm-1am, Su 5-11pm.

SHOOT THE CROWS PUB, LIVE MUSIC

1 Grattan St.

Once the coolest bar on the block, this place has seen some better days. That said, the grungy rock 'n' roll vibe still pervades the place as a saving grace. The dark fairy ornaments and the skull murals certainly do their best to add to that desired image. Don't be intimidated, though, because at the end of the day, the best thing here is the music, which is a little more intense than your average pub entertainment. Just don't look too closely at the floor at the end of the night.

⇞ From Hyde Bridge, walk down Wine St. Turn left onto O'Connell St. Turn left onto Grattan St. The pub is on the left. ℹ Live music most nights. $ Pints €2.50-3.20. ⏰ Open daily 3pm-late.

VELVET ROOM NIGHTCLUB CLUB

Kempten Prom. ☎71 914 4721 www.velvetroom.ie

The newest and coolest of the up-and-coming clubs in Sligo, this particular one caters to every need that even the most hardcore Continental clubs are looking for. With crazy light shows, a writhing pit of a dance floor, extremely stylish lounging decor, and even more stylish cocktails (€5.50) this is the place to lose your mind on the weekend.

⇞ From Hyde Bridge, walk along Rockwood Parade until you reach Thomas St. Turn left over the bridge. Turn right after the bridge onto Kempton Prom. The club is on the left. ℹ ID required for entry. Check online for upcoming events. $ Cover €10. ⏰ Open F-Su 10pm-4am.

MCGARRIGLES PUB, LIVE MUSIC

11 O'Connell St. ☎071 917 1193

McGarrigles has a laid-back atmosphere that is as much about the delicious food it offers as it is about the obvious desire to listen to live music with a pint. During the evenings, the more musical elements come out, and you can expect anything from jazz to bluegrass to full-on Irish trad from whoever happens to take up the entertainment challenge.

➔ From Hyde Bridge, walk down Wine St. Turn left down O'Connell St. The pub is on the left. ℹ Live music most nights. [$] Pints €2.50-3.20. ⏰ Open M-Th noon-12:30am, F-Sa noon-2:30am, Su 3pm-1:30am.

ARTS AND CULTURE

👍 **MICHAEL QUIRKE** WOOD CARVER

Wine St. ☎71 914 2624

Describing himself as a "guide and witness to the power of myth and legend," this elderly master craftsmen is as skilled in storytelling as he is with the tools of his trade. He can weave a tale of heroes and heroines, Fergus or Deirdre, Naoise or Red Hugh O'Donnell, which will make you want to sit and listen on one of the stumps for hours. As if his encyclopedic knowledge of Gaelic lore were not enough, he can knock out a traditional carving while you talk to him. We recommend asking for a small corner with your favorite **animal** and a message on the other side (€10).

➔ From Hyde Bridge, walk down Wine St. The shop is on the left. [$] Wood carvings €10-200. ⏰ Open Tu-Sa 10:30am-5pm.

👍 **HAWK'S WELL THEATRE** THEATER

Temple St. ☎71 916 1518 www.hawkswell.com

The center of the theatrical scene in Sligo, this fantastic local theater puts on anything from ballet to concerts to dramas. Notably, Seamus Heaney has been known to give poetry readings here, so don't miss checking online for an excellent night out should you have the the opportunity.

➔ From Hyde Bridge, walk down Wine St. Turn left onto Adelaide St. Continue onto Temple St. The theater is on the left. ℹ Call or go online to book. Tickets sell out quickly. [$] Tickets €10-30. ⏰ Box office open M–F 10am-5:30pm, Sa 2-5pm. Most shows start at 8pm.

SHOPPING

THE RECORD ROOM MUSIC

Grattan St. ☎71 914 4765

Stacked floor to ceiling with music memorabilia, CDs, vinyl, and pretty much anything musical you could be looking for, provided it doesn't have famous hair and a name that sounds like beaver. This particular place has a tenuous connection to the band Westlife. Whether that is a negative or positive point is really up to you.

➔ From Hyde Bridge, walk down Wine St. Turn left onto O'Connell St. Turn left onto Grattan St. The shop is on the right. [$] Prices vary. ⏰ Open M-Sa 9am-5pm.

ESSENTIALS

Practicalities

- **TOURIST OFFICE: Sligo Tourist Office.** (Temple St. ☎71 916 1201 www.sligotourism.ie ➔ From the Sligo Bus Station, turn left down Lord Edward St. Turn right onto Adelaide St. Continue onto Union St., then Temple St. The office is on the left. ℹ Free travel literature. Accommodation bookings system. ⏰ Open June-Aug M-F 9am-6pm, Sa-Su 10am-4pm; Sept-May M-F 9am-5pm, Sa 10am-2pm.)

- **INTERNET ACCESS: Sligo Central Library.** (Stephen St. ☎71 911 1675 $ Free. ⏰ Open Tu 9:30am-7pm, W-Sa 9:30am-5pm.)
- **POST OFFICE AND CURRENCY EXCHANGE: An Post.** (31 Castle St. ☎071 914 3078 ➜ From Sligo City Hall, turn left onto Quay St. Turn left onto Wine St. Turn right onto O'Connell St. Turn left onto Grattan St. Continue onto Castle St. The post office is on the right. ⏰ Open M-F 9am-5:30pm, Sa 9am-1pm.)

Emergency

- **POLICE: Garda Station.** (Pearse Rd. ☎71 915 7000, ☎999 for emergencies www.garda.ie ⏰ 24hr. assistance.)
- **HOSPITAL: St. Joseph's Hospital.** (Ray MacSharry Rd. ☎71 916 2649, ☎999 for emergencies. ⏰ Open 24hr.)
- **PHARMACY: Boots Pharmacy.** (31 O'Connell St. ☎71 9149445 www.lifepharmacy.ie ⏰ Open M-W 8:30am-6:30pm, Th-F 8:30am-8pm, Sa 8:30am-6:30pm, Su 11am-6pm.)

Getting There

BY BUS

Bus Éireann runs services from **Mac Diarmada Station** daily. Buses arrive from Belfast, Derry, Donegal, Dublin, Galway, and Westport bus stations. (☎74 912 1309 www.buseireann.ie $ €8-15, students €6-13.)

BY TRAIN

Mac Diarmada Railway Station in Sligo is the major entry point for trains from all over the country, particularly from Dublin. (Lord Edward St. ☎71 916 9888 www.irishrail.ie $ Tickets from Dublin cost €32-44, with discounts available for students. ⏰ 4 trains per day from Dublin.)

Getting Around

BY BUS

Local bus services are operated by the national **Bus Éireann** and run throughout town and to nearby locations (☎71 916 0066 www.buseireann.ie $ €4-15, students €1 off) Buses generally depart daily from Lord Edward St., across the street from **Mac Diarmada Station,** and take you to other regions of the county.

BY TAXI

Metered **taxis** run through town; call **Sligo Taxis** to book. (☎086 121 9111.)

westport ☎98

Were you to see a leprechaun casually walking down the street flipping a golden coin, it wouldn't seem all that out of place in this stereotypical Irish town. Loaded with more Irish pubs than is necessarily healthy and boasting enough Celtic designs to last even ardent enthusiasts a lifetime, Westport is a fantastic spot to sit back and let Irish tradition wash over you, from the kooky accents to the local sing-alongs. Dublin is bustling, Belfast is British now, but Westport has retained its small-town charm. While you won't be doing much sightseeing here, except the bottom of your Guinness pint, people-watching in a contagiously joyous atmosphere more than makes up for it. While you might opt for a shorter trip here, consider it a respite from a breakneck schedule and relax in one of the pleasant and plentiful B&Bs throughout the area. Sometimes you just need to kick back, and when you do, Westport is here.

WESTPORT

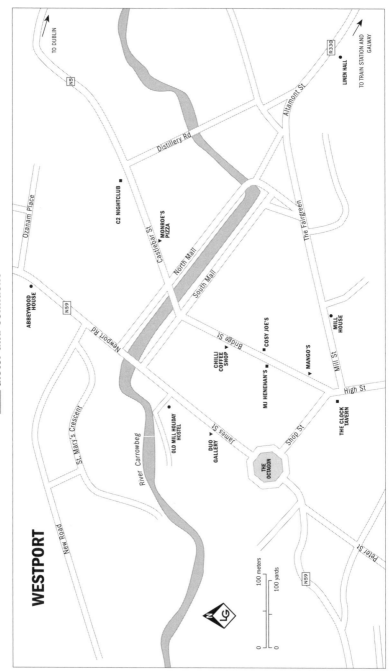

- TO DUBLIN
- N5
- Distillery Rd
- R330
- LINEN HALL
- TO TRAIN STATION AND GALWAY
- Altamont St
- Ozanam Place
- C2 NIGHTCLUB ■
- MONROE'S PIZZA ▶
- Castlebar St
- North Mall
- The Fairgreen
- South Mall
- ABBEYWOOD HOUSE ●
- N59
- Newport Rd
- Bridge St
- COSY JOE'S ■
- MILL HOUSE ■
- CHILLI COFFEE SHOP ▶
- MANGO'S ▶
- Mill St
- MJ HENEHAN'S ■
- High St
- St. Mary's Crescent
- River Carrowbeg
- OLD MILL HOLIDAY HOSTEL ●
- DUO GALLERY ▶
- James St
- Shop St
- THE CLOCK TAVERN ■
- THE OCTAGON
- New Road
- Peter St
- N59
- 100 meters
- 100 yards
- N LG

ORIENTATION

Most of the town is situated on the side of a hill, with the main streets sloping down from two small plazas. **James Street** runs from the **Octagon,** while Bridge St. goes downhill from **The Clock Tower.** These roads lead toward **South Mall, North Mall,** and a small river running through the town center, which can provide a scenic spot for a picnic. Most buses arrive on **Mill Street,** which is a side road off of the Clock Tower plaza, while the train station is a little farther away in the same direction on **Altamount Street.**

ACCOMMODATIONS

With B&Bs at every turn, many above local pubs, you should never go wanting for a bed.

👍 ABBEYWOOD HOUSE — HOSTEL $$

Newport Rd. ☎98 25496 www.abbeywoodhouse.com

This expansive ex-manor now offers some of the best budget accommodations you will find in Westport, which is almost entirely dominated by B&Bs. The plain but brightly colored hallways stretch out in all directions. The dorms themselves are clean, with modern, sturdy bunks, though for such a large building you might expect a bit more stretching room. All of that extra space goes to the hotel-quality twins and doubles, which have wonderful views over the lawn and town. Let the smell of freshly baked bread at breakfast clear out the fog of last night, and enjoy this country retreat.

➔ From the Octagon, walk down James St. Continue over the bridge onto Newport Rd. The hostel is on the left. ℹ Breakfast included. Free Wi-Fi. Kitchen available until 11pm. [$] 10-bed dorm €20; quads €24; doubles €60. ⏰ Reception 7am-11pm. Open May-Sept.

THE OLD MILL HOLIDAY HOSTEL — HOSTEL $$

James St. ☎98 27045 www.oldmillhostel.com

One of two hostels in town, the Old Mill Holiday Hostel is not quite as luxurious as the other option, crammed as it is between the main drag, James St., and the Westport Cineplex. The clientele consists mainly of backpackers and travelers, so you can happily swap stories on the broken-in sofas in the sitting room. For all that, though, this hostel will probably blend in with the next.

➔ From the Octagon, walk down James St. The hostel is on the left in a short alleyway. ℹ Free Wi-Fi. Breakfast included. Kitchen available. [$] Dorms €18-22. ⏰ Reception 24hr.

THE ELEPHANT GUEST HOUSE — B&B $$$$

Mill St. ☎87 226 6767 www.elephantguesthouse.net

Disappointingly, this is not a guest house for elephants. Rather, it's so named because the owner happens to keep an enormous collection of elephant figurines. Claiming this is one of the best B&Bs in Westport is quite something when there is one B&B for every five people in town, but we'll make that assertion. The gorgeous rooms generally feature super king-sized beds, Irish knit throws, and high windows that will allow the sun to gently wake you from your slumber in your comfortable bed. Make your way downstairs to enjoy the enormous and varied breakfast buffet, including the "Jumbo Elephant" fried breakfast.

➔ From the Clock Tower, walk down Mill St. The B&B is on the right. [$] Singles €50; doubles €45. ℹ Breakfast included. Free Wi-Fi. TV in all rooms. ⏰ Reception 7am-midnight.

SIGHTS

Pretty light on sights of the traditional variety, Westport is much more about immersing yourself in the community and embracing the local vibe. But if the tourist in you is begging for some sightseeing, there are a few options.

CLEW BAY HERITAGE CENTRE — MUSEUM

The Quay ☎98 26852 www.westportheritage.com

Offering a bit of historical insight into this gorgeous piece of coastline in County Mayo, Clew Bay Heritage Centre provides perspective on all that traditional style you have been so enjoying. Read about coopers and spinners, and hear a little about the famous pirate queen who roamed the waters outside this sheltering bay. Should you have the time and the inclination, you can research your genealogy to see whether your family actually hails from Westport. You might walk out feeling like Mayo's heritage is suddenly your own.

From the Octagon, walk up the hill on Peter St. Continue onto Quay St. Continue onto Quay Rd., then onto The Quay. The center is ahead. ℹ *Guided tours available. Guided walks of the area available. Inquire for details.* $ *€2 donation.* ⏰ *Open M-F 10am-2pm, Sa 2-5pm.*

CLEW BAY NATURE WALK

The Quay

Should you be mysteriously blessed with sunny weather, there are few things more beautiful than this stretch of shallow water, interspersed with fingers of verdant green land. Small boats skim the surface, occasionally dotting the horizon as they sail out into deeper water. But you, landlocked as you probably are, can just find a quiet corner in one of the stretching fields along this lush coastline. If you're immune to hypothermia, you can even try swimming, but you are going to want a warm, fluffy towel for when you get out.

From the Octagon, walk up the hill on Peter St. Continue onto Quay St. Continue onto Quay Rd., then onto The Quay. Follow the waterline as long as you want to.

WESTPORT HOUSE HISTORIC BUILDING, GARDENS

Quay Rd. ☎98 27766 www.westporthouse.ie

Generally considered to be the major tourist attraction in Westport, this grand old manor house is a pristine example of Irish architecture, with the most luxurious furnishings to be found in the country. The gardens are beautiful, tastefully sweeping around the house. Normally, this would make for an excellent visit, and we would whole-heartedly support it. Unfortunately, at some point in the recent past, someone with dollar signs tattooed on his eyelids found Westport House and decided to transform it into a commercial goldmine. The surrounding gardens now include log flumes, a "pirate adventure park," a small zoo, swan boats, and an old train. The poor house suffers on, valiantly attempting to add a stylish twist to the increasingly garish theme park growing up around it.

From the Octagon, walk up the hill on Peter St. Continue onto Quay St., then Quay Rd. The park is on the right. $ *House and gardens €12, students €9. With adventure park €20, students €18.* ⏰ *Open Apr-May Sa-Su 2-5pm; June M-Sa 11am-5pm (only house and zoo open), Su 11am-5pm (everything open); July-Aug daily 11:30am-5pm.*

Outside of Westport

CROAGH PATRICK MOUNTAIN

Teach na Miasa, Murrisk ☎98 64114 www.croagh-patrick.com

Soaring above Clew Bay, Croagh Patrick is the holiest mountain in Ireland. St. Patrick himself was said to have taken his 40 days and 40 nights of Lent fast at its peak, after which he had a heated argument with an angel and then decided snakes were no longer welcome in Ireland. Standing at its summit, you will certainly feel powerful enough to cast out any species at all from the gorgeous country spread out below. The church of St. Patrick at the peak is the most important pilgrimage site in Ireland, and on the last Sunday of July every year, thousands of devotees make the difficult climb to the top. While you don't need any equipment more special than a walking stick, the sliding rocks and steep final climb make for a tough ascent. But once you arrive, all that struggle fades away. Even if Catholicism goes against your grain of belief, there is something purifying and timeless in purging yourself from the year's worries in a climb, only to come to the top and feel clean. Of course, after that you have to figure out how to get down.

Easiest to take a cab (☎353 98 5305) from Westport or rent a bike (☎98 37675). ℹ Visitor center offers lockers (€5), a gift shop, cafe, and directions to the summit. ⏰ Visitor center open M-Sa 10am-5:30pm, Su 10am-6pm.

saints alive!

Everything you know about Saint Patrick is a lie. Well, maybe not—if you're a Celtic hagiographer, you might know this stuff, but otherwise, listen up. He's not the chill, friendly Irishman you think he was. For one thing, he wasn't even Irish. Born to a relatively well-off Roman family in Britain, he was captured by the Irish and sold as a slave to a Druid priest. When he managed to escape six years later, he hightailed it to Britain faster than you can say "apostle of Ireland." It was only after he started seeing mystical visions of children calling him back that he returned—you know, to save them from hellfire and all that. From there, it was all good works, miracles, and devoted poverty. Note that snake banishment was not included on that list; despite legends, it's believed that there would have been no snakes on the island, even before St. Pat arrived. But the biggest lie of all? Green probably has nothing to do with the saint. Although there are records of some 17th-century supporters wearing green ribbons, it's St. Patrick's blue that is the official color. Now you can feel all superior as you watch green-clad goons down pints of Guinness.

FOOD

Pub grub, and plenty of it, is the special of the day in this pub-dominated culinary landscape. While that will certainly satisfy you for the first hundred or so meals, after traveling through Ireland for a while, you might be eager for something more. Here are a few alternative options.

MANGO'S SEAFOOD, IRISH $$$$

Bridge St. ☎98 24999

This modern, stylish bistro is famous within the town for being one of the best dining options for nights when you are looking to impress that special someone. Offering a more sophisticated range of flavors than your standard Irish cuisine, Mango's takes the traditional seafood favorites and puts a modern and surprising twist on them. Try the delectable *moules frites* (mussels and fries), served with lemon butter and chives (€17) for a real taste of what can be done with the fruits of the Atlantic. Almost all of what you're eating was hauled in only a few miles from where you're sitting.

From the Clock Tower, walk down Bridge St. The restaurant is on the right. ℹ Reservations recommended F-Sa. $ Entrees €9-27. ⏰ Open M-Sa 5:45-10pm.

CHILLI COFFEE SHOP CAFE $$

Bridge St. ☎98 27611 www.chillicoffeeshop.ie

Generally considered a local favorite, head to Chilli Coffee Shop when midday stomach pains prevent you from walking any farther. The specialty here is sandwiches: delicious, belly-warming, and beautifully prepared. Try their cajun-style panini with mozzarella cheese, pesto, and Cajun spiced chicken (€7) or bite into one of their sinfully creamy pastries (€1.80). While the prices aren't cheap, any one of their signature dishes will keep you going all day.

From the Clock Tower, walk down Bridge St. The cafe is on the left. ℹ Free Wi-Fi. $ Sandwiches €6-7. ⏰ Open M-F 9am-10pm, Sa 10am-10pm, Su 10am-5pm.

MONROE'S PIZZAPIZZA
PIZZA $$

Castlebar St.   ☎98 25000 www.monroespizza.com

Monroe's PizzaPizza fills the necessary niche of sizzling hot pizza at prices that will make the tomatoes seem sweeter and the cheese all the more melted. While it may not be gourmet, you can expect to leave with your stomach well sated after a couple slices of comfort food.

✯ *From the Clock Tower, walk down Bridge St. Continue over the Mall onto Castlebar St. The restaurant is on the right.* ***i*** *Free Wi-Fi in store. Call for delivery.* Ⓢ *Pizza €6-15. €1 extra per topping.* Ⓞ *Open daily noon-midnight.*

DUO GALLERY
CAFE $$$

James St.   ☎87 971 9830 www.facebook.com/DuoGalleryWestport

While black turtlenecks and berets are generally frowned upon in Westport, you may be tempted to whip out the one you've been carrying around since leaving Paris here. Imagine a small, local art gallery, whose minimalist walls are best suited to display the works of many artists. Now imagine that space filled with a small cafe, with tables and chairs for patrons to relax with their triple espresso in peace. The result is something like the DUO Gallery, which is undoubtedly an island in Westport, but at least a neat island.

✯ *From the Octagon, walk down James St. The cafe is on the left.* ***i*** *Occasional visits from local artists.* Ⓢ *Coffee €1.80-3.20.* Ⓞ *Open M-Sa 10am-6pm.*

NIGHTLIFE

🖾 MJ HENEHAN
BAR

77 Bridge St.   ☎98 25561 www.mjhenehan.com

Probably the biggest of the seemingly innumerous pubs down Bridge St., Henehan's will not disappoint. Join the crowd thronging around the traditional bar in the front or enjoy the buzz in the small beer garden in the back. For later in the night, go to **The Bakehouse** at the very back, so-named for the smoky dry ice that floats over the crowds of reveling dancers, raging to some of the latest hits. It may not live up to Continental, hardcore clubbing, but it certainly will do for a few pints and a bit of a dancing to disco lights.

✯ *From the Clock Tower, walk down Bridge St. The bar is on the left.* ***i*** *Live music on weekends.* Ⓢ *Pints €3.50-4.20. Cocktails €9.* Ⓞ *Open Th-F 6pm-2am, Sa 3pm-2am, Su 6pm-1am.*

COSY JOE'S
PUB, BAR

Bridge St.   ☎98 29403 www.cosyjoesbar.ie

"Cosy" is probably the understatement of the century—immobilizing might be more appropriate as the swollen mass of people will have you hot under the collar after a few seconds. The traditional pub furnishings are perfectly offset by some modern touches, like blue floor-level lighting and some expertly mixed cocktails. Try to squeeze between the stag party directly next to the hen party chattering away to see the local light rock or trad band bashing out some tunes to the cheering crowd beyond. DJs spinning out the latest hits also appear as the night's entertainment.

✯ *From the Clock Tower, walk down Bridge St. The bar is on the right.* ***i*** *Live music on weekends. Sometimes closed in mid-afternoons during the week.* Ⓢ *Pints €3.50-4.20. Cocktails €10.* Ⓞ *Open M-Tu 1-8pm, W 2-11pm, Th 1pm-3am, F-Sa 11am-3am, Su 1-5pm and 9pm-midnight.*

C2 NIGHT CLUB
CLUB

Castlebar St.   ☎98 55088 www.facebook.com/c2niteclub

As one of the only nightclubs in the area, you can enjoy competing for space at C2 with all of the other people who just want to disappear in the crowd for a little while. This place can get surprisingly rowdy, if only because it is one of the very few places where down-and-dirty behavior will not be met with a bartender chasing you out armed with a broomstick. Come to enjoy a good mix of electronic, rock, and chart hits. Just don't get too carried away, though; chances are you'll see the people in here again the tomorrow morning in the street.

From the Clock Tower, walk down Bridge St. Continue over the Mall onto Castlebar St. The club is on the left inside the Castlecourt Hotel. i Lines can get long around 1am. $ Cover €10. Drinks €4-12. ⏰ Open F midnight-2:30am, Sa-Su 11:30pm-2:30am.

THE CLOCK TAVERN PUB

High St. ☎098 26870 www.theclocktavern.ie

One of the more run-of-the-mill pubs in the area, the Clock Tavern has a reputation for being cheap and popular with a younger bunch (read: those who can't chat their way past the doormen at the others). Despite this, or maybe because of it, you can rest assured you will have a lively and interesting night on the well-beaten leather couches and very well-polished bar. Stick around on the weekends for occasional live music, which tends to be a little wilder than the trad you'll find at the others.

Directly adjacent to the Clock Tower. i Open mic every M. $ Pints €3.50-4.20. ⏰ Open M-Th 5-11:30pm, F-Sa 1pm-12:30am.

ARTS AND CULTURE

THE WRIGHT GALLERY GALLERY

Lower Quay ☎87 771 9380 www.thewrightartists.blogspot.ie

Showcasing selections of local art around from the group council known as the Wright Artists, the gallery allows you to admire pieces inspired by the surrounding Clew Bay and St. Patrick. While the pieces are theoretically for sale, you probably are better served leaving the wallet at home should the artist overcome the banker in you.

From the Octagon, walk up Quay St. Continue onto Quay Rd. Bear left onto Upper Quay. The gallery is on the left. i Occasional late-night art openings. ⏰ Open M 11am-6pm, Th-Su 11am-6pm.

SHOPPING

JOHN O'BRIEN'S IRISH KNIT

Shop St. ☎98 27015

Offering enough Irish knit products to ensure that your grandmother never feels the need to knit you another sweater again, O'Brien's offers excellent quality for shockingly affordable prices. Probably the best bargain here is an Irish knit scarf for only €15. Get all your souvenir shopping out of the way here—unless you want Guinness memorabilia. For that, go next door to the town gift shop.

From the Octagon, walk toward the Clock Tower. The shop is on the left. $ Knitted items €8.50-90. ⏰ Open M-Sa 10am-6pm.

ESSENTIALS

Practicalities

- **TOURIST OFFICE: Westport Tourist Information Office** provides all the travel literature you need, along with accommodation recommendations and bookings. (James St. ☎98 25711 www.discoverireland.ie From the Octagon, walk down James St. The center is on the left. ⏰ Open Apr-June M-Sa 10am-5:45pm; July-Aug M-Su 10am-5:45pm; Sept-Oct M-Sa 10am-5:45pm; Nov-Mar M-F 9am-5:45pm.)
- **INTERNET ACCESS: Westport Public Library** offers computers and wireless internet. (The Crescent ☎98 25747 $ €3 for 30min. on computer. Free Wi-Fi. ⏰ Open Tu-W 10am-8pm, Th-F 10am-5pm, Sa 10am-4pm.)
- **POST OFFICE AND CURRENCY EXCHANGE: An Post: North Mall.** (North Mall ☎98 27210 From the Octagon, walk down James St. Cross the bridge and turn right onto North Mall.

The office is on the left. 🕐 Open M 9am-5:30pm, Tu 9:30am-5:30pm, W-F 9am-5:30pm, Sa 9am-1pm.)

Emergency

- **POLICE: Westport Garda Station.** (Fairgreen ☎98 25555, ☎999 for emergencies www.garda.ie 🕐 24hr. assistance.)

- **MEDICAL SERVICES: The Grove Medical Center.** (Mill St. ☎98 27666, ☎999 for emergencies. 🕐 Open M-F 9am-6pm.)

- **PHARMACY: Treacy's Pharmacy.** (James St. ☎98 25474 🕐 Open M-F 9:15am-6:30pm, Sa 9:30am-6pm.)

Getting There

BY BUS

Bus Éireann stops at Mill St. daily. Routes come from anywhere between Derry, Dublin, Galway and Sligo bus stations. (☎98 25711 www.buseireann.ie Ⓢ €8-15, students €2 off.)

BY PLANE

Knock Airport (NOC; ☎94 936 8100 www.irelandwestairport.com) brings in flights from the United Kingdom and Western Europe. From the airport, take bus #66 toward Westport.

BY TRAIN

Westport Railway Station serves the town, with most trains coming from Dublin's **Heuston Station.** (☎98 25253 www.irishrail.ie 🕐 Open daily 6am-11pm.)

Getting Around

Public transportation in such a small town is next to nonexistent, so if you are looking to go a little farther afield, you will have to provide your own means.

BY TAXI

There is no true taxi rank in Westport, but you can call for one. Try **O'Toole Taxis.** (☎353 985 305)

BY BIKE

Bicycle rentals are available from **Clew Bay Bike Hire.** (Distillery Rd. ☎983 7675 Ⓢ Prices from €20. 🕐 Open daily 9am-6pm.)

galway ☎091

Galway is an intimate city; more a sprawling town than a booming metropolis. Filled with college students, international travelers, and now you, Galway's eclectic population is reflected in the city's diversity. There are enough restaurants, bars, and nightclubs to have your pick whether you're a vegan or a Viking. The city is less tourist-oriented than Dublin, but that doesn't mean there isn't anything to see. Most of the sights are integrated into the city, yet they brim with history. While a two-hour walk around Galway might suffice for a sightseer, you'll need to delve deeper in order to capture the real vibe of the city. Make sure to spend plenty of time in the outdoor terraces of the local pubs, diving into some of the freshest seafood in Ireland.

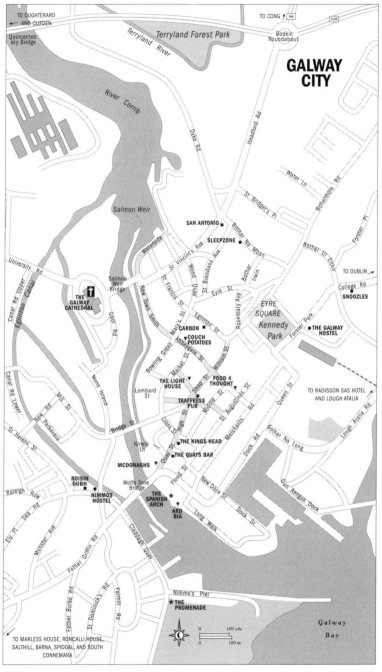

GALWAY CITY

TO OUGHTERARD AND CLIFDEN

TO CONG

Terryland Forest Park

Terryland River

Quincentenary Bridge

Bodkin Roundabout

River Corrib

Salmon Weir

University Rd

Canal Rd Upper

Eglinton Canal

Salmon Weir Bridge

THE GALWAY CATHEDRAL

Gaol Rd

Nuns Island

Canal Rd Lower

Mill St

New Rd

St Helens St

Raleigh Row

Elv Pl Sea Rd

Munster Ave

Father Griffin Rd

Claddagh Quay

TO MARLESS HOUSE, RONCALLI HOUSE, SALTHILL, BARNA, SPIDDAL, AND SOUTH CONNEMARA

Waterside

New Town Smith

St Francis St

Bowling Green

Mary's St

Market St

Abbeygate St

Lombard St

Bridge St

Pardvara

St Vincent's Ave

St Brendan's Ave

Quay

Eglinton St

SAN ANTONIO

SLEEPZONE

CARBON

COUCH POTATOES

THE LIGHT HOUSE

Shop St

TAAFFEESS PUB

Cross St

High St

Kirwin Lh

Quay St

MCDONAGHS

Flood St

Wolfe Tone Bridge

ROISIN DUBH

NIMMOS HOSTEL

THE SPANISH ARCH

ARD BIA

Long Walk

St Bridger's Pl

Bothar Na Mban

Bothar Irwin

Eyre St

Rosemary Ave

Bothar

Headford Rd

Water Ln

Bohermore Rd

Forster Pl

Bothar Ui Eithir

TO DUBLIN

College Rd

SNOOZLES

EYRE SQUARE

Kennedy Park

Forster Park

THE GALWAY HOSTEL

William St

FOOD 4 THOUGHT

Middle St

St Augustines St

Merchants Rd

Queen St

Dock Rd

Bothar Na Long

TO RADISSON SAS HOTEL AND LOUGH ATALIA

Lough Atalia Rd

Dun Aengus Dock

THE KINGS HEAD

THE QUAYS BAR

New Dock St

Dock St

Nimmo's Pier

THE PROMENADE

0   100 yds
0   100 m

Galway Bay

galway

ORIENTATION

The **Corrib River** and **Eyre Square** sandwich Galway's eastern bank. Follow **Quay Street** from the river to get to Eyre Square, or take **Abbeygate Street** if you are coming from the north. The western bank is home to the historic **Claddagh Quay;** follow it all the way out of the city to the **Salthill Promenade. Dominick Street Upper and Lower** host most of the western bank's businesses, which are tightly clustered on those two streets. **Wood Quay,** on the northern side of the eastern bank, is the center of the quieter, more residential area of Galway.

ACCOMMODATIONS

👍 KINLAY — HOSTEL $

Merchants Rd., Eyre Sq. ☎091 565 244 www.kinlaygalway.ie

If you're looking for somewhere to stay with 200 of your closest friends, Kinlay is the hostel for you. It's so big that it loses some of the intimacy typically expected of a hostel, but the small common room and wraparound kitchen nevertheless make it easy to meet fellow travelers.

🧭 On the edge of Eyre Sq. From the bus station, head down Victoria Pl. (a continuation of Eyre Sq. Rd). ℹ Breakfast included. Free Wi-Fi. Reception does tour bookings. $ Dorms 8-bed €10-12; 6-bed €21; 5-bed €23; 3-bed and 4-bed €26. Singles and doubles €29 per person. ⏰ Reception 24hr.

THE GALWAY HOSTEL — HOSTEL $

Eyre Sq. ☎091 290 1250 www.galwaycityhostel.com

Located across the street from the bus station, this hostel doesn't offer the best of views but makes up for it with a pretty convenient location, ideal for someone staying just a night or two. The creaky old stairs make this hostel sound a bit tired, but the colorful walls work to create a more fun atmosphere.

🧭 Across the street from the bus station. ℹ Breakfast included. $ 8-bed dorms M-Th €11, F-Sa €22, Su €11; 4-bed M-Th €17/26/17. ⏰ Reception 24hr.

SNOOZLES — HOSTEL $$

Forster St. ☎091 530 064 www.snoozleshostelgalway.ie

This brand-new hostel definitely revels in the 21st century: sleek lines, a contemporary kitchen, and an up-to-date flat screen TV and sound system can all be found here, which is perfect, because you must be sick of crumbling stone walls and antiquities anyway. This is the hostel for the young professional, the tech junkie, or anyone else who is striding boldly into the future.

🧭 From the bus station, take a right onto Forster St. ℹ Breakfast included. Free Wi-Fi. $ 10-bed dorms €14-30; 4-bed €22-40. ⏰ Reception 24hr.

SLEEPZONE — HOSTEL $

Bóthar na mBan ☎091 566 999 www.sleepzone.ie

One of the best hostels in Galway, this is a great place to meet fellow travelers. In a tribute to the Irish theater greats, framed playbills and bios of famous playwrights decorate the walls.

🧭 From the bus station, cross Eyre Square and take a right onto Prospect Hill, then a left onto Bóthar Irwin, which will turn into Bóthar na mBan. ℹ Breakfast included. Free Wi-Fi. $ 10-bed dorms M-Th €9, F-Sa €20, Su €9; 8-bed €12/20/12; 4- and 5-bed €15/25/15. Doubles €50. ⏰ Reception 24hr.

SAN ANTONIO — B&B $$

5 Headford Rd. ☎091 564 934

This B&B looks like it's been through a lot. The entryway is weary from years of travelers trekking through, but the rooms have a more upbeat vibe. Floral bedspreads brighten the room with the help of the sunlight streaming through the windows. It may not be home, but the prices look awfully homey to penny-pinching travelers.

➡ From the bus station, cross Eyre Square and take a right onto Prospect Hill, a left onto Bóthar Irwin, and then a left onto Headford Rd. ℹ Breakfast €5. [$] €25 per night per person. ⏰ Reception 9am-9pm.

NIMMOS HOSTEL $

1 Upper Dominick St. ☎091 586 661 www.nimmoshostel.com

The interior could use some love, but this is the cheapest hostel in Galway: you're not here for the atmosphere. The security is good and the beds are definitely up to par, and while the aesthetics may be off, the price is dead on.

➡ From the Wolfe Tone Bridge, take the 1st right and continue 2 blocks. ℹ Cable TV, storage facilities, and kitchen available. [$] 10- and 12-bed dorms M-Th €10, F-Sa €15, Su €10. ⏰ Reception 24hr.

SIGHTS

👍 **THE SALTHILL PROMENADE** WALK

Salthill

Get the best views of Galway and the bay as you walk toward the famous suburb of Salthill. The cold wind and unrelenting sea are every bit the harsh beauty of Ireland's western coast you've imagined in your shamrock-filled dreams. Keep on trekking until the bitter end; legend has it you have not completed the walk until you've kicked the wall at Blackrock. Dress warmly, even on sunny days.

➡ From Galway, follow Claddagh Quay as it turns into Grattan Rd. and then becomes the promenade. [$] Free.

👍 **THE SPANISH ARCH** MONUMENT

Quay St.

Believed to be the last place Columbus stopped before landing in America, the Spanish arch traces its origins to the 16th century. It was built to protect merchant ships from looting and to encourage trade with Spain; nowadays it serves as a reminder of centuries past. It also makes a great background for a photo shoot.

➡ From Eyre Square, take Williamsgate St. and continue as it becomes William St., then Shop St., then High St., and finally Quay St. [$] Free.

GALWAY CATHEDRAL CATHEDRAL

Church Ln. ☎091 563 577 www.galwaycathedral.ie

If it weren't for us, you would never know that Galway Cathedral was only built in 1965. (You're welcome.) The soaring stone arches may not bring you back to the era of plastic dresses and 15-cent hamburgers, but the too-vibrant-to-be-real stained-glass windows are pretty psychedelic. Expect to spend a fair amount of time craning your neck, staring at the 145ft. dome.

➡ From Eyre Sq., take Williamsgate St. Make a right onto Eglinton St. and continue as it becomes St. Francis St. Turn left onto St. Vincent's Av., which will turn into University Rd.; the Cathedral will be on your left. [$] Free. ⏰ Open daily 9am-5pm. Mass Su 10am.

EYRE SQUARE PARK

Eyre Square

Coming into Galway by bus, you'd be hard-pressed to miss this park. On sunny day, the grassy area fills up with children, dogs, and 👍**shirtless Irishmen** alike. The park is officially called the Kennedy Memorial Park, as JFK visited the square shortly before his assassination.

➡ Directly in front of the bus station. [$] Free. ⏰ Open 24hr.

KIRWAN'S LANE STREET

Kirwans Ln.

Though you're likely to stumble upon this early modern gem on your own, we're here to tell you what you've found. The original heart of old Galway (we're talking hundreds of years old), its architecture still reflects the 16th- and 17th-century city. Just one quaint lane, the street plays host to pottery shops, cafes, and restaurants.

 # Off of Quay St and Cross St. From Eyre Sq., take Williamsgate St. and continue as it becomes Shop St., then High St., and finally Quay St.

FOOD

ARD BIA CAFE, RESTAURANT $$

Spanish Arch ☎091 561 114 www.ardbia.com

Ard Bia offers fresh, mouth-watering food for a social crowd. Just in for coffee? We dare you to resist the cakes on display as you walk in. Evening turns the place into an intimate dinner setting, perfect for that first date with the hottie from your hostel or a more culinary crush, like the St. Tola goat's cheese and lovage gnocchi (€16).

 # From Eyre Sq., take Victoria Pl., and turn right onto Merchants Rd. Follow it to the end and turn right. i Free Wi-Fi. $ Sandwiches €7-12. Salads €7-9. Appetizers €6-10. Entrees €16-25. Coffee €1.80-2.90. ⏰ Open daily 9am-3:30pm and 6-10pm.

MCDONAGH'S SEAFOOD BAR $

22 Quay St. ☎091 565 001 www.mcdonaghs.net

If you ever want to try fried stingray, this is the best place to do it. Choose your protein source (anything from mackerel to ray to plaice) and get it fried up and served with chips. Sit down at the picnic tables inside, or take it out to the river for a relaxing meal overlooking the water.

 # From Eyre Square, take Williamsgate St. and continue as it becomes William St., then Shop St., then High St., and finally Quay St. $ Fish €5.60-6.20. Chips €2.55. Oysters 3 for €5. ⏰ Open M-Sa noon-11pm, Su 2-9pm.

CAVAS RESTAURANT $$

51 Lower Dominick St. ☎091 539 884 www.cavasrestaurant.ie

Relaxed elegance best describes this top-notch restaurant. Exposed stone walls and rich, dark-wood tables, combined with the soft piano music, are welcoming and refined. The extensive tapas menu is only rivaled by the wine options; give yourself some time to go through both menus thoroughly. With tapas options averaging around €6, you won't have to limit yourself.

 # From the Wolfe Tone Bridge, take your 1st right and walk 1 block, then take a right onto Lower Dominick St. i Live flamenco music W 7-9pm. $ Tapas €3-16. Bottles of wine €17-70. ⏰ Open daily noon-5pm and 6-10pm.

COUCH POTATOES CAFE, POTATOES $

40 Upper Abbeygate St. ☎091 561 664

It's hard to believe cafes like this don't exist all over Ireland. Starters aside, every menu item starts with a baked potato; we had no idea you could stuff so many things into one starchy tuber. The names of the dishes don't give much away; what do you think the Nina, the Pinta, or the Santa Maria baked potato tastes like? But the vegetarian Lord of the Dance (broccoli, carrots, corn, mushrooms, topped with cheddar; €8.25) will have you walking out to a decidedly Irish step.

 # From Eyre Square, take Williamsgate St., which turns into William St. Take a right onto Upper Abbeygate St. i Free Wi-Fi. $ Appetizers €5-8. Entrees €9.50-10. ⏰ Open daily noon-10pm.

THE LIGHT HOUSE CAFE $$

40 Lough Atalia Rd.

This must be where the delicate take their afternoon tea. Floor-to-ceiling windows allow light to stream onto the white tablecloths and walls, creating an ethereal look. The cakes and scones, however, are more reminiscent of sin. The blackboard displays the daily menu; expect local ingredients and plenty of vegetarian options.

🪧 From Eyre Square, take Victoria Pl. and continue as it curves right and turns into Queen St. Make a left onto Bóthar na Long, then another left onto Lough Atalia Rd. $ Lunch €4.50-8.50. Tea and coffee €2-2.50. Cakes and scones €2.50-4.50. ⏰ Open M-Sa 10am-8pm, Su 8am-8pm.

FOOD FOR THOUGHT — CAFE $$

5 Lower Abbeygate St. — ☎091 565 854

Picky eaters will have no trouble finding something to eat here. Gluten-free, vegetarian, and vegan options accompany the more caloric plates. Calorie-counters have an easy time of it: nutritional information is listed on each menu item for the health-conscious.

*🪧 From Eyre Square, take Williamsgate St., which turns into William St., then left onto Lower Abbeygate St. **i** Free Wi-Fi. $ Appetizers €4.25-7.50. Entrees €7.50-9. Coffee €1.80-3. ⏰ Open M-F 7:30am-6pm, Sa 8am-6pm, Su 11:30am-4pm.*

NIGHTLIFE

👍 **RÓISÍN DUBH** — BAR, CLUB

Lower Dominick St. — ☎091 586 540 www.roisindubh.net

Hipster hats reign here, as do the tight jeans and leather jackets. Galway's number-one alternative bar is an alternatively good time, whether or not you roll your own cigarettes. Two levels, three drinking areas, and a stage (with no one dancing) allow for all types of fun. Expect either live music or DJs Thursday through Saturday night.

*🪧 From Wolfe Tone Bridge, take the 1st right, then the next right onto Lower Dominick St. **i** Comedy shows on occasion. $ Pints from €4. Mixed drinks €5. ⏰ Open M-Th 5pm-1am, F-Sa 5pm-3am, Su 5pm-midnight.*

👍 **THE QUAYS** — PUB

11 Quay St. — ☎091 568 347

Wooden pointed arches give the Quays a medieval look, but the scene is anything but premodern. A thriving restaurant during the day, this pub turns into a true rager at night. With three bars on the main floor and one on the second level, no one ever stays thirsty. Live bands play regularly, so put on your dancing shoes.

*🪧 From Eyre Sq., take Williamsgate St. and continue as it becomes William St., then Shop St., then High St., and finally Quay St. **i** Free Wi-Fi. Traditional music every night. $ Pints from €4.20. Mixed drinks €5.10. ⏰ Open M-Th 10:30am-1am, F-Sa 10:30am-3am, Su noon-1am.*

THE KINGS HEAD — PUB

15 High St. — ☎091 566 630 www.thekingshead.ie

It may look like an unassuming Irish pub from the outside, but walking through the doors is like walking into Narnia. That is, if Narnia had a giant stage and a crazy band playing rock hits from the past ten years. So really, nothing like Narnia, but the transition is jarring. This place is too big to not be frequented by tourists and too fun to not be a regular haunt for locals, so you never know what sort of crowd you'll find here.

*🪧 From Eyre Sq., take Williamsgate St. and continue as it becomes William St., then Shop St., then High St. **i** Free Wi-Fi. Traditional music every night. $ Pints from €4.15. Mixed drinks from €8. ⏰ Open M-Tu 10:30am-11:30pm, W-Sa 10:30am-2am, Su 10:30am-11pm.*

TAAFFES — PUB

19-20 Shop St. — ☎091 564 066

Taaffes doesn't try to compete with the giant, touristy bars just down the street; it has much more of a small, local-bar feel. The lights are a little brighter, the atmosphere more friendly, and the percentage of Irishmen higher. The drinks cost a little less as well.

☞ From Eyre Sq., take Williamsgate St. and continue as it becomes William St., then Shop St. *i* Traditional music every night at 5:30 and 9:30pm. Ⓢ Pints from €3. Mixed drinks from €4.50. Ⓒ Open M-Th 11:30am-12:30am, F-Sa 11:30am-1:30am, Su 12:30pm-11:30pm.

CARBON ◆ CLUB
21 Eglinton St. ☎091 449 204

If you're worrying that your dress doesn't cover your butt or that your shirt has too many sequins, then you're appropriately dressed for Carbon. We're assuming it has its name because people come in as coal and leave as diamonds. Don't worry, a basic knowledge of chemistry isn't required to get in.

☞ From Eyre Square take Williamsgate St., then turn right onto Eglinton St. Ⓢ €5 cover. Shots from €2.50. Pints from €3. Ⓒ Open M 11pm-2am, W 11pm-2am, Th-Sa 11pm-2:30am.

ARTS AND CULTURE

GALWAY ARTS CENTRE ◆ ARTS CENTER
47 Lower Dominick St. ☎091 565 886 www.galwayartscentre.ie

The Galway Arts Centre is home to the avant-garde art shows of Western Ireland. It's hard to tell if the bare sheetrock walls and half-polished floors are part of the look of the gallery or if the place is actually unfinished. Nonetheless, it does create a nice minimalist setting for the shows.

☞ From Wolfe Tone Bridge, take the 1st right, then the next right onto Lower Dominick St. Ⓢ Free. Ⓒ Box Office open Tu-Sa 10am-5:30pm.

TOWN HALL THEATRE ◆ THEATER
Courthouse Sq. ☎091 569 777 www.tht.ie

The epicenter of arts and culture in Galway, the Town Hall not only regularly puts on plays by Irish playwrights but also plays a crucial role in many of Galway's festivals. The theater does more than plays: dance, film, and comedy shows all make appearances as well.

☞ From Eyre Sq., take Williamsgate St., then take a right onto Eglinton St. and continue as it turns into St. Francis St., then take a left onto St. Vincent's Av. Ⓢ Tickets from €10. Ⓒ Box office open M-Sa 10am-7:30pm; tickets available online.

SHOPPING

◆ THOMAS DILLON'S CLADDAGH GOLD ◆ JEWELRY
Quay St. ☎091 566 365 www.claddaghring.ie

The internationally known Facebook status on your finger, the Claddagh ring, was first made in Galway. This is the only place to get one stamped "original." Learn about the origins of this tradition in the back-room museum before picking out your ring.

☞ From Eyre Sq., take Williamsgate St. and continue as it becomes William St., then Shop St., then High St., and finally Quay St. *i* Museum in the back room. Ⓢ Rings from €65. Ⓒ Open M-F 10am-5:30pm, Sa 10am-4pm.

◆ PUBLIC ROMANCE ◆ CLOTHES
52 Upper Abbeygate St. ☎091 568 771

This is the place to find leather hot shorts. Seriously. There's a pretty large selection of them here. They also have a good amount of outrageously American sweatshirts—the ones that have bald eagles holding the flag that scream, "tourist." That's just the beginning. Get ready to spend some time here.

☞ From Eyre Sq., take Williamsgate St., which turns into William St. Take a right onto Upper Abbeygate St. Ⓢ Sweatshirts from €25, leather from €30. Ⓒ Open M-F 9:30am-5:30pm, Sa noon-4pm.

ESSENTIALS

Practicalities

- **TOURIST OFFICE: Galway Tourism** on Forster St., is just a 2min. walk from the bus station; it books tours and hostels and provides information on Galway and the surrounding area. (☎353 93 52467 www.galway-ireland.ie ⏰ Open daily 9am-5pm.) There is also an information center in the middle of Eyre Square. (⏰ Open daily 9am-4pm.)
- **INTERNET ACCESS:** For internet access, the **public library** offers free Wi-Fi as well as computers. (St. Augustine St. ☎091 561 666 www.galwaylibrary.ie ⏰ M 2-5pm, Tu-Th 11am-8pm, F 11am-5pm, Sa 11am-5pm.) **Net Café** does all things that require a computer: sends and receives faxes, CD/DVD burning, webcam set ups, etc. (Olde Malte Arcade ☎091 395 725 www.netaccess.ie ➡ From Eyre Sq., take Williamsgate St. and continue as it becomes Hop St. and then High St. $ Internet €1 per 15min., €2.50 for 45min., €3 for 1hr., €5 for 2hr. ⏰ M-F 10am-9pm, Sa 10am-7pm.)
- **POST OFFICE:** Located at 3 Eglinton St., just off of Eyre Square. (☎091 563 768 ⏰ M-Sa 9am-5:30pm.)

Emergency

- **POLICE:** A **Garda station** is located on the western bank on Mill St. Cross O'Briens bridge and continue on the slight right, look for it on your left. (☎091 538 000 www.garda.ie ⏰ 24hr.)
- **HOSPITAL: University Hospital Galway** is just outside the city on Newcastle Rd. (☎091 524 222 guh.hse.ie ⏰ Emergency care 24hr.)
- **PHARMACY:** Pharmacies are located around the city, look for the flashing cross. **O'Flaherty's** is centrally located on Eglinton St. just off of Eyre Square. (15 Eglinton St. ☎091 569 090 www.oflahertyspharmacy.com ⏰ M-Sa 10am-7pm.) On the western bank, follow Claddagh Quay away from the sea up the river to get to **O'Beirn's.** (11 Henry St. ☎091 563 768 ⏰ M-Sa 10-7pm.)

Getting There

BY BUS

Bus Éireann runs buses from: Cork ($ €18, students €16 ⏰ 3 buses daily at 9:25am, 12:25, 3:25pm); Dublin ($ €14, students €12 ⏰ Departs every hr. 8am-9pm); Limerick ($ €15, students €12 ⏰ Departs every hr. 8am-9pm); Belfast ($ €30, students €24 ⏰ Daily at 5am).

BY TRAIN

Trains arrive from Dublin ($ €33.50, students €22.50 ⏰ 7 daily) and Limerick ($ €21, students €13.50 ⏰ 7 daily).

BY PLANE

The nearest **airport** is in Dublin; see **Dublin: Getting There** (p. 51). The Shannon airport also offers many flights; see **Shannon: Getting There** (p. 94).

Getting Around

On the off chance that you need a taxi to get around (how many pints did you have?), expect to pay €5-7. **Big-O-Taxis** are the most used. (☎091 585 858 www.bigotaxis.com) **City Direct** runs a **bus** service that hits some of the major spots in the Galway city center, including Jury's Inn on the Quay and Eyre Square. (Rahoon ☎091 860 814 www.citydirectgalway.ie $ €1.90, 13-16 €1.40, children €1.)

MUNSTER

This is probably what you were thinking of when you settled on Ireland. At the very least, it's likely what everyone you know back home has in mind. At times, it'll seem too magical to be real—projections of your imagination fulfilling the wildest hopes of your wanderlust-fueled brain. Sheer cliffs dropping off into the sea, appearing to be the true end of the world and making you rethink the whole "round earth" theory; towering castles filled with history and charm and superstition; miles and miles of hauntingly beautiful bare rocky landscape with patches of vegetation powering through, stretching all the way to the ocean in the distance. But no: those cliffs, those castles, that unendingly beautiful wilderness—they're actually there, and so are you. Whether you use the cities included in this chapter as launching points for outdoor excursions or whether you stay within their limits and enjoy everything they have to offer, you'll leave this region with the true Irish experience.

greatest hits

- **TELL ME MOHER:** One of the greatest natural wonders of the world, don't miss out on the grandiose Cliffs of Moher (p. 86) in Ennis.

- **THE VILLAGE PEOPLE:** Greet your fellow Irishmen at Bunratty Castle and Folk Park (p. 92), a fully functional village representing 19th-century Irish life.

- **STUCK IN THE MUCK:** Just because Muckross Traditional Farm (p. 107) replicates history doesn't mean it's stuck in the past; this farm is still up and running after a long history.

- **PUCKER UP:** Whether you think it's a load of blarney or not, visit Blarney Castle (p. 116) to explore the ruins or kiss the legendary stone.

student life

If you're in Munster and on the hunt for some buddies to take on the town with, you're in luck: both Limerick and Cork are home to major universities. University College Cork, just west of the city center, is surrounded by solidly student-friendly food and nightlife options. Mingle with some students and tag along as they lead you to the best watering holes in the neighborhood. The University of Limerick is located a few miles east of the city center, but luckily there are a number of bars surrounding the campus. The Hurlers and The Lodge are two nightlife haunts where you're sure to meet some UL students. Follow them into town, where the most popular student hangouts are Angel Lane and Molly Malone's. Costelloes Tavern is a good place to go if you're looking for a more indie crowd.

ennis ☎065

Ennis musters up all the urbanity a small town can. The place teems with boutiques, nightlife, and streetside musicians, but it still doesn't lose its small-town friendliness. Locals fill the restaurants and pubs, always making sure tourists feel welcome (and usually asking the ladies for a dance). Keep your eye out for what looks like professional graffiti—it is. Artists recently flooded Ennis, taking everyday sights and transforming them into works of art (www.wallcandy.ie). Coupled with the crumbling ruins of years past, this town's youth, zest, and playfulness set it apart.

ORIENTATION

The **Fergus River** runs through Ennis, forming the town center's northern border, with **O'Connell Street** and **Carmody Street** bounding the center's remaining sides. Outside this triangle, the scene becomes largely residential. **O'Connell Square,** located at the intersection of O'Connell St., **Bank Place, High Street,** and **Abbey Street,** is an easy meeting point, with the **O'Connell Monument** visible from all over the city.

ACCOMMODATIONS

THE ROWAN TREE HOSTEL $

Harmony Row ☎65 686 8687 www.rowantreehostel.ie

With rooms that overlook the river—and by "overlook," we mean when you stick your head out the window, you're directly over the river—this could be one of the most relaxing hostel experiences in Ireland. The bedrooms are hardly spectacular, but they do provide much more space than the average hostel. The common room is sometimes used by local musicians as a practice room; if you're lucky, you'll catch a front-row seat for the best bar performers in Ennis.

From the O'Connell Monument follow Abbey Rd., and turn left over the bridge as the street becomes Harmony Row. The hostel is just past the bridge, on the left. ℹ Breakfast included. Free Wi-Fi. $ 10-bed dorms M-Th €12, F-Sa €16, Su €12; 6- and 8-bed €15/22/15; 3-, 4-, and 5-bed private rooms M-Th €14 per person, F-Sa €25 per person, Su €14 per person. Singles M-Th €35, F-Sa €40, Su €35; doubles €50/70/50. ⏰ Reception 24hr.

GREY GABLES BED AND BREAKFAST

Station Rd.

B&B $$$

☎065 682 4487 www.bed-n-breakfast-ireland.com

The rooms are all clean and simple, with modern bathrooms, and usually an Ikea-like shelf or chair to give the room some character. If you stay on the second floor, you get to use the super-cool wooden spiral staircase.

🚲 *From the bus station, take a left onto Station Rd.; the B&B is on the left after the intersection.*
i *Breakfast included. Free Wi-Fi.* Ⓢ *€35 per person.* 🕐 *Reception 24hr.*

BANNER LODGE

Market Sq.

GUESTHOUSE $$

☎065 682 4224

If Don Draper came to Ennis, this is where he'd stay. The dark green carpet and old leather chairs are accented by the lingering smell of smoke and the knowledge that whiskey is not far off. The random totem poles and wooden

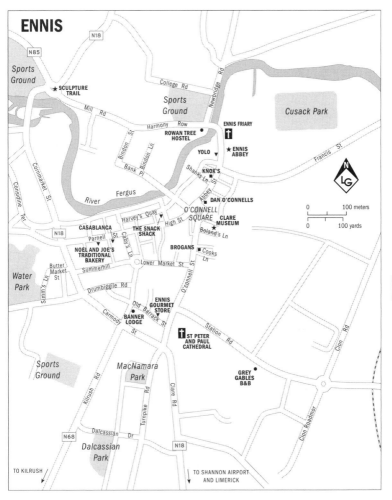

ENNIS

Native American statues suggest an aborted attempt at decor, but at least they keep things interesting.

✈ *From the O'Connell Monument, take O'Connell St., then turn right onto Barrack St. Banner Lodge is at the intersection of Market Pl. and Barrack St.* **i** *Breakfast included. Free Wi-Fi.* Ⓢ *€20 per person.* ☒ *Reception 24hr.*

SIGHTS

▨ ENNIS ABBEY   RUINS
Abbey St.   ☎065 682 9100
The crumbling ruins of the old Ennis Friary remind everyone how ancient this town really is. Although the roof is gone, the walls and empty window spaces that still remain speak of a grander time for the friary. Founded in 1240 by the King of Thomond, the striking structure was used until 1871 before being cast aside for the new Ennis Friary.

✈ *From O'Connell Sq., take Abbey St.; the ruins are on the right.*

CLARE MUSEUM   MUSEUM
Arthur's Row   ☎065 682 3382
Home to artifacts over 6000 years old, this museum contains a good deal of ancient weaponry and jewelry that was probably pretty impressive for its time but really wouldn't cut it in today's market. Visitors wander through "earth-," "power-," "faith-," and "water-" themed exhibits before reaching the top two levels of artwork on loan from the National Museum of Ireland. This museum is good for a rainy day if shopping isn't your thing.

✈ *From O'Connell Sq., take Friar's Walk to Arthur's Row.* Ⓢ *Free.* ☒ *Open Tu-Sa 9:30am-1pm and 2-5:30pm.*

SCULPTURE TRAIL   WALK
Mill Rd. Roundabout   www.clarelibrary.ie/eolas/cominfo/arts/sculpture
The trail follows the river along a nature path for a while (no, that's not a sculpture, that's a live blue heron) before twisting through the streets of Ennis and ending just above St. Peter and Paul Cathedral. This walk provides a wealth of photo opportunities, both of the regal sort befitting Ennis and of the funny, I'm-on-a-statue variety; it's also a great way to get your bearings in the city.

✈ *To get to the start, take Abbey St. from O'Connell Sq. and follow it as it turns over the river and becomes Harmony Row, then Mill Rd. The walk starts at the roundabout.* **i** *Download the map online or ask for one at the tourist office.* Ⓢ *Free.* ☒ *Open 24hr. but best enjoyed in daylight.*

ST. PETER AND PAUL CATHEDRAL   CATHEDRAL
O'Connell St.   ☎065 682 4043
Pastel stained glass and soft yellow walls give this cathedral a less intimidating look than most. The Virgin Mary grotto, just to the left of the entrance, contains the cathedral's main draw for tourists: the cathedral clock. The glass cabinet displays the giant mechanisms necessary for making this timepiece run, which means you can literally see and hear time tick by.

✈ *From O'Connell Sq., take O'Connell St.; it's on the right.* Ⓢ *Free.* ☒ *Open daily 8am-7pm.*

THE GREAT OUTDOORS

▨ THE CLIFFS OF MOHER   NATURAL WONDER
Liscannor   ☎065 708 6141 www.cliffsofmoher.ie
Considered one of the greatest natural wonders of the world, the Cliffs of Moher teeter on the edge of human comprehension. It's as though your eyes can't take in the full size and majesty of the 702ft. sheer cliff side. The official path is quite short, just 200m or so, but offers all the best views of the cliffs. More tourists than not brave the unofficial path that follows the edge of the cliffs for another kilometer with no guardrail to keep them safe. Some travelers report that on

munster

a nice day it's the best 30min. hike of your life. *Let's Go* recommends staying behind the safety of the walls; on windy days, a few daring tourists are blown off the edge every year. Finish your hike with a walk through the Interpretive Centre to get an idea of the influences of ocean, rock, nature, and man on the cliffs.

➜ Bus Éireann runs buses from Ennis bus station to the Cliffs of Moher. (Dir.: Doolin. 50min.; M-Sa 4 per day 10:25am-6:25pm, Su 3 per day 9:25am-7:55pm.) [$] €6, students €4. ⏰ Hours vary by month; open daily appx. 9am-7:30pm.

👍 BURREN NATIONAL PARK — NATIONAL PARK

Kilfenora — ☎01 888 2000 www.burrennationalpark.ie

The harsh beauty of Ireland is exemplified by the rocky countryside of the Burren. The deteriorating limestone rocks that dominate the terrain create inimitable landscape patterns on the hills soaring up from Galway Bay. The park is still home to many farmers who have been on the same land for hundreds of years; moss-covered rock walls are evidence of the area's age. The Burren is a heaven for botanists, and has a unique variety of plants, many of which are rarely found outside this rocky home. The early purple orchid dominates the area—as much as an alpine flower can dominate a rocky landscape—creating a contrast of delicate beauty with that of the rocks' harsher aesthetics.

➜ The Galway Tour Company operates driven tours (€29) out of Ennis, Galway, and Dublin.

FOOD

👍 ENNIS GOURMET STORE — CAFE $$

1 Barrack St. — ☎065 684 3314

This cafe looks like it's straight out of the hipster handbook: it's full of old men with long beards wearing the same thing as young men with mustaches who are doing it more ironically. The food for sale is a hodgepodge of hard-to-find meats, homemade jams, and alcohol. Watch the cooks chop off a slice of that foot-long hunk of cheese to make your bacon and brie sandwich (€6).

➜ From O'Connell Sq. take O'Connell St., then turn right onto Barrack St.. [$] Sandwiches €6. Salads €8.50-14. Specialties and tapas €7-18. Drinks €1.50-3. Beer and wine €3.50-6.50. ⏰ Open M-W 10am-7pm, Th-Sa 10am-11pm, Su 10am-7pm.

👍 NOEL AND JOE'S TRADITIONAL BAKERY — BAKERY $

70 Parnell St. — ☎065 682 1310

When you walk into this bakery, it'll probably be unstaffed. Noel and Joe spend most of their time in the back baking. Instead of clamoring for attention, take these few private moments to drink in the chocolate-dipped chocolate muffins (yes, that's chocolate twice; €1.60) and the loaves upon loaves of fresh-baked bread. We dare you to not buy something.

➜ From O'Connell Sq., take High St., which bends to the right and becomes Parnell St. [$] Baked goods €1.50-4. ℹ Day-old goods ½-price. ⏰ Open M-Sa 8:30am-2pm and 2:30-5pm.

CASABLANCA — BISTRO $$

56 Parnell St. — ☎065 684 3873

Come to Casablanca to get your funk on. Exposed white brick and green leather sofas create the vibe here, but the real attraction (other than the food) is the chairs. We know, it sounds weird, but they really bring the place together. The backs swoop down, seemingly disconnected from the rest of the chairs, making the entire dining area seem like a work of art. The food keeps up with the decor: the personal sized 10-inch marinara pizza is made with squid, smoked salmon, and shrimp—you can't get that just anywhere.

➜ From O'Connell Sq., take High St., which bends to the right and becomes Parnell St. [$] Starters €4-5.50. Flatbreads €7. Wraps and sandwiches €6. Salads €4.50-5.50. Specialty dishes €8-10. Pizzas and pasta €7-10. ⏰ Open M-W 9am-9pm, Th-Su 9am-10:30pm.

THE SNACK SHACK SANDWICHES $

Abbey St. Car Park ☎065 682 0750

This is the place to get big sandwiches for little prices. We're not sure why it's called the Snack Shack; even the smallest menu items can make for a full meal. Choose from the menu or make your own from the mega-list of ingredients. Is a corn, pineapple, and Nutella bagel your thing? There's only one way to find out.

🧭 From O'Connell Sq., take Bank Pl. and turn left onto Wood Quay, which is also the Abbey St. Car Park. [$] Sandwiches and bagels €3.50-6. Coffee and tea €1.50-3. Milkshakes €3.75. ⏰ Open M-Sa 9am-8pm, Su 10am-1pm.

YOLO RESTAURANT, BAR $$

Lower Abbey St. ☎065 679 7999

"You only live once," the sign explains to those neither fluent in acronyms nor familiar with Drake. Big meals for small prices best define this restaurant, although the menu choices are hardly once-in-a-lifetime material. It's the drinks that make this place adventurous. Three euro for a Sex on the Beach? Ten euro for four Jager Bombs? Don't mind if we do. Just be sure to fill up on some good Irish cooking beforehand.

🧭 From O'Connell Sq., take Abbey St.; the restaurant is on the left. ℹ Outdoor beer garden. [$] Starters €2.75-8. Entrees €3.75-11.75. Drinks from €3. ⏰ Open M-W 10am-midnight, Th-F 10am-2am, Sa 11am-2am, Su 11am-1am.

NIGHTLIFE

👍 **DAN O'CONNELLS** PUB

2 Abbey St. ☎065 684 9914

Dan O'Connells is a sports bar that always has Gaelic football or rugby on the tube and is redolent of strong Irish tradition. Sports, beer, and Home Rule are the three things that matter most here. In addition to the games always on TV, expect to find no small number of elderly Irishmen happy to discuss their opinions on the War for Independence. The decor looks like it hasn't been updated in 50 years, but don't be fooled—this pub is less than five years old.

🧭 From O'Connell Sq., take Abbey St.; it's at the corner of Abbey St. and Bank Pl. [$] Pints from €4. Spirits from €4.40. ⏰ Open M-Th 10am-11pm, F-Sa 10am-1am, Su 10am-11pm.

BROGANS BAR, LIVE MUSIC

24 O'Connell St. ☎065 682 9480 www.brogansbarandrestaurant.com

A watering hole for locals and tourists alike, the pub itself has little to distinguish it from others; instead, it's the music that sets it apart. You'll look less like a tourist if you sit at the bar next to the old men. If you've come for the live music, push your way past the crowd of tourists to get a better view of the ever-growing band. It starts with just two people, but musicians appear out of nowhere every 30min. or so with a new instrument and a Guinness, ready to join in.

🧭 From O'Connell Sq., take O'Connell St.; the bar is on the left. [$] Pints from €4. Spirits from €3.90. Bar menu €4-12. ⏰ Open M-Th noon-midnight, F-Sa noon-2am, Su noon-midnight.

KNOX'S PUB BAR, CLUB

18 Abbey St. ☎065 682 2871 www.knoxs.ie

Live music, a DJ on the weekends, young and beautiful patrons—this bar belongs in Dublin. Serving as a popular sports bar during the week, Knox's is transformed into a bumpin' nightclub on weekends. The sleek wooden bar and exposed brick walls give the place a modern, chic feel. Get your red shoes on and get ready to dance; Knox's is waiting.

🧭 From O'Connell Sq., take Abbey St.; the bar is on the left. [$] Pints from €5, Spirits from €5.50. ⏰ M-Th 10am-midnight, F-Sa 10am-2am, Su 10am-midnight.

ARTS AND CULTURE

GLÓR IRISH MUSIC CENTRE MUSIC CENTER

Causeway Link ☎065 685 3103 www.glor.ie

This auditorium/theater/gallery combines Irish music and shows with a chic, creative look, seamlessly melding modernity and tradition. Glór does children's theater, radio shows, and hosts musicians and comedians, to name just a few of its many offerings. The upstairs gallery changes every few months, but it always provides a spectacular view of the building's interior, a work of art in itself.

➔ From O'Connell Sq., take Abbey St., turn right onto Francis St, then another right onto Causeway Link. ℹ Free Wi-Fi. $ Tickets generally €10 for shows, though prices vary. Gallery free. ⏰ Box office and gallery open M-Sa 10am-4pm.

ENNIS ART GALLERY GALLERY

2 Francis St ☎065 689 2760

Irish artwork is found on the first floor, while the second floor is up for grabs for international artists to showcase their work. Stark white walls and a limited number of pieces make the ones that are here really stand out.

➔ From O'Connell Sq., take Abbey St., then turn right onto Francis St. $ Free. ⏰ Th-Sa noon-5pm.

SHOPPING

👍 **A. HONAN ANTIQUES** ANTIQUES

14 Abbey St. ☎065 682 8137

Literally every surface in this store is covered with something. And every one of those things has something else on top of it. It's almost magical, the way everything is piled so high that it towers over you—leaning, creaking, constantly threatening to fall. There is not enough time in the day—or in a lifetime—to take in every item in this store. There's barely enough room to walk through it. After a few minutes of letting your eyes adjust to what appears to be pure chaos, the fascination sets in. Lamps, paintings, old violins, an umbrella stand full of swords—we are fairly certain that anything that has ever existed can be found in this store.

➔ From O'Connell Sq., take Abbey St.; the store is on the left. ⏰ Open M-Sa 10am-6pm.

👍 **SOMALIA SHOP** THRIFT STORE

Wood Quay ☎065 682 4882

Ennis has more than its fair share of thrift stores, but this one has the most variety and the best selection. One room is dedicated to home furnishings, while the other is filled with clothes, shoes, and books. Prices appear on some items, but the implied agreement is that everything can be haggled, so get your bargain pants on. Don't have a pair? We bet you can find some here.

➔ From O'Connell Sq., take Bank Pl., then turn left onto Wood Quay. $ Most items €5-10. ⏰ Open M-F 11am-6pm, Sa 11am-1pm.

ESSENTIALS

Practicalities

- **TOURIST OFFICE:** The **Ennis Tourist Office** is located inside the **Clare Museum** on the 1st floor. (☎65 682 8366 ➔ From O'Connell Square, take Friar's Walk to Arthur's Row. ⏰ Open M-Sa 9:30am-5:30pm, Su 10am-1pm.)
- **TOURS:** Ennis walking tours leave from the **Tourist Office** M-Tu and W-Sa at 11am.
- **ATM:** There is a **24hr. ATM** at O'Connell Sq. There is also an ATM in the Ennis Shopping Center on Francis St.
- **INTERNET ACCESS:** There is free Wi-Fi available in the **Glór Music Centre.** (☎065 685 3103 www.glor.ie ⏰ Open M-Sa 10am-4pm.) Computers and Wi-Fi are available in the **De**

Valera Public Library. (Harmony Row ☎065 684 6353 🕐 Open M 10am-5:30pm, Tu 10am-8pm, W-Th 10am-5:30pm, F 10am-8pm, Sa 10am-2pm.)

- **POST OFFICE:** There is a post office located on Station Rd., a 2min. walk from the bus station. (☎065 682 0606 www.anpost.ie 🕐 Open M-F 9am-1pm and 2-5:30pm, Sa 9am-1pm.)

Emergency

- **POLICE:** The Ennis **Garda Station** is located at the end of Abbey St., just past the Abbey St. Bridge. (☎065 684 8100 www.garda.ie ⚑ Take Abbey St. from O'Connell Sq., and bear right at the bridge. 🕐 Open 24hr.)

- **HOSPITAL:** The **Mid-Western Regional Hospital** is located north of the city. (Gort Road ☎065 686 3100 ⚑ Take Abbey St. from O'Connell Sq., bear left on Harmony Row to cross the bridge, then make a quick right onto Newbridge Rd. Follow that until the roundabout; it's on the left. 🕐 Emergency care 24hr.)

- **PHARMACY: Flynn's Pharmacy** is on O'Connell St. (☎065 682 8666 🕐 Open M-Sa 9am-7pm.) **C&F Pharmacy** is on Market Pl. (☎065 682 9328 ⚑ From O'Connell Sq., take O'Connell St., right on Lower Market St., and left onto Market Pl. 🕐 Open M-F 8am-6pm, Sa 9am-1pm.)

Getting There

BY BUS

Bus Éireann runs buses from: Cork (💲 €14, students €11 🕐 Daily every hr. 7:25am-6.25pm); Galway (💲 €12, students €9 🕐 Daily every hr. 7am-8pm); and Limerick (💲 €6.80, students €4.20 🕐 Daily every hr. 7:25am-7:25pm).

BY TRAIN

Trains arrive from: Dublin (💲 €50, students €25 🕐 3-3½hr., 6 per day 7:30am-7:30pm); Galway (💲 €19.50, students €9.75 🕐 1½hr., 6 per day 6.20am-6:30pm); and Limerick (💲 €11.90, students €5.40 🕐 40min., 10 per day 6am-10:20pm).

BY PLANE

The nearest **airport** is in Shannon; see **Shannon: Getting There**.

Getting Around

Ennis has no city bus service; the best way to get around the city is to walk. **Taxis** line up at Harvey's Quay, right on the river past the Bank Pl. bridge.

shannon ☎061

The largely residential town of Shannon hides a few gems for travelers tucked away at the ends of its many culs-de-sac. A relatively new town, Shannon is still coming into its own: the convenient Shannon Airport and the proximity of castles and other day-trip activities makes Shannon a great place to fly into. It's the gateway to County Clare, so get ready for adventure.

ORIENTATION

The **Shannon River** borders Shannon to the south, with **Airport Road** forming the north and west boundaries. The area in between is divided up into various neighborhoods, any one of which contains more culs-de-sac than most travelers see in a lifetime. Unfortunately, several streets also share the same name. For example, **The Shannon Town Centre,** where nearly all the city's businesses and shops can be found, has four different streets named Shannon Town Centre.

ACCOMMODATIONS

MOLONEY'S B&B $$

21 Coill Mhara ☎061 364 185

This B&B has a real family atmosphere to it, so expect a child or two to be running around at all times, though never through guests' rooms. The accommodations are all ensuite, with modern bathrooms, and each room has a balcony. Soft pastel-colored comforters and sunlight streaming through the many windows make for a very comfortable stay.

🧭 Coming from the airport on Airport Rd., turn right onto Shannon Town Centre Rd., past the shopping center, then take the 4th left; Moloney's is at the end of the cul-de-sac. ℹ Breakfast included. Free Wi-Fi. 💲 Singles €42; doubles €66. ⏰ Reception hours vary; call ahead.

OAKWOOD ARMS HOTEL $$$$

Airport Rd. ☎061 361 500 www.oakwoodarms.com

As you walk into the Oakwood Arms's reception, three things will likely catch your attention: the rich, dark green carpet; the throne that serves as the reception area's sole chair; and the antique rifles decorating the walls. You might think you've just walked into an antique hunting lodge—that feeling doesn't go away. The hotel certainly doesn't let the antiquity impede on luxury, though. The rooms are nothing short of totally extravagant—we're talking too-many-pillows-on-the-bed and towels-in-the-shapes-of-swans extravagant.

🧭 On the left side of Airport Rd. coming from the Airport. ℹ Breakfast included. Free Wi-Fi. Special rates available online. Restaurant and bar in the hotel. 💲 Singles €75; doubles €79-95. Suites €90-115. Family €119. ⏰ Reception 24hr.

AIRPORT MANOR B&B $$

Ballycasey ☎061 363 010 www.airportmanorbandb.com

This B&B has the softest comforters we have ever had the pleasure of running our hands over, and luxuriant bed covers that are nearly impossible to get out off. Combine that with TVs in every room and you just might decide to stay inside all day. If you're looking for some human contact, though, the owners are more than happy to have a conversation over some tea or coffee.

🧭 Coming from the airport on Airport Rd., turn right onto Ballycasey Rd., then turn left into Ballycasey Park. ℹ Breakfast included. Free Wi-Fi. Complimentary ride to the airport. 💲 Singles €40; doubles €60. ⏰ Reception 24hr.

SIGHTS

★ BUNRATTY CASTLE AND FOLK PARK — CASTLE, VILLAGE

Bunratty — ☎061 360 788 www.shannonheritage.com

The grounds surrounding Bunratty Castle have been turned into a "folk park": a village representing typical Irish life in the 1800s. It's not just a representation, however—it is a fully operational village, which means, yes, you can buy a Guinness here. See how all types of Irish craftsmen and farmers lived, wander past the cathedral with sheep and goats grazing in the garden, and peek into the pig hut—but only if you're willing to come face-to-face with a mama hog. Take a break in one of the pubs lining the village's main street, or get a little shopping done before finishing your tour with Bunratty Castle itself. The most extensively renovated castle in Ireland, Bunratty gives visitors a good idea of just how awful it must have been to actually live in a castle. Stone walls are warmed slightly by French and Flemish tapestries, and the darkness is mildly alleviated by the slits that act as windows, but you still can't escape the reality that castles are cold, dark, and dreary places. Nevertheless, the only thing worse than living in a castle is not living in a castle. In the soldiers' dining hall, be sure to look up at the "murder hole"—let's hope you're an invited guest. Wind your way up the impossibly small winding stone staircase to the Earl's Hall and check out the entrance to the dungeon while you're there. Keep climbing the spiral staircase to reach the castle's battlements and a stunning view of the Shannon River. Spend a few minutes imagining that you own this castle and all the surrounding land before being ushered back downstairs to reality. Twice nightly, the soldiers' dining room is turned into a medieval banquet hall, where guests are served a four-course meal by the castle help while being entertained by theater and song ([$] €58 ⏰ Daily 5:30 and 8:45pm).

➔ 4km outside of Shannon. Take Bus Éireann (dir.: Limerick; €3.70) to Bunratty Castle. [$] Admission €15, students €10, families €38. ℹ Cafes, bars, and gift shop inside. ⏰ Open June-Aug M-F 9am-5:30pm, Sa-Su 9am-6pm; Sept-May M-F 9am-5:30pm.

FOOD

★ ROWAN BERRY CAFÉ — IRISH $$

Ballycasey Crafts Centre — ☎061 360 590

Few tourists make it to this gem of a local haunt, which is nothing if not off the beaten path. Dogs run freely in the courtyard while their owners grab a cup of tea or a hot lunch inside. A mix of fishermen, craftsmen, and slightly over-the-hill patrons gives this place a good variety of conversation. Breakfasts and lunches are artistically served in rather large portions, and the desserts are nearly a meal unto themselves.

➔ Coming from the Airport on Airport Rd., turn right just before Shannon Court Hotel. Take the 2nd left and then the 2nd right onto Ballycasey Crafts Centre. Many signs make it easy to find. [$] Starters €2-7. Sandwiches €6-9. Entrees €8.50-14. Coffee and tea €1.80-2.20 ⏰ Open M-F 8am-4pm, Sa 8am-3pm.

TASTY PIZZA — TAKE-AWAY $

Murphy's Cottage — ☎061 362 121

Only in Ireland are there enough thatched-roof cottages that one can be sacrificed to be converted into a takeout pizza joint. Sit down in the tiny one-room restaurant or order at the even tinier takeout counter. Take a minute to ponder how old the building is compared to how long it took you to get your kebab.

➔ Coming from the Airport on Airport Rd., it's on the right, just past the Oakwood Arms Hotel. ℹ Delivery available. [$] Breakfast €2-6. Pizza €7-12. Entrees €2-4 (€5-11 for meal deals). ⏰ Open daily 9am-midnight.

CHINA DINE CHINESE $

1-2 Ballycasey Crescent ☎061 703 333

It may not be the most gourmet meal you have in Ireland, but it will probably give you the most bang for your buck. The Chinese music playing in the background and chatter from the servers just might make you believe you're on the other side of the globe, although we're not sure you'd find the likes of this place in China. It's closer to the Western interpretation of Chinese food, with crispy fried wonton (€4) and, of course, the classic fish-and-chips platter (€4.50).

🚏 Coming from the airport on Airport Rd., turn right onto Ballycasey Rd., then left into Ballycasey Park. [$] Starters €3.50-5. Entrees €6-10. ℹ Takeout available. BYOB (€2 corking fee). ⏰ Open M-Sa 4:30pm-11pm, Su 1pm-10pm.

NIGHTLIFE

☑ SHANNON KNIGHTS INN TERRACE BAR BAR

☎061 361 045 www.shannonknights.ie/terrace-bar

Multicolored tile floors and dark-wood paneling give this pub a traditional Irish feel, but the vast space component combats that. This pub is massive, with huge open spaces between the bar and wall booths, so the place never really seems that full. Claustrophobes rejoice—we finally found a traditional Irish pub you can enjoy. Live bands bring a crowd of every age on the weekends.

🚏 Coming from the Airport on Airport Rd., take the 1st right past the 2nd roundabout into the parking lot; the bar is on the left. [$] Bar menu €4.50-14. Pints from €4. Spirits from €4. ⏰ Open M-Th 9am-11:30pm, F-Sa 9am-12:30am, Su 9am-11:30pm.

DARCY'S BAR, RESTAURANT

Sky Court Centre ☎061 708 149

Serving as an all-you-can-eat restaurant during the day, Darcy's comes alive as a sports bar at night. Brand-new flat screen TVs play the latest football game while the neon-lit bar serves pint upon pint. The large, open area hints at a dance floor weekend nights…will you be the one to start the party?

🚏 Coming from the Airport on Airport Rd., take the 1st right past the 2nd roundabout into the parking lot. Walk past the Subway into the courtyard; it's on the left. [$] Starters €4.50-9. Lunch entrees €6-12; dinner entrees €8-15. Pints from €4. Spirits from €4.20. ⏰ Open M-Th 11am-3pm and 4:30-11pm, F-Sa 11am-3pm and 4:30pm-11:30pm.

SHOPPING

BALLYCASEY CRAFT CENTRE SHOPPING CENTER

Ballycasey Craft Centre ☎061 362 105

Goldsmiths, woodworkers, candle makers, bakers, and many more craftsmen and women set up shop here. About a 0.5km walk off the main road down a quiet, wooded lane, the Ballycasey Craft Centre seems to be in another world: a world where everyone still makes things by hand. Wander the two small courtyards, chat up the shop owners, and check out their goods. (No, not those goods. Get your mind out of the gutter.) It doesn't get much more authentically Irish.

🚏 Coming from the Airport on Airport Rd., turn right just before the Shannon Court Hotel. Take the 2nd left, then the 2nd right onto Ballycasey Crafts Centre. Many signs make it easy to find. ⏰ Open M-Sa 8am-9pm. Individual shops keep their own hours.

SKY COURT CENTRE MALL

Shannon Town Centre ☎061 361 590

This new shopping center is a few years away completion: there are still several empty storefronts. However, it already has a thriving boutique lane, a gigantic Dunnes grocery store, and a food court on the second level. Stop by Prego Menswear (yes, that's the name; no, it doesn't appear to be a male maternity store) for some cheap jeans or check out the produce market to get a quick, locally grown snack.

✈ *Coming from the Airport on Airport Rd., take the 1st right past the 2nd roundabout into the parking lot.* 🕖 *Open M-Sa 9am-6pm, Su noon-6pm.*

ESSENTIALS
Practicalities

- **TOURIST OFFICE:** There is no tourist office in Shannon, but there is a website, **www.shannon. ie.** Some of the information is out of date, but it can still be useful.

- **ATM:** There is a 24hr. ATM at the entrance to the Sky Court Centre and another inside the MACE grocery store in Ballycasey Crescent.

- **INTERNET ACCESS: Sean Lemas Public Library** has computers available for use in exchange for an ID. (Shannon Town Centre ☎061 364 266 🕖 Open M 10am-1pm and 2-5:30pm, Tu 10am-8pm, W-Th 10am-5:30pm, F 10am-8pm, Sa 10am-2pm.) There are also computers available for use on the 2nd floor of the Sky Court Centre next to the food court. (€1 per 10min. 🕖 Open M-Sa 9am-6pm, Su noon-6pm.)

- **POST OFFICE:** There is a post office inside the Sky Court Centre. (☎185 057 5859 www.anpost.ie 🕖 Open M-F 9am-5:30pm, Sa 9am-1pm.)

Emergency

- **POLICE:** The **Garda** station is located down in Shannon Town Centre. (☎061 361 212 www.garda.ie 🕖 Open 24hr.)

- **HOSPITAL: Shannon Medical Centre** is located right next to the library and Sky Court Centre in Shannon Town Centre. (☎061 705 000 www.shannonmedicalcentre.wordpress.com 🕖 Emergency care 24hr.)

- **PHARMACY: Ballycasey Pharmacy** is located on Ballycasey Crescent, right next to the MACE grocery store and across from the Airport Manor. (☎061 363 853 www.ballycaseypharmacy.ie 🕖 Open M-Sa 9am-7pm.) **Unicare Pharmacy** is located in the Sky Court Centre. (☎061 360 716 www.unicarepharmacy.ie 🕖 Open M-W 9am-7pm, Th 9am-8pm, F 9am-9pm, Sa 9am-6pm, Su noon-6pm.)

Getting There
BY BUS

Bus Éireann runs buses from: Cork (💲 €14, students €11 🕖 Every hr. daily 7:25am-8:25pm); Ennis (💲 €6.70, students €5.50 🕖 10 per day 6:55am-11:05pm); Galway (💲 €14, students €10 🕖 2 per day at 3:40 and 4:40pm); and Limerick (💲 €3.70, students €3 🕖 Every 30min. daily 5am-11pm).

BY PLANE

The **Shannon Airport** (SNN; www.shannonairport.com) is small but a great place to fly into for those interested in exploring Ireland's west coast. **Aer Lingus** (☎061 715 400 www.aerlingus.com) and **Ryanair** (www.ryanair.com) have some of the cheapest flights in Ireland. **United** (www.united.com) and **Delta** (www.delta.com) also fly into Shannon.

Getting Around

Bus Éireann has a route that runs through the city, with buses every 30min. **Taxis** can be called or found at the Shannon Airport, with **McLoughlin Taxi** being the most popular in Shannon. (☎086 247 3712 www.mcloughlintaxi.com 🕖 Available 24hr.) Shannon is very walkable, and bike paths often accompany sidewalks.

limerick ☎061

There once was a woman from Lim'rick…We can't finish, but assure you it's bawdy. Aside from its poetry, Limerick is a city most famous as the location of Frank McCourt's impoverished childhood and the setting for *Angela's Ashes*. The legendary curse of St. Munchin, however, makes it a wonderful place for travelers. The story goes that when the residents of Limerick refused to help build St. John's Cathedral 1500 years ago, passing travelers helped to complete the work. St. Munchin cursed the residents to lives of grief and pain while blessing all travelers with good fortune. All the more reason to stop by. Curse or not, the city is thriving today with many a shopping center, hotel, and flashy restaurant bringing in a fair amount of tourism. We think it's the troubled past, however, that makes this city so fascinating. There's more to see here than museums and castles: there's a deeper history, a character that makes this city atypical in a good way.

ORIENTATION

O'Connell Street and **Henry Street** run parallel to each other through the city center and are home to the busy-city part of Limerick. O'Connell St. becomes **Patrick Street,** which turns into **Bridge Street** at the bridge to the medieval **English Town. Bridge Street** and the perpendicular **Nicholas Street** are host to everything that one might want to see or do in this smaller, older part of Limerick. **Bedford Row,** which connects O'Connell St. and Henry St., has some of the best but most expensive shopping, while **Denmark Street** is host to a few more boutiques. The junction of High St. and **Cornmarket Row** is where you will find the legendary **Milk Market,** as well as a few smaller pubs and restaurants.

ACCOMMODATIONS

RAILWAY HOTEL
HOTEL $$

Parnell St. ☎061 413 653 www.railwayhotel.ie

Located right across from the bus station and less than a 5min. walk to the city center, this hotel has got our best-location award all cinched up. The rooms themselves are not all that special; big white beds and classic wood accents make them unexciting. Then again, who really wants their bed to be too exciting? Televisions in all the rooms make homebodies happy and rainy days pass faster.

 # Right across the street from the bus station. i Free Wi-Fi. $ Singles €25; doubles €40. ⏰ Reception 7am-12:30am.

NO. 1 PERY SQUARE
HOTEL $$$$

1 Pery Sq. ☎061 402 402 www.oneperysquare.com

When you walk into No. 1 Pery Square, you are greeted with luxury. A slight scent of lavender soothes you and permeates the entire hotel. The standard rooms (still bigger than most hostels' entire 10-bed dorms) are all named after Irish legends. The period rooms, such as the Victorian Room, have bathrooms that you could easily fit a family of four in. Mostly they just contain period pieces and giant tubs to soak away any encounters you may have had with the commonfolk. Oh yeah, the bedrooms are pretty nice, too. Who would have thought that all you really needed to truly relax is a king-sized bed and pot of lavender?

 # From the bus station, take a left onto Parnell St., followed by a right onto Upper Mallow St., and finally a left onto Pery Sq. i Breakfast included. Free Wi-Fi. Spa in basement. $ Doubles €120-165; period rooms €195; suites €200. ⏰ Reception 24hr.

COURTBRACK ACCOMMODATION
HOSTEL $

Courtbrack Ave. ☎061 302 500 www.courtbrackaccom.com

The closest thing Limerick has to a hostel, this place rents out rooms to travelers in the summer at Limerick's lowest rates. About a 20min. walk to the city center,

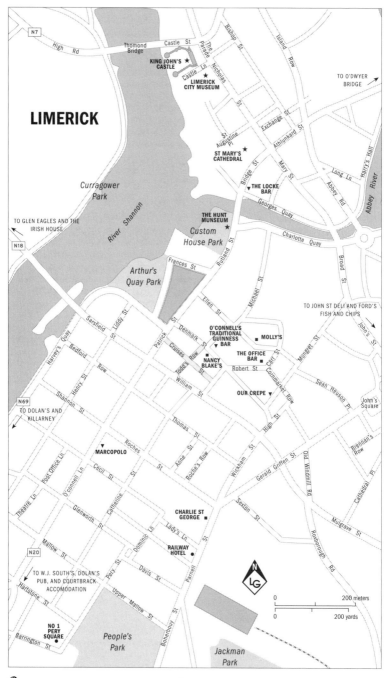

LIMERICK

you pay in calories what you don't pay in actual money. The rooms may not be ensuite, but the Wi-Fi extends throughout the entire hotel, and there are sinks in all the rooms.

From the bus station, turn left onto Parnell St., then turn right onto Upper Mallow St. Follow it as it becomes Lower Mallow St. Turn left onto Dock Rd., follow for 10min., then turn left onto Courtbrack Ave. i Breakfast included. Free Wi-Fi. Sept-May most rooms occupied by students. $ Singles €30; doubles €45, family rooms €23.50 per person. ⏰ Reception 24hr., call if there is no one there.

GLEN EAGLES B&B $$

12 Vereker Gardens ☎061 455 521

The rooms are hotel-like, with comforters that look a little worn, but there is a familial atmosphere. It is all too easy to spend all day in the sitting room, drinking tea and chatting with Helen, the owner, about your daily itinerary. Breakfast here is an event; Helen believes you cannot start the day without a good meal. Full Irish home-cooked breakfast, with a jar of Nutella on the table to go with anything you want? That makes this world worth living in.

From O'Connell St., turn left onto Sarsfield St. Head over the bridge and follow it as it becomes Ennis Rd., then turn left onto Vereker Gardens. i Breakfast included. Free Wi-Fi. TVs in all rooms. $ Doubles €33-36; singles €45. ⏰ Reception hours vary, call ahead.

THE IRISH HOUSE B&B $$

Ennis Rd. ☎061 277 795

Located in an old Victorian home, touches of the past seep into the B&B today, including the smoky smell from years ago. Other than that, this is a top-notch place to stay. A beautiful flower garden greets you out front and the rooms are certainly nothing to complain about: spacious, all ensuite, and beds big enough to fit a burly man.

From O'Connell St., turn left onto Sarsfield St. Head over the bridge and continue as it becomes Ennis Rd. The Irish House is on the right. i Breakfast included. Free Wi-Fi. $ Doubles/twins €40-45 per person; family rooms €60. ⏰ Reception varies, call ahead.

SIGHTS

THE HUNT MUSEUM MUSEUM, GALLERY

Rutland St. ☎061 312 834 www.huntmuseum.com

Take in the collection of 13th- to 15th-century pottery, admire the jewelry from the Iron Age (those ladies had good taste, if a bit overstated), and learn how the death penalty used to be carried out (hint: it involved being dragged behind wild horses). This museum keeps things fun by having drawers to open as well as combining history and art in unexpected ways. It will keep you on your toes. Finish up with the art exhibit in the basement; the material changes every few months but the high quality never does.

Follow O'Connell St. as it becomes Patrick St., then Rutland St. The museum is on the left. $ €5, students and seniors €3.50, children €2.50, families €12. Admission free Su. 2-for-1 admission on M. ⏰ Open M-Sa 10am-5pm, Su 2-5pm.

THE PEOPLE'S PARK PARK

Pery Sq. ☎061 407 100

The groomed gardens in The People's Park swoop up and down, providing glorious lawns for children and dogs to run free. The playground is often frequented by schoolchildren on field trips—the ever-present phallic monument to the Irish freedom fighters doesn't deter them and completes this classic Irish city park.

From the bus station, turn left onto Parnell St. The park is on the right. $ Free. ⏰ Open daily 8am-9pm or dusk.

KING JOHN'S CASTLE MUSEUM

Nicholas St. ☎061 411 201

It's part museum, part historical building, but all, well, kind of fun. The museum itself is a little confusing. Walk into a 5min. slideshow that reads more like an audio-visual work of art, with drawn recreations of the castle set to traditional Irish music. The upstairs part of the museum is a little more engaging, with random wooden statues of castle characters and an occasional voice-over booming your way (although the exhibit it's referencing is a mystery to us). The fun part is the castle grounds itself. It takes very little imagination to recreate the (only slightly) crumbling castle in its years of glory. Climb up the spiral stone staircases and walk the battlements up to the top. We heartily suggest trying your hand at pretending to be a castle guard.

🚏 From Bridge St., turn left onto Nicholas St. The castle is on the left. $ €9, students and seniors €6.25, children €5.25, families €20.60. ⏰ Open M-F 10am-5pm, Sa-Su 9:30am-5pm.

ST MARY'S CATHEDRAL CATHEDRAL

St. Augustine Pl. ☎061 310 293 www.cathedral.limerick.anglican.org

For 840 years, this cathedral has been a house of prayer, and those years hang heavily inside. The cobblestone path that leads to the entrance is the very same that worshippers have been walking on for centuries and tourists for at least the past 30 years. A slightly musty smell greets you as you walk in, but it's the kind that makes you feel as though you've stepped back in time. The dusty sunlight streaming in illuminates the aging stone walls and high-arched ceilings.

🚏 From the Bridge St. bridge, take Bridge St., then turn left onto Mary St., and then turn left onto St. Augustine Pl. i Book exchange inside. $ €3 donation expected. ⏰ Open M-Sa 9am-4:30pm and Su 2-5pm.

LIMERICK CITY MUSEUM MUSEUM

Castle Ln. ☎061 417 826 www.limerickcity.ie/citymuseum

The kind of place that makes for a short and sweet visit, the free Limerick City Museum focuses on the economic history of the city. The amount of period-piece fabrics and silver on display makes it feel a little like an antique store, but the plethora of ancient records of sale reminds you you're supposed to be learning. Those with a heavy interest in the monetary happenings of early Limerick will be in heaven; everyone else will spend a few minutes admiring the old rifles on the wall and then leave.

🚏 From the Bridge St. bridge, take Bridge St and then the 1st left; walk through the parking lot and turn right onto Castle Ln. $ Free. ⏰ Open Tu-Sa 10am-1pm, 2:15-5pm.

FOOD

👍 MARCO POLO RESTAURANT $$

O'Connell St. ☎061 412 888 www.marcopolo.ie

This is it. This is the ultimate restaurant. It's like someone put on the "I put no effort into being this cool" playlist, made a restaurant based off of neutral colors, modern art, and leather, and then lowered all prices to rival the neighboring McDonald's. Giant portions of quite literally mouth-watering international choices mean you're never going to want to leave. And when you do, you're going to want to go back.

🚏 From the point at which O'Connell St. and Patrick St. meet, take O'Connell St. It's 3 blocks down on the left. i Lunch and dinner deals, check website for details. $ Starters €4.50-8.50. Entrees €8.50-15.50. ⏰ Open Tu-Sa noon-10:30pm, Su 1-9:30pm.

👍 THE LOCKE BAR RESTAURANT, BAR $$$

2A Georges Quay ☎061 413 733 www.lockebar.com

It's possibly Limerick locals' favorite bar, but it's definitely a tourist hotspot. The pub itself is just a little too elegant to be all that authentically Irish, but the food's good, the music's better, and the crowd is worth every penny. Stone walls inside and soft-arched windows make you feel like you're dining in a castle basement. Then you'll notice the bottles stacked behind the bar and realize it's probably more like the castle's wine cellar. The food's not all that cheap, but as far as river-view dining goes, it's worth it.

Follow Patrick St. as it becomes Rutland St., then Bridge St. Turn right onto Georges Quay just over the bridge; The Locke Bar is on the left. ℹ *Traditional music sessions nightly 6pm-8pm and 9:30pm-late. Outdoor patio.* [$] *Lunch €8-12. Appetizers €5.50-11. Entrees €13-25. Desserts €4-9. Pints €4.20-6.* ⏰ *Open M-Th 10am-12:30am, F-Sa 10am-1am, Su 10am-12:30am.*

OUR CREPE CREPERIE $

High St. ☎085 833 2220 www.ourcrepe.ie

This restaurant does crepes like Canada does hockey players: there are a lot of them and they all look delicious. Keep close to your Irish roots with a boiled vegetable and cheese crepe (€4) or get a little crazy with a Nutella and coconut dessert crepe (€3). Hockey players not included.

From Patrick St., with the shopping center on your left, turn right onto Denmark St. and then turn left onto High St. ℹ *21 different dessert crepes, 30 different dinner crepes.* [$] *Dinner crepes €4-6.40. Dessert crepes €3-5.* ⏰ *Open M-Sa 8am-6pm.*

FORD'S FISH & CHIPS TAKE-OUT $

22 John's St. ☎061 418 545

This place does good fish and no frills; we mean no tables, chairs, wall decorations, or ambient music. You walk in, you order some delicious fish and chips, maybe some cheesy garlic fries if you're spicing things up, and you walk right back out. That's it.

From Charlotte's Quay, turn away from the river onto Broad St. and follow it as it becomes John's St. [$] *Fish and chips €0.60-2.80.* ⏰ *Open daily 11am-10pm.*

JOHN STREET DELI DELI $

16 John's St. ☎085 228 9740

This is where the young and budget-conscious come to get a nice meal, making this place as authentically Irish as they come. The red booths that dominate the place make you think of a '50s diner—they even sell slushies. With a full breakfast menu served until 2:30pm, you better believe more than one hung-over youngster makes it in here every day.

From Charlotte's Quay, turn away from the river onto Broad St. and follow it as it becomes John's St. [$] *Breakfast €4.50-7. Soups and sandwiches €3-5. Entrees €7. Drinks €1-4.* ⏰ *Open M-F 7:30am-4pm, Sa 8:30am-3pm, Su 9:30am-2pm.*

O'CONNELL'S TRADITIONAL GUINNESS BAR RESTAURANT, BAR $$

3 Little Ellen St. ☎061 401 190 www.oconnellsbar.ie

A bar dedicated to Guinness may not be an unusual find in Ireland, but the food that comes with this one is. It may not need to be said that a traditional Guinness bar does, in fact, serve traditional Irish meals, like full Irish breakfasts (€8) and a nice bacon and cabbage main dish (€9.50), but that is as far as the authentic Irish pub feel extends. The restaurant is large, making meals there efficient but not intimate. Guzzle enough Guinness, though, and you just might start getting intimate with everyone around you.

From Patrick St., turn onto Denmark St. and then turn left onto Little Ellen St. ℹ *Outdoor patio with roof.* [$] *Breakfast €2-8. Lunch €4.20-10.* ⏰ *Open M-Th 9:30am-11:30pm, F-Sa 9:30am-12:30am, Su 1-11pm.*

NIGHTLIFE

👍 DOLAN'S PUB PUB

3-4 Dock Rd. ☎061 314 483 ext. 1 www.dolans.ie

Serving lip-smacking good pub food by day and playing traditional Irish music by night (when there's not an important game on, that is), Dolan's is everything an Irishman could want in a pub. The final touch? It's popular enough to bring in a young crowd of travelers every night, adding an international touch to the locale.

 # From the bus station, turn left onto Parnell St., then right onto Upper Mallow St. Follow it as it becomes Lower Mallow St., then turn right onto Dock Rd. The pub is on the left. ℹ Live music daily at 9pm. $ Appetizers €4.50-6.50. Entrees €10.50-14.50. Desserts €4. Tea and coffee €2-2.70. Pints from €4. Spirits from €4. ⏰ Open M-F 5pm-2am, Sa 9am-2am, Su 10am-2am.

👍 W.J. SOUTH'S BAR

4 Quinlan St. ☎061 318 850

If you're looking for a relatively quiet scene (we mean quieter than ear-damaging music and grind-fests), then W.J. South's should do the trick. Irish music plays in the background while the 30-something patrons grab a pint or four, usually with an eye on whatever sports game is on. Named after an IRA fighter and a favorite of Frank McCourt, this pub has more Irish flavor to it than most.

 # From the point at which O'Connell St. and Patrick St. meet, take O'Connell St. Follow it as it turns into The Crescent and then Quinlan St. $ Pints from €4. Spirits from €3.90. ⏰ Open daily 10am-midnight.

THE OFFICE BAR PUB

Carr St. ☎086 777 9955

The Office Bar teeters on the line between traditional Irish pub and raging nightclub. With live music every night, one's inclined to think pub, but the giant stage and dance floor area that tends to fill up on weekends screams nightclub. Ponder the difference over your first three pints; dance the night away on your next four. You'll leave wishing this were your office.

 # From Patrick St., with the shopping center on your right, turn left onto Denmark St. Take the left fork onto Robert St., and then take a slight left onto Carr St. ℹ Live music weekly, check their Facebook page. $ Pints and spirits from €3.90. ⏰ Open M-W noon-11:30pm, Th-Sa noon-2am, Su noon-midnight.

CHARLIE ST. GEORGE PUB

41 Parnell St. ☎061 418 072

The ceilings hang low, and hurling and rugby teams of years gone by stare down from the walls in this 140-year-old pub. Sidle up to the bar and strike up a conversation with one of the many locals, or just drink silently while watching whatever sports game happens to be on. Don't expect any other tourists here; this is a local haunt.

 # From the bus station, turn right onto Parnell St. The bar is on the left. $ Pints and spirits from €4. ⏰ Open daily noon-11pm.

NANCY BLAKE'S PUB

Denmark St. ☎061 416 443

Nancy Blake's beer garden is its biggest draw. It's big, it's green, and it's packed with what seems like half of Limerick on a nice day. Don't worry; the inside's not bad to look at for the other 360 days of the year. Come early for a pint in a traditional pub atmosphere; stay late for a crowded, lively time.

 # From Patrick St., take Denmark St. The pub is on the right. ℹ Live music W, Th, and Su nights. $ Pints from €4.10. Spirits from €3.90. ⏰ Open M-W noon-midnight, Th-Su noon-1am.

MOLLY'S BAR, CLUB

Ellen St. ☎061 468 444

Sick of traditional Irish pubs? Looking for a place to get a pint without having to hear "Whiskey in the Jar" again? This is the place. The clientele are mostly locals in their mid-20s and 30s, and the music is Top 40s hits. It has enough space to dance if the mood strikes, but expect a lot more standing and schmoozing than popping, locking, and dropping.

🪧 From Patrick St., turn onto Ellen St. The bar is on the left, as the road curves. $ Pints and spirits from €4. ⏰ Open M-Th 7pm-midnight, F-Sa 7pm-2am, Su 7pm-midnight.

ARTS AND CULTURE

👍 **LIMERICK CITY GALLERY OF ART** GALLERY

Pery Sq. ☎061 310 633 gallery.limerick.ie

You might not be surprised to find another modern art gallery here—Ireland has a love of these. The Limerick City Gallery of Art features exhibits that border on the absurd using material from everyday life. The combination of the normal and the artistic is both disconcerting and fascinating.

🪧 From the bus station, turn left onto Parnell St., right onto Upper Mallow St., and left onto Pery Sq. $ Free. ⏰ Open M 10am-5:30pm, Tu 11am-5:30pm, W 10am-5:30pm, Th 10am-8:30pm, F 10am-5:30pm, Sa 10am-5pm, Su noon-5pm.

THE GALLERY GALLERY

13 Bedford Row ☎087 675 0754 www.slyonsart.com

Prints and originals from strictly Irish artists are for sale in this gallery. Follow the stairs up the three levels past a myriad of paintings and photographs of everything Irish until you reach a not very imposing orange tree at the top with a stop sign on it (not for sale).

🪧 From the point at which O'Connell St. and Patrick St. meet, take O'Connell St., followed by a right onto Bedford Row. $ Pieces generally range from €60-200. ⏰ Open Tu-Th noon-5pm, Sa noon-5pm.

THE BELLTABLE ARTS CENTER

69 O'Connell St. ☎061 319 866 www.belltable.ie

This stage is host to theater, music, and comedy, and the gallery showcases what most often tends to be a modern audio-visual exhibit with a social or political goal. Here, you can get educated on current events while being able to claim a cultural experience.

🪧 From the point at which O'Connell St. and Patrick St. meet, take O'Connell St. It is 6 blocks down on the left. $ Gallery exhibits free; ticket prices for theater, music, and comedy generally adults €8.50, students €6.50. ⏰ Open M-F 9:30am-5pm, Sa-Su noon-5pm.

SHOPPING

👍 **THE MILK MARKET** MARKET

Cornmarket Row ☎086 028 1828 www.milkmarketlimerick.ie

During the week it is home to a few tiny shops and restaurants barely big enough to fit two people at once. On the weekends the courtyard opens up and the Milk Market floods with shoppers, merchants, and craftsmen, just as it has for the past 150 years. Friday is the City Market, with booths ranging from antiques to traditional Irish food. Foodies, however, should make sure to come during the Saturday Food Market, when booths sell local and gourmet treats. Sunday is the Variety Market, where anything goes.

🪧 From Patrick St., turn onto Denmark St. and take a slight left at the fork onto Robert St. The Milk Market is at the intersection with Cornmarket Row. You can't miss it. ⏰ During the week the shops all have their own hours. Friday Market 10am-3pm, Saturday Market 8am-4pm, Sunday Market 11am-4pm.

26 Patrick St.   ☎061 415 504 www.irish-handcrafts.com

This is the best place in Limerick to get a famous Aran Islands wool sweater. Their selection includes sweaters and scarves for both men and women as well as a selection of non-wool items for those looking for something a bit less itchy. If you're having trouble finding the color that best brings out your eyes, the shop assistant is available for consultation. Compliments are free; the sweaters, however, are not.

✚ *From the point at which O'Connell St. and Patrick St. meet, take Patrick St. It is on the left.* i *Sweaters also available for purchase from their website.* Ⓢ *Sweaters from €50.* ⌚ *Open M-Sa 10am-6pm.*

EXCURSION

🏴Adare

ACCOMMODATIONS

It's pretty easy to find a place to stay in Adare, although the town caters to the well-off, so the rooms may not be cheap. **Station Road,** just off **Main Street,** has a fair amount of B&Bs to choose from. We suggest the **Abbey Villa** for a more modern, hotel-like stay (☎061 396 113 ✚ From the tourist information office, turn right onto Main St. and then turn right onto Station Rd. Ⓢ Doubles/twins €30 per person; singles €40; family rooms €80-100) or **Berkeley Lodge** if you're looking for a home-style experience. (☎061 396 857 ✚ From the tourist office, turn right onto Main St. and then right onto Station Rd. Ⓢ Singles €45-50; doubles €33-35 per person; family rooms €80-90.) For those who can't sleep without a portrait of Jesus watching over their bed, the **Churchview House B&B** has you covered. (☎061 396 371 ✚ From the tourist information office, turn onto Main St. and then turn right onto Station Rd. Ⓢ Doubles €35 per person; singles €60; family rooms €75-85.) The best non-B&B is the **Adare Village Inn,** which is family owned and in conjunction with Séan Collins and Sons Bar. The rooms are modern and the beds are big, but breakfast is not available. (☎061 396 400; www.adarevillageinn.com ✚ From the tourist information office, turn right onto Main St. and a take a slight left onto Rathkeale Rd. Ⓢ Doubles €30 per person; singles €40. ⌚ Reception 24hr., calling ahead is suggested.)

SIGHTS

Colloquially known as Ireland's most beautiful town, there are enough thatch-roofed houses and medieval architecture to make you believe you've stumbled back a thousand years or so. The half restored and partly overgrown ruins of **Desmond Castle** (☎901 396 114 ✚ Tours leave from the tourist information office i Entrance by guided tour only Ⓢ €6, students €5 ⌚ Tours daily between 10am-5pm) are both beautiful and haunting, offering glimpses of lives long past. To complete your tour of the castle grounds, head over to the ruins of the **Franciscan Friary,** located near hole six of the golf course. (Adare Manor Golf Club ☎061 396 204 ✚ From the castle entrance turn right onto Limerick Rd., then the next right into the Adare Manor Golf Club parking lot.) **Adare Manor** is now a hotel, but the 840-acre grounds, which include the **Maigue River** and **French Gardens,** are always open for exploration. (☎061 396 566; www.adaremanor.com ✚ From the tourist information office, turn left onto Limerick Rd. and then turn right into the entrance to the manor grounds.)

FOOD

Groceries are sold at **Londis** on Station Rd. (☎061 396 611 ⌚ M-Sa 7am-9:30pm, Su 7:30am-9pm), but Adare has a gourmet selection of restaurants to choose from as well as the classic pub fare. A good breakfast can always be found at **The Good Room,** and a good lunch is a safe bet as well. (☎061 396 298 ✚ From the tourist information office, turn left onto Limerick Rd. Ⓢ Sandwiches and salads €4.50-8.95.

munster

Pastries €2.99-4.75. Smoothies €4. Tea and coffee €2.20-2.95. ⏰ Open M-W 9am-5pm, Th-Sa 9am-5:30pm, Su 11am-5pm.) **The Wild Geese** has a half Irish, half French, and all delicious menu. (☎061 396 451; www.thewild-geese.com ➡ From the tourist information office, turn left onto Limerick Rd. $ €29 for 2 courses, €35 for 3 courses. Sunday lunch €20 for 2 courses, €25 for 3 courses. ⏰ Open Tu-Sa 6:30-10:30pm, Su noon-4pm.) **Séan Collins and Sons Bar** does lunch and dinner as well as live Irish music Monday, Friday, and Saturday nights. The food is simple and filling, and it is a local favorite. (☎061 396 400; www.seancollinsbaradare.com ➡ From the tourist office, turn right onto Main St. and take a slight left onto Rathkeale Rd. $ Appetizers €3.50-6.50. Wraps and salads €8.50-11.90. Pizza €10.50. Desserts €4. Pints from €3.90. ⏰ Open daily noon-midnight.) **Aunty Lena's** has a jazzy flair with their pub food for a few extra euro. (☎061 396 114; www.auntylenas.com ➡ From the tourist information office, turn right onto Main St. ℹ Free Wi-Fi. Live music Th, F, Su. $ Appetizers €4-6.50. Sandwiches, wraps, and salads €8.95-11.95. Entrees €10.95-11.95. Desserts 5.50. Pints from €4.10. ⏰ Open daily noon-midnight.)

ESSENTIALS

The **tourist office** is located on Main St., and is right where the bus from Limerick drops you off. It's inside the **Adare Heritage Center,** which also does Desmond Castle tours, traces family crests, and is host to restaurants and souvenir shops. (☎061 396 255 ⏰ Open daily 9am-6pm.) There is a 24hr. **ATM** on the corner of Main St. and Station Rd. The **Garda Station** is also located on Main St. and is open 24hr. for emergencies. (☎061 601 630; www.garda.ie) The **post office** is right across the street from the Garda Station. (☎061 396 120; www.anpost.ie ⏰ Open M-F 9am-1pm and 2-5:30pm, Sa 9am-1pm.) **Buses** depart from the Limerick bus station every hr. 8:35am-9:35pm. $ €12 roundtrip, students €8.50.

ESSENTIALS

Practicalities

- **TOURIST OFFICE:** The **tourist information office,** located off of Arthur's Quay, handles accommodation and tour bookings. (☎061 317 522 www.limerick.ie ➡ From the junction of O'Connell St. and Patrick St. meet, take Patrick St. and then turn left onto Arthur's Quay. ⏰ Open daily 9am-6pm.)
- **ATMS:** There are several **24hr. ATMs** located at the junction of O'Connell St. and Lower Cecil St.
- **INTERNET ACCESS:** Limerick has a wealth of free Wi-Fi hotspots. There is free Wi-Fi within 50m of all payphones. For computer access, the **Bethel Business Centre** (John's St. ☎061 467 809 ➡ From Charlotte's Quay, take Broad St. and follow as it turns into John's St. $ €1 per 30min. ⏰ M-Sa 10am-9pm) has internet access and does computer repairs, fax services, and printing.
- **POST OFFICE:** There is a post office located on Cecil St., just off of O'Connell St. (☎061 212 055 ⏰M-Sa 9am-5:30pm.) There is another post office located in **English Town** on Bridge St. (☎061 414 383 ➡ Take the 2nd right after crossing Matthew Bridge. ⏰ M-F 9am-1pm and 2-5:30pm, Sa 9am-1pm.)

Emergency

- **POLICE:** There is a centrally located **Garda station** on Henry St. (☎061 212 400 www.garda.ie ⏰ Emergencies 24hr.)

- **HOSPITAL: St. John's Hospital** is the nearest emergency care to the city center. (St. John's Sq. ☎061 415 822 www.stjohnshospital.ie ⚲ From O'Connell St., turn right onto William St. Turn left onto Cathedral Pl. 🕐 Emergency care 24hr.)

- **PHARMACY: O'Sullivans Late Night Pharmacy** is located at the corner of Liddy St. and Sarsfield St. (19-20 Sarsfield St. ☎061 413 808 www.osullivanspharmacy.com ⚲ From where O'Connell St. and Patrick St. meet, take Sarsfield St. 🕐 Open daily 9am-midnight.) To get to **Widdess Pharmacy,** take O'Connell St. from Patrick St. and turn left onto Roches St. (55 Roches St. ☎061 414 06 www.widdesspharmacy.com 🕐 Open M-Sa 9am-6pm, Su 2-6pm.)

Getting There

BY BUS

Bus Éireann runs buses from: Cork (💲 €15, students €12 🕐 13 daily); Dublin (💲 €13, students €12 🕐 6 daily); Galway (💲 €12 🕐 6 daily); Shannon Airport (💲 €7.20, students €6.30 🕐 6 daily).

BY TRAIN

Trains arrive from Dublin (💲 €60, students €26.50 🕐 3-3½hr., 6 per day 7:30am-7:30pm), Galway (💲 €28.50, students €17.50 🕐 1½hr., 6 per day 6.20am-6:30pm), and Cork (💲 €26, students €15.50 🕐 40min., 10 per day 6am-10:20pm).

BY PLANE

The nearest airport is in Shannon; see **Shannon: Getting There**.

Getting Around

Bus Éireann has 12 different routes that operate inside of Limerick. For exact routes, check the website. (☎061 313 333 www.buseireann.ie 💲 Adults €1.60, students €0.74. 🕐 Buses run from 7am-11pm.) **Taxis** are also readily available, with fares starting at €2.40. To get across town is usually not more then €5-7. **Top Cabs** is the most popular. (☎061 417 417 🕐 24hr.)

killarney ☎021

Killarney is to travelers what a candy shop is to children—and with a little something for everyone, it's hard to be disappointed. The city fills up with bikers and cyclists, partiers and sightseers, city-lovers and tree-huggers. Killarney fits more shopping, restaurants, and cafes into its three main streets than most cities do in their entirety. If long walks by the lakeshore are more your thing, Killarney National Park has days' worth of trails to explore. As for nightlife, the locals crowd the bevy of pubs in the city center right along with the tourists, resulting in a delightful mix of fun and the occasional international romance.

ORIENTATION

One of the few Irish cities not split in half by a river, Killarney makes up for it by having a 26,000-acre **national park** bordering the city on the west. **New Street** connects the park to the city center and is where you can find a good mix of pubs, accommodations, and restaurants. Where **New Street, Main Street,** and **High Street** meet is the **town center;** from there you can go north on High Street for some great restaurants and pubs or south on Main Street for shopping and more restaurants. **College Street** cuts through the town center and connects with **Fair Hill,** which will get you to the bus station on **Park Road. Muckross Road,** to the south of the city, is home to more B&Bs than you will find anywhere else and is also the start of the bike path leading out to the **Muckross House** and **Ross Castle.**

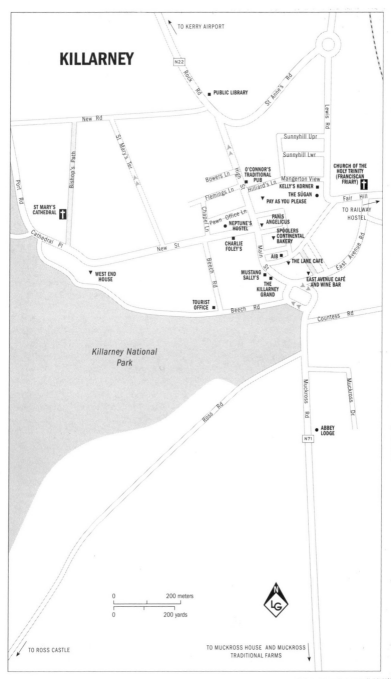

KILLARNEY

ACCOMMODATIONS

THE RAILWAY HOSTEL
HOSTEL $

Dennehy's Rd. ☎064 663 5299 www.killarneyhostel.com

Wooden floors, a brick oven, and some leather couches give this hostel a modern farmhouse feel. It is spacious here: the hallways are wide, the common room is uncluttered, and the beds, while still considered twins, border on doubles. Only a 5min. walk from the town center, the out-of-the-way street and natural surroundings make it feel miles away.

 # From the bus station, take a left onto Park Rd. and a right onto Dennehy's Rd., just before the road forks. i Breakfast and linens included. Free Wi-Fi in public areas. Kitchen and security safes available. [S] 10-bed dorms from €14; 8- and 9-bed from €14-16; 4- to 6-bed from €16-18; 2-to 3-bed from €18; private triples from €21 per person. ⏰ Reception 24hr.

NEPTUNE'S HOSTEL
HOSTEL $

Bishop's Ln. ☎064 663 5255 www.neptuneshostel.com

The common room is small, but that's about the only thing we have to complain about here. The kitchen is big enough to accommodate a German school group and modern enough that you won't feel like you're part of a living museum. While the TV room doesn't have Wi-Fi, it does have couches good enough to take a nap on if the giant flat screen isn't keeping you occupied. Tucked away from the main street, the hostel is quiet enough for a good night's sleep sans earplugs.

 # From the town center, take New St., then take the 1st right onto Bishop's Ln. i Breakfast and linens included. Free Wi-Fi in the kitchen and common room. Computer available for use. [S] 8-bed dorms M-Th €12, F-Sa €14, Su €12; 8-bed ensuite €13/15/13; 6-bed €13/14/13; 6-bed ensuite €14/15/14; 4-bed €13/15/13; 4-bed ensuite €15/16/15; 3-bed €14/16/14; 3-bed ensuite €16/18/16; twin/double-bed €17.50/20/17.50; twin/double-bed ensuite €20/25/20; singles €20/25/20; single ensuite €25/30/25. ⏰ Reception 24hr.

THE KILLARNEY SÚGÁN HOSTEL
HOSTEL $

Lewis Rd. ☎064 663 3104 www.suganhostelkillarney.com

The large, dimly lit common room and kitchen have the feel of either a cluttered wine cellar or a basement pub. The beds are a hybrid of doubles and twins; they are spacious enough, but just for one person (or two people getting real close). The sassy, Euro staff are a hoot to chat with, if you can keep up.

 # From the bus station, take a left onto Park Rd, follow it as it becomes Fair Hill. Turn right onto Lewis Rd. i Breakfast and linens included. Free Wi-Fi available in common areas. Bike rental available. [S] 8-bed dorms €15, 4-bed dorms €17, doubles/twins €20. ⏰ Reception 24hr.

ABBEY LODGE
B&B $$

Muckross Rd. ☎064 663 4193 www.abbey-lodge.com

The stone front and beautiful flower garden set this B&B apart from the rest lining the road. The interior might not be the most modern, but the rooms are large enough to actually fit two people and their luggage in at once—a rarity in B&Bs. Bring any questions, Killarney or otherwise related, to the owner, John: he's a fan of chatting.

 # From the town center, take Main St. and follow the curve slightly left onto Kenmare Pl. Then take a quick right onto Muckross Rd. i Breakfast included. Free Wi-Fi. [S] Singles €75; doubles/twins €55 per person. ⏰ Reception hours vary, call ahead.

SIGHTS

KILLARNEY NATIONAL PARK
PARK

Demesne ☎064 663 1440 www.killarneynationalpark.ie

The park serves as a good area to take a long walk, bike ride, horseback ride, or piggyback ride; really whatever form of transportation you prefer. The terrain varies from mossy, heavily wooded areas, to lakeside paths, to the rugged, green mountains Ireland is so famous for. The park is host to many sights in themselves, some of the more famous being **The Meeting of the Waters,** a quiet, lovely place where three lakes meet and home to the famous **Old Weir Bridge.** It's a strong contender for the most picturesque place in all of Ireland (with enough paintings and professional photographs to back it up). Make sure to check out **Dinis Cottage** and the 19-century "graffiti" (names carved into stone using diamonds).

⚑ *From the town center, take New St. until the end.* ⓘ *Check out the website for a full list of sights within the park.* ⓢ *Free.* ⏰ *Open 24hr.*

🏛 MUCKROSS TRADITIONAL FARM   FARM
Killarney National Park   ☎064 663 0804 www.muckross-house.ie

This farm serves as an historic and educational activity while still managing to act as a working farm. Props for multi-tasking. Five stone houses replicate how life was lived before electricity; women of the houses explain their lives and give you homemade bread and butter. In addition to that, the hour-long stroll through the countryside of Killarney National Park with breathtaking views of the mountains is never a bad way to spend your time.

⚑ *From the town center, take Main St. Turn slightly left onto Kenmare Pl. and then turn right onto Muckross Rd. (look for signs on the right to Muckross House).* ⓘ *A free coach service circles the farm at 15min. intervals. Cow milking at 10am and 4pm daily.* ⓢ *€7.50, students €4, seniors €6, families €22.* ⏰ *Open daily 10am-6pm.*

MUCKROSS HOUSE   ESTATE
Killarney National Park   ☎064 667 0144 www.muckross-house.ie

The name may make it sound unappealing, but this is one of the best-preserved and most fascinating estates we have ever been to (and we've been all over Ireland). Basically unchanged since the early 1900s, the guided tour of the house leaves you with an accurate idea of exactly how the residents lived, as well as a pretty good idea of how talented a hunter the last owner, Arthur Vincent, really was. The many stuffed fish, stags, and birds are all from the houses' grounds, now better known as the Killarney National Park. Grab a horse-drawn carriage tour of some of the grounds' most impressive sights or get a boat tour for the best views of the house itself.

⚑ *From the town center, take Main St. Turn slightly left onto Kenmare Pl. and then turn right onto Muckross Rd. (look for signs on the right to Muckross House).* ⓘ *Admission to the house with guided tour only.* ⓢ *House tour €7, students €3, seniors €6, families €18. Carriage tour €30 for 1-3 people, €40 for 4 people. Boat tours €10, children €5.* ⏰ *Open daily July-Aug 9am-7pm; Sept-June 9am-5:30pm. Carriage tours daily 9am-7pm. Boat tours daily 11am-6pm.*

ROSS CASTLE   CASTLE
Ross Rd.   ☎064 663 5851

Ross Castle is an Irish tower house used by the English in the struggle to maintain control over Irish lands in the 16th through 18th centuries. The guided tour is just long enough to give you a good idea of castle life, but short enough to keep everyone's attention. The renovations have left a much more modern castle but still give a good idea of how dreary, dark, and disease-infested castle life really was. The ever-pleasant tour guide does not shy away from the dirty details— learn how the castle inhabitants ate, slept, and pooped.

⚑ *From the town center, take Main St. Turn slightly left onto Kenmare Pl. and then turn right onto Muckross Rd. Take another right onto Ross Rd. and follow the castle signs.* ⓘ *Admission through guided tour only.* ⓢ *€4, students and seniors €3, families €10.* ⏰ *Open mid-Mar to Oct 9:30am-5:45pm.*

Killarney

FOOD

👍 PAY AS YOU PLEASE
RESTAURANT $

New Market Ln. ☎086 306 8253 www.payasyouplease.ie

Let's Go is not quite sure how a restaurant can stay afloat implementing this business model, but we aren't complaining! Yup, it's just as the name implies—pay whatever you think is a fair price for your experience here. Mismatched furniture, mismatched tableware, and a half-torn-apart piano-turned-bookshelf come together for amazingly eye-catching décor. The staff is as eccentric as the restaurant's look and equally passionate about their place. We would pay just to interact with them, whether or not we get a meal (which you always do). The menu changes week to week but always includes local foods that you can see being made from your seat.

➡ From the town center, take High St. and then turn right onto New Market Ln. i Free Wi-Fi. $ Wine €10-20 a bottle. Beer €5. ⏰ Open Th 12:30pm-4pm, F-Sa 12:30-4pm and 7-10pm, Su noon-4pm.

👍 SPÖGLERS CONTINENTAL BAKERY
CAFE $

Glebe Pl. ☎064 663 0202

We warn you that when you walk in here you are going to have a strong urge to eat everything in your line of sight. This family-owned bakery specializes in almost-too-good-to-be-true sweets and cakes but serves up a mean toasted sandwich as well. Be prepared for a bit of a line; the locals are all well aware this is the best place for a tea break in town.

➡ From the town center, take Main St. Turn left onto Plunkett St., which turns into College St., then a right onto Glebe Pl. i Made-to-order cakes available. $ Sandwiches €4. Hot lunches €5.50. Desserts €1.50-3. Tea/coffee €1.50-2.50. ⏰ Open M-Sa 9am-6pm.

THE LANE CAFÉ BAR
CAFE $$

Town Center ☎064 663 1855 www.theross.ie

This restaurant looks like what would happen if mystery and funk had a baby and taught it how to cook. The dark wood and fire-lit rooms demand your curiosity, while the pink and green leather chairs and giant couches lighten the mood. Three split-levels to the cafe make it seem like there is always something going on in the other room that you just can't quite see. The food? It's high-class, moderately-priced, international fare. We suggest the vegetarian falafel burger for just €10.50.

➡ From the town center, take Main St., a left onto College St., then a right into the alley just past Reen's Phamacy. i Outdoor patio. $ Lunch €4.30-16.25. Appetizers €6.50-13. Salads €9.50-14. Sandwiches €10.50-15. Entrees €10.50-16. Drinks €2.50-3.50. Free Wi-Fi. ⏰ Open daily 12:30-9:30pm.

EAST AVENUE CAFÉ AND WINE BAR
CAFE $$

East Ave. ☎064 663 9996

Love yourself some seafood in the morning? Or, for that matter, any time of day? The East Avenue Café does all meals with a heavy seafood influence. Grab the pan-fried fish (€10.95) in the morning, some of their famous seafood chowder (€6.95) for lunch, and finish up with "The Cod Father" (€14.95) for dinner. The high-backed black leather seats and mirror walls class up the place; eat on the sidewalk patio for some good people-watching.

➡ From the town center, take Main St. and take a slight left onto Kenmare Pl.; continue straight as it becomes East Ave. $ Breakfast €2.50-11. Appetizers €4-11. Fish €13-23. Other entrees €11-15. Sandwiches and wraps €10-15. Coffee and tea €1.80-2.70. Wine bottles €16.50-19.50. ⏰ Open M-F 9am-10pm, Sa 9am-11:30pm, Su 10am-6pm.

NIGHTLIFE

👍 THE KILLARNEY GRAND — BAR, CLUB

Main St. ☎064 663 1159 www.killarneygrand.com

The Grand somehow operates as both a traditional Irish pub and a Top-40 nightclub. Want to hang out with some middle-aged folks and listen to a live band? The pub half has it covered. Want to get low on a smoky dance floor with the young and the beautiful? Boom—the nightclub provides the perfect atmosphere for that. If you can't make up your mind, don't worry. A mere hallway divides the two; you can switch back and forth as much as you'd like.

🧭 From the town center, take Main St. and look to the right. ℹ Live music every night. $ Pints and spirits from €4. ⏰ Open M-Sa 7:30pm-2:30am, Su 7:30pm-1:30am.

👍 O'CONNOR'S TRADITIONAL PUB — BAR

7 High St. ☎064 663 1115

This pub has live Irish music, an upstairs comedy show, and enough Irishmen that the party tends to spill out on the street most summer evenings. We don't recommend going here for a quiet drink; the friendly locals won't let that happen, especially if you are a single lady.

🧭 From the town center, take High St. and look to the right. ℹ Live music every night from 9pm. Comedy show Th, F, Sa 9pm. $ Pints and spirits from €4. ⏰ Open daily 4pm-midnight.

MUSTANG SALLY'S — CLUB

15 Main St. ☎064 663 5790 www.mustangsallys.ie

The music is loud, the dance floor has a stripper pole, and the drink of choice is a vodka Red Bull. Relive your all-too-impulsive late teen years to Top 40 mash-ups and laser lights. You know you want to.

🧭 From the town center, take Main St. and look to the right. ℹ Live music Th, F, Su 9-11pm. $ Pints from €4. Mixed drinks €5. ⏰ Open M-W 7pm-1am, Th-Su 7pm-2:30am.

CHARLIE FOLEY'S — BAR

101 New St. ☎064 663 4311 www.charliefoleys.com

Considering the pubs that sandwich it on either side, Charley Foley's should be chock full of middle-aged American tourists, but for some reason it has escaped the tourist trap label. During the day, the pub operates as a sports bar and old man hang-out. Evening music brings in a younger crowd and the tourist or two who are wise to the area.

🧭 From the town center, take New St. and look to the left. ℹ Live music F and Su from 9pm. $ Pints from €4. ⏰ Open M-Th noon-midnight, F-Su noon-1am.

KELLY'S KORNER — PUB

Michael Collins Pl. ☎064 663 5966

The sign on the front of this pub advertises "Drinking Consultants." This ought to be good. Located right next to the Súgán Hostel, Kelly's Korner fills up nightly with a young international crowd. The place isn't huge and it's rarely quiet enough to hear the traditional Irish music playing in the background. It's a great place to get a little rowdy before heading out to the clubs.

🧭 From the bus station, turn left onto Park Rd. and follow it as it becomes Fair Hill. Turn right onto Lewis Rd. and look left for Michael Collins Pl. ℹ Live music upstairs. Outdoor patio. $ Pints and spirits from €4. ⏰ Open M noon-11:30pm, Tu-Th 4-11:30pm, F-Sa noon-12:30am, Su noon-11pm.

ARTS AND CULTURE

THE BACK LANE GALLERY — GALLERY

New Market Ln. ☎087 321 2948 thebacklanegallery.blogspot.ie

Featuring Irish artists, the tiny Back Lane Gallery is located in the bursting-with-culture Milk Market. With almost exclusively paintings on display, it's a great place to support local artists and find an authentic Irish souvenir. The gallery also does classes and music festivals. Check the website for more details.

⇞ From the town center, take High St. and then turn right onto New Market Ln. $ Prices vary, generally €20-200. ⏰ Open Tu-Sa 11am-7pm, Su noon-6pm.

DERMOT MCCARTHY ART GALLERY GALLERY

Barry's Ln. ☎064 663 9995

Part studio, part gallery, you can either browse the paintings on display or watch the slightly wild-haired Mr. McCarthy at work. The watercolor works he does are a little fantastic, a little whimsical, and always very colorful. Get an original for a splurge or settle for a print and a better price.

⇞ From the town center, take High St. and then turn left onto Barry's Ln. $ Originals €100-200, prints from €60. ⏰ Open M-Sa 11am-6pm.

SHOPPING

ARAN SWEATER MARKET OUTLET CLOTHES

College St. ☎064 663 9756

Other than the actual Aran Islands, this is the best place to get one of those famous Irish wool sweaters. They have every style from biker hoodie (yes, in wool) to sleeveless vests. Those of Irish descent will be delighted to find last-name-specific patterned sweaters. What's in a name? Apparently a wool sweater pattern, available here.

⇞ From the town center, take Main St. then turn left onto College St. $ Generally €40-80. ⏰ Open M-Sa 9am-10:45pm, Su 10am-10:45pm.

VARIETY SOUNDS MUSIC

College St. ☎064 663 5755

This is the place to find any traditional Irish instruments you many want as well as many non-traditional Irish ones. (Anyone on the hunt for a good banjo?) A selection of both Irish traditional and pop CDs are for sale. There is a good selection of music books so you can get ready to impress with that new penny whistle of yours.

⇞ From the town center, take Main St. then turn left onto College St. ⏰ Open daily 9am-9pm.

ESSENTIALS

Practicalities

- **TOURIST OFFICE:** The **Discover Ireland Killarney** tourist office is located on Beech Rd. They do accommodation and tour bookings and have information on the entire southern region of Ireland. (☎64 663 1633 ⇞ From the town center, take New St. and then turn left onto Beech Rd. ⏰ Open M-Sa 9am-6pm, Su 9am-5pm.)
- **ATMS:** There are several 24hr. ATMs in Killarney. There is one on the corner of New St. and Beech Rd., as well as one kitty-corner to that on Beech Rd. There is also one in the town center at the junction of New St., High St., and Main St.
- **POST OFFICE:** Coming from the town center, it's just past Beech Rd. on New St. (☎064 663 1461 www.anpost.ie ⏰ Open M-F 9am-5:30pm, Sa 9am-1pm.)

Emergency

- **POLICE:** To get to the **Garda Station,** take High St. from the town center, then turn left onto New Rd. (New Rd. ☎064 663 1461 www.garda.ie ⏰ Open for emergencies 24hr.)
- **HOSPITAL:** The **Killarney Hospital** is located north of the city. To get there, take High St. from the town center. Follow it as it turns into Rock Rd., then turn left onto St. Margaret's Rd. Take another left onto St. Margaret's Rd, and a left into the hospital driveway. (St. Margaret's Rd. ☎064 663 1076 www.hse.ie ⏰ Open for emergencies 24hr.)

- **PHARMACY: Reen's Pharmacy** does consultations and regular pharmaceutical functions. (Plunkett St. ☎064 663 2630 ☒ Open M-Sa 9am-6pm and Su 2-6pm.)

Getting There

BY BUS

Bus Éireann runs buses from: Cork (Ⓢ €17, students €14.50 ☒ 13 daily); Dublin (Ⓢ 25.50, students €20.50 ☒ 6 daily); Galway (Ⓢ €23.50, students €19.50 ☒ 6 daily); Limerick (Ⓢ €18, students €15 ☒ 6 daily); and Shannon Airport (Ⓢ €19.50, students €16 ☒ 6 daily).

BY TRAIN

Trains arrive from: Dublin (Ⓢ €62, students €34.50 ☒ 3-3½hr., 6 per day 7:30am-7:30pm); Galway (Ⓢ €36, students €25 ☒ 1½hr., 6 per day 6.20am-6:30pm); and Limerick (Ⓢ €24, students €14.50 ☒ 40min., 10 per day 6am-10:20pm).

BY PLANE

The nearest **airport** is in Shannon; see **Shannon: Getting There.**

Getting Around

Killarney is a small town and has no city bus service (as well as no need for it). To get to sights outside of the city, one can walk, rent a **bike** (College St. ☎087 962 922 Ⓢ Adults €15, students €12.50, children €10 ☒ Open daily 9am-7pm), or rent a **⌂horse-drawn carriage.** (Kenmare Pl. Ⓢ €30 for 1-3 people, €40 for 4.) Tours and taxis can be ordered from **Killarney Tour and Taxi.** (☎086 389 5144 www.killarneytaxi.com ☒ 24hr.)

cork ☎021

Visiting Cork is like popping one from a bottle of champagne—exciting, celebratory, and a bit damp. The most vital city in the eponymous "rebel county," Cork's city center is located between the two channels formed by the River Lee, which flows into Cork Harbour. So while the spray from the bubbly may be more delicious, the views in this water-dependent city are nothing short of picturesque. With a culture that very much embodies the Irish appreciation for song and dance, you'll want to drink in Cork's arts scene faster than the champagne. But the city isn't all fun and games (this is where our metaphor breaks down slightly); its history is tied to Ireland's War of Independence, as the city center was destroyed by British fires. Yet Cork gives its past a nod while fully embracing the present. This is not a city to sip from a flute; drink it in straight from the bottle.

ORIENTATION

The city's metropolis can be found between **St. Patrick's Street** and **South Mall,** bordered on either side by **Grand Parade** and **Parnell Place.** The entire city center is enveloped by the channels formed by the divided **River Lee.** Across the river, **Wellington Road** and **MacCurtain Street** hold the fast food joints and cheaper accommodations. **Washington Street** is the place to be at night as every other building is a pub or club, while **Western Road** leads out to the city's edge. Out there you can find Fitzgerald Park, Cork Public Museum, and University College Cork.

ACCOMMODATIONS

▨ BRÚ BAR AND HOSTEL   HOSTEL $

57 MacCurtain St.   ☎21 455 9667 www.bruhostel.com

It's every pub crawler's dream come true: a bar you can sleep in. Well, you don't actually sleep in the bar, you sleep upstairs in the slightly cramped dorms, but a

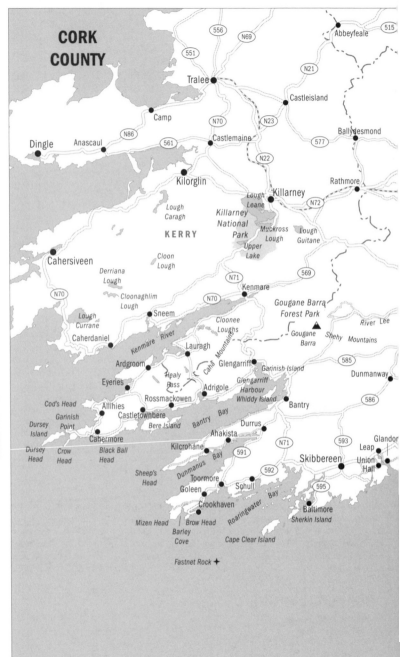

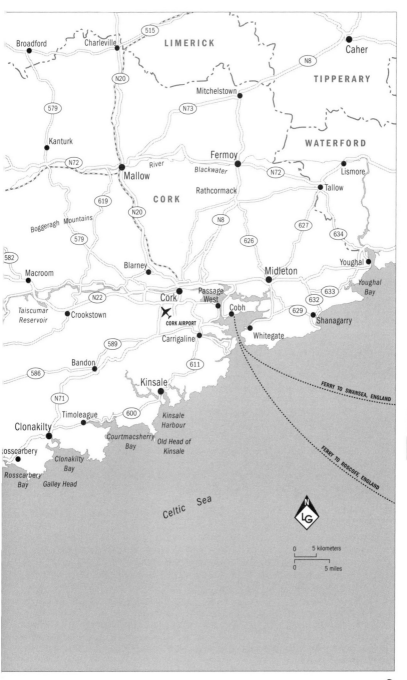

full bar is just a staircase away. The smaller kitchen-and-common-room combo ensures that most hostel guests spend their downtime with a Guinness, either listening to the weekly live music or keeping an eye on the game.

 # From the bus station, take Clontarf St. over the bridge as it becomes Summerhill. Turn left onto MacCurtain St. **i** *Breakfast, linens, and Wi-Fi included. Computers with internet available.* [$] *6-bed dorms €15-17; 4-bed €17-20. Triples €48.* ⏰ *Reception 24hr.*

KINLAY HOUSE HOSTEL HOSTEL $

Bob and Joan's Walk ☎21 450 8966 www.kinlayhousecork.ie

Kinlay certainly has character. The purple reception is accented with painted Irish flags on the wall, and the colorful combinations on the beds' comforters liven up the rooms. The brand-new internet cafe looks over their garden, which is accessible from the kitchen. Famous travel quotes cover the walls, practically daring you to do something spontaneous.

 # From the bus station, turn left onto Merchant's Quay and follow as it become Lavitt's Quay. Turn right over the bridge onto Carroll's Quay, and left onto Pope's Quay, then take a slight right onto Mulgrave Rd. Continue straight onto Upper John St. and turn left up a flight of stairs at the fork with Roman St. (Look for the hostel's sign). **i** *Breakfast, linens, and Wi-Fi included.* [$] *7- to 16-bed dorms €15, 8- to 10-bed dorms ensuite bath €16; 4-bed €16, 4-bed ensuite bath €20. Singles €30, ensuite bath €40. Doubles €46, ensuite bath €52.* ⏰ *Reception 24hr.*

ACORN HOUSE B&B $$

14 St. Patrick's Hill ☎21 450 2474 www.acornhouse-cork.com

This B&B does modern with floor-to-ceiling windows in each room and abstract carpet designs that will keep you staring. The warm Irish welcome is all traditional, though, as is the breakfast served every morning.

 # From the bus station, turn left onto Merchant's Quay then turn right onto Bridge St. Follow it over the bridge as it becomes St. Patrick's Hill. **i** *Wi-Fi included. Tea and coffee facilities in every room. All rooms with ensuite bath.* [$] *Singles €40; doubles €50; family rooms €60-80. Breakfast €7.* ⏰ *Reception hours vary; call ahead.*

SHEILA'S HOSTEL HOSTEL $

4 Belgrave Pl. ☎21 450 5562 www.sheilashostel.ie

This may be one of the cheapest hostels in Cork, but you're going to need to do some pre-visit thighmaster training. The climb from the bus station to the hostel may be less than 10min., but we're betting a few beads of sweat will trickle down your forehead on even the coldest Irish day. The hostel itself is quite standard: bunk beds; clean, if slightly aged, bathrooms; and a not-quite-home common room. The kitchen is surprisingly spacious and modern, so if cooking's your thing, this is the place to stay.

 # From the bus station, take Clontarf St. over the bridge as it becomes Summerhill. Turn left onto MacCurtain St, then turn right onto York St. Turn right onto Wellington Rd., then a quick left onto Belgrave Ave. **i** *Breakfast, Wi-Fi, and linens included. Luggage storage €1.* [$] *6-, 8-, and 14-bed dorms €16; 4-bed €17; 4-bed ensuite €18.50. Doubles €23 per person, with bath €26; singles €30/35.* ⏰ *Reception 24hr.*

GARNISH HOUSE GUESTHOUSE $$$

Western Rd. ☎21 427 5111 www.garnish.ie

This guesthouse has very up-to-date rooms and bathrooms, all slightly offset by the '70s color scheme that dominates the place. If the deep purple rugs and burnt orange accents are doing it for you, then you won't be distracted by the luxuries this place has to offer. Giant beds, two sitting rooms, and over thirty choices for breakfast keep Garnish House a step above the rest.

 # From the tourist office, turn right onto Grand Parade, then left onto Washington St. Follow it as it becomes Lancaster Quay, then Western Rd. **i** *Breakfast and Wi-Fi included, all rooms with ensuite bath.* [$] *Singles €55; doubles €78; triples €115; quads €120; quints €140.* ⏰ *Reception hours vary; call ahead.*

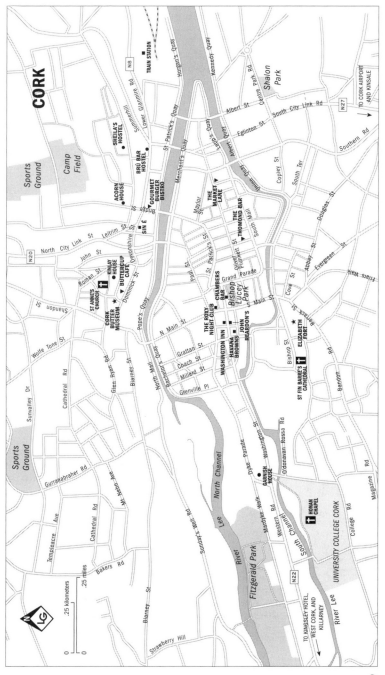

CORK

cork

SIGHTS

🏰 BLARNEY CASTLE
CASTLE

Blarney   ☎21 438 5252   www.blarneycastle.ie

The Blarney Castle is the stuff of Irish legends, and we're not exaggerating. The moss-covered ruins shoot up from the river, getting more impressively tall the closer you get. This is one of those rare tour-guide-free opportunities to run rampant through some castle ruins. If you want to crawl through the cold, cramped passages underneath the castle, go for it. If you want to lean a little too far out of the ruin's half of a window, you can do that too (*Let's Go* does not recommend leaning too far out of any windows, ever). The top of the castle hosts the ever-so-revered Blarney Stone. A kiss, legend has it, gives the visitor eloquence with words. That's just the start of your adventure. The castle grounds hold hours more of discovery, the best of which include the Witch's Cave and a poison garden. Seriously, don't eat anything. All the plants are poisonous.

☀ *Take the bus to Blarney from the Parnell St. bus station (€4.70 round-trip). From the bus stop in Blarney, cross The Square to the castle grounds' entrance.* ℹ *Cafes and souvenir shops throughout the grounds.* 💲 *€12, students €10, children €5, families €30.* 🕐 *Open May M-Sa 9am-6:30pm, Su 9am-6pm; June-Aug daily 9am-7pm; Sept M-Sa 9am-6:30pm, Su 9am-5:30pm; Oct-Apr M-Su 9am-sundown.*

ST. FIN BARRE'S CATHEDRAL
CATHEDRAL

10 Dean St.   ☎21 496 3387   www.cathedral.cork.anglican.org

The inside of this church is downright intimidating, although Gothic architecture has never really been known to be warm and welcoming. It will take a minute for your eyes to comprehend the massive arches holding up the impossibly high arched ceiling. Once they've adjusted to the light streaming in from the darkly colored stained-glass windows, take a moment to admire the historic artifacts waiting to be discovered, such as the 24lb. cannonball from the 1690 siege of Cork.

☀ *From the tourist office, turn left onto Grand Parade and follow it over the bridge. Turn right onto Sullivan's Quay. Continue as it becomes French's Quay, then Proby's Quay, then Bishop St. The cathedral is on the left.* ℹ *Guided tours upon request.* 💲 *€5, students €3.* 🕐 *Open Apr-Sept M-Sa 9:30am-5:30pm, Su 12:45-5pm; Oct-Mar M-Sa 10am-12:45pm and 2-5pm.*

munster

ELIZABETH FORT FORT

Barrack St.

Built in the oldest part of Cork as a defensive fort for an English garrison, it's rather fitting that it is now home to a Garda station. Those not on the run from the police can still take a look around. The original wall dates back to 1601, but due to some pesky sieges, attacks, and fires, it has been rebuilt several times. Not to worry, though, the original model has stuck: apparently 6ft. thick stone walls were a lasting design.

 # From the tourist office, turn left onto Grand Parade, cross the bridge, and turn right onto Sullivan's Quay. Continue as it becomes French's Quay, then Proby's Quay, and turn left into the alley; there is a sign. [$] Free. ⏰ Open daily 10am-5pm.

FITZGERALD PARK PARK

The Mardyke ☎021 427 0679

The immaculately groomed lawns and flower gardens center around a neglected pond with an overgrown fountain in the middle. The water lily-filled water and grass-filled fountain are reminiscent of the ruins of castles scattered across the Irish countryside. The wildlife and landscape make the park simply enchanting. If dreaming at a pond isn't fast-paced enough for you, there are walking paths along the river, a playground, and a skate park to keep you moving. Keep an eye out for the sequined tree.

 # From the tourist office, turn right onto Grand Parade, then turn left onto Washington St. Continue as it becomes Lancaster Quay, then Western Rd. Turn right onto Dyke Parade, then left onto Mardyke Walk. The park is on the right. [$] Free.

CORK PUBLIC MUSEUM MUSEUM

Mardyke Walk ☎21 427 0679

This is the best place to get a history of Cork and its surrounding areas. It's an even better place to gawk at how spiky keys were once used (they would make great self-defense devices today) and wonder how many of the famous Cork glass vases, some on display, have been broken by rowdy children over the years.

 # From the tourist office, turn right onto Grand Parade, then turn left onto Washington St. Follow it as it becomes Lancaster Quay, then Western Rd. Turn right onto Dyke Parade, then left onto Mardyke Walk. [$] Free. ⏰ Open M-F 11am-1pm and 2:15-5pm, Sa 11am-1pm and 2:15-4pm.

CORK BUTTER MUSEUM MUSEUM

O'Connell Sq. ☎21 430 0600 www.corkbutter.museum

We know what you're thinking, and no, it's not the biography of Paula Deen. Butter may not seem important enough to get an entire museum, but the exhibits are more of a history of Cork (with a heavy butter influence). Where else are you going to learn about the fabled Butter Road? Not your history books, that's for sure.

 # From the bus station, turn left on Merchant's Quay and continue as it become Lavitt's Quay. Turn right over the bridge onto Carroll's Quay, turn left onto Pope's Quay, then take a slight right onto Mulgrave Rd. Turn left onto John Redmond St., which leads to O'Connell Sq. [$] €4, students €3, children €1.50. ⏰ Open daily Mar-June 10am-5pm, July-Aug 10am-6pm, Sept-Oct 10am-5pm.

FOOD

GOURMET BURGER BISTRO RESTAURANT $$

8 Bridge St. ☎21 450 5404 www.gourmetburgerbistro.ie

This bistro is what would happen if a regular old burger joint mated with the House of Chanel. Meals are artfully designed on the plates and presented by the impeccably dressed staff. The menus, though laminated and left on the tables, describe meal options more commonly found in a 5-star hotel (chestnut and goat cheese burger anyone?) and offer a plentiful selection of vegetarian options.

*From the bus station, turn left onto Merchant's Quay, then turn right onto Bridge St. Follow it over the bridge. **i** Take-out available. $ Appetizers €3-9. Salads €13-14. Burgers (vegetarian, beef, lamb, and poultry) €10.50-13.50. Other entrees €14.50-17. Desserts €2.50-7.50. Tea and coffee €1-6. Beer and wine €5-6. ⏰ Open Tu-Sa 10am-midnight, Su 2-9pm.*

THE FISH HATCH TAKE-OUT $$

S. Mall ☎21 427 4040

Ireland's famous fish and chips get made right at The Fish Hatch. There are only eight menu choices, and we're going to tell you right now: they are all some sort of fish with chips on the side. The restaurant is just a hole in the wall (literally) big enough to order from, but these giant meals will leave you with one of those super satisfying, I-don't-ever-have-to-eat-again tummy aches.

*From the tourist office, turn left onto Grand Parade, then left onto S. Mall. **i** Meals come with side of mushy peas. $ Fish and chips €8-9.50. ⏰ Open M-Sa noon-3pm and 4:30-11pm, Su 4:30-11pm.*

BUTTERCUP CAFÉ CAFE $

19 Dominick St. ☎21 455 1888

The collage-art menu out front lets you know that this cafe has a little more character than most. The yellow flowers on each table add just the right splash of color to the monochromatic white tables and black chairs. It's the coffee people come for, but we wouldn't be surprised if one or two people stay for their cupcake selection as well.

*From the bus station, turn left onto Merchant's Quay and continue as it become Lavitt's Quay. Turn right over the bridge onto Carroll's Quay, turn left onto Pope's Quay, then make a slight right onto Mulgrave Rd. Turn left onto Dominick St. **i** Free Wi-Fi. $ Breakfast €1.50-2.75. Soups €3. Sandwiches €4-5. Pizza €6. Baked goods and desserts €1.50-3.75. Beverages €1-2.75. ⏰ Open M-F 10am-5pm, Sa 9:30am-4:30pm.*

THE MARKET LANE RESTAURANT $$$

5 Oliver Plunkett St. ☎21 427 4710 www.marketlane.ie

The clash of the feminine floral wallpaper with the masculine wooden tables mirrors the tension found in the menu choices: Irish meals done in not-so-Irish ways. The restaurant is busy almost all the time, but it doesn't get distracting—just enough for people-watching to keep you occupied until your ox cheek pie (€14) is ready.

*From the tourist office, turn right onto Grand Parade and then right onto Oliver Plunkett St. **i** Uses local ingredients bought across the street at the English Market. $ Starters €4.80-8. Sandwiches and salads €6.75-13. Entrees €11-25.50. Desserts €6. Beer €5-5.60. Wine €5-6.50. ⏰ Open M-Sa noon-late, Su 1-9pm.*

THE THOMOND BAR BAR $$

Marlboro St. ☎21 427 9747 www.thomond-bar.20m.com

Thomond serves traditional Irish grub in a traditional Irish pub. Grab some bacon and cabbage (€10.50) and plop down within viewing range of the game/live music/hot bartender.

*From the tourist office, turn right onto Grand Parade. Turn right onto Oliver Plunkett St., then turn left onto Marlboro St. **i** Free Wi-Fi. $ Entrees €8.50-10.50. Desserts €3-4. Pints €4-7. Spirits €4-6. ⏰ Open M 10:30am-1:30am, Tu-Th 10:30am-11:30pm, F-Sa 10:30am-12:30am, Su noon-11pm.*

NIGHTLIFE

SIN É BAR

8 Coburg St. ☎21 450 2266

This is not the place for claustrophobics, but man, this bar has character. Letters, photos, and bank notes from past customers decorate every spare surface of this bar (that is, every surface that isn't decorated with Irish paraphernalia). This pub has been loved. Even though the only walkway winds around the bar, the not-so-traditional yet somehow very Irish live music can be heard no matter where you are.

⇟ From the bus station, turn left onto Merchant's Quay, then turn right onto Bridge St. Follow it over the bridge and turn left onto Coburg St. ℹ Music most nights; call ahead to be sure. $ Pints €3.90-7.50. Spirits €3.90-9. ⏰ Open M-Th 12:30-11:30pm, F-Sa 12:30pm-12:30am, Su 12:30-11pm.

CHAMBERS BAR, GLBT

Washington St. ☎21 422 2860 www.chambersbar.ie

Plush white leather seats line the bar while high-backed booths offer a little more privacy for a midnight nuzzle. The dance floor is big enough to host a small village, but with either a live band or a DJ every night, Chambers keeps it full. Weekly events can range from trivia night to the Pride Prom; it's hard to know what to expect next. Keep an eye on their website and we bet you'll find something worth going out for.

⇟ From the tourist office, turn right onto Grand Parade, then left onto Washington St. $ Pints €3.50-7. Spirits €4-8. ⏰ Open W 9pm-2am, Th-F 9pm-late, Sa 9pm-2am, Su 9-11:30pm.

JOHN REARDEN'S BAR

26 Washington St. ☎21 427 4445 www.reardens.com

Located right in the middle of the pub and club center of Cork, Rearden's seems to collect anyone still standing past midnight. You may start at other bars, you may have other plans, but at some point Rearden's will call. Don't worry, it calls to everyone else, too, so those neon-lit dance floors and smooth leather couches will be filled up with college students, internationals, and a few daring middle-aged tourists.

⇟ From the tourist office, turn right onto Grand Parade, then left onto Washington St. ℹ Live music M, W, and F. $ Pints €4.20-8. Spirits €4-10. ⏰ Open M-W 10am-11:30pm, Th-Sa 10am-12:30pm, Su noon-11:30pm.

WASHINGTON INN PUB

30-31 Washington St. ☎21 427 3666

With exposed brick, stone walls, and a fireplace, the Washington Inn is about as cozy and old-fashioned as an Irish pub could be. The entire inside is composed of a half circle bar, and the small space around it is more often than not filled with college students. There could be raucous conversations at one end of the bar and a live band at the other and no one would know what the other was missing.

⇟ From the tourist office, turn right onto Grand Parade, then left onto Washington St. $ Pints €4-4.50. ⏰ Open M-Th 10am-11:30pm, F 10am-12:30pm, Sa noon-10:30pm, Su noon-11:30pm.

THE ROXY NIGHT CLUB CLUB

1-3 S. Main St. ☎87 271 0710

Exposed brick walls are entirely lit by multi-colored neon lights around the club. This ultra-sleek, ultra-chic club has a larger playlist than most. Sure, you might find a Top 40 hit every once in a while, but expect a Flaming Lips song just as often. Break out of your tired nightclub routine here.

⇟ From the tourist office, turn right onto Grand Parade, turn left onto Washington St., then turn right onto S. Main St. $ Pints €4-7. Mixed drinks €5-9. ⏰ Open Th-Su 11pm-2am.

HAVANA BROWNS CLUB

Hanover St. ☎21 427 1969 www.havana-browns.com

This club sure does focus on its geometric shapes. Box-shaped chairs and booths dominate the scene offset by the back-lit circular wall decorations. The place tends to fill up on weekends, so head to the exclusive VIP room to get away from it all (if you can get in). Otherwise, enjoy the hot, sweaty nightclub atmosphere while the DJs spin Top-40 hits.

⇞ From the tourist office, turn right onto Grand Parade, then turn left onto Washington St. Turn left onto S. Main St., then turn right onto Hanover St. [$] Pints €4-7. Mixed drinks €4.50-10. ⏰ Open Th-Sa 9pm-2:30am, Su 9pm-1am.

an irish music primer

Maybe you saw Riverdance with your aunt when it came to town that time back in '02. Or maybe your mom gets teary-eyed whenever the Irish tenors are on PBS. You may have tried to respectfully distance yourself from the whole *Celtic Women* thing, but you're going to Ireland now and it's time to get serious. Chances are if you're in a pub at night (which you will be), you'll run into a jam session. The group will consist of a couple of instruments, perhaps including a **bodhrán** (traditional drum) or **uilleann** (Irish bagpipes). It might grow into a **céilí,** a music and dance session, or pub-goers may break out into a drunken **sean nos** (ballad). But don't show up to the party unprepared, dear reader. Our picks span from the traditional to the commercial hits—so load up your iPod for the plane ride.

- **THE CLASSICS:** Bands responsible for bringing traditional Irish music to audiences around the world in the mid-20th century include **The Chieftains, Sweeney's Men, The Clancy Brothers,** and later, **The Bothy Band.** You'll probably recognize them from Public Television.
- **DRUNKEN FAVORITES:** It's hard to pick a favorite (most Irish songs are about drinking), but **The Dubliners** and Canadian band **The Irish Rovers** are two. Both performed the classic "Whiskey on a Sunday."
- **HAUNTING FEMALE VOICES OF THE '90S:** Really, no list would be complete without crooners **Sinéad O'Connor** ("Nothing Compares to You"), **The Cranberries** ("Linger"), and, of course, **Enya** ("Orinoco Flow," another Mom favorite).
- **COMMERCIAL FAVORITES:** It's a hard road from Top 40 to The Drug Store sessions, and don't **Westlife** and **The Corrs** know it? Flip on Westlife's "If I Let You Go" and be transported to a middle school dance floor, or imagine yourself the heroine of an early-2000s rom-com with The Corrs's breakout hit "Breathless."
- **THE BEST OF YOUR MOM'S IPOD:** When she's not crying it out in front of the Tenors or jamming to Enya, let's face it, your mom is listening to **Van Morrison** or **U2** and absolutely loving it. And we love your mom.
- **COLLEGE RADIO:** Ireland has also made significant contributions to the punk rock and indie pop played on your college radio. Some favorites include **The Undertones** and **Stiff Little Fingers.**

ARTS AND CULTURE

🏆 CORK OPERA HOUSE — OPERA

Emmet Pl. ☎21 427 0022 www.corkoperahouse.ie

The Cork Opera House is the Mt. Everest of theaters in Ireland: no other theater compares in size. When you see the 1,000-seat theater and impressively sized orchestra pit, one thought comes to mind: this isn't amateur hour. Combined with its smaller, no less impressive half-moon theater, the Cork Opera House hosts some of the best creative shows to ever make it to Ireland.

*➹ From the bus station, turn left onto Merchant's Quay. Located at the intersection of Lavitt's Quay and Carroll's Quay. **i** Tickets purchased online or over the phone are charged a €2.50 booking fee. [$] Tickets generally €5-30. ⏰ Open M-Sa 10am-5:30pm, 7:30pm on performance nights.*

CORK ARTS THEATER — THEATER

Camden Ct. ☎021 450 5624 www.corkartstheatre.com

A theater based largely on community, the Cork Arts Theater has become an integral part of the city's artistic scene. "Let words flow where cities meet," whispers their logo, tempting you to enjoy one of their now nightly shows in the intimate, 100-seat theater. At as low as €5 a ticket, we say why not?

➹ From the bus station, turn left onto Merchant's Quay; continue as it becomes Lavitt's Quay. Turn right over the bridge onto Carroll's Quay. The theater is on the left. [$] Tickets vary, usually €5-10. ⏰ Ticket booth open M-F 10am-6pm.

THE FIRKIN CRANE — DANCE

John Redmond St. ☎21 450 5624 www.firkincrane.ie

The large, circular, battlement-like building you see is no war museum; it's a dance studio. Performances and classes take place in the upstairs studio and theater, while the converted theater downstairs now serves as an exhibition on the Firkin Crane's founding. Tutus and ballet slippers of bygone years surround you as videos of their dances play.

➹ From the bus station, turn left onto Merchant's Quay; continue as it becomes Lavitt's Quay. Turn right over the bridge onto Carroll's Quay, left onto Pope's Quay, and take a slight right onto Mulgrave Rd. Turn left onto John Redmond St., which will lead you to O'Connell Sq. [$] Tickets usually free; exhibition always free. ⏰ Open M-F 10am-6pm.

SHOPPING

🏆 THE ENGLISH MARKET — MARKET

Grand Parade ☎21 492 4586 www.englishmarket.ie

The English Market is a covered boutique market that has been operating (quite successfully) since 1788. You can find just about anything you might want to eat here. A skinned pig's head? Sure, right at the corner booth. For the less adventurous eaters, they have a huge selection of meat, produce, and seafood. We advise uneasy stomachs to stay outside; there are a whole lot of smells going on at once here.

*➹ From the tourist office, turn right. **i** Public toilets inside. ⏰ Open M-Sa 8am-6pm.*

LISA — CLOTHES

19 Oliver Plunkett St. ☎21 427 9619

Ladies, this is the place to get your clubbin' clothes. Lisa's is all about crop tops, short skirts, and even shorter dresses. The most up-to-date going-out clothes can be found here along with a pretty large selection of USA gear: we're talking red, white, and blue leggings, crop tops, and see-through sweaters. We're pretty sure they're only cool if you're not American, but we've got our 4th of July outfit on lock regardless.

➹ From the tourist office, turn right onto Grand Parade, then turn right onto Oliver Plunkett St. [$] €10-25. ⏰ Open M-W 9:30am-6pm, Th 9:30am-7pm, F 9:30am-8pm, Sa 9:30am-6pm, Su 1-5:30pm.

ESSENTIALS

Practicalities

- **TOURIST OFFICE:** The **Discover Ireland Tourist Information Office** books accommodations and tours. (Grand Parade ☎21 425 5100 ⇄ From the bus station, right onto Parnell Pl., right onto S. Mall, and right onto Grand Parade. ⏰ Open M-Sa 9am-6pm.)
- **ATM:** There are two 24hr. ATMs located on either end of Grand Parade and three 24hr. ATMs on St. Patrick St.
- **INTERNET ACCESS:** **Wired to the World** is an internet cafe that does computer repairs as well as faxing. (28 N. Main St. ☎21 453 0383 www.wiredtotheworld.ie ⇄ From the tourist office, turn right onto Grand Parade, left onto Washington St., and right onto N. Main St. $ Wi-Fi €1 per hr. ⏰ Open M-Sa 9am-midnight, Su 10am-midnight.) The **City Library** also has Wi-Fi and free computers for use. It's located just across the street from the tourist office. (Grand Parade ☎21 492 4908 ⏰ Open M-Sa 10am-5:30pm.)
- **POST OFFICE:** The main post office is located on Oliver Plunkett St. (☎21 485 1042 www.anpost.ie ⇄ From the tourist office, turn right onto Grand Parade, then turn right onto Oliver Plunkett St. ⏰ Open M-Sa 9am-5:30pm.)

Emergency

- **POLICE:** The **Garda station** is located inside Elizabeth Fort. To get there from the tourist office, turn left onto Grand Parade, cross the bridge, and turn right onto Sullivan's Quay. Continue as it becomes French's Quay, then Proby's Quay. Turn left into the alley; there's a sign. (Barrack St. ☎21 432 7300 ⏰ Open for emergencies 24hr.)
- **HOSPITAL:** To get to **Mercy Hospital** from the tourist office, turn right onto Grand Parade, turn left onto Washington St., then right onto Woods St., which turns into Grenville Pl. (Grenville Pl. ☎21 427 1971 ⏰ Open in case of emergency 24hr.)
- **PHARMACY:** To get to **O'Learys Pharmacy** from the tourist office, turn right and head down the street. (8 Grand Parade ☎21 427 4563 ⏰ Open M-W 8:30am-6:30pm, Th-F 8:30am-7pm, Sa 9am-6pm.)

Getting There

BY BUS

Bus Éireann runs buses from: Dublin ($ 14, students €12 ⏰ 6 per day 8am-6pm); Galway ($ €15, students €12 ⏰ 12 per day 7:05am-6:05pm); Killarney ($ €18, students €15.20 ⏰ 11 per day 9:30am-8:30pm); Limerick ($ €15, students €12 ⏰ 14 per day 7:25am-8:35pm); and Waterford ($ €20, students €16.20 ⏰ 15 per day 8am-9pm).

BY TRAIN

Trains arrive from: Dublin ($ €60, students €30 ⏰ 14 per day 7am-9pm); Galway ($ €54.50, students €30 ⏰ 6 per day 6:20am-6:30pm); and Limerick ($ €26, students €15.50 ⏰ 10 per day 6am-10:20pm).

BY PLANE

The Cork Airport (ORK; ☎21 431 3131 www.corkairport.com) is only slightly smaller than the Dublin Airport and handles many regional and international flights. **Aer Lingus** (☎0818 365 044 www.aerlingus.com) and **Ryanair** (☎0818 303 030 www.ryanair.com) are always the best bets for cheap flights around Ireland. **Wizz Air** (www.wizzair.com) and **Jet2** (www.jet2.com) also run flights to and from Cork.

Getting Around

Cork is slightly too big of a city to be easily walkable, although the determined walker won't have any problems. There is a city **bus** service that runs 19 routes around Cork; it costs just €1.70 to get anywhere within the city. There are also **taxis,** which are easy to hail down. To be sure of a ride, call ahead to **Cork Taxi Co-op.** (☎21 472 2222 www.corktaxi.ie [$] Fares start at €4.)

waterford ☎051

For such a small town, Waterford is home to a huge number of attractions. It's that super-involved kid in high school that makes everyone think, "How does he have time for all this? Does he ever sleep?" Claiming to be Ireland's oldest town, home to Waterford Crystal, and host to at least seven different festivals each year, Waterford stays busy. Its history starts in 914 CE, making the city nearly irresistible to Viking lovers, history buffs, and battle aficionados.

ORIENTATION

The **Viking Triangle,** the original city of the 10th century, is located between three points: **Reginald's Tower,** the junction of **The Mall** and **Parnell Street,** and the **People's Park.** This is the most historic part of Waterford. The town square, located at the intersection of **Broad Street** and **Barronstrand Street,** is flanked by several smaller streets. Between Broad St. and Olaf St., with High St. connecting the two, lies most of the town's action, including the City Square Shopping Centre.

ACCOMMODATIONS

RIVERWALK ACCOMMODATION APARTMENTS $

Inner Ring Rd. ☎051 856 704 www.riverwalkwaterford.com

With no river nearby, this apartment's name is a bit of a mystery. But these rooms are just a 15min. walk from the city center and include a desk, bathroom, and single-room privacy. Do you want to jump on the bed naked? No one will know (just be sure to close your curtains first). This apartment-style housing fills up during the school year with students, so don't expect to find a room then.

From Reginald's Tower, take The Mall; continue as it becomes Parnell St. Turn left onto John St. and continue as it becomes Johnstown. Take a slight right onto Ballytruckle Rd., then turn right onto Inner Ring Rd. i Wi-Fi and linens included. [$] Singles €30, with kitchen €85; doubles €60/150. Reception daily 8am-5pm.

HAZELBROOK BED AND BREAKFAST B&B $$

10 Cork Rd. ☎051 379 815

Hazelbrook's rooms are modern without losing their homey feel and have enough space that two people can walk around without constantly having to grind all up on each other. There is a nicely kept garden as well as a glass-enclosed sunroom out back for some rain-free, almost outdoors time. Oh, and there's an actual brook too, although the Hazel part of the name will have to be provided by your eyes.

From Reginald's Tower, take The Mall and continue as it becomes Parnell St., then Manor St., then Cork Rd. i Breakfast and Wi-Fi included. [$] Singles €40; doubles €65; family rooms €100-160. Reception hours vary; call ahead.

PORTREE HOSTEL HOSTEL $$

11 Mary St. ☎051 874 574 www.portreehostel.ie

This hostel, located in the basement of a guesthouse, makes you feel like you're living in your parents' basement. Before you start thinking that's a bad thing,

waterford

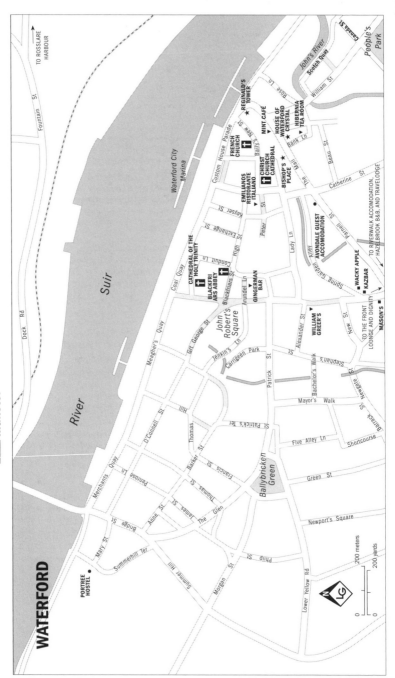

WATERFORD

munster

TO ROSSLARE HARBOUR

River Suir

Waterford City Marina

Custom House Parade

REGINALD'S TOWER

MINT CAFÉ ★

HOUSE OF WATERFORD CRYSTAL

HIBERNIA TEA ROOM ★

FRENCH CHURCH 🕇

CHRIST CHURCH CATHEDRAL 🕇

BISHOP'S PLACE ★

EMILIANOS RISTORANTE ITALIANO ▶

Bally's Ln

New St

Bank Ln

Rose Ln

John's River

Scotch Quay

Canada St

People's Park

William St

Beau St

Catherine St

The Mall

Peter St

Keyser St

Exchange St

Lady Ln

Parnell St

Spring Garden Alley

AVONDALE GUEST ACCOMODATION ▶

WACKY APPLE ■

KAZBAR ■

MASON'S ■

TO RIVERWALK ACCOMODATION, HAZELBROOK B&B, AND TRAVELODGE

TO THE FRONT LOUNGE AND DIGNITY

WILLIAM GREER'S ▶

Alexander St

New St

High St

Conduit Ln

Blackfriars St

Arundel Ln

CATHEDRAL OF THE HOLY TRINITY 🕇

BLACKFRIARS ABBEY 🕇

GINGERMAN BAR

Coal Quay

John Robert's Square

Jenkin's Ln

Carrigeen Park

Patrick St

Grt George St

Meagher's Quay

Merchants Quay

Penrose Ln

Mary St

Bridge St

Anne St

James St

Thomas St

Francis St

Barker St

Hill St

Thomas St

D'Connell St

Summerhill Ter

Summer Hill

PORTREE HOSTEL ●

Morgan St

Philip St

The Glen

St Patrick's Ter

Mayor's Walk

Bachelor's Walk

Stephen's Walk

Five Alley Ln

Shortcourse

Green St

Newport's Square

Ballybricken Green

Lower Yellow Rd

Barrack St

Newgate St

Fountain St

Dock Rd

200 meters

200 yards

0

LG

remember that your parents' house has an awesome sitting room with leather couches, a full kitchen, and a backyard. But you'll have to continue to share the two bathrooms with everyone else, just like at home.

🍴 *From the town square, take Barronstrand St., then turn left onto Meagher's Quay. Follow it until it becomes Grattan Quay, then turn left onto Suir St., which becomes Mary St.* ℹ️ *Continental breakfast €5, full Irish €7. Wi-Fi, lockers, and linens included.* 💲 *6- and 8-bed dorms €25.* 🕐 *Reception 7am-10pm.*

TRAVELODGE
HOTEL $$

Cork Rd.   ☎051 358 885 www.travelodge.ie/waterford-hotel

We will admit that the Travelodge does rooms well. They have a little more dancing space than most, and the beds can easily fit two people without forcing them to spoon. The rest of the hotel, however, is nothing to brag about. Reception is pretty drab and there are no social spaces to chill out in. With all rooms running the same rate, this is a better deal for groups.

🍴 *From Reginald's Tower, take The Mall; continue as it becomes Parnell St., then Manor St., then Cork Rd.* ℹ️ *Wi-Fi €5 per day.* 💲 *All rooms are the same rate: start at €39, can go as high as €150.* 🕐 *Reception 24hr.*

SIGHTS

🖼️ WATERFORD CRYSTAL FACTORY TOUR
FACTORY

The Mall   ☎051 317 006 www.waterfordvisitorcentre.com

I bet you're wondering, "Is Waterford Crystal really that famous? What do they even make?" A couple of sports awards, the People's Choice awards, and, oh yeah, 🏆**the millennium ball** in Times Square. Waterford Crystal is kind of a big deal. The tour goes through the working factory, so you get to see products being made that will be on sale later that week. Try not to knock anything over. Once you see just how many people it takes to make one wine glass, you're going to feel a lot worse about breaking anything (never mind the price tag).

🍴 *From Reginald's Tower, take The Mall.* ℹ️ *The tour ends in the Waterford Crystal Store, which has the best selection and cheapest (read: still expensive) products.* 💲 *€12, students and seniors €9, families €30.* 🕐 *Open M-F 9:30am-4:15pm.*

🖼️ REGINALD'S TOWER
MUSEUM

Parade Quay   ☎051 304 220 www.waterfordtreasures.com

The stone monument overlooking the harbor originated in the 10th century as a Viking tower. Duck low through the doorway to enter the cool, dimly lit basement, then work your way up through the three levels of the tower. The exhibits are almost as interesting as exploring the little nooks and crannies found in the 5ft. thick walls. When your inner child has had enough exploring, take some time to learn about Waterford's war-torn start. *Game of Thrones* has nothing on this city.

🍴 *At the junction of The Mall and Parade Quay.* 💲 *€3, children €2, students €1, families €8.* 🕐 *Open daily 10am-6pm.*

CHRIST CHURCH CATHEDRAL
CATHEDRAL

Cathedral Sq.   ☎051 858 958 www.christchurchwaterford.com

The cathedral is most famous for being the location of the marriage of Strongbow, a famous English warrior, to Aoife, a beautiful Irish princess sold into marriage by her father. The current cathedral, the fourth one built on this site, does not have the signature moody, Gothic vibe. Instead with pastel wall colors, stucco ceilings, and the light-catching crystal chandeliers, this cathedral is a prime example of Georgian architecture.

🍴 *From Reginald's Tower, take Parade Quay and turn left onto Greyfriars. Continue into Cathedral Sq.* 💲 *Free.* 🕐 *Open M-F 10am-5pm, Sa 10am-4pm.*

BISHOP'S PALACE MUSEUM

The Mall ☎051 304 500 www.waterfordtreasures.com

The first-floor guided tour brings you through an exact replica of an 18th-century Georgian house. Learn just how uncomfortable everyday life was; those couches were not conducive to afternoon naps. The second-floor exhibit is a history of the town including local artifacts like a Waterford jail window. Take a peek through it just so you can experience how much the bars blocked vision (though the crippling sense of defeat must be imagined on your own).

⇟ From Reginald's Tower take The Mall; the museum is on the right. ℹ 1st fl. exhibition by guided tour only. [$] €5, seniors €4, students €2. ⏰ Open June-Aug M-Sa 9:30am-6pm, Su 11am-6pm; Sept-May M-Sa 10am-5pm, Su 11am-5pm.

THE PEOPLE'S PARK PARK

Park Rd. and Newtown Rd. ☎051 870 813

Glorious on a sunny day and dreamy the other 360 days of the year, the People's Park provides an easy escape from the city bustle. There's a fountain for the dreamers to stare at; a gazebo for those requiring shade, shelter, or *Sound of Music* memories; and a playground for the young (at heart). Large expanses of lawn encircle the park and are used for everything from quick soccer games to tanning.

⇟ From Reginald's Tower, take The Mall, then turn left onto Lombard St., which becomes William St., then Newtown Rd. [$] Free. ⏰ Open daily 8am-dusk.

FOOD

✓ EMILIANOS RISTORANTE ITALIANO ITALIAN $$$

21 High St. ☎051 820 333

With a menu entirely in Italian and a staff that almost exclusively speaks the language, you'll feel like you've plopped down in Rome. All you Irish food lovers need not worry; amid the pizza selection and pages of pasta dishes, we found a few traditional Irish meals as well.

⇟ From the town square, take Barronstrand St., then turn right onto Blackfriars, which becomes High St. ℹ Reservations strongly suggested. [$] Appetizers €7.50-9.50. Salads €5-8. Pizzas €11-15.50. Pastas €10-15. Entrees €16.50-27. ⏰ Open Tu-Th 5:30-10:30pm, F-Su 12:30-2:30pm and 5:30-10:30pm.

✓ MINT CAFÉ CAFE $

33 The Mall ☎051 855 500

Mint's main goal is to get its customers to relax. Potted grass on each table sets the mood, the light mint green walls are quite calming, and Norah Jones coos over a loudspeaker to complete the scene. It's actually the coffee, though, that will soothe your troubled soul. If one of their specialty Black Forest Lattes with whipped cream and marshmallows (€3.40) doesn't calm you right down, we don't know what will.

⇟ From Reginald's Tower, take The Mall. ℹ Free Wi-Fi. [$] Soups €5. Sandwiches, wraps, bagels, ciabattas €4-7. Salads €6.50-7.25. Coffee and tea €1.20-3.40. ⏰ Open M-Sa 8:30am-6pm.

WILLIAM GREER BAKERY $

17 Michael St. ☎051 874 616

Family-owned for the past five generations, it's not a stretch to say that the Greer family has mastered the art of baking. They have a window display that is excruciatingly difficult to walk past without succumbing to the pastries that seem to be calling to you. When you walk in (you *will* walk in), the sweet smell of sugar and unhealthy baked goods fills your nose. You're not walking out of here without at least four pastries and you know it.

⇟ From the town square, take Broad St., which becomes Michael St. [$] Baked goods €1.60-7. ⏰ Open M-Sa 9am-5:30pm.

THE GINGERMAN BAR IRISH $$

6 Arundel Ln. ☎051 879 522

Tucked in the nook of an alleyway, this place is not the easiest to find, although the locals sure do know about it. The Gingerman's interior decorator must have had Guinness on his mind: it's all dark walls and dark furniture, with a lighter brown accent here and there. The food may not be the most adventurous, but this top-notch pub food sure does pair well with that famous stout.

From the town square, take Arundel Ln. [i] Free Wi-Fi. [$] Breakfast €1.50-8. Sandwiches €4.50-10. Salads €7-10. Entrees €9-12. Desserts €4.50. Tea and coffee €1.50-5.60. ⏰ Open M-Sa 10am-6:30pm.

HIBERNIA TEA ROOM CAFE $

Bank Ln. ☎051 843 884

You won't find the youngest crowd in here; in fact, this seems to be the lunch hotspot for the class of '43. But you will find the best lunch deal in Waterford, and, if you're lucky, someone will explain what the Great Depression was like first-hand. Where else can you get that kind of educational experience over lunch?

From Reginald's Tower, take The Mall, then turn left onto Bank Ln. [$] Sandwiches, ciabattas, wraps €5. Entrees €7-10. Desserts €2-4. Coffee and tea €1.50-3. Wine €4.75-5.50. ⏰ Open M-Sa 10am-6pm, Su noon-4pm.

NIGHTLIFE

DIGNITY BAR, GLBT

John St. ☎051 879 631 www.dignitybar.com

This GLBT-friendly bar is heavy on the erotica and light on…well, nothing. This club is fueled by lust and neon lights (and possibly a bit of vodka). Racy posters of scantily clad beautiful people make up the wall decorations. With events like "Waterford's raunchiest Valentine's Day party" and "XXX," dignity is perhaps lacking in subtlety. Shirts are optional.

From Reginald's Tower, take The Mall; continue as it becomes Parnell St. Turn left onto John St. [i] Weekly events, check the website. [$] Pints €4-8. Mixed drinks €5-10. ⏰ Open Tu-F 8pm-midnight, Sa 6pm-2am, Su 6pm-midnight.

WACKY APPLE BAR

27 Michael St. ☎051 875 100

Like every other bar in Waterford, Wacky Apple features live music on the weekends. Their niche is Irish tunes, drawing in a more traditional Irish, middle-aged crowd. The pub is smaller than most, and the seemingly purposefully unfinished walls make the place feel old in a traditional way. Get your sass ready—these Irish men have years of experience.

From the town square, take Broad St., which becomes Michael St. [$] Pints €4-7. Spirits €4-9. ⏰ Open M-Th 10:30am-11:30am, F-Sa 10:30am-12:30am, Su 10:30am-11:30pm.

KAZBAR BAR

57 John St. ☎051 843730 www.kazbar.ie

This is where all the young people hang out or, more specifically, where all the young, mainstream people hang out. If you like being well liked by most people, are unashamed of that fact that your taste in music is pretty unoriginal, and are under the age of 30, you will probably have a blast here. The live music at the upstairs stage rolls out some pretty danceable pop rock every weekend.

From the town square, take Broad St., which becomes Michael St., then John St. [i] "Pour your own pint" tables available. [$] Pints and spirits €4-8. ⏰ Open M-W 10am-11:30pm, Th-Su 10am-2am.

MASONS PUB BAR

97 Manor St. ☎051 875 881

Masons takes their music a little bit more seriously than the surrounding pubs. With music every night, Masons manages more diversity in its playlists. Expect some alternative rock, possibly a bit of punk, and was that dubstep we heard? The spacious bar may suggest dancing, but the upstairs stage and dance floor insists upon it.

➡ From Reginald's Tower, take The Mall; continue as it becomes Parnell St., then Manor St. ℹ Live music almost every night. Call ahead for specifics. $ Pints €4.20-7. Mixed drinks €5-10. ⏰ Open daily 9pm-2am.

THE FRONT LOUNGE — BAR

John St. — ☎051 303 550

This is where the working stiffs come for their after-work drinks. The vibe can be one of solitary, slightly drunk contemplation earlier in the evening, but after everyone's first beer or four, the place gets a lot more lighthearted. It fills up with an older crowd when there's a game on, but the mid-20s crowd dominates when the live music is playing.

➡ From Reginald's Tower, take The Mall; continue as it becomes Parnell St. Turn left onto John St. ℹ Live music F and Sa at 9pm. $ Pints €4-7. Spirits €4-9. ⏰ Open M-Th 11:30am-11:30pm, F-Sa 11:30am-2am, Su 11:30am-12:30am.

ARTS AND CULTURE

GREYFRIARS GALLERY — GALLERY

Greyfriars — ☎051 860 856

Housed in a cathedral, the rooms in this gallery still have the classic wooden floors and white walls you would expect. You can occasionally peek past and see the stone walls or high arched ceilings of the church. The lower gallery's exhibition is always changing, usually focusing on the unsettling audio-visual art so popular in Ireland today. The upstairs gallery, although still modern art, focuses on paintings. The gallery has a little something for everyone.

➡ From Reginald's Tower, take Parade Quay, then turn left onto Greyfriars. $ Free. ⏰ Open Tu-Sa 11am-5pm.

THEATRE ROYAL — THEATER

The Mall — ☎051 874 402 www.theatreroyal.ie

This 220-year-old Georgian theater offers a venue to showcase the best Ireland has to offer and a few international shows as well. Expect to find performances in everything from theater to dance to music. On non-show days, you can admire the gallery art on the walls and read a short excerpt on the history of the theater.

➡ From Reginald's Tower, take The Mall. $ Ticket prices vary; check the website. ⏰ Box office open Tu-Th 2-5pm.

SHOPPING

👍 **KITE DESIGN STUDIOS** — CRAFTS

11 Henrietta St. — ☎051 858 914

If the Waterford Crystal was a bit too pricey, you'll find more of a variety of local artisan crafts here. The work isn't just local—the artists themselves are actually at work in the back of the shop. Five artists have studios here, so feel free to wander, chat, and request your own custom design during your visit.

➡ From Reginald's Tower, take Parade Quay, which becomes Custom House Quay, then turn left onto Henrietta St. ⏰ Open M-F 9am-5pm, Sa 10am-5pm.

FITZGERALDS MENSWEAR — CLOTHES

6 Barronstrand St. — ☎051 855 055

This men's store has anything anyone who has an extra €100 to throw down on clothes absolutely needs. The staff, in their own perfectly tailored suits, are there to help you pick out exactly which pastel colored shirts you can't live without and which of the eight shades of pink necktie you need to go with it.

Suit and pant fittings are free, but tomfoolery is not permitted. This store caters to serious buyers.

➔ From the town square, take Barronstrand St. ⏰ Open M-Th 9am-5:30pm, F 9am-8pm, Sa 9am-5:30pm.

EXCURSION

👍 New Ross

New Ross is the Irish-American capital of Ireland. Most famous for being the departure point for millions of Irish emigrants during the Great Famine, New Ross has a 4th of July celebration every year to celebrate its ties with America. The celebration focuses around the **Dunbrody Experience,** which provides visitors with insight into the mass exodus to America aboard the *Dunbrody.* (The Quay ☎051 425 239 ➔ At the bus stop. ℹ Buy tickets at Tourist Office. $ €8.50, students €5, families €20. ⏰ Open daily 9am-6pm.) Starting with accounts of how and why the Irish emigrated, the tour moves out to a replica of the ship that over 100 passengers spent upwards of 50 days aboard. The **Discover Ireland Tourist Office** is home to the Irish-American Heritage center. Get a brief run-down of the Irish in America and admire photographs of the more famous emigrants. (The Quay ☎051 421 857 ⏰ Open daily 9am-6pm.) The world's most famous Irish-American, 👍**John F. Kennedy,** has a whole arboretum in New Ross dedicated to him. Take some time to wander around the 623 acres of the **John F. Kennedy Arboretum** (☎051 388 171 $ €3, students €1, families €8 ⏰ Open daily 10am-8pm) and soak up some sun, nature, and good ol' American patriotism. **Ros Tapestry** (Priory Ct. ☎051 445 396 www.rostapestry.com ➔ From the tourist information office take a right onto The Quay then a left onto Priory Ln. $ €6, students €5, families €16 ⏰ Open daily 10am-5pm) has probably the most time-consuming and interesting tale of New Ross's founding. Twenty tapestries, all vibrantly colored and intricately woven are a completely new (for you—actually quite archaic) way to get a history lesson. St. Michael's Theatre's upstairs **Gallery Bistro** serves lunch, and if you're lucky you can catch a show as well. (South St. ☎051 421 255 ➔ From the tourist office, take a left onto The Quay, a right onto Sugar House Ln., and a right onto South St. $ Starters €4.50. Sandwiches €4-5. Entrees €3.50-6. ⏰ Open M-Sa 10am-6pm.) **O'Brien's Bar** is the place to go for a strong beer and some equally as hearty food. (13 South St. ☎051 421 903 ➔ From the tourist office, turn left onto The Quay, a right onto Sugar House Ln., and a right onto South St. $ Entrees €3.50-7. Pints €3-5. ⏰ Open M-Th 10:30am-11:30pm, F-Sa 10:30am-12:30am, Su 10:30am-11pm.) Craving something sweet? Grab a fresh-baked bite of sin at **The Bakehouse.** They make sandwiches, too, so make a meal out of it (67 South St. ☎051 422 951 ➔ From the tourist office, turn left onto The Quay, a right onto Sugar House Ln., and a right onto South St. $ Sandwiches €3-4.10. Bread and pastries €2.80-5.50. ⏰ Open M-Sa 7am-6pm.) If you're looking for a more exciting dining experience, **The Galley River Cruising Restaurant** (North Quay ☎051 421 723 ➔ From the tourist office, turn right onto The Quay and continue as it becomes John St., turn left onto North Quay $ Lunch €25; afternoon tea €12; dinner €40 ⏰ Open daily Apr-Oct; lunch 12:30pm, tea 3pm, dinner 6:30 and 7pm) does a tour of the Barrow River during your meal—for those who don't get seasick.

GETTING THERE

Bus Éireann runs buses to New Ross from Waterford ($ One-way €6.65, students €6; round-trip €9.70 ⏰ 20min.; M-F 16 per day 6:50am-7:30pm, Sa 14 per day 6:50am-6pm, Su 8 per day 7am-7:30pm) and Wexford ($ One-way €7.60, students €6.65; round-trip €14.25 ⏰ 40min.; M-F 7-9 per day 7:25am-7:25pm, Sa 6 per day 7:25am-7:25pm, Su 5 per day 7:40am-7:25pm).

ESSENTIALS
Practicalities

- **TOURIST OFFICE:** The **Discover Ireland Tourist Office** is located on Merchants Quay directly across the street from the bus station. (☎051 875 823 ☒ Open M-Sa 9:30am-5:30pm.)

- **ATMS:** There are three different banks with **24hr. ATMs** located on Broad St., and there's a **Bank of Ireland** with a 24hr. ATM on Meagher's Quay.

- **INTERNET ACCESS: RF Internet Café and Computer Repairs** does everything its name would suggest. (31 Parnell St. ☎051 583 837 *i* €1.50 per hr. ☒ Open M-F 9:30am-7pm, Sa 11am-6pm.) **The Waterford City Council Central Library** has Wi-Fi and computers available for use. (Lady Ln. ☎051 849 975 ⚡ From the town square, take Broad St., then follow the curve left onto Michael St., which becomes Lady Ln. ☒ Open M-Tu 10am-5:30pm, W 10am-8pm, Th-F 10am-5:30pm, Sa 10am-1pm and 2-5:30pm.)

- **POST OFFICE:** The **post office** may not be large, its letter-sending and stamp-selling abilities are up to par. (19 O'Connell St. ☎051 874 444 ⚡ From the tourist office, turn right onto Merchants Quay, right onto Hanover St., left onto O'Connell St. ☒ Open M-W 9am-1pm and 2-5:30pm, Th 9am-1pm, F-Sa 9am-1pm and 2-5:30pm.)

Emergency

- **POLICE:** To get to the **Garda station** from the town square, take Broad St., then turn right onto Patrick St. (Patrick St. ☎051 305 300 ☒ Emergencies 24hr.)

- **HOSPITAL:** The nearest hospital is **Waterford Regional Hospital** on Dunmore Rd. (☎051 848 000 www.hse.ie ☒ Emergencies 24hr.)

- **PHARMACY** To get to **Mulligans Pharmacy** from the town square, head toward the river on Barronstrand St. (40-41 Barronstrand St. ☎051 875 211 ☒ Open M-Sa 9am-6pm.)

Getting There

BY BUS

Bus Éireann runs buses from: Dublin (Ⓢ €15, students €13 ☒ 18 per day 7:30am-11:45pm); Galway (Ⓢ €24.50, students €20.50 ☒ 5 per day 7:05am-6:25pm); Cork (Ⓢ €20, students €16.50 ☒ 14 per day 8:40am-8:40pm); Shannon Airport (Ⓢ €17, students €16 ☒ 8 per day 7am-6:50pm); and Limerick (Ⓢ €16, students €14 ☒ 6 per day 8:25am-8:40pm).

BY TRAIN

Trains arrive from: Dublin (Ⓢ €28, students €18.50 ☒ 8 per day 7:20am-9:20pm); Galway (Ⓢ €59, students €32.50 ☒ 2 per day 7:05am and 1:05pm); Limerick (Ⓢ €39, students €18.50 ☒ 1 daily at 6pm).

BY PLANE

The nearest airport is in Cork; see **Cork, Getting There**.

Getting Around

Waterford is very walkable; it hardly takes more than 20min. to traverse the entire town. To travel farther outside the city center, **taxis** are available but usually only when called. **Rapid Cabs** is the most popular. Fares start at €3.50 and it's hardly more than €7 for a 10min. drive. (Parnell St. ☎051 858 585 www.rapidcabs.com.) **Bus Éireann** does a Waterford City service with five different routes starting from the city center and going as far as the hospital. Tickets are €1.20-3 depending on how far you are going.

LEINSTER

You may not come across many surprises in this region, but that's only because by now you've come to expect picturesque castles, quiet, fog-covered harbors, and ruined abbeys sitting peacefully by the lakeshore. Even the idea of a city founded around a brewery doesn't seem too bizarre; if anything, it's surprising that such a town plan isn't more common. Perfect for a quick jaunt away from Dublin, the cities in this chapter will charm you so thoroughly they won't even need to buy you dinner before you decide to give in and spend the night.

greatest hits

- **EPISODE II: ATTACK OF THE CLONMACNOISE:** A Christian heritage site, Clonmacnoise (p. 148) is less popular with the Jedi and more popular with tourists looking to soak in some ancient history.

- **FA LA LA:** Break out your horned hat and hit the Wexford Opera House (p. 142) to experience some culture in this grand building.

- **OH MY GOD, YOU KILKENNY...CASTLE:** Visit the Picture Gallery Wing at Kilkenny Castle (p. 134) and then wander around the manicured landscape.

student life

If you're in this part of Ireland and looking for a solid student scene, just head to Dublin.

kilkenny ☎056

Kilkenny is a city founded around an ancient Franciscan abbey that brewed beer to survive—the water was unclean. So yeah, of course this is one of the top college student destinations in Ireland. Beyond the beer, medieval sights like Kilkenny Castle and St. Canice's Cathedral provide plenty of opportunities to pack your days with history and mystery. As for nightlife, nearly every other building is a pub. The scene focuses on live bands and equally lively whiskey-fueled traditional settings. Grab a Jameson, meet a local, and get out on that dance floor. The cover band singing Bon Jovi demands it.

ORIENTATION

During the day, **High Street** and **St. Kieran's Street** are the busiest parts of Kilkenny. Little-known boutiques and great pubs can be found on the several small lanes off of High St. St. Kieran's St. is home to hungry travelers—several great pubs and cafes can be found here. **The Parade,** which turns into **Castle Road,** is where you will find **Kilkenny Castle,** its sprawling grounds, and **Castle Yard. Rose Inn Street,** which turns into **Lower John Street** across the bridge, sees its fair share of drunken college students on any given Friday. Head there for a good time.

ACCOMMODATIONS

MACGABHAINNS BACKPACKERS HOSTEL HOSTEL $

24 Vicar St. ☎056 777 0970 www.macgabhainns-backpackers.hostel.com

You will feel like more than just a customer here—guests are fully welcomed into the slightly sassy and always entertaining Macgabhainns family. Sure, there's not a whole lot of extra space in the rooms, but that just means you'll spend more time in the kitchen having dinner with the staff or in the common room watching movies with your new roommates. There are no bickering Germans or loud Australians to interrupt you in the private bathrooms—sing away, my friend. It's just you, so go ahead and belt out some Adele.

 # From the tourist office, turn left onto Rose Inn St., then turn left onto St. Kieran's St. Follow St. Kiernan's St. as it becomes Parliament St., then Irishtown. Turn right onto Vicar St. $ 10-bed dorms €15-17.50; 16-bed €16-€18.50; 4-bed €17-18.50. Doubles €17.50 per person. i Breakfast, Wi-Fi, linens, and parking included. Computer available for use. ⏰ Reception open 7am-10pm. All other times, call ahead.

KILKENNY TOURIST HOSTEL HOSTEL $

35 Parliament St. ☎056 776 3541 www.kilkennyhostel.ie

Kilkenny Tourist Hostel feels much more like you're staying in a home than in a hostel—an old home with staircases that creak and an upstairs that you share with about 50 other people. The kitchen and dining room are far from industrial; it feels like Grandma is going to pop out at any moment to make you breakfast. The bad news is that unless you bring your own grandma, breakfast must be found outside the hostel. The good news is that it's located just two doors down

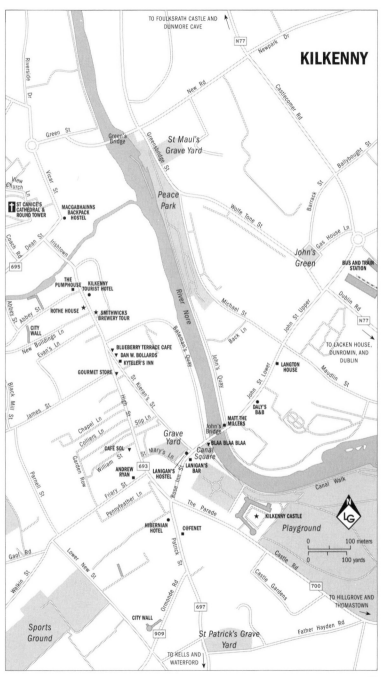

KILKENNY

TO FOULKSRATH CASTLE AND
DUNMORE CAVE

N77

Newpark Dr

New Rd

Castlecomer Rd

Riverside Dr

Green St

Greensbridge St

Green's Bridge

St Maul's
Grave Yard

Ballybought St

Barrack St

View
Church

ST CANICE'S
CATHEDRAL &
ROUND TOWER

MACGABHAINNS
BACKPACK
HOSTEL

Peace
Park

Wolfe Tone St

Gas House Ln

John's
Green

Vicar St

Dean St

Irishtown

Coach Rd

695

BUS AND TRAIN
STATION

THE
PUMPHOUSE

KILKENNY
TOURIST HOTEL

River Nore

Michael St

John St Upper

Dublin Rd

N77

Abbey St

ROTHE HOUSE

SMITHWICKS
BREWERY TOUR

TO LACKEN HOUSE,
DUNROMIN, AND
DUBLIN

CITY
WALL

New Buildings Ln

Evan's Ln

BLUEBERRY TERRACE CAFE
DAN W. BOLLARDS
KYTELER'S INN

Bateman's Quay

Back Ln

John St Lower

Maudlin St

GOURMET STORE

St Kieran's St

High St

John's Quay

LANGTON
HOUSE

Black Mill St

James St

Chapel Ln

Colliers Ln

Slip Ln

DALY'S
B&B

MATT THE
MILLERS

CAFE SOL

William

693

Mary's Ln

Garden Row

ANDREW
RYAN

Grave
Yard

John's
Bridge

BLAA BLAA BLAA

Canal
Square

Canal Walk

Parnell St

LANIGAN'S
HOSTEL

Rose Inn St

LANIGAN'S
BAR

Friary St

Pennyfeather Ln

The Parade

KILKENNY CASTLE

N
LG

Playground

HIBERNIAN
HOTEL

C@FENET

Gaol Rd

Lower New St

Patrick St

0   100 meters
0   100 yards

Castle Rd

Watkin St

Ormonde Rd

Castle Gardens

700

TO HILLGROVE AND
THOMASTOWN

697

CITY WALL

909

Sports
Ground

St Patrick's Grave
Yard

Father Hayden Rd

TO KELLS AND
WATERFORD

kilkenny

from the Smithwick's Brewery and directly across from a few god pubs, so if you like beer for breakfast, you should be set.

🧭 From the tourist office, turn left onto Rose Inn St., then turn left onto St. Kieran's St. Continue as it becomes Parliament St. Ⓢ 8- and 12-bed dorms M-Th €15, F-Su €17; 4-bed dorms €17/€19; doubles €36/€42; triples €52.50/€60. ℹ Free Wi-Fi. Parking and linens included. Computer provided for use. ⏰ Reception 24hr.

DALY'S B&B B&B $$

82 John St. ☎056 776 2866

Reception at Daly's is reminiscent of a greenhouse; there are plants on every available surface and sun streams in through the skylights. An open wooden staircase in the corner leads to the slightly less exciting rooms. Standard double beds, wooden furniture, and forest-green bedspreads may not be unique, but you'll be comfortable nonetheless. Daly's does a great job of being a giant B&B without anyone really knowing it.

🧭 From the tourist office, turn left onto Rose Inn St. Follow it over the bridge as it becomes John St. ℹ Breakfast €5. Free Wi-Fi. Parking included. All rooms ensuite. Ⓢ Singles €40; doubles and triples €25 per person. ⏰ Reception hours vary; call ahead.

LANIGAN'S HOSTEL HOSTEL $

Mary's Ln. ☎056 772 1718 www.hostelkilkenny.ie

Lanigan's Hostel appears to believe strongly in no frills, no decor, and no color. Completely blank tan walls look onto completely white beds, although the common room spices things up with some red patterned chairs. While it can certainly be said that Lanigan's takes full advantage of its space, it means that some of the beds are only accessible by squeezing between two columns, while somehow vaulting onto the top bunk. If you aren't a gymnast, you can get to those beds by climbing over the bunks in front of it. You better hope everyone has the same bedtime.

🧭 From the tourist office, turn left onto Rose Inn St., then turn left onto St. Kieran's St. Turn left immediately onto Mary's Ln. ℹ Free Wi-Fi. Linens included. Ⓢ 5-, 10-, and 12-bed dorms M-Th €18, F-Sa €20, Su €18; B&B rooms F-Sa €30 per person. ⏰ Reception 24hr.

SIGHTS

👍 ST. CANICE'S CATHEDRAL AND ROUND TOWER CATHEDRAL

Coach Rd. ☎056 776 4971 www.stcanicescathedral.com

As far as cathedrals go, St. Canice's is up to par. It has classic Gothic architecture, which is simultaneously so intimidating and awe-inspiring that you just want to sit down and soak it up. St Canice's, however, has even more to offer. The top of the **Round Tower** boasts the best views of Kilkenny, but it's the life- or death-climb to the top that Let's Go really enjoys. Wooden structures that start as stairs get progressively steeper and the light gets progressively darker. At one point, you need to climb a ladder in complete darkness. As you get closer to the light (hopefully the sun, not the bright light at the end of some dark tunnel), get ready to squeeze through the foot-wide opening while climbing some slippery stone steps before finally reaching the top. That's just getting up. Going down is a whole lot more exciting.

🧭 From the tourist office, turn left onto Rose Inn St., then turn left onto St. Kieran's St. Continue as it becomes Parliament St., then Irishtown. Turn left onto Dean St., then turn right onto Coach Rd. Ⓢ Tower €3, students €2.50. Cathedral €4, students €3. Combined ticket €6. ℹ Gift shop inside the cathedral. ⏰ Open Apr-May M-Sa 10am-5pm, Su 2-5pm; June-Aug M-Sa 9am-6pm, Su 2-6pm; Sept-Mar M-Sa 10am-4pm, Su 2-4pm.

👍 KILKENNY CASTLE CASTLE

Castle Rd. ☎056 772 1450 www.kilkennycastle.ie

Recently renovated from crumbling ruins to living museum, the castle recreates the splendor of the 1800s. A must-see is the Picture Gallery Wing. Yes, it is a whole wing of the castle. Keep an eye out for the intricately carved wooden ceilings that steal attention from the trussed up nobility on the walls. The castle interior may only take about 40min. to explore, but the grounds will take all day. On one side, the rolling hills of the perfectly groomed lawn stretch beyond your line of vision and end a few kilometers down in a lake. On the other side, rose gardens surround a fountain and necessitate a photoshoot. Seriously. Roses, shooting streams of water, and a castle in the background? That's profile picture material right there.

➡ From the tourist office, turn right onto Rose Inn St., then turn left onto The Parade, which turns into Castle Rd. ***i*** *Castle tours available upon request. Castle grounds free and downstairs cafe free. $ €6, seniors €4, students €2.50, families €14. ⏰ Open daily Apr-May 9:30am-5:30pm, June-Aug 9am-5:30pm, Sept 9:30am-5:30pm, Oct-Feb 9:30am-4:30pm, Mar 9:30am-5pm.*

ROTHE HOUSE AND GARDEN TOUR

Parliament St. ☎056 772 2839 www.rothehouse.com

The tour of the house and gardens is self-guided, meaning if you want to run up and down the creaky wooden stairs, give orders to imaginary servants, and act like you own the place, you can. If you'd rather admire the 17th-century architecture and portraits of the previous owners—well, to each his own. The gardens are surprisingly large considering the house is planted in the middle of town. The lower gardens have herbs, flowers, and a few wild strawberry plants that we're pretty sure you're not supposed to sample from, while the upper garden contains the orchard, the cherry trees, and six ducks that act like they own the place.

➡ From the tourist office, turn left onto Rose Inn St., then turn left onto St. Kieran's St. Continue as it becomes Parliament St. ***i*** *Guided tours available upon request. $ €4.80, students €3.80; gardens only €2. ⏰ Open M-Sa 10:30am-5pm, Su 2-6pm.*

SMITHWICK'S BREWERY TOUR

Parliament St. ☎056 779 6498 www.smithwicks.ie

The beginning of the tour is a bit dull for anyone not very interested in the economic history of Smithwick's beer, but get re-focused when the guide begins to explain why Smithwick's holds claim to the title "Ireland's oldest brewery." The brewery was started over 300 years ago by the monks of St. Francis Abbey. They brewed a nutrient-rich dark beer out of necessity—as the water was undrinkable—and survived on five beers a day during their 40 days and nights of fasting…suddenly becoming a monk doesn't seem all that bad. The tour continues with a look inside the factory and then, of course, a perfectly poured pint of Smithwick's in their cellar bar.

➡ From the tourist office, turn left onto Rose Inn St., then turn left onto St. Kieran's St. Continue as it becomes Parliament St. ***i*** *Must be 18+ to drink. $ €10. ⏰ Tours daily at noon, 1, 3, and 3:30pm.*

FOOD

👍 **GOURMET STORE** DELI $

56 High St. ☎056 777 1727 www.thegourmetstorekilkenny.com

This is the place to get organic, gourmet jams, pickles, olives, and really anything that comes in a jar. There are a number of non-jar items as well, like organic kettle chips, pasta, and herbs. Not adept enough to cook for yourself? The Gourmet Store has you covered. They use their own gourmet ingredients to make sandwiches and baked goods as well.

➡ From the tourist office, turn right onto Rose Inn St., then turn right onto High St. ***i*** *Gluten-free and vegetarian options available. $ Cold sandwiches €3.40. Hot sandwiches €3.50. Pastries €1.50-2.30. Tea and coffee €2-2.50. ⏰ Open daily 9am-6pm.*

DANIEL W. BOLLARDS IRISH $$

31-32 St. Kiernan's St. ☎056 772 153

Believe it or not, you can't get a beef and Guinness casserole just anywhere. You can here, though, and it's the best darn beef and Guinness casserole you'll have for a while. Come during busy lunch hours when the pub fills up with laughing locals. If you prefer a more subdued atmosphere, the pub quiets down between 3pm and 7pm. It'll just be you and that old Irish guy.

✈ *From the tourist office, turn left onto Rose Inn St., then turn left onto St. Kieran's St.* ℹ *Free Wi-Fi. Live music F and Sa 9:30pm.* Ⓢ *Appetizers €4-5.50. Entrees €10-12. Salads €8.50-13. Sandwiches €6-7.50. Pints €4-5.* ⌚ *Open M-Th 10:30am-11:30pm, F-Sa 10:30am-12:30am, Su 12:30-11pm.*

BLUEBERRY TERRACE CAFE   BISTRO $$
Parliament St.

The sidewalk sign will catch your eye, advertising seafood salad pasta and blueberry beef lasagna. Your mouth will start to water, and a little voice in your head will tell you you need to be eating that food. The downside is that you're going to have to navigate your way through three levels of a super-sized home store to get here; the upside is that your taste buds' wildest dreams will come true. On days when it's not raining like the world is ending, you can sit in their outdoor terrace and soak up the meager bits of sun that manage to shine through while admiring Kilkenny from above—that is, if you can concentrate on anything other than the food.

✈ *From the tourist office, turn left onto Rose Inn St., then turn left onto St. Kieran's St. Continue as it becomes Parliament St.* ℹ *Gluten-free options available upon request.* Ⓢ *Breakfast €4-8. Sandwiches €7.50. Entrees €3-8. Pastries and desserts €1-3.50. Tea and coffee €1.20-3.* ⌚ *Open M-Sa 10am-5pm.*

BLAA BLAA BLAA SANDWICHES   TAKE-OUT $
3 Canal Sq.   ☎056 775 2112

This take-out sandwich place takes hole-in-the-wall quite literally: there is only enough room for one person at a time to order. On sunny days, enjoy their patio seating, but on rainy days you have no option but to take your bacon, Brie, and cranberry sandwich (yum) somewhere else.

✈ *From the tourist office, turn left onto Rose Inn St., then turn right just before the bridge onto Canal Sq.* Ⓢ *Soup €2.50. Sandwiches €3.50-5. Drinks €1-2.* ⌚ *Open M-F 8:30am-3:30pm, Sa 9am-4pm.*

CAFÉ SOL   CAFE $$$
William St.   ☎056 776 4987 www.restaurantskilkenny.com

With sleek, light-colored wooden tables and artwork on the wall, this cafe does casual elegance just right. At night the lighting dims, boosting the romance factor but also the prices.

✈ *From the tourist office, turn right onto Rose Inn St., then turn right onto High St., then turn left onto William St.* ℹ *Lunch menu daily noon-5pm.* Ⓢ *Lunch: Vegetarian options €5-10. Salads €6.50-10. Sandwiches €10-11. Entrees €11-13. Dinner: Appetizers €6-8. Entrees €16-22. Desserts €7. Wine €5.50 a glass, €20 a bottle. Tea and coffee €2-3.20.* ⌚ *Open daily noon-5pm and 5:30-9pm.*

NIGHTLIFE

📷 LANIGAN'S   BAR
29 Rose Inn St.   ☎056 772 1718 www.lanigans.ie

Lanigan's is a sports bar on weeknights and a packed, drunken dance bar on weekends. You're not only elbow-to-elbow with everyone around you, but also back-to-back, foot-to-foot, and close enough to have no idea where that awful body odor is coming from. Rock out to the live music on the first floor or Top 40s hits on the second floor; either way you'll be surrounded by neon lights, a dance floor, and drunk Irish locals.

✈ *From the tourist office, turn left onto Rose Inn St.* ℹ *Live traditional Irish music W-F and Su.* Ⓢ *Pints €4-6. Spirits €4-7.* ⌚ *Open M-Th 11am-11:30pm, F 11am-12:30am, Sa 11am-2am, Su 11am-11:30pm.*

📷 THE PUMPHOUSE   BAR
26-28 Parliament St.   ☎056 776 3924 www.pumphousekilkenny.ie

The Pumphouse is the paradox of Kilkenny: it's always filled with locals but has more tourist events than most of the other bars around. Don't expect the

leinster

Irishmen to look up from their pool game while you're being taught how to Irish dance; wait until the live music and the €3.50 beers have set in. With your new Irish dancing skills, we're sure you'll blend right in.

🚏 From the tourist office, turn left onto Rose Inn St., then turn left onto St. Kieran's St. Continue as it becomes Parliament St. ℹ Free Irish traditional dance lessons every M-W at 9pm. $ Pints €3.50-5. Spirits €4-6. ⏰ Open M-Th 11am-11:30pm, F-Sa 11am-12:30am, Su 11am-11:30pm.

👍 RYAN'S BAR BAR

3 Friary St. ☎056 776 2281 www.ryanskilkenny.com

This pub looks like any other kind of dive-but-a-great-local-find pub at first. Walk in on weeknights to find a few regulars drinking quietly, and on weekends the bar ups the volume a few notches. What sets Ryan's apart is the ceiling; the entire thing is covered with photos. Candid shots of people who have frequented the bar in the past, old men, young men, bikers, Irishmen, and internationals… anyone who had a drink had a chance to make the ceiling. The real stuff though, is behind the bar. Yup, we mean the boobie pictures. Try to keep your mind on what you want to drink and not the boobs on boobs on boobs staring at you from behind the bar. Just try.

🚏 From the tourist office, turn right onto Rose Inn St., then turn right onto High St., then turn left onto Friary St. $ Pints €4-5. Spirits €3.70-6. ⏰ Open M-Sa 3-11:30pm, Su 3-11pm.

MATT THE MILLERS BAR

1 Lower John St. ☎056 776 1696 www.mattthemillers.com

We bet that somewhere between the two dance floors, three bars, and live band, you'll find yourself having fun. If that's not exciting enough for you, wait for Monday nights when the themed parties go down. There's nothing quite like a costume party to get grown men in tutus and women without pants.

🚏 From the tourist office, turn left onto Rose Inn St., then follow it over the bridge as it becomes John St. ℹ Music every night. Live Irish traditional music Tu and W at 6:30pm. $ Pints and spirits €4-7. ⏰ Open M-Sa 9:30am-2am, Su 9:30am-1am.

KYTELER'S INN BAR

St. Kieran's St. ☎056 772 1064 www.kytelersinn.com

Kyteler's has a reputation of being the best place to drink in Kilkenny. Dame Alice Kyteler established the bar in 1324 and was later condemned for witchcraft, partly because her "place of merriment" was a little too merry by some people's standards. Live music inside gets pretty crowded; head out to the massive downstairs courtyard beer garden for some not so fresh air (it's the only place people can smoke) but some oh-so-fresh company. By fresh, we mean tourists. Locals can hardly be bothered with Kyteler's.

🚏 From the tourist office, turn left onto Rose Inn St., then turn left onto St. Kieran's St. ℹ Live Irish traditional music every night at 6:30 and 8:30pm. $ Pints €4.10-7. Spirits €4-6. ⏰ Open M-Sa noon-12:30am, Su noon-11pm.

LANGTON HOUSE HOTEL BAR

69 John St. ☎056 776 5133 www.langtons.ie

Langton's has real flowers in vases on the bar. As in, never does it get rowdy enough here for anyone to knock over a pitcher of fragile beauty. The bars here seem to go on forever; endless rooms of black leather, marble fireplaces and mirrored walls. Pick one of the seven bars (they don't differ much) to grab a pricey drink and hope that someone starts paying for yours soon. With the amount of men in suits and women in matching sweater sets here, we imagine it won't take long.

🚏 From the tourist office, turn left onto Rose Inn St., then follow it over the bridge as it becomes John St. $ Pints €4.20-7. Spirits €4-8. ⏰ Open M-Th 10:30am-11:30pm, F-Sa 10:30am-2am, Su 10:30am-11pm.

ARTS AND CULTURE

NATIONAL CRAFT GALLERY GALLERY

Castle Yard ☎056 779 6147 www.nationalcraftgallery.ie

Get ready for this space to blow your mind. Part art gallery, part art project, the gallery's goal is to nurture arts and crafts in Ireland. To do this, they offer classes and workshops for artists. We don't mean workshops of the this-is-how-you-use-papier-mâché variety, we mean actual workspaces behind the gallery where the artists can create and sell their art on their own. Take some time to browse the gallery, but our favorite part is watching the silversmith work in his shop.

From the tourist office, turn right onto Rose Inn St., then turn left onto The Parade. Castle Yard is on the right. $ Free. Open Tu-Sa 10am-5:30pm, Su 11am-5:30pm.

BUTLER GALLERY GALLERY

The Castle ☎056 776 1106 www.butlergallery.com

To get to the Butler Gallery you have to walk down some ancient stone steps and wander through a castle basement, so it's a surprise to go from the dimly lit stone corridor to the brightly lit, modern art gallery. The sparseness of the room is amplified by the stark art on the walls, but that's not the only thing that will catch your attention. The four rooms are set up so that every noise, from the clicking of the computer keys to the whisperings from a room away, can be perfectly heard. The gallery itself turns eavesdropping into art.

From the tourist office, turn right onto Rose Inn St., then turn left onto The Parade. The Castle is on the right. $ Free. Open daily May-Sept 10am-5:30pm; Oct-Feb 10am-1pm and 2-4:30pm; Mar 10am-1pm and 2-5pm; Apr 10am-1pm and 2-5:30pm.

SHOPPING

KILKENNY DESIGN CENTRE DESIGN CENTER

Castle Yard ☎056 772 2118 www.kilkennydesign.com

The design center is gigantic, so much so that it needed to be divided into categories. There is the "If You Make a Wrong Move Everything Will Break" room, also known as the pottery and glass room. There is the "I Wonder How Many Sheep Gave Their Lives for This Sweater" room (none, don't worry). Lastly, wander through the "Maybe I Could Afford Something If It's Not Framed" paintings and sketches room. Even if you come out empty handed, it's worth admiring the best Ireland has to offer.

From the tourist office, turn right onto Rose Inn St., then turn left onto The Parade. Castle Yard is on the right. i Restaurant on the 2nd level. Open daily 10am-7pm.

KILKENNY CRYSTAL SHOP CRYSTAL

19 Rose Inn St. ☎056 772 1090 www.kilkennycrystal.com

Unlike Waterford Crystal, Kilkenny Crystal is still entirely made in Ireland. The shop sells some of the company's more famous products, such as stemware and lamps. As much fun as it is to dream about a lighthouse-shaped lamp, if you don't have to cash to lay down on it, the shop offers a few souvenir products for under €20 as well. The lighthouse lamp can wait.

From the tourist office, turn right onto Rose Inn St. $ Generally €40-200. Open M-Sa 10am-6pm.

ESSENTIALS

Practicalities

- **TOURIST OFFICE:** The **Discover Ireland Tourist Office** does tour and accommodation bookings and offers general information. (Rose Inn St. ☎056 775 1500 From the bus and train station, take Dublin Rd. and turn left onto Upper John St. Continue as it becomes Lower John

St., then cross the bridge and continue as it becomes Rose Inn St. Look to the right. 🕐 Open M-Sa 9:45am-6pm.)

- **ATMS:** There are 3 24hr. ATMs located on High St. Two Bank of Ireland ATMs are at the intersection of High St. and Parliament St. and the AIB 24hr. ATM is located between Chapel Ln. and Colliers Ln. on High St.

- **INTERNET ACCESS:** The **Kilkenny Library** has Wi-Fi and computers free for use. (John's Green ☎056 779 4160 🚶 From the bus and train station, take Dublin Rd. and continue straight onto Wolfe Tone St. Turn right onto John's Green. 🕐 Open M-F 9am-1pm and 2-5pm.)

- **POST OFFICE:** There is a post office located near the library on John's Green. To get there from the bus station, take Dublin Rd. Continue straight onto Wolfe Tone Rd., then turn right onto John's Green. (John's Green ☎056 772 2963 🕐 Open M-W 9am-5:30pm, Th-F 9am-7pm, Sa 9am-3pm.)

Emergency

- **POLICE:** To get to the **Garda station** from the tourist office, turn left onto Rose Inn St., then left onto St. Kieran's St. and follow it until it becomes Parliament St. Turn left onto High St., then turn right immediately onto James's St. Follow it as it becomes James's Green, then Kickham St. Turn right onto Dominic St. (Dominic St. ☎056 772 2222 🕐 Open for emergencies 24hr.)

- **HOSPITAL:** The **Aut Evan Hospital** is located on Freshford Rd. and is too far to walk to. To drive there from the tourist office, turn right onto Rose Inn St, then right onto High St. Follow High St. as it becomes Parliament St., then Irishtown. Turn right onto Vicar St. and continue as it becomes Troy's Gate. Turn left onto Bishops Hill and continue as it becomes Loreto Lodge, then Freshford Rd. (Freshford Rd. ☎056 777 5275 🕐 Open for emergency care 24hr.)

- **PHARMACIES:** There are several pharmacies located on High St. To get there from the tourist office, turn right onto Rose Inn St., then right onto High St. There is **O'Connell's Pharmacy** (89 High St. ☎056 772 1309 🕐 Open M-Sa 9am-6pm) and **Whites Pharmacy.** (5 High St. ☎056 772 1328 🕐 Open M-Sa 9am-5:30pm.)

Getting There

Bus Éireann runs buses from: Cork (💲 €19, students €16 🕐 14 per day 8:40am-8:40pm); Dublin (💲 €12, students €10 🕐 11 per day 7:30am-11:45pm); Galway (💲 €24, students €20 🕐 9 per day 7:30am-7:30pm); Limerick (💲 €19.50, students €16 🕐 6 per day 7am-7:50pm); Shannon Airport (💲 €21, students €18 🕐 5 per day 7am-5:50pm).

BY TRAIN
Trains arrive from Dublin (💲 €24, students €14.50 🕐 8 per day 7:20am-9:20pm) and Limerick (💲 €50, students €26.50 🕐 daily at 6pm).

BY PLANE
The nearest **airport** is in Cork; see **Cork: Getting There**.

Getting Around

Whip out those walking boots because that's the best way to get around Kilkenny. It takes less than 10min. to walk from one end of the town to the other, so we wouldn't worry about getting worn out. **Kilkenny Cycling Tours** rents bikes that come with helmets, maps, and suggested routes. (Rose Inn St. ☎086 895 4961 www.kilkennycyclingtours.com 🕐 Open M-Sa 10am-7pm, Su noon-6pm.)

wexford ☎053

With the morning fog still heavy in the air and the twin cathedrals dominating the skyline, Wexford is a quiet harbor town. Pretty sleepy during the week, people go about their daily business and dodge the rain, but on the weekend, this town gets a shot of adrenaline. The pubs fill up, the whiskey bottles empty out, and when Monday rolls around, everyone is grateful for the quiet week ahead.

ORIENTATION

Nearly anything worth seeing in Wexford is located somewhere between **North Main Street** and **South Main Street,** with a few notable establishments branching off of these two roads. The area stretching from **Custom House Quay** through **Crescent Quay** to **Paul Quay** has a few good restaurants and art galleries with great views of the harbor. **The Bull Ring,** so named for its Saturday Bull Ring Market, is located where N. Main St. intersects with **Cornmarket.** The accommodations tend to be sprinkled on the edge of the city center. **George Street** and **Barrack Street** both have a few good options as well.

ACCOMMODATIONS

⬛ ST. GEORGE GUEST HOUSE   B&B $$

Upper George St.   ☎053 914 3474   www.stgeorgeguesthouse.com

It's the people, in conjunction with the rooms, that make this B&B unique. Don't get us wrong, the rooms are great—big beds, modern ensuite bathrooms, and enough space to do your morning yoga or build a fort with your covers. The personal touches, such as daily cookies with your tea and custom breakfast orders, give this B&B that little bump into luxury. The owner, Michael, is absolutely great. Don't be surprised if you end up ditching your friends to grab a beer with him instead.

⎯ *From the bus station, take Slaney St. Turn left onto Selskar St., then take the 2nd right onto Lower George St. and continue as it becomes Upper George St.* ***i*** *Breakfast included. Free Wi-Fi. TV, tea and coffee available in every room.* Ⓢ *Singles €40; doubles €35; family rooms €80.* ⚅ *Reception open 7am-10pm. All other times, call ahead.*

⬛ STAYING IN WEXFORD   SHARED   APARTMENTS $

38 William St.   ☎087 233 3891   www.stayinginwexford.com

Staying In Wexford is apartment housing for travelers. Yes, you get an actual house to use to your liking and yes, the actual house comes with one to three roommates. It also comes with your own private room, a fully equipped kitchen, complimentary washer and dryer, a backyard, and a puppy. Okay, we were kidding about the puppy. Wooden floors, tiled bathrooms, and an unalarming cream color on the walls make it hard to disagree with the decor, but we'll take dull decor over a snoring Brazilian on the bottom bunk any day.

⎯ *From the tourist office, turn left onto Paul Quay. Follow it as it becomes Trinity St., then William St.* ***i*** *Free Wi-Fi. Towels, linens, tea, and coffee included.* Ⓢ *Each room is €28 per night; can sleep singles or doubles.* ⚅ *Reception hours vary; call ahead.*

MCDONALD'S PUB/B&B   B&B $

114 S. Main St.   ☎ 053 912 3457

We're not saying that McDonald's is the most aesthetically pleasing B&B you'll ever stay in, but your wallet will be tickled pink. There's nothing to complain about: the rooms are fully equipped with beds, desks, wardrobes and bathrooms. There's also nothing to rave about: the walls are bare, the rooms are dull, and the decor is about as exciting as a ◪**Lonely Planet** guidebook. This is a no frills, "I'd rather spend my money in the pub" B&B.

⎯ *From the tourist office, take Oyster Ln., then turn left onto S. Main St.* ***i*** *Breakfast €7. Free Wi-Fi. Linens included. TV, tea, and coffee in every room.* Ⓢ *Singles €25; doubles €40; triples €50.* ⚅ *Reception 7am-12:30am; call all other times.*

leinster

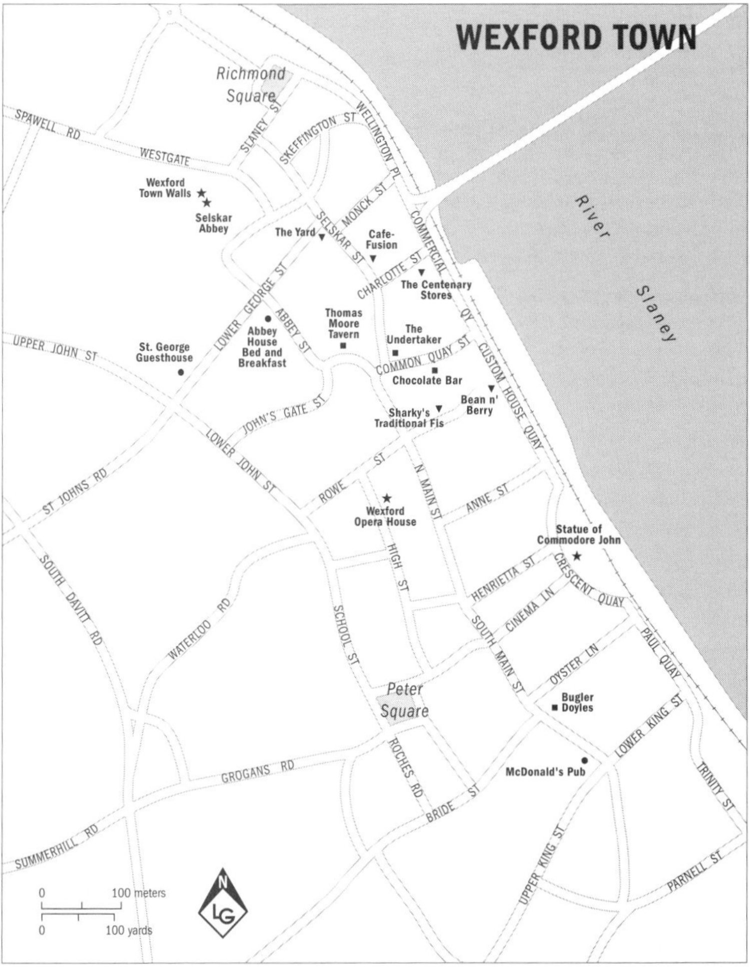
WEXFORD TOWN
Richmond Square
SPAWELL RD
WESTGATE
SLANEY ST
SKEFFINGTON ST
WELLINGTON PL
Wexford Town Walls
Selskar Abbey
MONCK ST
SELSKAR ST
The Yard
Cafe-Fusion
COMMERCIAL QY
CHARLOTTE ST
The Centenary Stores
River Slaney
LOWER GEORGE ST
ABBEY ST
Thomas Moore Tavern
Abbey House Bed and Breakfast
The Undertaker
UPPER JOHN ST
St. George Guesthouse
COMMON QUAY ST
Chocolate Bar
CUSTOM HOUSE QUAY
Bean n' Berry
Sharky's Traditional Fis
JOHN'S GATE ST
LOWER JOHN ST
ST JOHNS RD
ROWE ST
N MAIN ST
ANNE ST
Wexford Opera House
Statue of Commodore John
HIGH ST
HENRIETTA ST
CRESCENT QUAY
SOUTH DAVITT RD
WATERLOO RD
SCHOOL ST
CINEMA LN
SOUTH MAIN ST
PAUL QUAY
OYSTER LN
Peter Square
Bugler Doyles
LOWER KING ST
ROCHES RD
McDonald's Pub
GROGANS RD
BRIDE ST
TRINITY ST
SUMMERHILL RD
UPPER KING ST
PARNELL ST
0
100 meters
0
100 yards
N
LG

ABBEY HOUSE B&B $$

34-36 Abbey St. ☎053 912 4408

This is everything you've imagined a B&B to be. The owner is attentive but not nosy, there are fresh flowers in the hallways, and the dining room includes a nice sitting area in front of a fireplace. Recently renovated, Abbey Court maintains a classic wood-furniture-and-flowers-on-the-windowsill B&B look, just sleeker than before.

🚏 From the bus station, take Slaney St. Turn left onto Selskar St., then take the 2nd right onto George St. Turn left onto Abbey St. ℹ Breakfast included. Free Wi-Fi. All rooms ensuite. $ €35 per person per night. ⏰ Reception hours vary; call ahead.

SIGHTS

🏛 WEXFORD OPERA HOUSE — OPERA HOUSE

High St. ☎053 912 2144 www.wexfordoperahouse.ie

For such a small city, Wexford has one hell of an opera house. The semicircle, multi-level seating soars above the stage, and upon seeing it you'll begin to understand why the shows sell out all the time. In addition to three bars, the Opera House's Sky View Café has legendary views of the Wexford harbor as well as some legendary soup selections. Tours of the Wexford Opera House give you exclusive access to the orchestra pit, green room, and dressing rooms. We can't promise any half-dressed actors, but maybe you'll get lucky.

⇆ From the tourist office, turn right onto Crescent Quay and continue as it becomes Custom House Quay. Turn left onto Church St., then turn left onto High St. ℹ Hosts the Wexford Festival Opera in October. $ Tours €5. ⏰ Box office open Tu-Sa 10am-4pm. Tours Sa at 2:30pm.

STATUE OF COMMODORE JOHN BARRY — STATUE

Crescent Quay

The Statue of Commodore John Barry is the focal point of the Wexford Quay. Born in Wexford, Commodore Barry is credited as the father of the American Navy as well as the guy who fired the last shot of the American Revolution. Yeah, he's kind of a big deal. The statue was a gift from the United States and was visited by JFK in 1963 on his Ireland tour. If you're visiting on June 27th, head down to the statue for Barry Day, an Irish Navy commemoration ceremony.

⇆ From the tourist office, turn right onto Crescent Quay. $ Free. ⏰ Open 24hr.

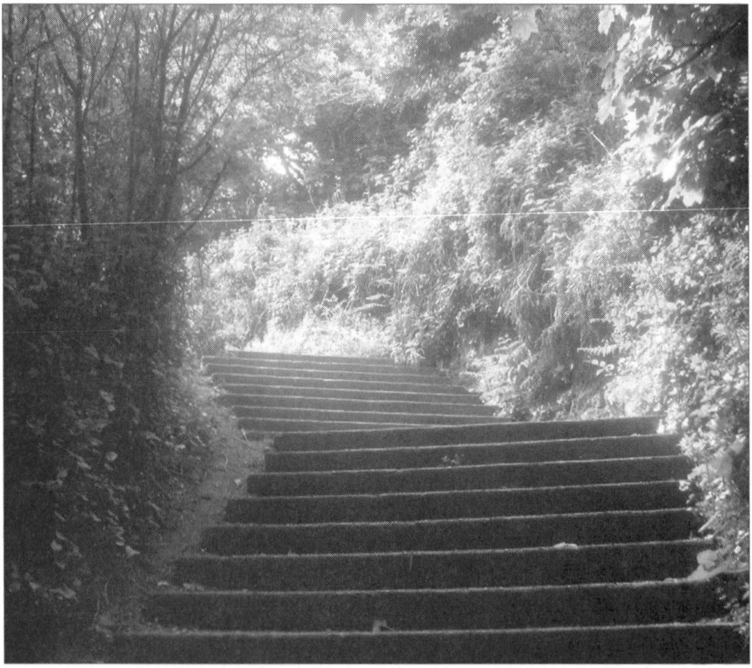

SELSKAR ABBEY
RUINS

Temperance Row

This abbey is the very spot where the Irish signed the first treaty with the English, surrendering the town of Wexford into Irish rule. The cathedral was later destroyed by Oliver Cromwell in 1649. Not really a win for the cathedral, but in Ireland it's almost an honor for something to have been destroyed by Cromwell. Today, the abbey is some really pretty ruins with a real good story behind them.

⚶ *From the bus station, take Slaney St. and turn left onto Temperance Row.* ⓘ *Entrance by guided tour only.* ⓢ *Free.* ⌚ *Tours daily, see tourist office for times.*

WEXFORD TOWN WALLS
MONUMENT

Temperance Row

Dating back to the 10th century, the Wexford Town Walls have seen their fair share of Viking deaths, bad weather, and secret smooches. Two of the three still happen regularly. While the first walls were wooden, the foundation of today's walls date back to their Norman reconstruction.

⚶ *From the bus station, take Slaney St. Turn left onto Temperance Row.* ⓘ *Where the walls have been rebuilt, the original techniques were used.* ⓢ *Free.* ⌚ *Open 24hr.*

FOOD

▨ SHARKY'S TRADITIONAL FISH AND CHIPS
IRISH $

Church St. ☎053 912 1990

A classic fish and chips place, Sharky's fries its way through the fish market. If you're not feeling a giant hunk of fish, enough chips to feed a small family, and mushy peas and coleslaw to boot, order a kids meal (you're allowed, we promise). It includes a smaller portion of fish and chips and doesn't include the sides. Take-out is the most common here, but feel free to soak up the '50s style diner feel while you add three inches to your hips.

⚶ *From the tourist office, turn right onto Crescent Quay and continue as it becomes Custom House Quay. Turn left onto Church St.* ⓘ *Take-out available.* ⓢ *Fish meals €9-10. Burgers €2.20-5.50. Chips €2.40-5.40. Beverages €1.20-1.80.* ⌚ *Open M-Th 10am-11pm, F-Sa 10am-midnight, Su 11am-11pm.*

▨ CAFE-FUSION
CAFE $

109 N. Main St. ☎086 243 4360

The red, white, and black couches have a few lime-green and purple, fuzzy throw pillows on them, and the walls are decorated with paintings from what we think must be every genre of art. By virtue of nothing matching, everything in the room matches; decor can only be that haphazard on purpose. Don't let any of that distract you from the food, though. Fusion makes a darn fine scone, and there is nothing haphazard about their coffee.

⚶ *From the bus station, take Slaney St. Turn left onto Selskar St., then a slight left onto N. Main St.* ⓢ *Coffee and tea €1.30-3.50. Desserts and pastries €1.20-3.* ⌚ *Open M-W 10am-5pm, Th-F 10am-9pm, Sa 10am-5pm, Su noon-5pm.*

THE YARD
IRISH $$$$

3 Lower George St. ☎053 914 4083 www.theyard.ie

Try not to swoon with pure adoration as the smell of perfectly spiced roasting meat hits you. The Yard offers elegantly crafted Irish cuisine for lunch and dinner, as well as a few just as elegantly done adventure meals (at least for the non-Irish.) Our suggestion: peppered squid (€11) as a starter with confit of pork belly steak (€25) for the main course. Holy cow, The Yard makes good meals.

⚶ *From the bus station, take Slaney St. Turn left onto Selskar St., then turn right onto Lower George St.* ⓘ *Early-bird special set meals: M-W 6-8pm, Th-Sa 6-7pm. 2 courses €22, 3 courses €25. Outdoor patio seating available.* ⓢ *Starters €5-12. Entrees €17-29. Desserts €6-6.50.* ⌚ *Open M-F noon-3pm and 5:30-9:30pm, Sa noon-3pm and 5:30-10pm.*

BEAN N' BERRY
CAFE $

Church St.   ☎053 917 4899

Bean n' berry politely suggests a make-your-own-sandwich bar, allowing the creative to run free here. The less creative can also have a good meal as there are hot options, salads, and smoothies to choose from as well.

⌗ *From the tourist office, turn right onto Crescent Quay and continue as it becomes Custom House Quay. Turn left onto Church St.* ⓘ *Free Wi-Fi.* Ⓢ *Breakfast €2-9. Soups and sandwiches €5-8. Entrees €8. Salads €6-9.50. Desserts €4-5.50. Tea and coffee €2-3.75.* ⌚ *Open M-Sa 10am-5pm.*

THE CENTENARY STORES
IRISH $$

Charlotte St.   ☎053 912 4424 www.thestores.ie

There is nothing on The Centenary Stores's menu that doesn't go well with a Guinness. The pork and mushroom pie served with potatoes (€10) is our favorite meal to soak up the beer, but the cream of potato and bacon soup (€4.25) is a close second. Stay in the dimly lit bar if you want the full pub experience or take your meal out to the large stone- and tree-filled patio for some fresh sea air.

⌗ *From the tourist office, turn right onto Crescent Quay and continue as it becomes Custom House Quay, then Commercial Quay. Turn left onto Charlotte St.* Ⓢ *Starters €4.25-7. Sandwiches €5-8. Salads €10. Entrees €8-12. Desserts €4.25. Tea and coffee €2.20-2.80.* ⌚ *Open M 10:30am-9pm, Tu 10:30am-2am, W 10:30am-9pm, Th-Sa 10:30am-2am, Su 10:30am-1:30am. Kitchen open daily 10:30am-8pm.*

NIGHTLIFE

🖾 THE UNDERTAKER
PUB

Cornmarket   ☎053 912 2949

The old signs and silver steins may have been the only things they had hanging around, so they threw them up on the walls. The bar is filled with a mid- to late-twenties crowd who just got off work, have been in there since they got off work, or need a job. It may not be the most affluent of clientele, but with a little music and a lot of whiskey, they sure are the most fun.

⌗ *From the tourist office, turn right onto Crescent Quay and continue as it becomes Custom House Quay, then Commercial Quay. Turn left onto Common Quay St. and continue as it becomes Cornmarket.* Ⓢ *Pints €4-5. Spirits €3.80-6.* ⌚ *Open M-Th 10:30am-11:30pm, F-Sa 10:30am-12:30am, Su 10:30am-11pm.*

BUGLER DOYLES
BAR

83 S. Main St.   ☎053 912 2261 www.buglerdoyles.ie

Well there's not much to the decor, but we bet your eyes will be on the rowdy Irishman and young internationals that fill the pub, not the lack of wall decorations. Head over at about 10:30pm on the weekend, and we bet you won't want to leave.

⌗ *From the tourist office, take Oyster Ln. Turn left onto S. Main St.* ⓘ *Traditional Irish music F and Sa 9:30pm. Smoking patio and beer garden out back.* Ⓢ *Pints €4-5. Spirits €3.80-6.* ⌚ *Open M-Th 10:30am-11:30pm, F-Sa 10:30am-12:30am, Su 12:30-11pm.*

CHOCOLATE BAR
BAR

Common Quay St.   ☎053 912 1131 www.thechocolatebarwexford.ie

This is where American Apparel would go if it were a person; it's the mainstream of the alternative. Punky, hip music from ten years ago blasts loud enough to be heard from the outside, just upbeat enough to be alluring but not so upbeat that you'll be singing along. Backlit wall murals of cathedrals adorn the walls and a younger, in-vogue crowd hangs here. Don't expect any traditional Irish music sing-alongs here.

⌗ *From the tourist office, turn right onto Crescent Quay. Continue as it becomes Custom House Quay, then Commercial Quay. Turn left onto Common Quay St.* ⓘ *DJ or live band every M, W, and Sa night.* Ⓢ *Pints €4-5.10, Spirits €4-7.* ⌚ *Open M 9am-2am, Tu-Th 9am-11:30pm, F-Sa 9am-2am, Su 9am-11:30pm.*

THOMAS MOORE TAVERN PUB

Cornmarket ☎053 917 4688 www.thomasmooretavern.com

The traditional Irish music is finger-snapping-good and the white Christmas light-lit smoking room is magical. Most of the patrons look like they might have known Mr. Moore as a child, but at least you know things won't get too rowdy.

🚏 From the tourist office, turn right onto Crescent Quay. Continue as it becomes Custom House Quay, then Commercial Quay. Turn left onto Common Quay St. and continue as it becomes Cornmarket. ***i*** *Live music Tu, F, and Sa at 10pm. $ Pints €4-5.10. Spirits €4-7. ⏰ Open M-Tu 4-11:30pm, W-Th noon-11:30pm, F-Sa noon-12:30am, Su noon-11pm.*

ARTS AND CULTURE

👍 **GREENACRES** GALLERY

Selskar St. ☎053 912 2975 www.greenacres.ie/art-galleries

Wander around this gallery's white-walled, wood-floored room and admire the classic art with a modern touch. The bronze sculptures, landscape paintings, and woodcarvings are scattered delicately around the spacious rooms, making each piece an individual focal point.

🚏 From the bus station, take Slaney St. Turn left onto Selskar St. $ Works generally €60-500. ⏰ Open M-Sa 9am-10pm, Su noon-8pm.

WEXFORD ARTS CENTRE ARTS CENTER

Cornmarket ☎053 912 3764 www.wexfordartscentre.ie

Wexford Arts Centre does it all: jazz shows, improv, and some good ol' children's theater. That's not all, though; it has art classes and workshops, a cafe, and a gallery with exhibitions that change every few months. This center juggles more things at once than a working single mother. Shows range from free to affordable, so support the arts in Ireland and get an entertaining night out of it as well.

🚏 From the tourist office, turn right onto Crescent Quay. Continue as it becomes Custom House Quay, then Commercial Quay. Turn left onto Common Quay St. and continue as it becomes Cornmarket. ***i*** *Free Wi-Fi. $ Shows from free to €10. ⏰ Open Tu-Sa 10am-5:30pm.*

SHOPPING

👍 **WESTGATE DESIGN** ARTISAN GOODS

22A N. Main St. ☎053 912 3787 www.westgatedesign.ie

The majority of the products here are way beyond a poor college student's decor budget, but if you're going to splurge on something, do it here. We're not sure the Tipperary Crystal or Kilkenny Glass will match the tattered Bob Marley poster in your dorm room, but we sure bet it will please a parent or two. If you don't love your parents that much (or already blew all your cash), stick with the Wexford Home Preserves. They are thoughtful and about €250 cheaper.

🚏 From the tourist office, turn right onto Crescent Quay. Turn left onto Anne St., then turn right onto N. Main St. ⏰ Open M-Sa 8:30am-6pm.

WEXFORD SILVER SILVER

115 N. Main St. ☎053 912 1933 www.wexfordsilver.com

If you ever wanted your name, astrological sign, or favorite guidebook's name (cough) worked in silver, hit up Wexford Silver. The workshop is visible in the back; just give a shout if you need some help. Driftwood props display Celtic and Christian works already completed and on sale, but feel free to bring in your own custom designs.

🚏 From the tourist office turn right onto Crescent Quay and continue as it becomes Custom House Quay, then Commercial Quay. Turn left onto Charlotte St., then turn right onto N. Main St. Wexford Silver is on the left. $ €16-100. ⏰ Open Tu-Sa 10am-1pm and 2-5:30pm.

ESSENTIALS

Practicalities

- **TOURIST OFFICE:** The **Discover Ireland Tourist Office** is located on Crescent Quay. (Quayside ☎053 912 311 ➔ From the bus station, take Redmond Pl. and continue as it becomes Commercial Quay, then Custom House Quay, and finally Crescent Quay. ⏰ Open M-Sa 9:30am-5:30pm.)
- **ATMS:** There are 3 24hr. ATMs located on Main St. Two Ulster Bank ATMs are at the intersection of N. Main St. and Charlotte St. There is also an AIB ATM on S. Main St.
- **INTERNET ACCESS:** The **Wexford Town Internet Cafe** has computers available for use and does repairs as well. (26 Henrietta St. ☎053 915 2901 www.wexfordtown.ie ➔ From the tourist office, turn right onto Crescent Quay, then turn left onto Henrietta St. ℹ €2 for 30min. ⏰ Open M-Sa 10am-8pm, Su 2-6pm.)
- **POST OFFICE:** There is a post office on Anne St. To get there from the tourist office, turn right onto Crescent Quay, continue as it becomes Custom House Quay, then turn left onto Anne St. (Anne St. ☎053 912 2031 ⏰ Open M-F 9am-5:30pm, Sa 9am-1pm.)

Emergency

- **POLICE:** To get to the **Garda station,** take Oyster Ln. Turn left onto S. Main St., then turn right onto Bride St. Turn right onto Roches Rd. (Roches Rd. ☎053 912 2333 ⏰ Open 24hr. for emergency care.)
- **HOSPITAL:** To get to the **Wexford General Hospital** from the bus station, take Slaney St. Turn right onto Westgate. Continue as it becomes Spawell Rd., then take a slight left onto Old Hospital Rd. (Old Hospital Rd. ☎053 915 3000 ⏰ Open 24hr. for emergencies.)
- **PHARMACY: Sherwood's Pharmacy** is located on N. Main St. To get there from the tourist office, turn right onto Crescent Quay and continue as it becomes Custom House Quay. Turn left onto Anne St., then turn right onto N. Main St. (2 N. Main St. ☎053 912 2875 ⏰ Open 9am-9pm.)

Getting There

BY BUS

Bus Éireann runs buses from: Cork ($ €22, students €18.50 ⏰ 6 per day 7:10am-7:10pm); Dublin ($ €18, students €15 ⏰ 22 per day, buses run 24hr.); Galway ($ €22, students €18.50 ⏰ 15 per day 6:30am-5:30pm); Limerick ($ €17.50 ⏰ 5 per day 7:10am-6:40pm); Shannon Airport ($ €21, students €19.50 ⏰ 6 per day 7:10am-9pm).

BY TRAIN

Trains arrive from Dublin. ($ €25, students €17. ⏰ 8 per day 7:20am-9:20pm.) To get to other Irish towns and cities by train you must go through Dublin. See **Dublin, Getting There**.

BY PLANE

The nearest **airport** is in Cork; see **Cork, Getting There**.

Getting Around

Wexford is a small town and walking is more than sufficient for getting around. If the hill up to your B&B looks too daunting, call **TJ Taxis.** Rates are hardly ever more than €5-7. (Crossabeg ☎053 91 28 168 www.tjtaxis.com ⏰ Taxis available 24hr.)

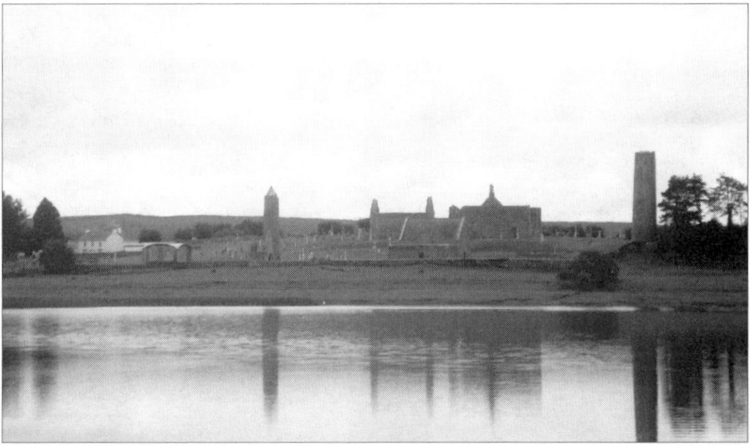

athlone ☎090

Just south of **Lough Ree,** on the border of **Counties Roscommon and Westmeath,** and close to one of Ireland's most famous historical sights, **Clonmacnoise,** this somewhat sleepy town is a nice break for those on the road between Galway and Dublin. **Athlone Castle** dominates the city and serves as a constant reminder of the city's historical significance. The **Siege of Athlone** in 1691 and the Viking activity on the **Shannon River.** are just two major events in Athlone's substantial past; but the city is by no means wizened. History lovers, walk the **Quay** and discover all that this picturesque little Irish town has to offer.

ORIENTATION

The **Shannon River** cuts through the middle of Athlone, dividing it into the right bank and the left bank. The **right bank** holds most of the town's shopping and restaurants and is centered on **Church Street.** The historical **left bank** is home to the **castle, Sean's Bar,** and the **Athlone Docks. Market Square** and **Main Street,** on either side of the castle, make for easy reference points.

ACCOMMODATIONS

👍 BASTION — B&B $$

2 Bastion St. ☎090 649 4954 www.thebastion.net

Bastion's Birkenstock-wearing brothers easily make you feel right at home. Follow them up the winding, old wooden stairs, past the ubiquitous plants, to your bed with crisp white sheets and still more decorative plant life. Make your way to the common room for some leather couches and good conversation with other travelers or with the owners themselves.

➹ From the castle, take High St. Follow it as it turns into Bastion St. ℹ Breakfast included. Free Wi-Fi. $ €35 per person per night. ⏰ Reception 24hr.

SHANNONSIDE HOUSE — B&B $$

Battery Rd. ☎090 649 4773 www.shannonsidehouse.ie

This is very much a "welcome to the family" bed and breakfast. Rooms with pastel walls and floral comforters reveal that this family's a bit more traditional, and decorates with a feminine touch. Located outside of the city center, the rooms are quiet, and the residential neighborhood makes it feel like you're there to stay with a long-lost aunt—hopefully not Petunia Dursley.

⇆ From the castle, take High St. Follow as it turns into Bastion St. and continue until it turns into Battery Rd. The B&B will be on your left. i Free Wi-Fi. $ €35 per person, per night.

ARCH HOUSE B&B $$

Sean Costello St. ☎090 647 7222 www.archhouse.ie

This bed and breakfast doesn't scream character, but it does tout, in a nice conversational manner, its own prices and great location. Ensuite rooms, complimentary in-room tea and coffee, and a homemade breakfast leave nothing to complain about. There's no place like home, but at least this B&B is comfortable.

⇆ From the bus station, take Ballymahon Rd., then turn left onto Sean Costello St. i Free Wi-Fi. $ €40 per person per night, €45 with breakfast. ⏰ Reception 8am-10pm.

RONCALLI B&B $$

42 St. Francis Terr. ☎090 647 4204

Located less than a five-minute walk from the city center, Roncalli feels worlds away in a quiet, residential neighborhood. The outdoor patio and garden promise a tranquil night's sleep. While the decor isn't anything to call home about, the rooms are more than adequate. And dog lovers will no doubt be entertained and enamored with Coco, the B&B's rambunctious mascot.

⇆ With your back to the bus station, head left on Southern Station Rd. Take a right onto Garden Vale, then turn right onto St. Francis Terr. i Dog in residence. $ €35 per person per night.

SIGHTS

CLONMACNOISE RUINS

Shannonbridge, County Offaly ☎090 967 4195 clonmacnoise@opw.ie

With history tracing back to 600 CE, this Christian heritage site has been a place of pilgrimage for over a millennium. St. Ciarán is credited with founding the first settlement here and building its first church, which would be followed by seven others. Clonmacnoise's prime location and wealth of resources made it a common destination for both Irish and Viking raids; today it no longer sees pillaging mobs, just tourist ones. Supposedly, sprinkling soil from St Ciarán's Cathedral onto the four corners of a field will help your crops grow.

⇆ 21km south of Athlone. You can get here either via the Viking Tour or a van (€20), which you can book at the tourist office. $ €6, students and children €2, seniors and groups €4. ⏰ Open daily June-Aug 9am-6:30pm, mid-March to May 10am-6pm, Sept-Oct 10am-6pm, Nov to mid-March 10am-5:30pm. Last entry 45min. before closing. Tours every hr.

ATHLONE CASTLE CASTLE

Castle St. ☎090 644 2109 www.athloneartandheritage.ie

Dominating the city center, the Athlone Castle is the number one reason to stop by this lovely city. The flowers that creep out of the cracks in the edifice soften the towering walls. The museums inside depict the history of Athlone as well as the biography of tenor John McCormack, Athlone's most famous export. The tourist office inside also offers information on the city and surrounding area.

⇆ With your back to the bus station, turn right and head down Southern Station Rd., which will turn into Northgate St. Take a right onto Custume Pl. and keep to the left. i Closed for renovations. Expected to reopen 2013. $ €8, students and seniors €6. ⏰ Open daily 10am-4:30pm.

BURGESS PARK PARK

Wolfe Tone Terr.

A playground, benches, little children feeding swans—you can't ask for much more from a park. Serving as the groomed border between the city and the expanse of Irish countryside that surrounds it. The park dishes out one of the best views of the castle, bridge, and the Shannon River. If you look in the other

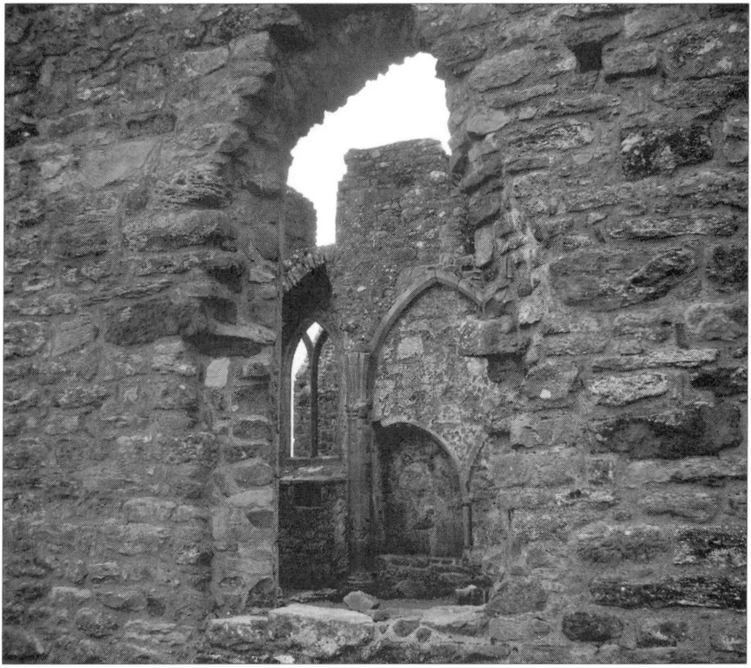

direction, you will mostly likely end up getting into a staring contest with the cow. Yup, the country starts right here.

⇞ From the Athlone Towncentre shopping center, take Griffith St. toward the river. Take a left onto Wolfe Tone Terr. You will run right into the park. ℹ You're not supposed to feed the swans. $ Free. ⏰ Open 24hr.

FOOD

🍴 PLANET LIFE — CAFE $

1 Bastion St. ☎090 649 0420

This isn't just a cafe—it's a lifestyle. It doubles as an organic market, so consult the holistic medicine menu to see what food will best cure your headache/nausea/hangover. Or just grab one of their locally famous pita sandwiches and enjoy the surrounding chatter.

⇞ From the castle, take High St. and continue as it turns into Bastion St. $ Coffee €1.60-3.20. Lunch €3-7. ⏰ Open M-Sa 9:30am-5:30pm.

🍴 THE LOCKE — IRISH $$$

The Quay ☎090 649 4517

Local and fresh are the key words here, which begs the question; just how fresh can a slow-roasted pork belly be? The menu has a host of traditional Irish menu items; stay downstairs for the late bar or head up to the lofted dining area for a rather holy eating experience—that's right, it's in a renovated church.

⇞ Follow The Quay down from the castle; the Locke will be on the right. $ Appetizers €6.30-9.50. Entrees €11.50-22.50. Pints from €3.90. ⏰ Open M-Sa 4:30-10:30pm.

SHANNON CRAFTS AND COFFEE CAFE $

The Strand ☎090 176 2552

This is where diets go to die. German chocolate cake (with a practically illegal number of layers) greets you as you walk in, while the blueberry crumble shyly peeks out from behind it. If, for some unfathomable reason, nothing on display appeals to you, cakes and scones can be made to order. Sit down and start getting fat; you'll enjoy every bite.

 # From the Athlone Towncentre shopping center, take Griffith St. and turn right onto The Strand. i Also sells flower arrangements. [$] Coffee and tea €2. Desserts from €3. Lunch from €3.90. ⏰ Open daily 9am-6pm.

SAVIO'S FAST FOOD $

16 Mardyke St. ☎090 649 5098

It's getting late. You may or may not have had a whiskey or two, you're walking back to your B&B, and whoa—what's that there? Fish and chips for €3? A sausage meal for €2? This may not be what your mother wants you eating for dinner, but it's too delicious for you to care. Enjoy those late-night garlic fries.

 # From the castle, take Custume Pl. and follow as it curves right, becoming Church St., then Dublin Gate St., then Mardyke St. i Student discounts available. Delivery available. [$] Pizzas €6-10. Kebabs €5-6. Burgers €2-5. ⏰ Open M-Sa noon-1am, Su 4pm-1am.

NIGHTLIFE

SEAN'S BAR PUB

13 Main St. ☎090 649 2358 www.seansbar.lightholderproductions.com

Dating back to 900 CE, Sean's claims to be **the oldest bar in Ireland,** and it has the *Guinness Book of World Records*'s certificate on the wall to prove it. The bar maintains a good local scene despite its big-time claim to fame. With live music every night, it's always a safe bet for a solid night.

 # Across the street from the castle, near the intersection of Main St. and High St. i Beer garden. [$] Pints from €4. ⏰ Open M-Sa 4pm-1am, Su 4pm-midnight.

GERTIE BROWNE PUB

9 Custume Pl. ☎090 647 4848

There isn't a spot on the walls or ceiling (and on busy nights, the floor) that isn't decorated. Originally a brothel, the pub has a tarty history; let the painting of former Mistress Gertie tell it to you with her eyes, as you recline in the smoking room's leather seats.

 # From the castle, head onto Custume Pl. and cross the bridge. It is on your right just before Church St. [$] Pints from €3.70. ⏰ Open M-Sa 4pm-1am, Su 4pm-midnight.

SHOPPING

LEFT BANK ANTIQUES ANTIQUES

15 Main St. ☎090 649 3377

Looking for an engagement ring? Maybe a really old bible? How about a shaving kit from the '50s? This shop's assortment of antiques guarantees something for everyone. That is, something for everyone willing to spend around €100. But hey, those engagement rings look like they're worth it.

 # Right across Main St. from the castle. ⏰ Open M-Sa 10am-6pm.

THE GOLDEN ISLAND MEGASTORE

Golden Island ☎090 647 6760

The name might be a bit optimistic (it's more like "Cheap Irish Stores Island"), but what this place lacks in class it makes up for in price. We're talking Tesco, the cheapest supermarket in Ireland, and of course, Penneys, the so-called **Irish Walmart.** A good place to restock on anything food- or clothing-wise.

➹ From the castle, take Custume Pl. Follow as it turns into Church St., then Dublin Gate St., then Mardyke St. Take a right onto John Broderick St., followed by a left onto Golden Island. ℹ Free Wi-Fi. ⏰ Open M-Sa 9am-6pm, Su noon-4pm.

OZANAM HOUSE THRIFT STORE
16-18 O'Connell St. ☎090 313 3798

Although not exactly haute couture, this thrift store is the perfect place to find those €4 jeans that fit well enough. The clothing selection is expansive, but the books are the real draw. A new train read for less than a euro? Sure thing.

➹ From the castle, take High St., follow as it turns into Bastion St., then O'Connell St. [$] Clothes €3-10. Shoes €5-8. Books less than €1. ⏰ Open M-F 10am-4:30pm, Sa noon-4pm.

ESSENTIALS

Practicalities

- **TOURIST OFFICE:** The tourist office for County Westmeath (Athlone's county) is located on Church St. between the Town Bridge and St. Mary's Church. (Church St. ☎090 649 4630 www.discoverireland.ie/westmeath ⏰ Open M-Sa 9am-6pm.)
- **TOURS:** Viking Tours go north to Lough Nee, or south to Clonmacnoise (by reservation only). Besides giving you a look at the Irish countryside, the 75min. tour includes local history, wildlife, environment, and even a little bit on current events. (Quay at Athlone Castle. ☎090 262 1136 www.vikingtoursireland.ie ➹ On the Quay side of the castle. With your back to the bus station, turn right and head down Southern Station Rd., which turns into Northgate St. Turn right onto Custume Pl. and keep to the left on Castle St. Follow the curve as it turns into Main St. and turn right onto The Quay. ℹ Viking hats and swords available for purchase; complimentary tea and coffee on board. [$] €10, students and children €5, families €30. ⏰ Tours usually run from 9:30am-4pm; check website for details.)
- **POST OFFICE:** The town's main post office is located just over the bridge next to St. Peter and Paul's Church in Market Square. (Barrack St. ☎090 643 5005 ⏰ Open M 9am-5:30pm, Tu 9:30am-5:30pm, W-F 9am-5:30pm, Sa 9am-1pm.)

Emergency

- **POLICE:** The **Garda station** is also located just over the bridge next to St. Peter and Paul's Church in Market Square. (Barrack St. ☎090 649 2609 www.garda.ie ⏰ Open 24hr.)
- **HOSPITAL:** To get to the **Athlone District Hospital,** cross the bridge from the castle and turn left onto Northgate St. (Northgate St. ☎090 647 5301 ⏰ Emergency care 24hr.)
- **PHARMACY:** **Concannon's** is just across from the Athlone Town Centre. (11 Church St. ☎090 647 8667 ⏰ Open M-Sa 9:30am-6pm.)

Getting There

BY BUS

Bus Éireann runs buses from: Cork ([$] €24.50, students €22.50 ⏰ 3 buses daily at 9:25am, 12:25, 3.25pm); Dublin ([$] €12, students €11 ⏰ Departs every hr. 8am-9pm); Galway ([$] €12, students €11 ⏰ Departs every hr. 8am-9pm); Belfast ([$] €28, students €22.50 ⏰ daily at 5am).

BY TRAIN

Trains arrive from: Dublin ([$]€24, students €20 ⏰ 7 daily) and Galway ([$] €24, students €20 ⏰ 7 daily). From all other cities, one must first get to Dublin or Galway, then transfer to the Galway-Dublin route.

BY PLANE
The nearest **airport** is in Dublin; see **Dublin: Getting There**.

Getting Around

Athlone doesn't have much in the way of public transportation; in fact, it doesn't have any. Brush off those walking boots; it's the easiest way to get around. The city itself is quite small, although there are several sights a short drive from the town center. There are several **car rental** agencies, such as **Enterprise.** (Dublin Rd. ☎090 649 1030 www.enterprise.ie ⌚ Open M-F 8am-6pm, Sa 9am-noon.) **Argus** will pick you up anywhere in Athlone. (☎090 888 3002 www.arguscarhire.ie ⌚ 24hr.) The main **taxi** service is **Taxis Athlone;** fares start at €3.45. (☎090 260 8571 www.athlonetaxis. com ⌚ 24hr.)

leinster

NORTHERN IRELAND

This isn't the Republic of Ireland. This is Northern Ireland, as in the United Kingdom of Great Britain and Northern Ireland. After centuries of colonization and violence, this corner of Ireland is what remains of the British presence on the island. Anchored by the cities of Belfast and Derry (or Londonderry, if you ask a Briton), Northern Ireland has its own character, unfortunately still marred by the political and religious strife that has not ceased to plague the region despite the relatively recent cessation of armed activities. See the effects of the Troubles (the violence between the mainly Catholic Irish and the mainly Protestant British) in the border city of Derry, or head to Northern Ireland's hub of up-and-coming Belfast—cosmopolitan but still rough around the edges. May you fare better than the *Titanic*.

greatest hits

- **YOU JUMP, I JUMP, JACK:** Reminisce about Leo and Kate while soaking in a bit of history at Titanic Belfast (p. 165).

- **RUMPELSTILTSKIN'S PARADISE:** The artists here aren't spinning straw into gold, but at the Golden Thread Gallery (p. 164) the modern art is just as lucrative.

- **PRETTY PLEASE, WITH A DERRY ON TOP:** Head on over to the Museum of Free Derry (p. 187) to embrace Northern Ireland's past and appreciate its present.

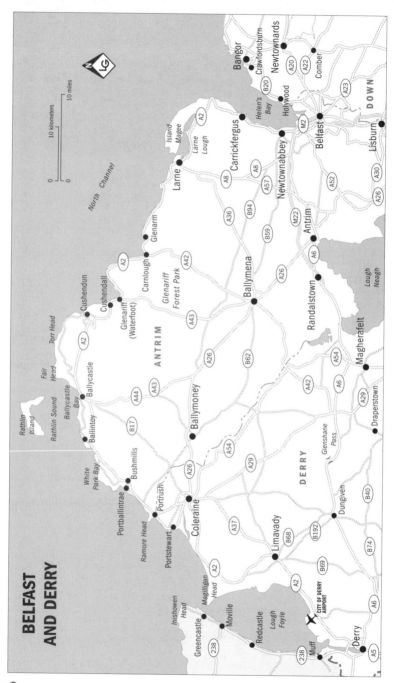

northern ireland

BELFAST AND DERRY

belfast ☎28

Think of Belfast as Dublin's badass older brother who plays in a band: he's cool, gritty, and gets tons of groupies. The city has an air left over from a history of recent war and strife, so don't be surprised if there is some enmity between members of the population on cultural lines. The city's people are some of the friendliest, though, and you only need to sit in one of the traditional pubs for a short while before you find someone who not only remembers "the Troubles" (as the conflict is called), but can also recall a time when a police frisking was requisite before entering the city center. But far from having resentment or a "hush-hush" attitude, the people of Belfast engage with their history; black cab tours of West Belfast, the area of hottest conflict, have become a popular tourist attraction. With all the history behind it, Belfast is reinventing itself as a tourist paradise, with a wonderful balance of sights, restaurants, and nightlife to make it a completely perfect starting point for an adventure through the island.

ORIENTATION

What's with all the Donegalls? Okay, get this: **Donegall Square** surrounds the city hall, **Donegall Road** runs from the west, crossing through town at **Shaftesbury Square** and becoming **Donegall Pass;** and finally, there's **Donegall Street,** which runs right through the heart of the **Cathedral Quarter.** Lesson to be learned? If someone gives you directions via a "Donegall" anything, make sure you get a second opinion. Belfast is a narrow city, running mostly north-south, with the previously conflicted **Falls** and **Shankill Roads** in West Belfast usually best visited hurriedly. The **University Quarter,** comprising **Queen's University,** lies south of the city center along **University Road** (follow Bedford St. and Dublin Rd. from city hall) and houses most of the student life and nearly all of the budget accommodations in Belfast. What was called the "Golden Mile" in past years—the triangle formed by Dublin Rd., Great Victoria St., and Bruce St.—is now pretty much dead. A few fast-food joints and the odd pub can be found there, but the new hotspot for nightlife is the **Cathedral Quarter,** the area above city hall near the **River Lagan.** The developing **Titanic Quarter** lies to the east and, while still not exactly a hotspot, is up and coming, with a new be-all and end-all **Titanic Exhibition** as its crown jewel.

The University Quarter

The University Quarter centers on **Queen's University** but extends into the residential neighborhoods to the west and south. The **Students' Union, The Botanic Inn,** and **Eglantine Inn** are all popular student bars, and there are several hostels and B&Bs on **Eglantine Avenue** and **Fitzwilliam Street. Lisburn Road** provides the other, far-side north-south channel, and also has several good restaurants and cafes. If you ever get disoriented, ask for either Lisburn Rd. or University Rd. and you'll be able to get yourself back toward the city center.

belfast

BELFAST

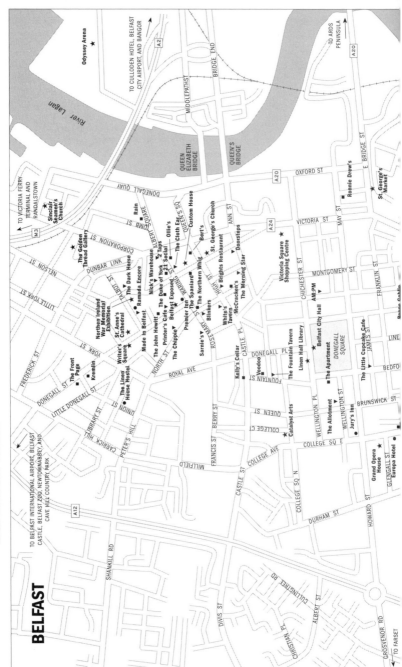

TO BELFAST INTERNATIONAL AIRPORT, BELFAST
CASTLE, BELFAST ZOO, NEWTOWNABBEY, AND
CAVE HILL COUNTRY PARK

River Lagan

Odyssey Arena ★

TO CULLODEN HOTEL, BELFAST
CITY AIRPORT, AND BANGOR

TO ARDS
PENINSULA

A2

A20

BRIDGE END

MIDDLEPATHS

QUEEN ELIZABETH BRIDGE

QUEEN'S BRIDGE

DONEGALL QUAY

OXFORD ST

A20

E BRIDGE ST

Ronnie Drew's ■

St. George's Market ★

VICTORIA ST

MAY ST

TO VICTORIA FERRY
TERMINAL AND
RANDALSTOWN

Sinclair Seamen's Church ★

M3

The Golden Thread Gallery ■

BMW ST

ALBERT SQUARE

Rain ■

CORPORATION ST

NELSON ST

LITTLE YORK ST

DUNBAR LINK

YACHT ST

The Dark Horse

3 Taps
Sacha!

Ollie's

The Cloth Ear

Custom House

QUEEN'S SQ

St. George's Church ★

Bert's

Doorsteps

ANN ST

A24

CHICHESTER ST

Victoria Square
Shopping Centre

MONTGOMERY ST

FRANKLIN

Nick's Warehouse
The Duke of York
Printer's Cafe ▼

Northern Ireland
War Memorial
Exhibition ■

Ramada Encore ●

St. Anne's Cathedral ★

HIGH ST

Belfast Exposed
WARING ST

Brights Restaurant

The Northern Whig ▼

The Morning Star ▼

AM:PM ▼

Banana

VICTORIA ST

Made in Belfast

The John Hewitt ▼

Premier Inn ●

The Spaniard ▼

McCracken's ▼

Blinkers ▼

White's Tavern ▼

Belfast City Hall ★

FREDERICK ST

YORK ST

NORTH ST

The Chippie ▼

Sarnie's ▼

ROSEMARY ST

Writer's Square ★

Kremlin ■

The Front Page ■

DONEGALL ST

The Linen House Hostel ●

UNION ST

LIBRARY ST

CARRICK HILL

LITTLE DONEGALL ST

PETER'S HILL

ROYAL AVE

Kelly's Cellar

CASTLE PL

DONEGALL PL

The Fountain Tavern ■

Linen Hall Library ■

The Apartment ■

DONEGALL SQUARE

The Little Cupcake Cafe

JAMES ST

LINE

BEDFO

Voodoo ▼

FOUNTAIN ST

FRANCIS ST

BERRY ST

MILLFIELD

Catalyst Arts ■

COLLEGE CT

QUEEN ST

WELLINGTON PL

The Allotment ▼

WELLINGTON ST

BRUNSWICK ST

Jury's Inn ●

CASTLE ST

COLLEGE AVE

COLLEGE SQ N

COLLEGE SQ E

DURHAM ST

HOWARD ST

Grand Opera House ★

GLENGALL ST

Europa Hotel ●

SHANKILL RD

DIVIS ST

CHRISTIAN PL

ALBERT ST

CULLINGTREE RD

GROSVENOR RD

TO FARSET

A12

belfast

The Titanic Quarter

Over the river to the east of the city center, the Titanic Quarter was once home to Belfast's massive shipbuilding industry. Indeed, it is still home to the historic **Harland & Wolff** shipyard, whose enormous cranes are still visible from almost any point in the area. Today, the Titanic Quarter is being subjected to a thorough redevelopment project, which includes the glowingly enormous **Titanic Exhibition** perched on the banks of the river. Most spots in this area can be seen from the **Titanic Trail** stretching from the Bridge End bridge along the river. While this is a small quarter at the moment, keep an eye on the website **www.titanic-quarter.com** for new events and openings.

Cathedral Quarter

Boasting the hottest nightclubs and independent restaurants, the Cathedral Quarter is the place for a night out. Here is where you'll find the newest pubs, the hippest crowds, and the sweetest cocktails. **High Street** provides a neat "bottom" to the neighborhood, which extends up to the **University of Ulster** and east over to **North Street.** The smaller streets have a lot to offer as well: Waring St., for instance, has some good bars and luxury hotels. It's all held together by the ubiquitous backbone known as **Donegall Street.**

City Center

Not one to mess around with misnomers, the City Center is indeed in the center of the city. Mostly focused around **Belfast City Hall** in **Donegall Square,** the **Cathedral Quarter** is to the north, while following **Dublin Road** all the way to the south will eventually lead to the **Queen's Quarter.** Most of the chain shopping areas and more upscale restaurants can be found between Donegall Sq. and **Castle Place,** while nightlife and accommodations are found from the square to **Donegall Pass.** If you don't get confused by the number of Donegalls around here, buy a Guinness, then see how you feel.

ACCOMMODATIONS

Belfast is home to a wide range of student hostels, B&Bs, commuter hotels, and luxury hotels whose decadence surpasses Midas. For the most part, look to the **University Quarter** for the best budget options, along with the promise of plenty of students to keep you company. While you might not even feel the need to leave the cozy shade of Queen's University, the only consideration might be the distance from the city center along less glamorous avenues. If your primary goal in Belfast is to sample the nightlife options, however, try to find a place in the **Cathedral Quarter,** which has at least one reasonably priced hostel. Should you decide to throw your budget out the window, splurge for the hyper luxurious **Merchant Hotel,** whose prime location is only matched by the fact that they own not one but three scorchingly hot nightlife options.

The University Quarter

Of all the districts in Belfast, this is where you will find the cheapest accommodations and hostels, naturally catering to the student-heavy population. It might be a slight trek from the city center's shopping complexes and quite the trek from the nightlife in the Cathedral Quarter, but the price and the quality of hostel comrades will more than make up for the extra minutes on foot.

☒ VAGABONDS   HOSTEL $$
9 University Rd.   ☎28 9543 8772 www.vagabondsbelfast.com

More focused on the glamorous and stylish elements of travel, rather than the rough-and-ready quality most backpackers adopt, Vagabonds conjures quite the modern and chic image. Clean dorms, comfy common spaces, and a friendly staff (mostly travelers just passing through themselves) are what you will find here. Most walls are covered with some celebration of traveling for travel's sake, from

northern ireland

globally sourced photos to quotes from greats like Paul Theroux. This is a break from the horror stories of the road. You might even want to stay home for a night and just relax. That's okay, though—Monday movie night means free popcorn.

⇞ From Shaftesbury Sq., walk down Bradbury Pl. Bear left onto University Rd. The hostel is on the right. ℹ Breakfast included. Free Wi-Fi. Bike hire available. Laundry available. [$] Dorms £13-16; doubles £40. ⏰ Reception 24hr. Check-in after 1pm. Check-out 11am.

GLOBAL VILLAGE HOSTEL $$

87 University St. ☎28 9031 3533 www.globalvillagebelfast.com

The newest addition to a quarter already teeming with hostels, Global Village is already making a name for itself. Rocking a very young, artsy vibe, every wall is exploding with some style, be it crazily patterned wallpaper or huge, carefully painted characters. The dorms themselves are more minimalist—with white bunks and linens, you can't help but admit it is clean. If you are traveling with someone you don't mind sharing a bed with, maybe spring for the double room, as the beds themselves are so enormous there might be a significant temporal gap between waking up and traveling to the edge of the bed. The crowd in the common area is welcoming and unimposing, so you will feel right at home.

⇞ From Botanic Station, walk left along Botanic Ave. Turn left onto University St. ℹ Free Wi-Fi. Bicycle hire available. [$] Mixed or female-only dorms £14; doubles £20. ⏰ Reception 24hr.

PADDYS PALACE HOSTEL $

68 Lisburn Rd. ☎28 9033 3367 www.paddyspalace.com

Part of a chain of fun-loving hostels, there is a definite feeling of rugged adventure at Paddys Palace. From the irony in calling this distinctly un-palatial accommodation a palace to the posters covering the reception walls, fun is the target of your stay. In terms of comfort, it doesn't get much better. The large glass conservatory is the perfect place to curl up with a book on those drizzling afternoons, or maybe whip up some simmering Irish stew in the enormous kitchen. Best of all, like the rest of the chain, this hostel packs only "Sleeptite" mattresses, which are super modern and comfy for all you non-mattress aficionados. All in all, you won't go wrong with this one.

⇞ From Shaftesbury Sq., walk down Bradbury Pl. Bear right onto Lisburn Rd. The hostel is on the left. ℹ Continental breakfast included. Free Wi-Fi. Free Giant's Causeway Tour available. [$] Dorms £8-13; doubles £25. ⏰ Reception 24hr. Breakfast 7:30-9:30am.

CITY BACKPACKER HOSTEL HOSTEL $$

53 Malone Ave. ☎28 9066 0030 www.ibackpacker.co.uk/belfast-hostel

Another new hostel, this one packs a few surprises. At first it seems to have all the usual amenities. Walk into a bedroom, though, and two things will immediately strike you. First, all the bunks are electric yellow, to the point that you are afraid to touch them; second, the bedspreads are hilarious. From Doctor Who to Playboy bunnies (logos, not girls), you can entertain yourself with a blast from the past. Other than the few little shocks, the rest of the facilities are all shiny, clean, and professional. It won't leave you with too great an impression in the end, but it is a nice place to stay for a few nights.

⇞ From the main gate of Queen's University, walk left on University Rd. Bear right onto Malone Rd. Turn right onto Malone Ave. The hostel is on the right. ℹ Breakfast included. Free Wi-Fi. Laundry available. [$] Dorms £14; doubles £20. ⏰ Reception 24hr.

ARNIE'S BACKPACKERS HOSTEL $$

63 Fitzwilliam St. ☎28 9024 2867 www.arniesbackpackers.co.uk

Less of a happy-go-lucky option compared to others in the area, this hostel focuses instead on the simple joys of a cuppa tea by the fire and other personal touches. Step inside this small, townhouse-style hostel for a haven from the partying and extroverted atmosphere that usually accompanies hostel life. The quiet cobbled garden is pleasant enough for sitting around in the cool afternoon sun, while the rooms are straightforward and simple. This is for the quieter traveler who doesn't mind a bit of dorm living as well.

➜ From Shaftesbury Sq., walk down Bradbury Pl. Bear right onto Lisburn Rd. Turn left onto Fitzwilliam St. The hostel is on the left. ℹ Free Wi-Fi. Computer £1 per 30min.; proceeds donated to charity. Kitchen available. 1st bunk in the 4-bed dorm is lofted and offers more privacy than the rest. $ 8-bed dorms £10-12; 4-bed £12-14. ⏰ Reception 24hr. Check-in from 9am. Check-out 11am.

LAGAN BACKPACKERS HOSTEL $$

121 Fitzroy Ave. ☎754 041 8246 www.laganbackpackers.com

Another small-ish option, this hostel has more of a tight-knit feeling. Expect to share your breakfast table with one or two other travelers and walk away with some new friends. The townhouse setting feels larger than it is thanks to some choice wall paintings as well as adroitly placed blocks of color. Most bedrooms are simple, with wide windows and thick comforters, which you will appreciate on those chilly Belfast nights. There usually seems to be a barbecue happening during the evening, so go buy some hamburgers and get your grill on with those new friends.

➜ From Botanic Station, turn left and walk down Botanic Ave. Turn left on College Green. Continue straight onto Fitzroy Ave. ℹ Breakfast included. Free Wi-Fi. Cinema room available. 2 kitchens available. Free international phone calls. $ Dorms £12-15.50; doubles £20. $ Reception 24hr.

MARINE GUEST HOUSE B&B $$$

30 Eglantine Ave. ☎28 9066 2828 www.marineguesthouse3star.com

A large brick building surrounded by a small garden, Marine Guest House is a good choice for those willing to pay a little bit extra for a more private option with a hotel-like feeling. Rooms look to be in minty fresh condition, well-appointed, and generally have a sprig of some flower in a vase. Luxurious hotel, no, but about as good as a simple B&B can be.

➜ From Shaftesbury Sq., walk down Bradbury Pl. Bear right onto Lisburn Rd. Turn left onto Eglantine Ave. The B&B is on the left. ℹ Full Irish breakfast included. TVs in rooms. All rooms ensuite. $ Singles £40-50; doubles £50-60. ⏰ Check-in 1pm. Check-out noon.

THE GEORGE B&B B&B $$$

9 Eglantine Ave. ☎28 9068 3212 the-george@hotmail.co.uk

A slightly less expensive option compared to The Marine, this cozy B&B offers all the usual expected courtesies—a bed and a breakfast. Lying in bed while rain patters on the window as you settle down with a good movie is sometimes exactly what you need. Not chock-full of character, but another option for those looking for a leafy retreat from hostel living.

➜ From Shaftesbury Sq., walk down Bradbury Pl. Bear right onto Lisburn Rd. Turn left onto Eglantine Ave. The B&B is on the right. ℹ Full Irish breakfast included. Free Wi-Fi. $ Singles £30; doubles £50. ⏰ Breakfast 7-9am.

Cathedral Quarter

This is not really the quarter for budget accommodations; options are very limited for those with a tight budget. But this is also the epicenter of some of the most happenin' nightlife, so it may be worth it.

👍 **THE LINEN HOUSE HOSTEL** HOSTEL $

18 Kent St. ☎28 9058 6400 www.belfasthostel.com

This hostel is undoubtedly the best value you will find in the Cathedral Quarter, and probably in Belfast as a whole. If you can put up with sleeping in a dorm with 20 other people, as well as the noise emanating from the late-night party crowd (it is in the heart of the Belfast nightlife, after all), you'll get more than your money's worth. With a reasonably comfortable, if not feathery-soft bunk, a kitchen whose major attraction is plenty of countertop surface area, and a simple, nondescript dining room, you will not be living in the lap of luxury. Fortunately, the price is definitely right.

From Belfast City Hall, walk up Donegall Sq. Continue straight until it becomes Royal Ave. Turn left onto Kent St. The hostel is on the left. i Free Wi-Fi. Laundry £4. Pizza £3. Linens included. $ Large mixed dorm £6.60; large female-only dorm £7.50; 8- to 10-bed £8; 6-bed £9. Singles £20; doubles £15; quads £11. ⏰ Reception 24hr. Check-in from 2pm. Check-out 10:30am.

RAMADA ENCORE HOTEL $$$$

20 Talbot St. ☎28 9026 1800 www.encorebelfast.co.uk

All the feigned panache you can expect from a commuter hotel, without any of the real vibrancy of a youth hostel. On the upside, however, staying here promises to be both comfortable and a retreat from the public lifestyle that accompanies hostel living. The click of the door behind you and the brightly shining tiles in the bathroom are always welcome—even if you do have to pay handsomely for the privilege.

From St. Anne's Cathedral, turn left and walk up Donegall St. Turn left onto Talbot St. The hotel is on the right. i Wi-Fi available, but only 1st 30min. free. $ Doubles from £59. ⏰ Reception 24hr. Check-in from 3pm. Check-out 11am.

PREMIER INN HOTEL $$$

2-6 Waring St. ☎87 1527 8070 www.premierinn.com

That clean and processed smell that pervades the commuter hotel community does not escape this case. One of a UK-based chain of hotels, Premier Inn is clean, comfortable, and essentially the same as every other chain hotel you've ever stayed in—except for the bright purple decor and a surprisingly lively bar in the evenings, that is.

On the corner at the top of Donegall St. i Free Wi-Fi. $ Doubles from £53. ⏰ Reception 24hr. Check-in from 2pm. Check-out 11am.

The Titanic Quarter

As it is home to the major redevelopment project of Northern Ireland, this isn't going to be where you find places to stay.

PREMIER INN HOTEL $$$

2 Queens Rd. ☎871 527 9210 www.premierinn.com

Like every other of its name, the Premier Inn will satisfy all the needs of your body, if none of those of the soul. Standardized rooms might be good for one night after a concert at the Odyssey Arena, but otherwise, make the walk to the Cathedral or University Quarters.

From the Bridge End bridge, turn left. Walk along the riverside footpath. The hotel is on the right. i Free Wi-Fi. $ Doubles £63-72. ⏰ Reception 24hr.

City Center

As in most city centers, only the wealthier franchises can afford real-estate here. As a result, you will either find boutiques or a forgettable commuter hotel.

BELFAST INTERNATIONAL HOSTEL (BIH) HOSTEL $$

22 Donegall Rd. ☎28 9031 5435 www.hini.org.uk

BIH is like a McDonald's—you only get it really late at night and you don't really want it, but you're in need, so you succumb, only to feel like you could have done better. Housed in a corporate, office-like space, it has over 200 rooms and less than a pint's worth of character. Still, if you can't find a room in Belfast, head here and you're guaranteed a clean place to stay for the night.

From the Europa Hotel, turn right and walk down Great Victoria St. Turn right onto Donegall Rd. The hostel is on the left. i Free Wi-Fi. Presentation of passport or other valid ID required for check-in. $ Dorms £10.50-15; singles £15-25. ⏰ Reception 24hr. Check-in 1:30pm. Check-out 11am.

JURYS INN HOTEL $$$

Great Victoria St. ☎28 9053 3500 http://belfasthotels.jurysinns.com

This commuter hotel has all the decor, leather, and light fixtures you can normally expect from one of its kind. Comfortable, if uninteresting, and with expensive Wi-Fi, Jurys Inn is pretty run-of-the-mill.

#From the Europa Hotel, turn left and walk up Great Victoria St. The hotel is on the left. i Wi-Fi £10. [$] Doubles £65-80. ⏰ Reception 24hr. Check-in 2pm. Check-out 11am.

EUROPA HOTEL HOTEL $$$$

Great Victoria St. www.hastingshotels.com/europa-belfast

The Europa hotel holds the dubious record for being the most bombed building in Belfast, with over 30 attempts and three explosions. They've put in some explosion-proof glass at this point and, fortunately, nobody's woken up in a rubble heap yet. Rooms here are actually quite luxurious, but be forewarned, they can run you well into the £100+ range.

#From the back of Belfast City Hall, turn right onto Howard St., then turn left down Great Victoria St. The hotel is on the right. i Free Wi-Fi. [$] Doubles from £85. ⏰ Reception 24hr.

SIGHTS

Belfast's sights are defined partially by its history and partially by its desired future. On the one hand, there are plenty of traditional monuments, like the impressively grand **Belfast City Hall** or the numerous churches scattered on every street, catering mostly to those of a Catholic disposition. However, Belfast's intense recent history has made it a vibrant city, constantly bent on creative reinvention. Nowhere is the shift more obvious than in the awesome array of modern art galleries, which house everything from contemporary sculpture to cinematographic displays.

The key re-development project in the city right now is focused in the newly named **Titanic Quarter,** so named as it is the place where the *Titanic* was born to the shipwrights of **Harland & Wolff.** Marking the beginning of this project is the towering crown of a building that houses the **Titanic Exhibition.** The shining steel of this beacon on the docks of Belfast is a sign of great things to come for this magnificent city in Northern Ireland.

The University Quarter

👍 **ULSTER MUSEUM** MUSEUM

Botanic Gardens ☎28 9042 8428 www.nmni.com/um

This museum can't decide whether it is a natural history museum, a human history museum, an art museum, or a local history museum. In fact, joyously, it is all four. Gaping Tyrannosaurus jaws will make you wonder why they seemed to have better dentists in the Jurassic era, while mummified remains might tempt you as a burial option. Prehistoric Irish river fish floating menacingly in formaldehyde will make you wonder why a minnow like Jaws was such a big deal, and sketches by Leonardo Da Vinci will put to rest any traditional artistic leanings you might have. In short, the sprawlingly extensive collection caters to any kind of whimsical desire you might find simmering within.

⇞ Just inside the Botanic Gardens, toward Queen's University. ℹ Free museum tours Tu-F 2:30pm and Su 1:30pm. $ Free. ⏰ Open July-Aug daily 10am-5pm; Sept-June Tu-Su 10am-5pm.

QUEEN'S UNIVERSITY UNIVERSITY

University Rd. ☎28 9097 5252 www.qub.ac.uk

Sprawling lawns and classic brick buildings could definitely make you wonder if you made the right university choice (i.e., the choice not to go here). While Queen's does have plenty of modern buildings, the older, central sections have to be walked through to be properly admired. We recommend calling ahead and getting a guided tour. Yes, you will be one of those touristy people intruding on a campus, but it is definitely worth the distasteful stares. If you don't want to bother with that, you can simply pick up the "Walkabout Queen's" pamphlet, which will take you through a similar route as that of the guided tours, without the obligation to tip the brochure when you're done—unless, of course, you thought the brochure was cute; then you could maybe ask it to dinner.

⇞ To get to the visitors' center, just walk through the main entrance. ℹ Tours available upon request at the Welcome Center. Tours last 1hr. $ Free. ⏰ Visitors' center open M-F 9:30am-4:30pm.

BOTANIC GARDENS PARK

Belfast Gardens Park ☎28 9031 4762 www.belfastcity.gov.uk

Not to be confused with "The Botanic Inn" sports bar across the street (serving relaxation of a different variety), the Botanic Gardens are an excellent spot to check out some scenery, watch people walk their dogs (or kids), or trot through the sweltering heat in one of the old-fashioned, Victorian greenhouses. Stay away from the center—there's a pine tree in a cage. You don't want to make it angry. You won't like it when it's angry.

⇞ Just south of Queen's University on University Rd. $ Free. ⏰ Gardens open daily 7:30am-sunset. Palm House open Apr-Sept M-F 10am-noon and 1-5pm; Oct-Mar M-F 10am-noon and 1-4pm. Last admission 15min. before close.

QUEEN'S FILM THEATER CINEMA

20 University Sq. ☎28 9097 1097 www.queensfilmtheatre.com

While there are movie theaters every few feet in the city center, get away from the popcorn-strewn minefield and fatty processed diet of Odeon, and spring for something that will remind you that movies are an artistic affair. The rich red carpet, brass door fittings, and clientele composed of well-dressed ladies and gents are worth a hundred Odeons. You are not spoon-fed entertainment; it is brought to you on a silver platter to be savored. This small theater is tucked into a building which could easily be mistaken for a townhouse, just off the main university lawn. You will be sure to catch the Sundance favorites or, at the very least, one or two flicks you've never heard of. If indie films are not your style, they usually show one or two cult favorites, like *Pulp Fiction* or the original *Rocky*. It will take old stand-bys to new heights.

✈ *From the University main gate, turn right. Turn right onto University Sq. The theater is on the left.* ℹ *Book tickets online.* Ⓢ *£6.20, students £4.* ⏰ *Open daily 6pm-late.*

CRESCENT CHURCH   CHURCH
6 University Rd.   ☎28 9024 4026 www.crescentchurch.org
As the most active church in the student community, it is interesting to peruse the Gothic architecture and imposing steps of this place at the heart of the university community. It is somewhat difficult to understand the central role of the church in a student setting without seeing, feeling, and experiencing exactly how the two work together. True, you will have your fair share of Bible bashing, but step carefully around it and look for the experience behind.

✈ *From the University main gate, turn right. The church is on the right.* Ⓢ *Donations welcome.* ⏰ *Open Tu-F 10am-4pm. Services Su 11:40am and 7pm.*

Cathedral Quarter

🖾 GOLDEN THREAD GALLERY   GALLERY
84-94 Great Patrick St.   ☎28 9033 0920 http://goldenthreadgallery.co.uk
Without question one of the most challenging and refreshing galleries of modern art, this out-of-the-way find is particularly impressive in a city where modern art is something of a rarity. While two continuously shifting exhibits occupy the main spaces, the real gem is the community art project space. It doesn't get much fresher than works finished one day, only to be on the wall the next. If there is a place to feel the glow of creativity, it is here.

✈ *From the Albert Clock, walk up Victoria St. Continue onto Dunbar Link. Turn right onto Great Patrick St. The gallery is on the left.* ℹ *Free guided tours available to book.* Ⓢ *Free entry.* ⏰ *Open Tu-F 10:30am-5:30pm, Sa 10:30am-4pm.*

BELFAST EXPOSED   GALLERY, PHOTOGRAPHY
23 Donegall St.   ☎28 9023 0965 www.belfastexposed.org
This gallery's original mission was to recount Belfast's history from local perspectives. While Belfast remains a crucial focus of plenty of exhibits, the original intent has since been extended to include sets of various other contemporary photographs. The prerequisites? They have to be intricate, interesting, and thought-provoking. You will pocket your disposable camera in shame as you see what really can be, and has been, achieved with a camera.

✈ *From St. Anne's Cathedral, turn left and walk down Donegall St. The gallery is on the left.* ℹ *Check online for current exhibitions.* Ⓢ *Free entry.* ⏰ *Open Tu-Sa 11am-4pm.*

NORTHERN IRELAND WAR MEMORIAL EXHIBITION   MUSEUM
21 Talbot St.   ☎28 9032 0392 www.niwarmemorial.org
Often, war museums become far too big, overwhelmed by the need to cover the entire breadth and depth of the realities of wartime experiences and tragedies. Usually, trying to do that ends up obscuring the real message. In this case, the intimate and real experiences of Ulster County and the rest of Northern Ireland shine through in such a way that you can truly feel the history, not simply read about it. This museum is a great monument to those men and women who were touched by the First and Second World Wars and how they overcame the dangers of the past.

✈ *From St. Anne's Cathedral, turn left and walk up Donegall St. Turn left onto Talbot St. The museum is on the right.* ℹ *Check online for current exhibitions.* Ⓢ *Free.* ⏰ *Open M-F 10:30am-4:30pm.*

northern ireland

WRITER'S SQUARE SQUARE

40 Donegall St.

Inscribed with quotes from the surprisingly numerous literary greats who hail from Belfast (including John Hewitt and CS Lewis), this central square occasionally transforms itself into the heart of cultural happenings in Belfast. With various kiosks, dancing, and maybe even impassioned poetry readings, there's a lot to see here. But, if you just need a rest from all that sightseeing or a spot to enjoy your slowly decaying sandwich, come and soak up the atmosphere in the shade of the mountainous **St. Anne's Cathedral.**

In front of St. Anne's Cathedral. ***i*** *Check online for upcoming events.*

SINCLAIR SEAMEN'S CHURCH CHURCH

Corporation Sq. ☎28 9071 5997

Bedecked in seafaring memorabilia, from the lifeboat-shaped collection boxes to the ship's shining wheel and compass, it might be a little distracting were you to come here for a service. But for a secular visit, you can enjoy the strong seafaring tradition in Belfast. Dating back to 1857, this particular church probably hosted some of the men who worked aboard the RMS *Titanic*, the fantastically ill-fated "Pride of Belfast."

From the Albert Clock, walk up Victoria St. Continue onto Dunbar Link. Turn right onto Corporation St. Turn right into Corporation Sq. ***i*** *Su services at 11am and 6:30pm.* $ *Donations welcome.* ⏰ *Open W 2-4:30pm.*

CUSTOM HOUSE HISTORIC BUILDING, SQUARE

Custom House Sq.

While the Custom House isn't exactly the most interactive sight to visit, there is certainly something to be said for sitting in its square. While doing so, you can either coo over Charles Lanyon's architectural work or you can enjoy the fact that novelist **Anthony Trollope** worked in the post office here for several years. But what you will probably be doing instead is spying on one of the many rallies, protests, or events that happen in the square, much to the chagrin of locals. Enjoy the atmosphere, even if you don't enjoy the cause.

With your back to city hall, head right on Chichester St., then turn left onto Victoria St.

ST. ANNE'S CATHEDRAL CATHEDRAL

Donegall St.

Mixing Gothic architecture with modern art installations can sometimes work in particularly interesting or arresting ways. Unfortunately, in St. Anne's Cathedral, it did not quite work out. The cavernous interior of the gaudy cathedral, with the requisite number of glowing candles and small side chapels, is broken up by the "Spire of Hope," a towering space needle jutting through the center of the ceiling and extending up into the sky above. Apparently they were trying to get the attention of someone overhead, but unfortunately all they got were some very confused birds and one perplexed aircraft.

On the corner of Donegall St. and Talbot St. 1 block south of the University of Ulster. $ *Donations welcome.* ⏰ *Open M-F 10am-4pm.*

The Titanic Quarter

TITANIC BELFAST MUSEUM

Queen's Rd. ☎28 9076 6399 www.titanicbelfast.com

This museum is a source of pride of Belfast, but hopefully this one won't sink. Vaunted as the most complete *Titanic* experience in the world, the shimmering sides and pointed prows (as they are best described) of this miracle of architecture dominate the Titanic Quarter. Once inside, though, the tourist machine will mobilize. After your (expensive) ticket has been purchased, take the escalator to the upper level, but beware, this is not an exhibit in which you are free to roam. It is an "experience" in the way that cattle herding is an "experience" for the cattle. Your cycle through the process includes a ride through a replica of the shipbuilding yards, a look out over the sea from a replica bow of the *Titanic* itself (above water), a glance at a holographic, quarrelsome first-class passenger, and then a full-blown movie dive to the wreckage. You might be struck by the amount of time spent on the engineering breakthroughs and building process compared to the more famous wreck, but as they say in Belfast "It was fine when it left us," and that is their focus. Less romantic than the movie (which you will undoubtedly want to watch afterward), but still everything you ever wanted to know about the unsinkable ship.

⚑ *From the Bridge End bridge, turn left. Walk along the riverside footpath until it ends. The museum is ahead.* **i** *Allow 2hr. to move through the exhibition. Audioguides available.* Ⓢ *£13.50, students £9.50.* Ⓣ *Open Apr-Sept M-Sa 9am-7pm and Su 10am-5pm; Oct-Mar daily 10am-5pm. Last admission 1hr. 40min. before closing.*

THE TITANIC DOCK AND PUMP HOUSE HISTORIC BUILDING
Northern Ireland Science Park, Queen's Rd.   ☎28 9073 7813 www.titanicsdock.com
Unlike the "Experience" located next door, this is a piece of real *Titanic* history. The only one, in fact, unless you happen to have the thousands of dollars necessary for a dive to the wreck itself. It is the sheer scale of the ship that really hits you here. It becomes apparent that this wasn't big in the old-fashioned sense, something which wouldn't actually seem so impressive today. No, this was a behemoth of steel and engineering. At the time, the Pump House launched the single largest ship ever to float in its day. When it was first released, it was the largest object ever moved by human beings. That's big. Wander through by yourself and enjoy the echoes of footsteps, or get the guided tour for plenty of tidbits and factoids you would have missed in the more grandiose "Experience."

⚑ *From the Bridge End bridge, turn left. Walk along the riverside footpath until it ends. Continue onto Queens Rd.* **i** *Tours commence on the hour, every hour.* Ⓢ *£4.50, students £3.60. With guided tour £4.50, students £5.40.* Ⓣ *Open M-Th 10am-5pm, F 9:30am-5pm, Sa-Su 10am-6pm.*

make it crane

Paris has the Eiffel Tower. Rome has the Colosseum. Belfast has... two industrial cranes? Yes, the Belfast skyline is a bit less architecturally refined compared with some other European cities, as two of its defining features are Samson and Goliath, the bright yellow shipbuilding cranes on Queen's Island on the largest dry dock in the world. Harland and Wolff, the industrial company who owns the pair of cranes, should probably brush up on their Biblical history—if they wanted to exude success, they probably should have went with David rather than Goliath. Samson (106m) and Goliath (96m) can collectively lift over 1600 tonnes, and while they are still used for ship repairs, they serve more as a cultural symbol than as industrial powerhouses, as Harland and Wolff has been on a downward slope. That makes sense, though, since the company has some history with things that go down—they built the *Titanic*.

HARLAND & WOLFF SHIPYARD
Queens Rd.   ☎28 9024 6609
Don't go wandering too far through here, as it remains a very active shipyard. Unless you happen to have a penchant for welding, probably best to give most of this a wide berth. But you can't be anywhere in Belfast without seeing the towering outfitting cranes **Samson and Goliath.** Indeed, there is a fair portion of

new stained glass in the city which features their yellow bulk in some corner. So wander in and get those definitive holiday snaps, while deepening your understanding of Belfast through the once single greatest employer of Belfastians in times gone by. And, yes, it is also a *Titanic* sight. It is its birthplace, in fact. For the best experience, get one of the **Laganside River Tours,** which will take you around the whole place by water.

From the Bridge End bridge, turn left. Walk along the riverside footpath until its end. Continue onto Queens Rd. The shipyard is on the right.

City Center

BELFAST CITY HALL — CITY HALL

Donegall Sq. ☎28 9032 0202 www.belfastcity.gov.uk/cityhall

Very pretty on the outside, but if you want to get at the fascinating stuff on the inside, we recommend the pro tour. Admire giant silver scepters and gawk at funny old clothing, even those still being used by a councilman. Maybe sit on the seats of all the bigwig politicos using that unusual garb or take time to touch furniture that missed the *Titanic*'s maiden voyage and wonder about their fellows at the bottom of the sea.

City Center, Donegall Sq. i Sign up for tours at reception. $ Free. ⏰ Exhibition open M-F 9am-4:30pm, Sa 10am-3:30pm. Tours M-F 11am, 2, and 3pm; Sa 2 and 3pm.

THE LINEN HALL LIBRARY — LIBRARY

17 Donegall Sq. ☎28 9032 1707 www.linenhall.com

Among the creaky bookshelves and deeply engraved reading desks, you can plunge yourself into the collected written history of Belfast and Northern Ireland. You could spend hours diving for buried factoids among dusty shelves, while all the time spying on the frolicking in Donegall Sq. below. But it is vacation time, so you probably aren't researching. In that case, come for the erudite atmosphere, strong coffee, and free Wi-Fi.

From Belfast City Hall, turn left along Wellington Pl. The library is on the right. i Free Wi-Fi. $ Donations welcome. ⏰ Open M-F 9:30am-5:30pm, Sa 9:30am-4pm.

CATALYST ARTS — GALLERY

5 College Ct. ☎28 9031 3303 www.catalystarts.org.uk

Attempting to introduce modern art in a "poly-vocal" style, Catalyst Art hosts a variety of attractions: a 24hr. cinema, a wrestling ring, and a nightclub—sometimes those last two get confused. All in all, though, the resilience of the group of artists running the gallery (they don't let managers or businessmen step in) gives it the rebellious and confrontational style we are always searching for in a gallery.

From Belfast City Hall, turn left and walk along Wellington Pl. Turn right onto Queen St. Turn left onto College Sq. Turn right onto College Ct. The gallery is on the left. i Check online for upcoming listings. $ Free. ⏰ Open Tu-Sa 11am-5pm.

ORMEAU BATHS GALLERY — GALLERY

18 Ormeau Ave. ☎28 9032 1402 www.ormeaubaths.co.uk

Housed in an old Victorian bathhouse, don't be skeptical if you see a couple tubs as you walk in the door—just hope that they're empty. The Ormeau Baths Gallery rotates between eight and 10 exhibits of all sorts throughout the year. It's a perfect space for a gallery: quiet, spacious, and full of odd echoes. You might come out feeling like you should pay a visit to a more modern bathhouse, but hopefully you'll be too concerned with the raw creativity still fresh on your canvas.

From Belfast City Hall, turn right onto Donegall Sq. Turn right onto Adelaide St. Turn right onto Ormeau Ave. The gallery is on the left. i Check online for current exhibits. Occasionally offers workshops for kids. $ Free. ⏰ Open Tu-Sa 10am-5pm.

ST. GEORGE'S MARKET MARKET

12 E. Bridge St. ☎28 9043 5704 www.belfastcity.gov.uk/stgeorgesmarket

First opened in 1890, some things about St. George's Market haven't changed—you'll still get a strong smell of raw fish and meat as you walk in the entrance, and catcalls from one vendor to another are still the norm. You'll now also find everything from handmade jewelry to pungent spices to questionable antiques. Check it out on Saturday mornings and listen to the live music that goes on right in the middle of everything.

⇞ From Belfast City Hall, turn right onto Chichester St. Turn right onto Victoria St. Turn left onto E. Bridge St. $ Prices vary. Haggle. ⏰ Open F 6am-2pm, Sa 9am-3pm, Su 10am-4pm.

GRAND OPERA HOUSE OPERA

2 Great Victoria St. ☎28 9024 1919 www.goh.co.uk

There are few opera houses you'd expect to see adorned with elephants and Hindu gods, least of all in Belfast. But indeed, inspired by England's former Indian territories, the architect of the Grand Opera House incorporated his experiences of the then-empire into this building's interior design. If you can't get in to see a show (which can be done on the cheap if you call in for standby tickets), at least try and get in to see the theater space. An elephant would never forget it.

⇞ Walk around to the back of Belfast City Hall. Turn right onto Howard St. Turn left onto Great Victoria St. The theater is on the right. ℹ Book tickets online. $ Prices vary, but expect to pay £8-30. ⏰ Box office open M-F 9:30am-5:30pm, Sa noon-5pm.

ST. MALACHY'S CHURCH CHURCH

24 Alfred St. ☎28 9032 1713

The third-oldest Catholic church in Belfast, St. Malachy's is a good place to start your Catholic education, with all the stained glass, holy water, and incense you could desire. And you won't even have to wear a plaid skirt and knee-highs. The church is not only home to believers but is also a haven for thinkers. Some time ago, the owners of a local whiskey distillery complained to the church that the peal of the bell in the tower was upsetting the distillation process. The solution? Muffle the bell, of course. *Let's Go* approves of this church's priorities.

⇞ From Belfast City Hall, turn right on Donegall Sq. Turn right onto Adelaide St. Turn left onto Alfred St. The church is on the right. ℹ Church open between services. $ Donations welcome. ⏰ Services M-F 8-9am and 1-2pm; Sa 6-7pm; Su 9:30-10:30am, 11:30am-12:30pm, 6-8pm.

ST. GEORGE'S CHURCH CHURCH

105 High St. ☎28 9023 1275 www.stgeorges.connor.anglican.org

Looking more like a Greek or Roman temple on the outside, this church shows another side to the liturgical Belfast and is this city's oldest Church of Ireland church. Opting for a simple decor (the classical exterior an obvious exception), there are still a fair number of frescoes and stained-glass windows to keep you interested.

⇞ From Belfast City Hall, walk up Donegall Sq. Turn right onto Castle Pl. Continue onto High St. The church is on the right. $ Donations welcome. ⏰ Services daily.

VICTORIA SQUARE SHOPPING CENTRE MALL, VIEWS

1 Victoria Sq. ☎28 9032 2277 www.victoriasquare.com

A mall is a mall is a mall. And a mall this is, albeit a really huge one. But if there is any shopping you need to do, here is the place. The reason it is a sight, however, is that the climb up five-plus stories to the dazzling dome at the top presents you with a panoramic view of Belfast. Get dizzy climbing the stairs or be lazy and take the elevator—personally, we're lazy.

⇞ From Belfast City Hall, turn right onto Chichester St., then turn left onto Victoria St. The mall is on the left. ℹ Get a Student VIP card for discounts at reception; valid student ID required. ⏰ Open M-Tu 9:30am-6pm, W-F 9:30am-9pm, Sa 9am-6pm, Su 1-6pm.

FOOD

Trying to pin down exactly what Irish cuisine is might take quite some time. Let's just say that it focuses on local ingredients fed in the pub-grub form. And there are Irish pubs aplenty, never fear. Should you decide to venture away from the safe confines of a memorabilia-decked bar, however, there are some savory options awaiting you.

A particular favorite around these parts is the all-day **Ulster Fry,** which includes a fried "farl" of soda bread, fried potato "farls," bacon, eggs, and sausage—all locally sourced, of course. Mix it all up and dive into the fried goodness.

The University Quarter

BOOKFINDER'S CAFE
CAFE $
47 University Rd.   ☎28 9032 8269

Long before the commercial chains started throwing coffee shops into their upper stories, this dusty bookshop was welcoming scholars from the nearby university into its tiny cafe. Let yourself be ushered through the once-loved, worn secondhand books piled high around you, before finding yourself in a small grotto among them all. There is nowhere better to sip on a latte reading your newest favorite.

✈ *From Shaftesbury Sq., walk down Bradbury Pl. Bear left onto University Rd. The cafe is on the right.* ***i*** *Free Wi-Fi.* Ⓢ *Coffee £2. Soup £4.* ⌚ *Open M-Sa 10am-5.30pm.*

BOOJUM
MEXICAN $
73 Botanic Ave.   ☎28 9031 5334   www.boojummex.com

For those familiar with the American chains like Qdoba or Chipotle, this burrito bar will have a comfortingly familiar feeling to it. But, there are some crucial differences, not the least of which happens to be its location in Northern Ireland. The number of burrito bars in Ireland would make you think St. Patrick drove them out along with the snakes. On the actual food front, the burritos are plentiful and more than a meal by themselves. We recommend trying the steak filling, with plenty of cheese and guacamole. There are also fajitas and tacos to choose from. Get your Mexican fix here, it doesn't come often.

✈ *From Botanic Station, walk left down Botanic Ave. The restaurant is on the right.* Ⓢ *Entrees £4.25-5.25. Extra fillings £0.40. Nachos £4.* ⌚ *Open M-F 11:30am-9pm, Sa noon-9pm.*

YUM
FUSION $$
157 Stranmillis Rd.   ☎28 9066 8020   www.yumbelfast.com

Fusion restaurants almost always tread a fine line between fusion and corruption, yet this particular restaurant manages to get the balance just right. Whether you are looking for a prawn and chicken stir-fry (£13) or a basic house lasagna (£10), you will undoubtedly find something worth chowing down on in here. It is a perfect choice for when everyone in your group seems to be in a different food mood.

✈ *From Shaftesbury Sq., walk down Bradbury Pl. Bear left onto University Rd. Bear left again onto Stranmillis Rd. The restaurant is on the right.* ***i*** *Special menus often replace the normal one.* Ⓢ *Entrees £8.25-16.* ⌚ *Open M-Th 9am-9pm, F-Sa 9am-10pm.*

THE MAD HATTER
BRITISH $$
2 Eglantine Ave.   ☎28 9068 3461

Join the rest of the local residents in their Sunday best for a solid fry up on a weekend morning. Ideal for soaking up the mistakes from last night, bite into the crisp fried bread and smother those sausages and bacon in plenty of ketchup. For the real experience, mix everything on your plate into one great big fried mess. Grab a paper from the rack by the door and settle in to munch contentedly, and then stay for a while longer while you try to move.

✈ *From Shaftesbury Sq., walk down Bradbury Pl. Bear right onto Lisburn Rd. Turn left onto Eglantine Ave. The cafe is on the left.* ***i*** *£5 credit card min.* Ⓢ *Ulster Fry £4.45. Entrees £4-7.50.* ⌚ *Open M-Sa 8am-6pm, Su 8:30am-5pm.*

belfast

THE BARKING DOG
FINE DINING $$$$

31 Malone Rd. ☎28 9066 1885 www.barkingdogbelfast.com

The black paw prints all over everything belie the real style and panache of this classic local restaurant. The darkened interior is held back by flickering candles, just enough light to snuggle up over a meal. True, most of the patrons are on the older side, but that only adds to the comfortably chic image. Try the homemade saffron linguini, with confit cherry tomatoes, basil, and crayfish (small £6, large £10.50).

✚ *From Shaftesbury Sq., walk down Bradbury Pl. Bear left onto University Rd. Bear right onto Malone Rd. The restaurant is on the right.* ℹ *Reservations recommended on weekends.* Ⓢ *Entrees £12-21. Pasta/salad £6-12.50.* ⌚ *Open M-Th noon-3:30pm and 5:30-10pm, F-Sa noon-3pm and 5:30-11pm, Su noon-9pm.*

MOLLY'S YARD
MICROBREWERY $$$$

1 College Green Mews, Botanic Ave. ☎28 9032 2600 www.mollysyard.co.uk

Once one of the cheaper options in the district, this little gem found its way into the Michelin guide and since then its prices have skyrocketed. But no matter, there are still some fantastically tasty morsels here, even if the lunch menu is more within your budget than the dinner one. Choose either the small homey interior or sit in the cool night air with everyone else in the cobbled courtyard. If you are stopping for a drink, try their signature chocolate stout ($3.30 per pint), for a flavor experience your palate won't soon forget.

✚ *From Botanic Station, walk left down Botanic Ave. The pub is on the left.* Ⓢ *Entrees £7.50-17.50.* ⌚ *Open M-Th noon-9pm, F-Sa noon-6pm. Evening menu available M-Th 6-9pm, F-Sa 6-9:30pm.*

CARLITO'S
ITALIAN $$$

78 Botanic Ave. ☎28 9024 2020 www.carlitosrestaurant.com

A classic Italian restaurant is never difficult to find near a college campus; enter Carlito's, which serves the classic favorites to hordes of students. True, you won't suddenly be inspired to hop on a plane to Italy, and it is not a restaurant that decided to deck itself out in memorabilia, but the pizzas are the real thing, and, for the true experience, add a Peroni alongside it—you won't be disappointed.

✚ *From Botanic Station, walk left down Botanic Ave. The restaurant is on the left.* Ⓢ *Pizzas £6.50-9.50. Entrees £9.50-16.50. Lunch £6.* ⌚ *Open M-Sa noon-10pm.*

THE HOUSE
GASTROPUB $$

12 Stranmillis Rd. ☎28 9068 2266 www.thehousestranmillis.com

While filling up with a louder population later in the night, the classic pub decor is matched with plenty of TVs, lighting up the rooms with whatever sports game happens to be on, and some solid pub classics, like Madras chicken or some truly juicy chargrilled burgers. While it isn't something you will be writing home about, it is cheap, fun, and filling.

✚ *From Shaftesbury Sq., walk down Bradbury Pl. Bear left onto University Rd. Bear left again onto Stranmillis Rd.* ℹ *Free Wi-Fi. Live music Su 8-11pm. Reservations recommended on weekends.* Ⓢ *Entrees £8-12. Burgers £8.50-10.* ⌚ *Open M-Sa 11am-1am, Su 11am-midnight.*

KOOKY'S CAFÉ
SANDWICHES, CAFE $

112 Lisburn Rd. ☎29 068 7338

Kooky's Café isn't so much "kooky" as it is a good place to get your morning coffee fix. There are some pieces of modern art adorning the walls and yes, those mirrors are wavy instead of square, but the overall feel is much more standard than its crazy name would have you believe. But, that doesn't change the quality of food. Grab a "Veggie Works" breakfast with a free-range egg and pull down the morning's paper from the rack.

✚ *From Shaftesbury Sq., walk down Bradbury Pl. Bear right onto Lisburn Rd. The cafe is on the left.* Ⓢ *Lunch sandwiches £3.25-4.25.* ⌚ *Open M-F 10am-5pm, Sa-Su 10am-3pm.*

SWEET CHILLI CANTINA $$$

54 Stranmillis Rd. ☎28 9050 9820 www.sweetchilli.weebly.com

Irish and Mexican cuisines are not two that spring to mind as a pair. However, they seem to have done an excellent job here at making the two work. The spicy Mexican flavors take on new forms and even climb to new heights when matched with local Irish ingredients. Try the spicy shredded beef sandwich topped with fried onions, cheese, and Mexican coleslaw (£10). Interesting foods are one attraction, but another is Sweet Chilli's BYOB status. You can choose your own bottles from a nearby liquor store, which will ensure that you will have a most rosily cheery evening.

From Shaftesbury Sq., walk down Bradbury Pl. Bear left onto University Rd. Bear left again onto Stranmillis Rd. The restaurant is on the left. i BYOB £2 per bottle. Free Wi-Fi. $ Entrees £10-15. ⏰ Open Tu-Sa noon-9:30pm, Su noon-6pm.

Cathedral Quarter

MADE IN BELFAST IRISH $$$

23 Talbot St. ☎28 9024 4107 www.madeinbelfastni.com

From the eclectic decor around you to the breakdown of the menu into "smalls" and "bigs," you know you have stumbled into a backpacker's paradise of a restaurant. With overstuffed pillows and wall hangings, the vibe is right—and we haven't even gotten to the food. Try the Irish dexter beef, Belfast black stout, and oyster pie (£12) for a succulent, drool-worthy, and deliciously Irish meal.

From St. Anne's Cathedral, turn left and walk down Donegall St. Turn left onto Talbot St. $ Entrees £9.50-22. ⏰ Open M-W noon-10pm, Th-Sa noon-11pm, Su noon-9pm.

THE DARK HORSE CAFE $$$

30 Hill St. ☎28 9023 7807

Outfitted in dark wood paneling, darker leather booths, and painted mirrors behind the bar, this little sister to the nearby Duke of York is reminiscent of an old-school gentlemen's club—think pipes rather than strippers. Putting some of the style back into coffeehouses, this place is perfect for a more refined sandwich at lunchtime or a proper sit-down meal in the evening before you join the fray in Commercial Ct.

From St. Anne's Cathedral, turn left along Donegall St. Turn left onto Talbot St. Turn right onto Hill St. The restaurant is on the left. $ Entrees £6.50-16.75. i Free Wi-Fi. Take-out available. ⏰ Open M-Th 9am-6pm, F-Sa 9am-1am.

WHITES TAVERN PUB $$

2-4 Winecellar Entry ☎28 9024 3080 www.whitestavern.co.uk

Tucked away in a side entry, this small public house is undoubtedly best described as a tavern. Whites Tavern has a warm heart and is full of the smell of freshly pumped Guinness and the chuckling of regulars on their well-worn wooden benches. The food is hot and pubby, just what you need on those rainy Belfast days. Sure, on weekends it swells full to bursting and even spills out onto the cobblestones, but the glowing golden light bathing the street keeps the party bright and merry.

From the top of Donegall St., turn right and follow Bridge St. to the left. Turn right onto Rosemary St. Turn left onto Winecellar Entry. The pub is on the right. i Live music F and Sa nights. $ Pints from £2. Entrees £4-12. ⏰ Open M-Th noon-11pm, F-Sa noon-1am, Su noon-11pm.

BLINKERS BRITISH $$

1 Bridge St. ☎28 9024 3330

This is a greasy spoon that serves up British home-style favorites. Blinkers is best known for their full, all-day Ulster Fry (£8), which pulls in plenty of children with eyes six or seven times the size of their stomachs. For a starving backpacker though, there isn't a much better breakfast than a huge plate piled high with fried, greasy wonderfulness. You certainly won't leave hungry.

From the top of Donegall St., turn right and follow Bridge St. to the left. The diner is on the right. *i* *Take-out available.* *$ Entrees £7-19.* *Open M-Sa 9am-7pm.*

THE CLOTH EAR PUB $$$

33 Waring St. ☎28 9026 2719 www.themerchanthotel.com

It seems almost impossible that the Merchant Hotel would have yet another offering to explorers of the Cathedral Quarter, but indeed they do. With a brightly lit bar set on light wood floorboards, this is a gastropub, but one that is not trying to be anything else. The large, white leather booths and occasional stained glass give the place exactly the right balance between restaurant and pub. It gets tirelessly busy from Thursday to Saturday, though, so either reserve a table or arrive with plenty of time to spare.

From the top of Donegall St., turn left and walk down Waring St. The pub is on the right. *i* *Live music Th. Reservations recommended for dinner.* *$ Entrees £9-19.* *Open M-W noon-11:30pm, Th-Sa noon-1am, Su 1-11:30pm.*

NICKS WAREHOUSE BISTRO $$$

35 Hill St. ☎28 9043 9690 www.nickswarehouse.co.uk

Expressionist paintings sit next to laughing family photos at this bistro-esque restaurant. With an enormous wine selection (£3-5 per glass) and a comfortable brick interior, Nicks Warehouse gives you all the frills of a high-end restaurant with none of the pretension. You'll be joining a healthy swath of people having a small bite and a swig before heading out to the teeming streets for the night.

From St. Anne's Cathedral, turn left and walk down Donegall St. Turn left onto Talbot St. Turn right onto Hill St. The bistro is on the left. *$ Entrees £8-15. Sandwiches £4. Wine £3.50-6.* *Open Tu-Sa noon-3pm and 5-10pm.*

THE CHIPPIE FAST FOOD $

29 North St. ☎28 9043 9619

Without question, the Chippie is the cheapest option around. With nothing over £3.50, we think it should be called the Cheapie. Several chip variations (that's "fries" to you Amur'can folk), including "gravy chip," "garlic chip," and "curry chip," are here to tempt. If that doesn't whet your palate, go for a ¼lb. Hawaiian burger (£2.85).

From the top of Donegall St., turn right. Turn right onto North St. The chip shop is on the right. *$ Fish £3.50. Everything else £3.* *Open M-Sa noon-11pm, Su 2-11pm.*

PRINTER'S CAFÉ CAFE $$

33 Donegall St. ☎28 9031 3406

The game plan here is char-grill it and put it in a bun. Get the Thai beef patties with Asian salad, warm pita bread, satay sauce, and Thai sweet chili sauce (£8.25). Or, if you have a need for speed before heading off to drink at the Duke of York, grab a sandwich from their take-out counter at the front of the building. The check-out line may slow you down a little, though.

From St. Anne's Cathedral, turn left and walk up Donegall St. *i* *Vegetarian options available.* *$ Lunch £4-13.* *Open M-Th noon-3pm, F noon-3pm and 5:30-9:30pm, Sa 6pm-midnight.*

2 TAPS TAPAS BAR $$$

42 Waring St. ☎28 9031 1414

No, we did not make a spelling mistake and, no, we don't know quite why it is called 2 Taps. Here, in the center of one of the most happening areas of the quarter, order yourself up some sizzling tapas from one of the wraparound booths and share a jug of sangria (£12) as it gets dark. If the night is mild, head outside to watch Waring St. start to heat up as the bars and clubs fill before diving in yourself.

From the top of Donegall St., turn left onto Waring St. The bar is on the left. *$ Lunch plates £7.50. Tapas £3.50-6.25. Entrees £12-15.* *Open Tu-Sa noon-late.*

City Center

ARCHANA
INDIAN $$

53 Dublin Rd. ☎28 9032 3713 www.archana.co.uk

With enormous plates of creamy, fragrant curries and rice, this is the Indian spot in Belfast. If an endorsement is needed, the Indian national cricket team themselves ate here when they were visiting Belfast on their world tour (apparently there is no higher endorsement as far as Indian food goes). The small size of the restaurant means that seats fill up quickly, even the rickety tables on the upper level, so arriving on the earlier side will ensure that you can enjoy your classic tikka masala with almonds and cashews (£10) like a cricketer.

⁂ *From the back side of the Belfast City Hall, turn right down Donegall Sq. Turn left onto Bedford St. Bear right onto Dublin Rd.* ⑨ *Entrees £10-12.* ⌚ *Open daily noon-2pm and 5-11pm.*

THE ALLOTMENT
BISTRO $$$$

48 Upper Queen St. ☎28 9023 3949 www.theallotment-ni.co.uk

Quality ingredients is certainly the name of the game, and the fresh fare here comes from nearby allotments and personal plantations. And they transform those local ingredients into stunning dishes of gastronomic excellence. The atmosphere remains relaxed, with light wood tables and chalkboards belying the exquisite menu, which is admittedly limited but changes frequently. While it might seem expensive at first, you are encouraged to BYOB and, with no corkage fee, you will have all the fun you want over great food with plenty of the bottle for good measure.

⁂ *From the Belfast City Hall, turn left and walk down Wellington Pl. Turn left onto Upper Queen St.* ⓘ *BYOB. Free Wi-Fi. Special student rates. Book a table online.* ⑨ *Entrees £10-17.* ⌚ *Open M-W 7:30am-6pm, Th-F 7:30am-4pm and 6-10:30pm, Sa 9am-4pm and 6-11pm, Su 9am-3pm.*

BRIGHTS RESTAURANT
BREAKFAST, CAFE $$

23 High St. ☎28 9024 5688 www.brightsrestaurantbelfast.co.uk

You know those mythical breakfast places with platters of scorchingly fried food just waiting to be slathered in ketchup and devoured by hordes of towering rugby players? Those myths are the shadowy reality of Brights. Serving all sorts of other foods throughout the day, the real find here is the "Brights Ulster Fry," a truly magnificent concoction of eggs, bacon, fried bread, black pudding, sausages, tomato, and mushrooms (to appease the herbivores). And at only £4 before noon, there is no better value across the land.

⁂ *From Belfast City Hall, walk up Donegall Sq. Turn right onto Castle Pl. Continue onto High St. The restaurant is on the right.* ⓘ *Cheap "Earlybird Breakfast" before noon.* ⑨ *Entrees £6.25-10. Full Ulster Fry £4 before noon.* ⌚ *Open M-W 9am-5:30pm, Th-F 9am-8pm, Sa 9am-5pm.*

POPPO GOBLIN
SANDWICHES $

23 Alfred St. ☎28 90246 894

A tiny sandwich shop tucked into a back street of central Belfast, the locals head here for a taste of the gourmet at less-than-gourmet prices. True, the size of the place limits the amount of real atmosphere you can pack in here, but thankfully the flavors of the food pack in enough to speak for themselves. Try the sesame chicken in spicy peanut sauce on pita (£3.25) for the biggest bang—both for your buck and your palate.

⁂ *From Belfast City Hall, turn right onto Donegall Sq. Turn right onto Adelaide St. Turn right onto Alfred St.* ⓘ *Expect a line at lunchtime.* ⑨ *Sandwiches £3.25-5.* ⌚ *Open M-Sa 9am-3pm.*

THE MORNING STAR
PUB $$

17 Pottinger's Entry ☎28 9023 5986 www.themorningstarbar.com

Part nightlife pub, part daytime restaurant, the Morning Star, while an excellent place to have a few afternoon beers or come for a slight crush in the evenings, is even better during the day because of its colossal trays of delectable fare from the overly ample buffet (£5.50). The menu changes almost daily, so if you want an updated version, you should call in, but rest assured you can expect the best local ingredients, particularly seafood, as everything is delivered fresh each day.

Walk up Donegall Pl., then turn right onto Castle St. Turn right onto Pottinger's Entry. The pub is on the right. [S] Entrees £8-15. Pints £2.50-3.10. ⏰ Open M-Th 10:30am-11pm, F-Su 10:30am-1am (you have until 1:30am to finish your drinks).

AM:PM IRISH $$$

38 Upper Arthur St. ☎28 9024 9009 www.ampmbelfast.com

Atmosphere is everything in this flowery and dark wood restaurant. Often playing host to a variety of themed nights, like a Cabaret Supper Club on Saturday, AM:PM has a touch of the Old World in its painted mirrors and plush red leather booths. During the week, you start to understand exactly what that elusive being "contemporary Irish cuisine" really is. There is fish involved.

From Belfast City Hall, turn right down Chichester St. Turn right onto Upper Arthur St. The restaurant is on the left. ⏰ Lunch plates £5-13. Pints £3.40. ⏰ Open M-Th 10am-11pm, F-Sa 10am-1am, Su noon-10pm.

THE FOUNTAIN BAR GASTROPUB $$$

16 Fountain St. ☎28 9032 4769 www.thefountainbar.com

A gastropub only in style of food, this mod-ish bar and grill brings the old favorites into the 21st century, featuring a sleek and elegant interior that matches the slate gray exterior. But there are still huge Guinness awnings on the outside to set the pub-going crowd at ease. Here's the place to go when you're looking for a great pub burger, with a fancy cocktail or Guinness on the side.

From Belfast City Hall, walk up Donegall Sq. Turn left onto Castle Ln. Turn right onto Fountain St. The pub is on the right. ℹ £5 pint and food 11:30am-7pm. Reservations for dinner recommended. [S] Entrees £8-15. ⏰ Open M-W 11:30am-9pm, Th 11:30am-11pm, F 11:30am-midnight, Sa 11:30am-11pm, Su 1-5pm.

THE LITTLE CUPCAKE CAFE CUPCAKES $$

8 Bedford St. ☎28 9024 1751 www.thelittlecupcakecafe.co.uk

Hiding just a minute's walk away from Belfast City Hall, this tiny cafe could definitely be your grandmother's house. Assuming your grandmother is awesome, that is. Flowered wallpaper and plaid couches encourage massive overconsumption of ultra-decadent cupcakes of all kinds (£1.70 each). Raspberry white chocolate? Latte? Cookies 'n' cream? Wash it all down with a deliciously swirled milkshake? Sure, just be sure to call a stretcher in case of a sugar coma.

From the back side of the Belfast City Hall, turn right and walk down Howard St. Turn left on Bedford St. The cafe is on the left. [S] Cupcakes £1.80 each. Milkshakes £2.50. Coffee £1-2. ⏰ Open M-F 8:15am-5:30pm, Sa 10:30am-5:30pm.

SARNIE'S DELI $

35 Rosemary St. ☎28 9024 8531

This is a real-deal deli. Squeeze yourself into the tiny interior, order your food (make sure you know what you want beforehand, these guys don't mess around), and you're done. None of this "atmosphere" everyone seems so keen on. How can you complain about atmosphere when this place serves up the best subs in town? Take your foot-long outside, though, or you'll be trying to get your sandwich to your mouth around somebody else's elbow.

From Belfast City Hall, walk up Donegall Sq. Continue onto Royal Ave. Turn right onto Rosemary St. The deli is on the left. ℹ Outdoor seating area available. [S] Sandwiches £3.50. Soups £2. ⏰ Open M-Sa 11:30am-11pm, Su 11am-11pm.

DOORSTEPS SANDWICHES $$

64 Ann St. ☎28 9024 3232

This is a great sandwich place with hearty breads and meats. Quick on the spot, Doorsteps allows you to grab and go with any of the cold cuts and either sit outside or take it away. The decor of the restaurant won't bolster your appetite nearly as much as the sight of the food.

From Belfast City Hall, walk up Donegall Sq. Turn right onto Castle Pl. Continue onto High St. Turn right onto Church Ln. Turn right onto Ann St. The cafe is on the right. i Vegetarian options available. $ Coffee £1.20-1.65. Sandwiches £3-4. ⏰ Open daily 7am-5:30pm.

NIGHTLIFE

Belfast's nightlife is thriving and lively, with pubs and clubs open every night of the week. The best to be found are in the **University Quarter** and the **Cathedral Quarter,** where on the weekends it'll seem like everyone from hipsters to hippies to hoary is out on the town. And that is all for the better. Belfast nightlife is not one for snobs, obnoxious drunks, or unfriendly aggression. When everyone is out, everyone wants to have a good time—nobody wants to be a buzzkill here. Toward one or two in the morning, you'll find it harder to get into clubs—and even harder to move once you get in. It isn't pumping and famous like London or Glasgow, and Dublin it certainly is not. Pints abound, Belfast at 3am sees a lot of singing, staggering, and general revelry. Taxi drivers seem to get a little bit picky in the early hours as well, so try and sober up (or at least look it) when attempting to hail a cab.

The University Quarter

THE BELFAST EMPIRE — VENUE

42 Botanic Ave. ☎28 9024 9276 www.thebelfastempire.com

Boasting two stage and bar areas, the Empire is not somewhere you go for a quick pint. With live performances advertised around the city that span from local tribute bands to classic artists, the small club's rock 'n' roll spirit is not dead. The dark wood interior is emphasized by the powerful spotlights trained on the stage. You can almost imagine you are at a petite rock concert all for you. Without even walking in, the large, stone front of the building is impressive, with plenty of gently curving balustrades and oak doors. For the most part, tickets are available on the night of, but book online to be safe.

From Botanic Station, walk left down Botanic Ave. The hall is on the left. i Check online for listings and to book tickets. $ Tickets £6-12. Beer from £3. ⏰ M-Sa 11:30am-1am.

LAVERY'S — PUB, CLUB

12-18 Bradbury Pl. ☎28 9087 1106 www.laverysbelfast.com

Everybody has heard of it and mostly everyone has been, provided they aren't living in a ditch somewhere. With three floors, Lavery's is huge. The first floor is a traditional pub bar, with a great outdoor beer garden; the second floor is a black, compact music venue and bar, with all the finesse twirling bartenders can bring; and finally, a club with spinning green strobes and a serious dance floor sits up top. Each level feels spacious…that is, until the weekends, when the crowd spills out the door. Happy hours M-Th means all drinks are £2.85. During the week, the third floor, "The Ballroom," is a fantastic pool hall, where it is not a heinous crime to be less than world-ranked.

The far end of Shaftesbury Sq., away from the City Center. $ Pints £3.20. Top 2 floors £5 cover. ⏰ Open M-Sa 11:30am-1am, Su 12:30pm-midnight.

THE ELMS — BAR, VENUE

36 University Rd. ☎28 9050 9840 www.theglobebar.com

The music is the all-important component here, mostly sticking to the classics of rock and alternative. If you are a fan of anything from Jimi Hendrix to The Black Keys, you will feel right at home in here. With all the hard rock feel, but none of the potentially upsetting grunge, true diehards might feel a bit out of place. But forget the funky-patterned wood bar…and the classy cocktails…and the perfectly arranged posters on the walls, just let the beat of those classic tracks take over as you swig something strong and sharp.

From Shaftesbury Sq., walk down Bradbury Pl. Bear left onto University Rd. The bar is on the left. ***i*** *Live music most nights.* $ *Beer from £3.20. Cocktails £5. Food £5-7.* ⏰ *Open M-W 4pm-1am, Th-Sa 7pm-1am, Su 7pm-midnight.*

CUCKOO BAR

149 Lisburn Rd. ☎28 9066 7776 www.facebook.com/cuckoobelfast

Wickedly cheerful and wildly colorful, Cuckoo makes no apologies for itself. Indeed, it proclaims its motto very clearly over the front entrance: "Stop making sense." Inside, there is a brilliantly inspired mixture of graffiti art combined with more traditional dark wood, wicker, and leather fittings. Check out the layers of artistry covering the floor from the comfort of a leather armchair. You can't beat this place on its eclecticism, its passion, or its style. And, with a theme for every night of the week, you will rarely go astray here.

From Shaftesbury Sq., walk down Bradbury Pl. Bear right onto Lisburn Rd. ***i*** *M trivia night. Tu ping-pong tournament. W open mic. Th-Sa indie, electronic, club, and house music. Su acoustic night.* $ *Pints from £3. Cocktails £4.50.* ⏰ *Open M-Sa noon-1am, Su noon-midnight.*

THE BOTANIC INN BAR, CLUB

23-27 Malone Rd. ☎28 9058 9740 www.thebotanicinn.com

Like a Swiss army knife of nightlife, "the Bot" has a little bit of everything. It gets packed on the weekends and during sporting events thanks to its reputation as Belfast's sports bar. Check out signed rugby jerseys, boxing gloves, and a shiny, shiny trophy case. On Saturday, the downstairs suddenly becomes a buzzing local watering hole, before those same customers head upstairs to the tightly packed dance floor in the club. Show up on Sunday for the carvery menu (£6) and wash it down with some local Belfast Ale. Framed photos of burly men in short-shorts abound. Don't catch the eye of the Toucan, though: there could be trouble.

From Shatesbury Sq., walk down Bradbury Pl. Bear left onto University Rd. Bear right onto Malone Rd. The bar is on the right. ***i*** *Nightclub upstairs open on the weekends from 10pm.* $ *Pints £3.10-3.60.* ⏰ *Open M-Sa 11:30am-1am, Su noon-midnight.*

QUEEN'S UNIVERSITY STUDENTS' UNION BAR, CLUB

75 University Rd. ☎28 9097 3106 www.qubsu.org

Impossible to get any more studenty than the student union, this one will make you wonder how Queen's students get any work done at all. With not one, but three bars, this complex can keep you entertained all night long, where new friends are not hard to come by. The **Speakeasy Bar** upstairs is generally the quietest of the three, but when the evening gets going, the space gets so packed that those comfy-looking chairs are a dream from long ago. Downstairs, meanwhile, there is the more lounging **Bar Sub,** with plenty of comfy couches and TVs, should you decide that you would rather not talk to your friends. Finally, there is **Bunatee Bar,** where most of the student-run organizations hold their "evening get-togethers"—over pints, of course.

From Shaftesbury Sq., walk down Bradbury Pl. Bear left onto University Rd. ***i*** *Check online for upcoming events.* $ *Pints £3-3.50.* ⏰ *Open M-Sa 8:30am-late, Su noon-midnight.*

THE EGLANTINE INN BAR

32-40 Malone Rd. ☎28 9038 1994 www.egbar.co.uk

Across the street from "the Bot" is "the Eg," a heavily student-patronized bar with chic red lighting and black leather couches. Sit near the wide windows facing the Bot and enjoy the cool darkness, a stark contrast to the other's cheery, loud merriment.

From Shaftesbury Sq., walk down Bradbury Pl. Bear left onto University Rd. Bear right onto Malone Rd. The bar is on the left. $ *Most pints £3.* ⏰ *Open M-Sa 11:30am-late, Su noon-late.*

SCRATCH CLUB

5 Lower Crescent ☎28 9050 9750 www.taphousebelfast.com

Breaking down the "clubbing experience" to its bare essentials, this particular spot focuses mostly on its sunken dance floor and plenty of panic attack-inducing light displays, going for lasers, beams, spotlights, and strobes. True, there are a few couches in the back corner for the exhausted (or maybe they are for those looking for stimulation of a different kind), but the epicenter is very much a crazy, writhing pit of wanton dancing.

➔ From Botanic Station, walk left down Botanic Ave. Turn right onto Lower Crescent. The club is on the right. $ Cover £5. Drinks £2. Mixed Drinks £4. ⏰ Open M 9pm-late, W-Su 9pm-late.

AVENUE BAR

59 Botanic Ave. ☎28 9050 9800 www.madisonshotel.com

Normally hotel bars stay on the quiet side out of respect for the well-paying customers upstairs. Well, either sound-proofing technology has come a long way or Madison's Hotel is not too worried about repeat customers, because the two-story bar below approaches late-night club status with pleasing (for us anyway) regularity. Come here for a good long drink or a mixed cocktail and enjoy the wide variety of radiant characters you can watch swing around with inhibition-releasing joy.

➔ From Botanic Station, walk left down Botanic Ave. The club is inside Madison's Hotel on the right. ℹ Guest DJs on Sa night. $ Drinks from £3.20. ⏰ Open Th-Sa 8pm-late.

Cathedral Quarter

👍 **OLLIE'S** CLUB

35-39 Waring St. ☎28 9023 4888 www.olliesclub.com

Below the undeniably opulent Merchant Hotel lies a basement that most hotels can only dream of. Low, exposed brick covers the ceilings and glowing, seductive art hangs out in the corners, while cheerful chattering can only just be heard over the bass reverberating through the tunnel walls. Here, you'll see all kinds, from students to some older folks who have definitely still got it. If all the dry ice, drums, and bass gets to be too much, take a break in the enclosed Heineken Lounge, where you can enjoy a chilled bottle of the stuff, surrounded by mounted, green-glowing bottles in the night air.

➔ From the top of Donegall St., turn left onto Waring St. The club is on the right. ℹ F-Sa 21+ only. $ M cover £3, all drinks £2.50; Th-F cover £5; Sa cover £10. ⏰ Open M 10pm-late, Th 9pm-late, F 10pm-late, Sa 9pm-late.

👍 **THE DUKE OF YORK** PUB

11 Commercial Ct. ☎28 9024 1062

You would be forgiven for thinking that the cramped entry of Commercial Court has exploded into a rowdy street party on a Saturday night. The outdoor cobblestones are flooded with light and slick with spilled drinks. A traditional pub downstairs, the Duke of York often sees its hubbub spill out into the street, whose cramped quarters would rival those of any club. If you can get there, though, the tiny upstairs club is complete with walls covered in framed Guinness ads and old portraits alike, along with spinning tinted disco lights.

➔ Walk down Donegall St. Turn right onto Commercial Ct. The pub is on the right. ℹ Buy club entrance early in the night, as they run out quickly. $ Beer from £3. ⏰ Open M 11:30am-11pm, Tu-F 11:30am-1am, Sa 11:30am-2am, Su 2-8pm.

21 SOCIAL RESTAURANT, BAR, CLUB

1 Hill St. ☎28 9024 1415 www.21social.co.uk

One of the most chic places on the block, 21 Social has three floors: the restaurant downstairs, the main bar upstairs and the VIP bar on the top floor—"Cigarette Girl," which you probably won't see unless you've got a big wad of cash in your pocket. This place will satisfy any time of day or night, so head here in the day to try the risotto with forest mushrooms and cashel bleu cheese topped with truffle foam (£9), or else go at night to join the heaving mass of the rest of Belfast.

From the top of Donegall St., turn left and walk down Waring St. The bar is on the left. $ Upstairs club cover £10-20. Entrees £9-17. ⏰ Open M-Tu noon-11pm, W noon-midnight, Th-Sa noon-1am, Su 1-9pm.

THE SPANIARD BAR

3 Skipper St. ☎28 9023 2448 www.thespaniardbar.com

Even if you can get in over the steep 25+ age requirement, you might have a difficult time squeezing into this miniature rumhouse, where there are so many people you'll worry the floor might collapse. If you manage to make your way upstairs, don't be disturbed by the omnipresent pictures of Jesus—no one quite knows why they're there, but they work oddly well as decor. Try the "Extraordinary," with Havana Cuba rum, squeezed lime, and ginger beer (£5.25).

From the top of Donegall St., turn left onto Waring St. Turn right onto Skipper St. The bar is on the right. ℹ 25+. $ Pints £3.30. ⏰ Open M-Sa noon-1am, Su noon-midnight.

THE NORTHERN WHIG BAR

2-10 Bridge St. ☎28 9050 9888 www.thenorthernwhig.com

Dominating the top of Donegall St., this large bar is housed inside an old bank building, which lends it a sprawling amount of floorspace, along with a high, echoing ceiling. During the day, these extravagances might seem somewhat presumptuous, but by the time night comes around, every inch of extra space is a blessing. Plenty of plush, scattered seating, nimble bartenders, and a diligent DJ discharging all sorts of favorites from the charts lends the place an atmosphere just shy of a club. If you're looking for a place to start your night, you just found it.

From the top of Donegall St., turn right and follow Bridge St. to the left. The bar is on the left. $ Cocktails £5.25-5.75. ⏰ Open M-Tu noon-11pm, W-Sa noon-1am, Su 1-11pm.

KREMLIN CLUB, GLBT

96 Donegall St. ☎28 9031 6061 www.kremlin-belfast.com

The self-described hottest gay experience in Europe, the Kremlin lives up to its boasts. Separated into three distinct areas, everyone will find somewhere to embrace the night regardless of their political leanings. First, there is "Tsar," the relaxed cocktail area that is most suitable for some conversation and a sweet drink before moving to the more lively areas. Next you might come to the "Long Bar," the louder alternative to the cocktail lounge—you can expect plenty of laughing and disco spinning over two levels while music blares. Finally, once courage is at its highest, ramp it up to the "Red Square," a two-level clubbing arena usually outfitted with a backdrop reflecting that night's theme. By the time you get to the arena, you will be a true member of the Party.

From the top of Donegall St., walk down Donegall St. The club is on the left. ℹ Check online for nightly themes. $ Free entry until midnight, £10 after. ⏰ Open Tu, Th-Su 10pm-2am.

BERT'S JAZZ BAR

16 Skipper St. ☎28 9023 4888 www.themerchanthotel.com

Another excellent offering from the Merchant Hotel, Bert's takes a turn back to an old world of *Mad Men* opulence, with red leather booths and small red lamps. You can be sure to find at least one fedora-clad cellist razzling up a bow, while a Ray-Ban wearing saxophonist swings out another classic. For a night of live jazz and snazzy cocktails, break out your smartest threads.

From the top of Donegall St., turn left onto Waring St., then right onto Skipper St. The bar is on the left. ℹ Live jazz F-Sa. $ Cocktails from £5. ⏰ Open M-F 5pm-late, Sa-Su noon-late.

RAIN CLUB

10-14 Tomb St. ☎78 1051 8625 www.rainnightclub.co.uk

Rain is undoubtedly a club powerhouse, spread over two-stories and complete with sunken dance floors, a packed beer garden, and a line out the door that gets long enough that you'll find yourself outside another club. While it's often praised as *the* place to be in Belfast, if it is a quiet night, you would be better off trying one of the places along Waring St. But, if packed full to bursting, this place will rage with the best of them.

➤ Near the River Lagan. ℹ Check online for night themes. M is student night. Arrive early if you want to pay a cheaper cover. $ Cover £5-10. M-Th and Su £2 drinks all night. Sa drinks full price. ⏰ Open daily 9pm-3am.

THE FRONT PAGE — PUB, CLUB

11 Donegall St. ☎28 9024 6369 www.thefrontpagebar.co.uk

One of the few remaining family-owned/operated pubs in the quarter, the Front Page is almost two different venues. The downstairs, with its tranquil atmosphere, is full of quiet beer drinking and murmured conversations covering subjects like darts, horse racing, and how tourists ruin everything. The club upstairs, on the other hand, caters to a much younger crowd that's less interested in conversing and more intent on getting as close as possible, in a thick, heavy atmosphere throbbing to punk and rock music.

➤ Near the intersection of Donegall St. and Academy St. $ Pints £3. ⏰ Open M-Sa 11:30am-1am, Su noon-11:30pm.

THE JOHN HEWITT — PUB

51 Donegall St. ☎28 9023 3768 www.thejohnhewitt.com

Housed in an old newspaper building and run by the neighboring unemployment office, this local landmark ensures all the money you spend at the Hewitt goes back to the community. With 14 different beers on tap, including drafts from all four of the local microbreweries, you'll have a hard time trying every one in a single visit. With live music six nights a week, this is a pub where you can easily while away a night.

➤ Walk down Donegall St. The pub is on the right. ℹ Live music 6 nights per week. W night "charity night." $ Pints from £3. ⏰ Open M-F 11:30am-1am, Sa noon-1am, Su 7pm-midnight.

City Center

👍 **MCCRACKEN'S** — PUB

4 Joy's Entry ☎28 9032 6711 www.mccrackenscafebar.co.uk

A newer, trendier version of the traditional Irish pub, McCracken's has substituted funky, green seats for boring bar stools and installed some portraits of famous Irish writers à la Andy Warhol. The crowd is trendier as well and tends to offer more for the well-dressed, young professionals han the older Irish regulars or crazy high school kids.

➤ Walk up Donegall Pl. and turn right onto Castle St., then right onto Joy's Entry. The pub is on the left. ℹ Su jazz night 6:30-8:30pm. $ Pints £3.15-3.25. ⏰ Open M-W 11:30am-9pm, Th-F 11:30am-11pm, Sa 11:30am-3am, Su 6:30-8:30pm.

👍 **VOODOO** — BAR, LIVE MUSIC

9-11 Fountain St. ☎28 9027 8290 www.facebook.com/VoodooBelfast

One of the best live music bars in the City Center, you can expect to be downing pints in good style at Voodoo. The downstairs bar is stylish, with red wood detailing and a full selection of whiskeys and beers. Delve farther into the venue, though, and you will quickly come across some long-haired punk rockers and beams of blue or green light exploding in a wild crowd.

➤ From Belfast City Hall, walk up Donegall Sq. Turn left onto Castle Ln., then right onto Fountain St. The bar is on the left. ℹ Check live music during the day. Free Wi-Fi. $ Prices vary depending on performance. Beer from £3.50. ⏰ Open M-Sa noon-2am.

FILTHY MCNASTY'S LOUNGE

45 Dublin Rd. ☎28 9033 3388 www.filthymcnastysbelfast.com

Mannequins in body suits and tutus guard the entrance to this hip and trendy club. An alternative crowd hangs out here, and if you wanna get really McNasty, shots are just £3.

🚶 From the back side of the Belfast City Hall, turn right down Donegall Sq. Turn left onto Bedford St. and right onto Dublin Rd. The pub is on the left. $ Pints £3.30. ⏰ Open M-W 11am-11pm, Th 11am-midnight, F-Sa 11am-1am, Su 11am-11pm.

THE STIFF KITTEN CLUB

1 Bankmore Sq. ☎28 9023 8700 www.thestiffkitten.com

On a Saturday the Stiff Kitten rivals Berlin or Amsterdam in terms of pulse-pounding tracks and streaming lights. When you get tired of dancing, head over to the Blue Bar, where you can sit down; if you really want to take a break from the sound, head next door to the SK bar, where all-age groups mingle in a much more relaxed environment.

🚶 From the Europa Hotel, turn right and walk down Great Victoria St. Turn left onto Bruce St. Turn right onto Dublin Rd. Turn right onto Bankmore Sq. The club is on the right. ℹ Come on Th and F for £1.50 and £2 drinks respectively. ⏰ Open M noon-1am, Tu noon-2am, W noon-1am, Th-F noon-2:30am, Sa noon-3am.

AUNTIE ANNIE'S PUB, LIVE MUSIC

44 Dublin Rd. ☎28 9050 1660 www.cdcleisure.net/annies.php

A stalwart standard of Central's nightlife, this particular pub venue is not nearly as sedate as its name makes it sound. If you ask us, they are severely lacking in pretzels. But we can't really complain. What else do you need apart from good food, better beer, and the best live music? Not much, to be honest (except maybe a pretzel—not that we're bitter). If you are in a more laid-back mood, though, grab a pint and sit outside on bustling Dublin Rd. before deciding that you want to have some live music blast your eardrums out of your head.

🚶 From the Europa Hotel, turn right and walk down Great Victoria St. Turn left onto Bruce St., then left again onto Dublin Rd. The pub is on the left. ℹ Buy tickets at the bar during the day. $ Prices vary depending on performance. Pints from £2.60. ⏰ Open daily noon-1:30am.

RONNIE DREW'S PUB

79 May St. ☎28 9023 0295 www.ronniedrews.com

Rebranded after a rather sordid past as Magennis's Bar, the sight of some less-than-pacifist IRA activity, Ronnie Drew's is doing an admirable job of overwriting its unfortunate history and starting fresh. You can lay back comfortably on leather couches in the huge, open-plan lounge pub, as the live Irish music playfully dances around your ears. This is a relaxed atmosphere for a relaxed night.

🚶 From Belfast City Hall, turn right onto Chichester St. Turn right onto Victoria St. Turn left onto May St. ℹ Live Irish music M and F. $ Pints from £2.60. ⏰ Open daily 11am-1am.

KELLY'S CELLARS PUB

30 Bank St. ☎28 9032 4835 www.facebook.com/kellys.cellars

A complete cliché of an Irish pub, this place could have been airlifted out of Dublin's Temple Bar. With plenty of memorabilia to keep your eyes happy, from old beer bottles to framed advertisements, you can engage in the most important pastime and do as the Irish do—drink Guinness (responsibly).

🚶 From Belfast City Hall, walk up Donegall Sq. Turn left onto Bank St. The pub is ahead. ℹ Check online for daily live music. $ Pints from £2.50. ⏰ Open daily 11am-1am.

APARTMENT BAR

2 Donegall Sq. ☎28 9050 9777 www.apartmentbelfast.com

On the top floor of Apartment, all that separates you from a nighttime view of City Hall are big glass panes. And while the exterior of City Hall is Victorian, the interior of this bar could have come straight out of 1972. Long, flat furniture and funky '70s soul music make this place a hotspot for an older, slightly more cash-heavy crowd.

✈ *From Belfast City Hall, walk to the left side of Donegall Sq. The bar is on the right.* **i** *Check online for live music listings.* ⑨ *Cocktails from £5.* 🕓 *Open M-Sa 11:30am-1am.*

LIMELIGHT
LIVE MUSIC

17 Ormeau Ave. ☎28 9032 7007

Serving the rock and alternative crowd, Limelight provides more of a live music experience than you might have found in the Cathedral Quarter. That crowd, though, is very much on the young side. Limelight is like that club everyone snuck into in high school, which is fine, provided you can deal with the gelled hair and obnoxious whine of youth. You probably won't be able to hear it over the blasting music anyway, so fear not. Go for the classic tunes, if not the company.

✈ *From Belfast City Hall, turn right onto Donegall Sq. Turn right onto Adelaide St. Turn right on Ormeau Ave. The venue is on the right.* **i** *Buy tickets in Katy Daly's pub.* ⑨ *Prices vary by performance.* 🕓 *Open daily 10pm-late, but depends on performance.*

KATY DALY'S
PUB

17 Ormeau Ave. ☎28 9032 7007

Attached to Limelight, Katy Daly's is a more laid-back alternative and usually hosts exhausted punters from the club above. They do have their fair share of music as well, though, along with pub night fallbacks, quiz nights, karaoke, and so on. The major draw here is location, though, given the club above and a less than 5min. walk to the hub on Dublin Rd.

✈ *From Belfast City Hall, turn right onto Donegall Sq. Turn right onto Adelaide St. Turn right onto Ormeau Ave. The pub is on the right.* ⑨ *Pints from £3.20. Occasional cover.* 🕓 *Open M-Sa noon-1am, Su noon-midnight.*

THE CROWN BAR
BAR

46 Great Victoria St. ☎28 9024 3187 www.crownbar.com

One of the most famous bars in Belfast, the Crown Bar has ornaments on its ornaments. This place also has a Victorian-era bar and 10 famous "snugs," or enclosed wooden booths, so you'll want to call ahead if you're with a group or want to get a snug at peak hours. Take pictures next to the impressive wood and tile work or simply get your snuggie on.

✈ *Directly across the street from the Europa Hotel.* ⑨ *Lunch menu £3-9. Pints £3.50-4.* 🕓 *Open M-W 11:30am-11pm, Th-Sa 11:30am-midnight, Su 12:30-10pm.*

ARTS AND CULTURE

🎪 BELFAST COMMUNITY CIRCUS SCHOOL
CIRCUS TRAINING

23 Gordon St. ☎28 9023 6007 www.belfastcircus.org

You're already traveling, so why not run away with the circus? Jugglers, unicycles, high-wires, "hat manipulation," and stilts—all those entirely useless and entirely entertaining skills you always secretly wanted to be incredible at, you can actually learn here. No one is going to rebuke you for clowning around. Adult classes every Wednesday night focus on a different skill and include a warm up and cool down. The school also runs Northern Ireland's only street festival, the Festival of Fools (www.foolsfestival.com).

✈ *From St. Anne's Cathedral, turn left. Turn left again onto Talbot St. Take the 1st right onto Hill St. Turn left onto Gordon St. The school is on the right.* **i** *Open to all skill levels, from "Itty Bitty" to "Pro."* ⑨ *Lessons from free to £5.* 🕓 *Lessons W 7:30-9:30pm.*

THE BLACK BOX
ARTS VENUE

18 Hill St. ☎28 9024 4400 www.blackboxbelfast.com

An established favorite in the Cathedral Quarter, this culture-heavy bar could easily be classified as nightlife in its own right. However, the variety of performance here makes it a cultural must-see. From traditional music to rock music,

belfast

intricate and incomprehensible Irish poetry readings to awkwardly hilarious stand-up comedy, dancing, drama, you get the idea: this place has it all. Just relax and enjoy a drink and some food while you take in the local flavor. Start in the downstairs cafe-bar-pizzeria, then make your way to the large venue upstairs with its lit stage and glowing faces.

➜ From the top of Donegall St., turn left down Waring St. Turn left onto Hill St. ℹ Check online for listings and ticket prices. $ Tickets £5-15. ⏰ Times vary depending on event. Cafe M-F 10am-3pm. Pizzeria 6-11pm.

THE MAC ARTS VENUE

10 Exchange St. ☎28 9023 5053 www.themaclive.com

The newest cultural center in Belfast and attached to the almost annoyingly artistic University of Ulster, this venue can do anything. From multimedia exhibits to delicate watercolors, live music events to declamations of artistic torment, this large, modern space can be adapted to suit any need. It is still an up-and-comer, however, so don't be surprised to wander into completely empty exhibition spaces. Or is that some artistic statement in and of itself?

➜ From the front of St. Anne's Cathedral, turn right. Turn right again onto Academy St. Take the 2nd right onto Exchange St. (careful, there are 2). The venue is ahead. ℹ Go online to book tickets and check listings. $ Free to Gallery. Event tickets vary, £5-20. ⏰ Box office open M 10am-7pm, Tu-Sa 10am-8pm, Su 10am-7pm. Gallery open daily 10:30am-7pm.

AN DROICHEAD CULTURAL CENTER

20 Cooke St. ☎28 9028 8818 www.androichead.com

Tasked with preserving the cultural heritage of Northern Ireland, like the language itself, this center may have seen better days. But still, the frequent live music and comedy shows in both Irish and English, will remind you that Belfast was Irish long before it was British. If you are truly a brave soul and have some time on your hands, sign up for a beginning Irish class to test your linguistic abilities. It might not help you very much in life generally, but it will certainly twist your tongue.

➜ From Botanic Station, turn left. Turn left again onto McClure St. Continue onto Cooke St., via the underpass. The center is on the left. ℹ Check listings online. $ Tickets from free to £15. ⏰ Times vary depending on event.

ULSTER HALL THEATER

34 Bedford St. ☎28 9033 4400 www.ulsterhall.co.uk

Quite the jack-of-all-trades, this famous music venue has seen the likes of everyone from **Van Morrison** and Rory Gallagher, to quite a different supergroup: the BBC Orchestra. Come in June and look for the £5 "lunchtime concerts" for a cheap shot of musical brilliance. Or, if you are in less of a cerebral and more of a brawling mood, come to watch people getting rough during the frequent boxing and wrestling matches: during most months, Sat. night is Fight Night.

➜ From the back of the Belfast City Hall, turn right onto Howard St. Turn left onto Bedford St. ℹ Check online for events listings. £1.50 surcharge for online bookings. $ Tickets £20-30. ⏰ Box office open M-Sa 10am-5pm, or 8:30pm on event days. Open before and during shows.

SHOPPING

👍 **NO ALIBIS** BOOKS

83 Botanic Ave. ☎28 9031 9601 www.noalibis.com

An aptly named bookseller specializing in crime fiction, this independent sight is a testament against the commercialization of bookshops. The electric blue front might seem a little in-your-face, but that is entirely the idea. If you have an inkling of the kind of murder mystery you happen to be feeling that day, ask one of the student employees, who will start pulling books off the shelves faster than you can follow. Along with an awesome selection, the shop also organizes a good number of book signings, readings, and even occasional live music. ⚐ *From Botanic Station, turn left and walk down Botanic Ave. The shop is on the right.* ⓘ *Check online for event listings.* Ⓢ *Books £3-20. Event tickets £5-10.* ⌚ *Open M-Sa 9am-5pm.*

FRESH GARBAGE CLOTHES
24 Rosemary St. ☎28 9024 2350

Priding itself on going against the designer clothes trend, don't expect to see any labels in here. Mostly hippie or goth clothing, you'll find that crazy purchase you know your mother would never approve of or maybe that style that you always wanted to try. Along with a clothing hunter's paradise, you can also find any number of other random things, like incense, metallic bracelets, and crazily striped socks. Try something new; worst that could happen is that you'll have to laugh at yourself. ⚐ *From the Belfast City Hall, walk up Donegall Sq. Turn right onto Castle Pl. Turn left onto Castle Arcade. Turn right onto Rosemary St. The shop is on the right.* Ⓢ *Clothes £5-25.* ⌚ *Open M-W 10am-5:30pm, Th 10am-9pm, F-Sa 10am-5:30pm, Su 1-5pm.*

ESSENTIALS
Practicalities

- **TOURIST OFFICES: Belfast Welcome Centre** is one of the only tourism offices (and by far the biggest) in Belfast and is also the only place to go for **luggage storage.** (Ⓢ£3 for up to 4 hr., £4.50 for over 4hr.) The BWC provides all the tourism info you could ever want, assistance booking tours, a gift shop, **currency exchange,** and an **internet cafe.** (47 Donegall Pl. ☎28 9024 6609 www.gotobelfast.com ⚐ From Belfast City hall, walk up Donegall Sq. The center is on the left. ⓘ Touch-screen information kiosk available. Two 24hr. ATMs located outside Belfast Welcome Centre. ⌚ Open Oct-May M-Sa 9am-5:30pm, Su 11am-4pm; June-Sept M-Sa 9am-7pm, Su 11am-4pm.)

- **TOURS:** Operating since 1992, 🟥**McComb's Tours** has the longest-running Giant's Causeway tour and their guides are friendly and knowledgable. Take the causeway tour (£25 full day, £18 express) or the City Tour (£11). 20% discount available for patrons of the International Youth Hostel, in which McComb's has their office. (22-32 Donegall Rd. ☎02890 315333 www.mccombstravel.com ⌚ Open daily 8am-10pm.) The **Titanic Walking Tour** is a 2½hr. tour that takes you on a leisurely walk through the Titanic Quarter and outlines the achievements of the designers and builders of the *Titanic* (every achievement except building a boat that floats). Purchase tickets online or at the start of the tour at Belfast Welcome Centre. (⚐ Meet outside the Titanic Exhibition. ☎790 435 0339 www.titanicwalk.com Ⓢ£10. ⌚ Tours 11am and 2pm.) **Black Cab Tours** offers taxi tours through the Falls and Shankhill neighborhoods, with a local guide to tell the history of "the Troubles." (☎7751 565 359 Ⓢ 1-2 people £25 total, 3-6 people £10 each.)

- **BANKS: Bank of Ireland.** (28 University Rd. ⓘ Two 24hr. ATMs. ⌚ Open M-Tu 9:30am-4:30pm, W 10am-4:30pm, Th-F 9:30am-4:30pm.) **First Trust Bank.** (Across the street from the front of city hall. ⓘ 2 24hr. ATMs. ⌚ Open M-Tu 9:30am-4:30pm, W 10am-4:30pm, Th-F 9:30am-4:30pm.) **Belfast Post Office** has currency exchange. (12-16 Bridge St. ☎28 9032 0337 postoffice.co.uk ⌚ Open M-Sa 9am-5:30pm.)

- **INTERNET ACCESS: Revelations** gives a discount to students and hostelers, if your hostel doesn't have internet already. (27 Shaftesbury Sq. ☎28 9032 0337 www.revelations.co.uk Ⓢ £1.10 per 15min. ⌚ Open M-F 8am-10pm, Sa 10am-6pm, Su 11am-7pm.)

- **POST OFFICES: Belfast Post Office.** (12-16 Bridge St. ☎28 9032 0337 postoffice.co.uk ⌚ Open M-Sa 9am-5:30pm.) You can also head to the **Bedford Street** branch. (16-22 Bedford St. ☎28 9032 2293 ⌚ Open M-F 9am-5:30pm.)

belfast

Emergency

- **POLICE:** (60 Victoria St. ☎845 600 8000 for switchboard, ☎999 for emergencies; www.psni.co.uk ⏰ 24hr. assistance.)
- **PHARMACY:** At **Boots,** wade through an enormous makeup section and head upstairs to get to the pharmacy. (☎28 9024 2332 www.boots.com ➜ From Belfast City Hall, walk up Donegall Sq. The pharmacy is on the left. 35-47 Donegall St. ⏰ Open M-F 8am-9pm, Sa 8am-7pm, Su 1-6pm.)
- **HOSPITALS: Belfast City Hospital.** (Lisburn Rd. ☎28 9032 9241 for switchboard, ☎999 for emergencies; www.belfasttrust.hscni.net ⏰ Open 24hr.)

Getting There

BY PLANE

Belfast International Airport (BFS; ☎28 9448 4848 www.belfastairport.com) has flights all over Europe, the US, and beyond, and hosts the following airlines: **Aer Lingus** (☎871 7185 000 www.aerlingus.com), with flights from Barcelona, Faro, Lanzarote (Arrecife), London Heathrow, Málaga, Munich, Rome, Tenerife; **Continental** (www.continental.com/uk), with flights from New York; **easyJet** (☎905 821 0905 www.easyjet.com), with flights from Alicante, Amsterdam, Barcelona, Bristol, Edinburgh, Faro, Geneva, Glasgow, Ibiza, Krakow, Liverpool, London Gatwick, London Stansted, Málaga, Newcastle, Nice, Palma de Mallorca, Paris Charles de Gaulle; **Jet2.com** (☎871 226 1 737 www.jet2.com), with flights from Blackpool, Chambery, Dubrovnik, Ibiza, Jersey, Leeds Bradford, Mahon, Murcia, Newquay, Palma de Mallorca, Pisa, Toulouse, Tenerife; **Manx2.com** (☎871 200 0440 www.manx2.com), with flights from the Isle of Man, Galway, Cork; **Thomas Cook** (☎871 895 0055 www.thomascook.com), with flights from Alicante, Antalya, Bodrum, Corfu, Cancún, Dalaman, Faro, Fuerteventura, Heraklion, Ibiza, Lanzarote, Larnaca, Las Palmas, Mahón, Monastir, Palma, Puerto Plata, Reus, Rhodes, Sanford Orlando, Sharm el Sheikh, Tenerife, Toulouse, Veronal; **Thompson Airways** (☎871 895 0055 www.thomson.co.uk), with flights from Bodrum, Bourgas, Dalaman, Grenoble, Lanzarote, Lapland, Las Palmas, Málaga, Naples, Palma de Mallorca, Reus, Tenerife. **Belfast City Airport** (BHD; ☎28 9093 9093 belfastcityairport.com) hosts **flybe.com** which runs from destinations within the UK, including London, Edinburgh, Manchester, and Glasgow.

BY TRAIN

Belfast Central Train Station takes trains from all over Northern Ireland and down to the Republic as well. Major origins include Dublin (2hr.), Londonderry (2¼hr.), and Neary (50min.). Check the website for times and prices, as both are subject to frequent change. (Central Station, E. Bridge St. ☎28 9066 6630 www.translink.co.uk ⏰ Open M-Sa 6:20am-8:10pm, Su 10am-7:30pm.)

Getting Around

Transportation cards and tickets are available at the **pink kiosks** in Donegall Sq. W. (⏰ Open M-F 8am-6pm, Sa 9am-5:20pm) and around the city.

BY BUS

Belfast has two bus services. Most local bus routes connect through **Laganside Bus Station, Queens Square.** Metro bus service (☎28 9066 6630 www.translink.co.uk) operates from Donegall Sq. Twelve main routes cover Belfast. **Ulsterbus** "blue buses" cover the suburbs. ($ Day passes £3.50. Travel within the city center £1, £2.50 beyond, under 16 £1.50). **Nightlink** buses travel from Donegall Sq. West to towns outside Belfast ($ £3.50 ⏰ Sa 1 and 2am).

BY TAXI

Metered taxis run through the city 24hr. Look for the following companies: **Value Cabs** (☎28 9080 9080), **City Cab** (☎28 9024 2000), and **Fon a Cab** (☎28 9033 3333).

BY BICYCLE

For bike rental, head to **McConvey Cycles.** (183 Ormeau Rd. ☎28 9033 0322 www.mcconvey.com *i* Helmets and locks supplied. $ £20 per day; £80 per week. £50 deposit. ⏰ Open M-W 9am-6pm, Th 9am-8pm, F-Sa 9am-6pm.)

derry ☎28

While Belfast's dark history has been well buried by now, Londonderry's is still very much alive and thriving. Whether in the enormous memorial murals commemorating the Bloody Sunday Massacre or in the bravely flying Irish flags, Londonderry's heritage will never be forgotten. Indeed, it is barely considered heritage—more like current events. However, you will find plenty of great spots to just sit and soak up the roiling atmosphere, perhaps in one of the numerous Irish pubs all around town. Or, if you are feeling more active, get up and dance the night away, jigging until you're out of breath. There is history, culture, and intense pride here, and you must feel it to understand it.

ORIENTATION

Most places in Londonderry can be located from **The Diamond,** which marks both the center of the town and the top of its major hill. From there, going down **Butcher Street** will eventually lead to the Bogside, which was the sight of the Bloody Sunday Massacre and which continues to be a resistant force against British incursion. Meanwhile, in the other direction, down **Ferryquay Street,** you will eventually reach the River Foyle Embankment, which can make for a pleasant walk. Down **Shipquay Street,** you will find the **Peace Bridge,** which leads across the river to the other, more residential half of Londonderry.

ACCOMMODATIONS

DERRY INDEPENDENT HOSTEL HOSTEL $

44 Great James St. ☎028 7128 0542 www.derry-hostel.co.uk

Greeted by Tintin and Snowy at the door, you will immediately feel at home in this friendliest of hostels. The fun-loving atmosphere is matched with a panoply of oddities from around the world scattered on every wall of the Middle Eastern-inspired reception area. If you happen to be traveling with a partner, splurge on one of the double rooms which, while not only simple and classic, are located at a second location with a quieter atmosphere and a spacious and high-tech basement kitchen. If traveling during the off-season months, you pay whatever you think is fair for your stay. What could be a better deal?

From The Diamond, walk down Shipquay St. Turn left onto Shipquay Pl. Turn right onto Waterloo Pl. Turn left onto Great James St. i Oct-Apr "Pay what you want" offer. $ Dorms weekdays £11, weekends £13; doubles £15. ⏰ Reception 24hr. Check-in 2-10pm. Check-out 11am.

PADDY'S PALACE HOSTEL $$

1 Woodleigh Terr. ☎028 7130 9051 www.paddyspalace.com

A chain of popular hostels, Paddy's Palace does its best to avoid fitting stereotypes. In this case, the interior goes for a wood-paneling and classic leather couches look, with books and board games galore. Should you feel the urge to stay in, a fully appointed kitchen and wide range of movies to choose from will

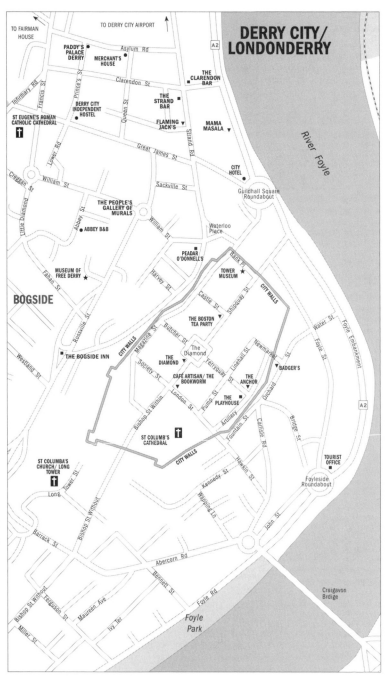

DERRY CITY/
LONDONDERRY

TO FAIRMAN
HOUSE

TO DERRY CITY AIRPORT

River Foyle

PADDY'S
PALACE
DERRY

MERCHANT'S
HOUSE

Asylum Rd

THE
CLARENDON
BAR

Clarendon St

Prince's St

THE
STRAND
BAR

DERRY CITY
INDEPENDENT
HOSTEL

FLAMING
JACK'S

MAMA
MASALA

ST EUGENE'S ROMAN
CATHOLIC CATHEDRAL

Queen St

Strand Rd

Great James St

CITY
HOTEL

William St

Sackville St

Guildhall Square
Roundabout

THE PEOPLE'S
GALLERY OF
MURALS

William St

Waterloo
Place

Abbey St

ABBEY B&B

PEADAR
O'DONNELL'S

Bank Pl

MUSEUM OF
FREE DERRY

Harvey St

TOWER
MUSEUM

CITY WALLS

BOGSIDE

Castle St

Shipquay St

THE BOSTON
TEA PARTY

Rossville St

CITY WALLS

Butcher St

The
Diamond

Linenhall St

Newmarket

Water St

Foyle Embankment

Westland St

THE BOGSIDE INN

Magazine St

Society St

THE
DIAMOND

Ferryquay St

CAFÉ ARTISAN/
THE
BOOKWORM

Pump St

THE
ANCHOR

Orchard St

BADGER'S

Foyle St

A 2

Bishop St Within

London St

THE
PLAYHOUSE

Artillery St

Fountain St

Carlisle Rd

Bridge St

ST COLUMB'S
CATHEDRAL

CITY WALLS

TOURIST
OFFICE

ST COLUMBA'S
CHURCH/ LONG
TOWER

Tower St

Kennedy St

Hawkin St

Foyleside
Roundabout

Long

Bishop St Without

Wapping Ln

Barrack St

John St

Abercorn Rd

Craigavon
Brdige

Bennett St

Bishop St Without

Ferguson St

Maureen Ave

Ivy Ter

Foyle Rd

Miller St

Foyle
Park

northern ireland

Tower Rd

Francis St

Infirmary Rd

Creggan St

Little Diamond

Fahan St

Faligan St

ensure an enjoyable night in one of the comfortably spacious dorms above. You may enjoy the atmosphere of quick travels, but not the discomfort.

➡ From The Diamond, take Shipquay St. Left onto Shipquay Pl., then right onto Waterloo Pl. Continue onto Strand Rd, then left onto Asylum Rd. ℹ Breakfast included. Free Wi-Fi. Free walking tours daily. $ Dorms £14-18; doubles £20-22. ⏰ Reception 24hr. Check-in 1pm. Check-out 10:30am.

FAIRMAN HOUSE HOSTEL $

2 Fairman Pl. ☎028 7130 8000 www.fairmanhouse.co.uk

A little bit of a trek from the center of town, this hostel prides itself on its independence and extremely comfortable beds. While perhaps not quite as well-appointed as the other two hostels, they make up for it with a cheerful, distinctly Irish atmosphere and an enormous kitchen that is frequently filled with the smell of sizzling onions on the stove. Fairman House is a good bargain for a great stay in Derry, provided you don't mind wearing in your boots a little bit more.

➡ From The Diamond, take Butcher St. Bear left onto Fahan St., right onto Rossville St., left onto Fahan St. At the traffic circle, continue onto Francis St. Left onto Academy Rd, then left onto Fairman Pl. ℹ Free Wi-Fi. $ Dorms £12; singles £16; doubles £32. ⏰ Check-in 1pm. Check-out 10:30am.

ABBEY B&B B&B $$$

4 Abbey St. ☎028 7127 9000 www.abbeyaccommodation.com

A pleasant little B&B, this one is only a stone's throw away from the recently war-torn Bogside, including the **Museum of Free Derry** and the **People's Gallery of Murals.** The rooms are extremely comfortable, perfect for a couple traveling together, and the bright, fresh feeling of the place can make for a flowery break from hostel living.

➡ From The Diamond, walk down Butcher St. Bear left onto Fahan St. Turn right onto Rossville St. Turn left onto Fahan St. Turn right onto Abbey St. The B&B is on the right. ℹ Free Wi-Fi. TVs in rooms. All rooms ensuite. $ Doubles £28-30. ⏰ Check-in 1pm. Check-out 11am.

THE MERCHANT'S HOUSE B&B $$$$

16 Queen St. ☎028 7126 9691 www.thesaddlershouse.com

The more luxurious option for a B&B in Derry, the Merchant's House's colorful walls and shiny breakfast china lend a particularly fancy air to the place while at the same time putting you at ease. The slowly collapsing Tartan sofa and the crooked drawings of local sights both add to the homey atmosphere. It is a splurge to be sure, but a welcome one for those who can afford it.

➡ From The Diamond, walk down Shipquay St. Turn left onto Shipquay Pl. Turn right onto Waterloo Pl. Continue onto Strand Rd. Turn left onto Clarendon St. Turn right onto Queen St. ℹ Breakfast included. Free Wi-Fi available. TVs in rooms. $ Doubles £50-60. ⏰ Reception 24hr.

SIGHTS

THE MUSEUM OF FREE DERRY MUSEUM

55 Glenfada Park ☎028 7136 0880 www.museumoffreederry.org

The tragedy of local history is never far beneath the surface in Derry. The feelings of oppression, subjugation, and, yes, occupation, are simmering, though no longer boiling. After seeing the 100th defiant Irish flag or the 13 crosses of Bloody Sunday, you will feel a need to understand exactly what all the discord is about, and this museum is dedicated to helping you do just that—if from a very one-sided point of view. But they make no apologies for their perspective, and you will very likely emerge from the small gallery wondering how on earth this was allowed to happen so recently and how the British got away with it in the first place. This museum is completely unmissable, but just remember to take it with a fistful of salt.

➡ From The Diamond, walk down Butcher St. Bear left onto Fahan St. Turn right onto Rossville St. Turn left at Glenfada Park. ℹ Free Derry tours daily Oct-Mar 10am, 2pm; Apr-Sept 10am, noon, 2pm; July-Aug 10am, 2, 4pm. $ £3, concessions £2. With tour £6/5. ⏰ Open Apr-July M-F 9:30am-4:30pm, Sa 1-4pm; July-Sept M-F 9:30am-4:30pm, Sa-Su 1-4pm; Oct-Mar M-F 9:30am-4:30pm.

TOWER MUSEUM MUSEUM

Union Hall Pl. ☎028 7137 2411 www.derrycity.gov.uk/Museums/Tower-Museum

The local history museum of the town, this ambitious project tells the story of the area from the time of the first signs of human habitation through to the peace process following the Northern Irish conflict. While the enormity of scope might limit the amount of coverage each intervening event receives, there is just enough to emerge feeling completely, comfortably informed about the place. An especially impressive collection details the wreck of *La Trinidad Valencera*, one of the Spanish Armada's ships, and its ensuing discovery and excavation by Derry divers. Fittingly, the top of the museum provides unparalleled panoramic views of the modern town as you gaze out over the comfortingly constant River Foyle.

⇄ From The Diamond, walk down Shipquay St. Turn left onto Union Hall Pl. The museum is on the left. $ £4, concessions £3. ⏰ Open Tu-Sa 10am-5pm. Last entry 30min. before close.

THE PEOPLE'S GALLERY MURALS

Rossville St.

A lasting statement of the group known as the "Bogside Artists," these enormous murals, often covering entire sides of houses, commemorate the war-torn era of Derry rebellion. They ensure that locals never forget, and the defiant black flag over the sign reading, "You are now entering Free Derry," tells the whole story.

⇄ From The Diamond, walk down Butcher St. Bear left onto Fahan St. Turn right onto Rossville St. Continue down Rossville St.; the murals are on the left. ℹ The Free Derry tours, which includes the murals, depart from the Museum of Free Derry.

ST. COLUMB'S CATHEDRAL

CATHEDRAL

17 London St.   ☎028 7126 7313 www.stcolumbscathedral.org

Less obviously revolutionary than other sights in Derry, this church was at the epicenter of the religious divisions between the residents of Derry. Today, those divisions are buried, but the church remains a towering edifice, with plenty of stained glass, organ pipes, and ominously frequent flowered memorials.

🔗 From The Diamond, walk down Ferryquay St. Turn right onto Pump St. The cathedral is ahead at the end of the street. Ⓢ £2. 🕘 Open Mar-Oct M-Sa 9am-5pm; Nov-Feb M-Sa 9am-4pm.

CITY WALLS

WALLS

Encircles The Diamond   ☎028 7126 7284 www.derryswalls.com

The old structures made of fortress-like bricks are all that remain of Derry's old defenses. Walk around the entire perimeter of the town on its ramparts, from which you can see most of the major sights of Derry. Look out over the Bogside and imagine the marching protesters amongst the murals, then arrive at the uncomfortable realization that the cannon you are sitting on was made in London.

🔗 Choose any of the main streets leading away from The Diamond. Climb to the walls via steps beside any of the gates. 𝒊 Download a walking tour MP3 of the Walls online. Ⓢ Free.

FOOD

🦑 MAMA MASALA

INDIAN, ITALIAN $$$

24 Queens Quay   ☎028 7126 6646 www.mamamasala.net

Mama Masala serves up two popular cuisines, even if they don't exactly go together. As with most Indian restaurants, the menu is all-encompassing, but you might not suspect that you could get a very decent pizza to go along with your curry. Thanks to the ridiculously large number of options as well as the fantastically large portions, you won't go hungry here. Go for something creamy with chicken tikka and you won't be disappointed by the sputtering, fragrant pot brought to the table with plenty of naan along with it. Or else decide on pizza or pasta, both as truly Italian as you can expect in Northern Ireland.

🔗 From The Diamond, walk down Shipquay St. Turn left onto the Foyle Embankment. Continue onto Queens Quay. The restaurant is on the left. Ⓢ Entrees £8.45-17. 🕘 Open daily 11am-10pm.

BOSTON TEA PARTY

TEA ROOM $

15 Craft Village   ☎028 7126 0329

Sit back in the cozy Craft Village in this traditional tea room, complete with chintzy chairs and lacy curtains. If you are feeling traditional, order the tea and scone ($2.50), which come readily prepared with an enormous dollop of cream and just enough jam to make its presence known. It is as deliciously classic as anyone could want.

🔗 From The Diamond, walk down Shipquay St. Turn left into The Craft Village. The shop is ahead. Ⓢ Cakes £1-3. Sandwiches £3-5. 🕘 Open M-Sa 9am-5:30pm.

FLAMING JACK'S

STEAKHOUSE $$$$

31 Strand Rd.   ☎028 7126 6400

The fiery sounds and smells of sizzling meats, still vigorously spitting as they come to the table, are top of the order here. Don't try to play the hero when the waiter informs you that the frying pan he places in front of you is "very hot"; it is, and you could go home with a scorched hand rather than a warm belly. For the house favorite, try the barbecue ribs ($15), smothered in sauce and still crackling as you tuck in.

🔗 From The Diamond, walk down Shipquay St. Turn left onto the Foyle Embankment. Bear left onto Great James St. The restaurant is ahead. Ⓢ Entrees £8.45-20. 🕘 Open M-Sa noon-10:30pm.

derry

BADGER'S PUB $$$

16 Orchard St. ☎028 7136 0763

Serving up traditional pub grub in a dark atmosphere of wood and stained glass, this is the perfect place to unwind over a pint of something strong while basking in the amber glow of pub traditionalism. Try the steak and Guinness pie (£13) for a beautifully flaky and creamy experience.

*➜ From The Diamond, walk down Ferryquay St. Turn left at Linenhall St. The pub is on the right. **i** Live music F-Sa. [$] Entrees £6-20. ⏰ M-Th noon-7pm, F-Sa noon-9pm, Su noon-4pm.*

THE DIAMOND PUB $$

23 The Diamond ☎028 7127 2880 www.jdwetherspoon.co.uk/home/pubs/the-diamond

You can always find a decent pub meal here, even after most other places stop serving. While it won't be the most inspiring grub, they offer good deals on a burger and pint (£5), or "club" meals for specials of the day (£5). The pub atmosphere, along with a cross-section of the population—from the grizzled older patrons to the more screeching hen parties—makes for a relatively agreeable experience.

*➜ Directly adjacent to The Diamond. **i** Free Wi-Fi. [$] Entrees £9-15. ⏰ Open daily 8am-11pm.*

NIGHTLIFE

👍 **PEADAR O'DONELL'S** PUB

59 Waterloo St. ☎028 7137 2138 www.peadars-gweedorebar.com

Positively crammed with memorabilia, this is definitely the place to be in Derry. With a sterling reputation for unbelievably good live Irish music and a thriving business that attracts tourists and locals alike, expect yourself to be pressed against the wall the entire night (assuming you even make it in, that is). If you are looking for a more contemporary scene, head to the brother pub next door, the **Gweedore,** for a more rock 'n' roll night out.

*➜ From The Diamond, walk down Shipquay St. Turn left onto Castle St. Turn right down Waterloo St. **i** Live music most nights. [$] Pints £2.80-3.40. ⏰ Open M-Sa 11am-late, Su 12:30pm-midnight.*

MASON'S BAR

10 Magazine St. ☎028 7136 0177

Boasting live music every night of the week, this darkened spot is popular with the younger student crowd from the surrounding area. While it might seem a little intimidating at first—when everyone suddenly looks at you as you walk in—persevere, and soon enough you will be accepted into the fold.

*➜ From The Diamond, walk down Shipquay St. Turn left onto Castle St. Turn right onto Magazine St. **i** Live music every night. Cash only. [$] Pints £2.80-3.50. ⏰ Open daily 11am-late.*

THE BOGSIDE INN PUB

21 Westland St. ☎028 7126 9300

Right at the heart of the Bogside, we challenge you to count the number of Irish flags you see around this pub. Undeniably a local joint, you will get a brutal shot of the bloody Derry history looking around at the walls. It can be a cozy pub to nurse a pint, however, provided you don't wear any British flags.

➜ From The Diamond, walk down Butcher St. Bear left onto Fahan St. The pub is on the left. [$] Pints £2.80-3.50. ⏰ Open daily 11am-late.

THE CLARENDON BAR BAR

44 Strand Rd. ☎028 7137 3014

More of a saloon than the traditional Irish pubs that you see scattered around, this one boasts plenty of bright brass, some plumply cushioned stools, and lots of TVs to watch the latest games. Probably not the best locale for a late night out, but definitely the place to curl up around a brew and whisper quietly into someone's ear.

*➜ From The Diamond, walk down Shipquay St. Turn left onto Shipquay Pl. Turn right onto Waterloo Pl. Continue onto Strand Rd. The bar is on the right. **i** Cash only. Live music some nights. [$] Beer*

£2.80-3.50. ☑ Open M-Sa 11:30am-1am, Su 1pm-midnight.

THE STRAND BAR   BAR, CLUB
35 Strand Rd.   ☎028 7136 6910

One of the very few nightclubs in Derry, this particular one gets the attention of all would-be club-goers lavished upon it. True, this can mean that you might run across one or two more shady characters, but all in all, the throbbing live music and flux of colored lights will ensure that the shine for the evening doesn't tarnish away. Go for a quick dance after a more sparkling time at one of the many pubs available.

*⚲ From The Diamond, walk down Shipquay St. Turn left onto Shipquay Pl. Turn right onto Waterloo Pl. Continue onto Strand Rd. **i** Live music most nights. ⓢ Cover for club £5. ☑ Open M 3-4pm and 8-11pm, Tu 8pm-3am, W 3pm-1am, Th 1-10pm, F 9-10am and 3pm-1am, Sa-Su 1pm-2am.*

SHOPPING

🔲 THE CRAFT VILLAGE   VILLAGE
Shipquay St.   ☎028 7126 0329 www.derrycraftvillage.com

Offering a haven for independent artists and boutique shops, the Craft Village is where you can find any number of cool things to send home to mom. For the truly souvenir-minded, check out **The Irish Shop** for all of the hand-knit Irish sweaters you can never afford. Otherwise, take a break in one of the many tea rooms in the traditional, old stone buildings around here. You will feel oh-so-bohemian.

⚲ From The Diamond, walk down Ferryquay St. ⓢ Prices vary.

THE DONEGAL SHOP   IRISH
8 Shipquay St.   ☎028 7126 6928

You know that wool sweater you absolutely promised all your friends back home when you left on your Irish adventure? Well, this is the place where you will finally find it. With everything from blankets to sweaters to throws to mittens, all the fine wools you could ever ask for cover the inside of this shop. We half-expect to see Mrs. Weasley in the corner.

*⚲ From The Diamond, walk down Ferryquay St. **i** Other hours available by appointment. ⓢ Prices vary. ☑ Open M-Sa 10am-6pm.*

AUSTIN'S   INDEPENDENT DEPARTMENT STORE
The Diamond   ☎028 7126 1817 www.austinsstore.com

The self-proclaimed "Oldest Department Store in the World," Austin's tries to emulate the style and class of some of its (younger) competitors, like Harrods (London) or Jenners (Edinburgh). The only problem with this idea seems to be that it is located in the middle of Londonderry and has been usurped by the far cheaper options in the nearby shopping center. Like Harrods, go for the experience and enjoy its status as a cornerstone of Derry for 200 years…even if you don't buy anything.

*⚲ Adjacent to The Diamond. **i** Cafe in the basement, restaurant on the top floor. ☑ Open M-Th 9:30am-5:30pm, F 9:30am-7pm, Sa 9:30am-5:30pm, Su 1-5pm.*

ESSENTIALS
Practicalities

- **TOURIST OFFICE: Londonderry Visitor Centre** provides all the useful information you could want. (44 Foyle St. ☎028 7126 7284 www.derryvisitor.com ⚲ From The Diamond, walk down Ferryquay St., then bear left onto Bridge St., then bear left. The center is ahead. **i** Free travel literature. Bureau de Change available. Bike lockers available. ☑ Open M-F 9am-5pm, Sa 10am-5pm.)

- **CURRENCY EXCHANGE:** Available at both the **Tourist Information Office** and the **Post Office** during their normal opening hours.
- **INTERNET ACCESS: Claude's Internet Cafe.** (4 Shipquay St. ☎ 028 7127 9379 ℹ Free Wi-Fi. ⏰ Open daily 9am-6pm.) **Londonderry Library.** (35 Foyle St. ☎ 028 7127 2310 www.ni-libraries.net/libraries/derry-central-library ℹ Free computers available. ⏰ Open M 8:30am-8pm, Tu 8:30am-5:30pm, W 8:30am-5:30pm, Th 8:30am-8pm, F 8:30am-5:30pm, Sa 9:30am-4:30pm.)
- **POST OFFICE: Park Avenue Post Office.** (10 Academy Terr. ☎ 028 7126 7896 postoffice.co.uk ⏰ Open M-F 8:45am-5:30pm, Sa 9am-12:30pm.)
- **POSTAL CODE:** BT47

Emergency

- **POLICE: Strand Road Police Station.** (81A Strand Rd. ☎0845 600 8000, for switchboard or ☎999, for emergencies www.psni.co.uk ⏰ 24hr. assistance.)
- **HOSPITAL: Altnagelvin Area Hospital.** (Glenshane Rd. ☎028 7134 5171, for switchboard or ☎999, for emergencies www.westerntrust.hscni.net ⏰ Open 24hr.)
- **PHARMACY: Boots Pharmacy.** (47 Great James St. ☎028 7126 7399 www.boots.com ⏰ Open M-F 9am-6pm.)

GETTING THERE

By Plane

City of Derry Airport (LDY; ☎028 7181 0784 www.cityofderryairport.com) receives flights from Tyrone and Donegal in the Republic of Ireland. **Flybe** offers flights from Manchester; **Ryanair** from Birmingham, Faro, Glasgow, London Stansted, Liverpool, and Tenerife. There is a bus service, the **Airporter** (☎028 7126 9996 www.airporter.co.uk), that takes you to the city center in about 25min. ($ £5, £8 round-trip.)

By Bus

Translink provides bus service to other major cities via its Goldline Express Service into **Londonderry Bus Station. Number 212** arrives from Belfast every 2hr. 24hr a day. **Number 274** arrives from Dublin several times per day. There is also a **Bus Éireann** service that runs from Sligo, Galway, and the rest of the island's west coast. Check online at www.translink.co.uk for more details.

By Train

Waterside Railway Station (☎028 7134 2228 www.translink.co.uk) receives most incoming trains. The station serves most of the county, but the main service is one from Belfast every 2hr. operated by Northern Ireland Rail.

GETTING AROUND

By Bus

County bus services are operated by **Ulsterbus** (24 Foyle St. ☎028 7126 2261 www.translink.co.uk) and operate from the Londonderry Bus Station. ($ Day passes £2.30. Travel within the city center £1.)

By Taxi

Metered taxis run through the city 24hr. **City Cabs Derry** (☎028 7126 4466); **Derry Taxis** (☎028 7126 0247); **Waterside Taxis** (☎028 7134 5858).

ESSENTIALS

You don't have to be a rocket scientist to plan a good trip. (It might help, but it's not required.) You do, however, need to be well prepared, and that's what we can do for you. Essentials is the chapter that gives you all the nitty-gritty you need to know for your trip: the hard information gleaned from 50 years of collective wisdom and several months of furious fact-checking. Planning your trip? Check. Where to find Wi-Fi? Check. The dirt on public transportation? Check. We've also thrown in communications info, safety tips, and a ☑phrasebook, just for good measure. Plus, for overall trip-planning advice from what to pack (money and as little underwear as possible) to how to take a good passport photo (it's physically impossible; consider airbrushing), you can also check out the Essentials section of www.letsgo.com.

So, flick through this chapter before you leave so you know what documents to bring, while you're on the plane so you know how you'll be getting from the airport to your accommodation, and when you're on the ground so you can find a laundromat to solve all your 3am stain-removal needs. This chapter may not always be the most scintillating read, but it just might save your life.

greatest hits

- **DON'T SMUGGLE IN ANY DRUGS.** Um, duh. Drug use is a major problem in Ireland and they will not be lenient with you if you are caught (p. 199).

- **BE WARY OF TERRORISM.** Although terrorism is less of a concern than it was during the height of the Troubles, it is still an issue in Ireland (p. 199).

- **NORTHERN IRELAND IS NOT THE SAME AS THE REPUBLIC OF IRELAND.** When people talk about the country "Ireland," they are typically referring to the Republic of Ireland, which uses the euro and the metric system. Northern Ireland is part of the UK, which uses the pound and the British Imperial system (p. 197, p. 203).

- **SHIP SOUVENIRS HOME BY SURFACE MAIL.** Our thrilling "By Snail Mail" section will tell you how (p. 202).

planning your trip

entrance requirements

- **PASSPORT:** Required for visitors from all countries except EU citizens (as well as those from Iceland, Liechtenstein, Norway, and Switzerland) who can show their national ID.

- **VISA:** Not required for citizens of most Western countries, including the US, Canada, Australia, the UK, and New Zealand. Required for citizens of many eastern European, Asian, and African countries. For country-specific information, go to www.dfa.ie/home/index.aspx?id=8777.

- **WORK PERMIT:** Required for citizens of non-EEA (European Economic Area) countries—except Switzerland—planning to work in Ireland.

DOCUMENTS AND FORMALITIES

We're going to fill you in on visas and work permits, but don't forget the most important one of all: your passport (which, if you are a citizen of a non-EEA country, must not expire for at least six months from the date of entry). **Don't forget your passport!**

Visas

Those lucky enough to be citizens of countries in the EU, Australia, Canada, New Zealand, and the US do not need a visa to globetrot through Ireland for up to 90 days. Those intending to stay for longer than 90 days must apply for a long-term visa; consult an embassy or consulate for more information. Citizens of certain eastern European, Asian, and African countries will need a visa to enter Ireland. A comprehensive list of the countries that require visas can be found at www.dfa.ie/home/index.aspx?id=8777. If you do need a visa to enter Ireland, note that a Schengen visa will not be adequate. Ireland opted out of the Schengen arrangement in order to maintain their Common Travel Area arrangement with the UK. The advantage of this is that non-EU citizens can visit Ireland without eating into the 90-day limit on travel within the Schengen area. Some travelers have been known to use Ireland as a convenient location for "stopping the Schengen clock" and extending their Eurotrip. The only real disadvantage of Ireland's non-Schengen status is that you will be subject to border controls on entry, so don't forget your passport.

Double-check entrance requirements at the nearest embassy or consulate of Ireland (listed below) for up-to-date information before departure. US citizens can also consult http://travel.state.gov.

Entering Ireland to study does not require a special visa if you do not need a visa to enter the country in the first place. Citizens of non-EEA countries who plan to spend more than three months studying in Ireland will need to register with the local immigration officer in the area in which they intend to live after arrival. If you do need a visa to enter Ireland and you plan to study there for less than three months, you should apply for a **D study visa.** If you plan to study in Ireland for more than three months, you should apply for a **C study visa.** A visa will typically cost about €60. For more information, see the **Beyond Tourism** chapter.

essentials

- **IRISH EMBASSY IN AUSTRALIA: Embassy.** (20 Arkana St., Yarralumla, ACT 2600 ☎+61 262 73 37 41 www.embassyofireland.au.com ☒ Open M-Th 9:30am-12:45pm and 2-5pm, F 9:30am-12:45pm and 2-4pm.)

- **IRISH EMBASSY IN CANADA: Embassy.** (Suite 1105, 130 Albert St. Ottawa, Ontario K1P 5G4 ☎+1 613-233-5835 www.embassyofireland.ca ☒ Open M-F 10am-12:30pm and 2-4pm.)

- **IRISH CONSULATE IN NEW ZEALAND: Consul General.** (7th fl., Citigroup Bldg., 23 Customs St. E., Auckland 1010 ☎+64 99 77 22 52 ☒ Open M-F 8:30am-5pm.)

- **IRISH EMBASSY IN THE UK: Embassy.** (17 Grosvenor Pl., London SW1X 7HR ☎+44 020 72 35 21 71 www.embassyofireland.co.uk ☒ Open M-F 9:30am-5pm.)

- **IRISH EMBASSY IN THE US: Embassy.** (2234 Massachusetts Ave. NW., Washington, DC 20008 ☎+1 202-462-3939 www.embassyofireland.org ☒ Open M-F 9am-1pm and 2-4pm.)

- **AUSTRALIAN EMBASSY IN IRELAND: Embassy.** (7th fl., Fitzwilton House, Wilton Terr., Dublin ☎+353 1 664 5300 www.ireland.embassy.gov.au ☒ Open M-F 8:30am-4pm.)

- **CANADIAN EMBASSY IN IRELAND: Embassy.** (7-8 Wilton Terr., Dublin 2 ☎+353 1 234 4000 www.canadainternational.gc.ca ☒ Open M-F 9am-1pm and 2-4:30pm.)

- **NEW ZEALAND CONSULATE IN IRELAND: Consulate.** (PO Box 9999, Dublin ☎+353 1 660 4233 www.nzembassy.com/united-kingdom.)

- **BRITISH EMBASSY IN IRELAND: Embassy.** (29 Merrion Rd., Ballsbridge, Dublin ☎+353 1 205 3700 www.britishembassyinireland.fco.gov.uk/en ☒ Open M-Th 9am-12:45pm and 2-5:15pm, F 9am-12:45pm and 2-5pm.)

- **AMERICAN EMBASSY IN IRELAND: Embassy.** (42 Elgin Rd., Ballsbridge, Dublin ☎+353 1 668 9946 www.dublin.usembassy.gov ☒ Open M-F 8:30am-5pm.)

Work Permits

Unless you are a citizen of an EEA country, admittance to Ireland as a traveler does not include the right to work, which is authorized only by a work permit. For more information, see the **Beyond Tourism** chapter.

money

EURO VS. POUND

When traveling in Ireland, the first thing you need to know is that the Republic of Ireland and Northern Ireland do not use the same currency. The Republic of Ireland uses the euro, while Northern Ireland uses the pound sterling.

embassies and consulates in northern ireland

- **BRITISH CONSULATE IN AUSTRALIA: Consulate.** (Commonwealth Ave., Yarralumla, ACT 2600 ☎+61 02 62 70 66 66 www.ukinaustralia.fco.gov.uk ☼ Open M-F 8:45am-12:30pm and 1:30-5pm.)

- **BRITISH CONSULATE IN CANADA: Consulate.** (80 Elgin St., Ottawa, Ontario K1P 5K7 ☎+1 613-237-1530 www.ukincanada.fco.gov.uk ☼ Open M-F 8:30am-5pm.)

- **BRITISH CONSULATE IN NEW ZEALAND: Consulate.** (Level 17, 151 Queen St., Auckland 1010 ☎ +64 9 303 2973 www.ukinnewzealand.fco.gov.uk ☼ Open M-F 9am-5pm.)

- **BRITISH EMBASSY IN THE US: Embassy.** (845 Third Ave., New York, NY 10022 ☎+1 212-745-0200 www.ukinusa.fco.gov.uk ☼ Open M-F 9am-5pm.)

- **AUSTRALIAN EMBASSY IN THE UK: Embassy.** (Australia House, Strand, London WC2B 4LA ☎+44 020 7856 1563 www.uk.embassy.gov.au ☼ Open M-F 9am-4pm.)

- **CANADIAN CONSULATE IN NORTHERN IRELAND: Consulate.** (Unit 3, Ormeau Business Park, 9 Cromac Ave., Belfast BT8 2JI, PO Box 405 ☎+353 28 91 27 20 60 www.canadainternational.gc.ca ☼ By appointment.)

- **NEW ZEALAND CONSULATE IN NORTHERN IRELAND: Consulate.** (The Ballance House, 118A Lisburn Rd., Glenavy, Co. Antrim BT294NY Northern Ireland ☎+44 71 35 84 35 www.nzembassy.com/united-kingdom)

- **AMERICAN CONSULATE IN NORTHERN IRELAND: Consulate.** (Danesfort House, 223 Stranmillis Rd., Belfast BT9 5GR ☎+44 28 90 68 13 01 www.belfast.usconsulate.gov/index.html ☼ Open M-F 8:30am-5pm.)

- **IRISH EMBASSY IN THE UK: Embassy.** (17 Grosvenor Pl., London SW1X 7HR ☎+44 020 7235 2171 www.embassyofireland.co.uk ☼ Open M-F 9:30am-5pm.)

GETTING MONEY FROM HOME

Stuff happens. When stuff happens, you might need some money. When you need some money, the easiest and cheapest solution is to have someone back home make a deposit to your bank account. Otherwise, consider one of the following options.

Wiring Money

Arranging a **bank money transfer** means asking a bank back home to wire money to a bank in Ireland. This is the cheapest way to transfer cash, but it's also the slowest and most agonizing, usually taking several days or more. Note that some banks may only release your funds in local currency, potentially sticking you with a poor exchange rate; inquire about this in advance. In Ireland, bank transfers can take up to eight days. Remember that you will need identification—typically a passport—to collect your money.

Money transfer services like **Western Union** are faster and more convenient than bank transfers—but also much pricier. Western Union has many locations worldwide. To find one, visit www.westernunion.com or call the appropriate number: in Australia ☎1800 173 833, in Canada 800-235-0000, in the UK 0808 234 9168, in the US 800-325-6000, or in Ireland 1800 395 395. Money transfer services are also available to **American Express** cardholders and at selected **Thomas Cook** offices.

essentials

US State Department (US Citizens Only)

In serious emergencies only, the US State Department will help your family or friends forward money within hours to the nearest consular office, which will then disburse it according to instructions for a US$30 fee. If you wish to use this service, you must contact the Overseas Citizens Services division of the US State Department. (☎+1 202-501-4444, from US 888-407-4747.)

WITHDRAWING MONEY

ATMs are widely available all across Ireland, but if you are traveling to a particularly rural area, stock up on cash before heading out. You should not have a problem accessing your personal bank account while in Ireland, but you should always check with your local bank at home to make sure that their systems are compatible with those used abroad. ATMs get the same wholesale exchange rate as credit cards, but there is often a limit on the amount of money you can withdraw per day (usually around US$500). There is typically also a surcharge of US$1-5 per withdrawal. American Express cards work at some ATMs, whereas MasterCard and Visa are the most frequently accepted.

To use a debit or credit card to withdraw money from a cash machine (ATM) in Europe, you must have a four-digit Personal Identification Number (PIN). If your PIN is longer than four digits, ask your bank whether you can just use the first four or whether you'll need a new one. Credit cards don't usually come with PINs, so if you intend to hit up ATMs in Europe with a credit card to get cash advances, call your credit card company before leaving to request one.

the euro

Despite what many dollar-possessing Americans might want to hear, the official currency of 16 members of the European Union—Austria, Belgium, Cyprus, Estonia, Finland, France, Germany, Greece, the Republic of Ireland, Italy, Luxembourg, Malta, the Netherlands, Portugal, Slovakia, Slovenia, and Spain—is the euro.

Still, the currency has some important—and positive—consequences for travelers hitting more than one eurozone country. For one thing, money-changers across the eurozone are obliged to exchange money at the official, fixed rate and at no commission (though they may still charge a small service fee). Second, euro-denominated traveler's checks allow you to pay for goods and services across the eurozone, again at the official rate and commission-free. For more info, check a currency converter (such as www.xe.com) or www.europa.eu.int.

TIPPING

Some restaurants in Ireland figure a service charge into the bill; some even calculate it into the cost of the dishes themselves. The menu often indicates whether or not service is included. If gratuity is not included, consider leaving 10-15%, depending on the quality of the service. Tipping is not necessary for most other services, such as taxis and concierge assistance, especially in rural areas. In most cases, people are usually happy if you simply round up the bill to the nearest euro. But if a driver is particularly courteous and helpful, consider tipping 5-10%. Hairdressers, at least for women, are typically tipped 10% of the bill. Never tip in pubs—it's considered condescending. In general, do not tip bartenders, though some bartenders at hip urban bars may expect a tip; watch and learn from other customers.

TAXES

Both the Republic and Northern Ireland charge a value added tax (VAT), a national sales tax on most goods and some services. In the Republic, the 23% VAT does not apply to many foods, health services, insurance and banking services, and children's clothing. A reduced VAT of 9% is added to restaurant meals. The VAT is almost always included in listed prices. The British rate, applicable to Northern Ireland, is 20% on many services (such as car rental, hairdressers, hotels, and restaurants) and on all goods (except food, children's clothing, medicine, medical supplies, and books). The prices stated in *Let's Go* include VAT unless otherwise noted. Refunds are available only to non-EU citizens and only for goods taken out of the country. In Ireland, VAT refunds are available on goods from stores displaying a "Cashback" sticker (ask if you don't see one). Request a voucher with your purchase, which you must present at the Cashback service desk in the Dublin or Shannon airport. Purchases greater than €635 must be approved at the customs desk. Your money can also be refunded by mail.

Visitors to Northern Ireland can get a VAT refund on goods taken out of the country within three months of purchase through the Retail Export Scheme. Look for signs like "Tax Free Shopping" or "Tax Free for Tourists" and ask the shopkeeper about minimum purchases (usually €65-130) and get a form. Keep purchases in carry-on luggage so a customs officer can inspect the goods and validate refund forms. Some places give on-the-spot refunds, but most require that you mail the stamped forms back to the store in the envelope provided.

safety and health

GENERAL ADVICE

In any type of crisis, the most important thing is to **stay calm.** Your country's embassy abroad is usually your best resource in an emergency; registering with that embassy upon arrival in the country is a good idea. The government offices listed in the **Travel Advisories** feature at the end of this section can provide information on the services they offer their citizens in case of emergencies abroad.

Local Laws and Police

Crime in Ireland is relatively low, though crowded or touristy areas attract pickpockets and thieves. In the Republic of Ireland, the police force is An Garda Síochána—typically referred to as the guards or Gardai (pronounced "gar-dee"). If you are the victim of a crime or need to report a crime, the Gardai are generally the people to turn to for help, but the Irish Tourist Assistance Service is also available to aid you. This nationwide service offers support and assistance to victimized visitors and can be reached by calling ☎+353 189 036 5700. In Northern Ireland, there is a single territorial police force, known as the Police Service of Northern Ireland (PSNI). In case of emergency, dial ☎999. This emergency number works in both the Republic of Ireland and Northern Ireland (in the Republic, ☎112 also works). Besides the PSNI, you can contact Victim Support Northern Ireland, a service that provides support and assistance to victims of crime, witnesses, and their families ☎+44 028 90 24 40 39. Call the Victim Support line ☎+44 084 53 03 09 00 if it is after 5pm, the weekend, or a public holiday.

If you're traveling throughout Ireland by car, there's no need to worry about security checkpoints; there are no longer border checkpoints throughout the Republic of Ireland and Northern Ireland.

Drugs and Alcohol

The Republic of Ireland and Northern Ireland both regulate the possession of recreational drugs, with penalties ranging from a warning to lengthy prison sentences. Possession of marijuana results in a fine, though repeated offenses can result in prosecution. Harder substances are treated with severity. If you carry prescription drugs with you, have a copy of the prescription and a note from a doctor readily accessible at country borders. The drinking age, 18 in both the Republic of Ireland and Northern Ireland, is more strictly enforced in urban areas. While there is no national legislation prohibiting drinking in public, local authorities may pass by-laws enforcing such a policy. Drinking is banned in many public places in Northern Ireland. Contact the local authority for more information.

SPECIFIC CONCERNS

Demonstrations and Political Gatherings

Although sectarian violence is dramatically less common than it was in the height of the Troubles, some neighborhoods and towns still experience unrest during sensitive political times. It's best to remain alert and cautious while traveling in Northern Ireland, especially during Marching Season, which reaches its height July 4-12. August 12, when the Apprentice Boys march in Derry, is also a testy period, so be cautious when traversing urban areas during this time. The most common form of violence is property damage, and tourists are unlikely targets (beware of leaving a car unsupervised, however, if it bears a Republic of Ireland license plate). In general, if traveling in Northern Ireland during marching season, prepare for transport delays and for some shops and services to be closed. Vacation areas like the Glens and the Causeway Coast are less affected. Use common sense in conversation and, as in dealing with any issues of a different culture, be respectful of locals' religious and political perspectives.

Border checkpoints have been removed, and armed soldiers and vehicles are less visible in Belfast and Derry. Do not take photographs of soldiers, military installations, or vehicles; the camera will be confiscated and you may be detained for questioning. Taking pictures of political murals is not a crime, although many people feel uncomfortable doing so in residential neighborhoods. Unattended luggage is always considered suspicious and is liable to confiscation.

Terrorism

Terrorism has become a serious international concern, but it is enormously difficult to predict where or when attacks will occur. Northern Ireland has its own domestic terrorist organizations. Most of these terrorist organizations set out to cause maximum monetary damage but minimum casualties. Travelers are almost never targeted, and, since the Good Friday Agreement in 1998, terrorism has ceased to be a major

safety and health

concern for most Irish people, even in the North, though Troubles-related violence still occurs—especially during the summer Marching Season.

Travelers should gather as much information as possible before and during their trips. The US Department of State website (www.travel.state.gov) is a good place to research the current situation anywhere you may be planning to travel. The UK Civil Contingencies Secretariat website at www.ukresilience.gov.uk features updates and warnings for citizens of and travelers to the UK. Depending on the circumstances, you may want to register with your home embassy or consulate when you arrive. The box (see above) lists contacts and webpages with updated government travel advisories.

PRE-DEPARTURE HEALTH

Matching a prescription to a foreign equivalent is not always easy, safe, or possible, so if you take **prescription drugs,** carry up-to-date prescriptions or a statement from your doctor stating the medications' trade names, manufacturers, chemical names, and dosages. Be sure to keep all medication with you in your carry-on luggage. It is also a good idea to check if the drugs you may need during your trip have different names in Ireland. For example, what is referred to as acetaminophen (brand name: Tylenol) in the US is known as paracetamol in Europe. A common brand name for this drug in Ireland is Panadol. Pseudoephedrine, a decongestant, is commonly known as Sudafed. Ibuprofen (known as Advil, Motrin, etc. in the US) is commonly referred to as Nurofen in Ireland.

Immunizations and Precautions

Travelers over two years old should make sure that the following vaccines are up to date: MMR (for measles, mumps, and rubella); DTaP or Td (for diphtheria, tetanus, and pertussis); IPV (for polio); Hib (for *Haemophilus influenzae* B); and HepB (for Hepatitis B). For recommendations on immunizations and prophylaxis, check with a doctor and consult the **Centers for Disease Control and Prevention (CDC)** in the US (☎+1 800-232-4636 www.cdc.gov/travel) or the equivalent in your home country.

keeping in touch

BY EMAIL AND INTERNET

Hello and welcome to the 21st century, where you're rarely more than a 5min. walk from the nearest Wi-Fi hotspot, even if sometimes you'll have to pay a few bucks or buy a drink for the privilege of using it. In Irish cities, Internet access is available in cafes, hostels, and usually in libraries. Though Internet is readily available in cities, it can often be hard to find in rural Donegal and Kerry. One hour of internet costs about €3-6 (an ISIC may win you a discount). Look into a county library membership in the Republic (€2.50-3), which will give you unlimited access to participating libraries and their Internet connections. Such membership is particularly useful in counties where Internet cafes are sparse, like Donegal, Kerry, and Mayo. For lists of cybercafes in Ireland, check out www.irelandyes.com/internet/html.

BY TELEPHONE

Calling Home from Ireland

If you have internet access, your best—i.e., cheapest, most convenient, and most tech-savvy—means of calling home is probably our good friend ▓Skype (www.skype.com). You can even videochat if you have one of those new-fangled webcams. Calls to other Skype users are free; calls to landlines and mobiles worldwide start at US$0.023 per minute, depending on where you're calling.

For those still stuck in the 20th century, **prepaid phone cards** are a common and relatively inexpensive means of calling abroad. Each one comes with a Personal Identification Number (PIN) and a toll-free access number. You call the access number and then follow the directions for dialing your PIN. To purchase prepaid phone cards, check online for the best rates; www.callingcards.com is a good place to start. Online providers generally send your access number and PIN via email, with no actual "card" involved. You can also call home with prepaid phone cards purchased in Ireland. Swiftcall phone cards or other prepaid Irish phone cards (available at post offices and newsstands) can score you great rates after 9pm, Irish time—often as low as €0.15-0.20 per minute. In Northern Ireland, Northern British Telecom Phonecards, in denominations of UK£2, £5, £10, and £20, are sold at post offices and newsstands, and are accepted at most public phones.

Another option is a **calling card,** linked to a major national telecommunications service in your home country. Calls are billed collect or to your account. Cards generally come with instructions for dialing both domestically and internationally.

Placing a collect call through an international operator can be expensive but may be necessary in case of an emergency. You can frequently call collect without even possessing a company's calling card just by calling its access number and following the instructions.

Cellular Phones

Cell phones are widely available in Ireland and if you are traveling for more than a few weeks, buying a cheap cell phone will likely be less expensive than using phone cards. For example, you can buy a cell phone from Tesco for €20 and load it with "pay as you go" minutes (€5-20).

The international standard for cell phones is **Global System for Mobile Communication (GSM).** To make and receive calls in Ireland, you will need a GSM-compatible phone and a **SIM (Subscriber Identity Module) card,** a country-specific, thumbnail-sized chip that gives you a local phone number and plugs you into the local network. Many SIM cards are prepaid, and incoming calls are frequently free. You can buy additional cards or vouchers (usually available at convenience stores) to "top up" your phone.

For more information on GSM phones, check out www.telestial.com. Companies like **Cellular Abroad** (www.cellularabroad.com) and **OneSimCard** (www.onesimcard.com) rent cell phones and SIM cards that work in a variety of destinations around the world.

international calls

To call Ireland from home or to call home from Ireland dial:

- **1. THE INTERNATIONAL DIALING PREFIX.** To call from **Ireland, New Zealand,** or the **UK** (including **Northern Ireland**), dial ☎00; from A**ustralia,** ☎0011; and from **Canada** or the **US,** ☎011.

- **2. THE COUNTRY CODE OF THE COUNTRY YOU WANT TO CALL.** To call the **Republic of Ireland**, dial ☎353; the **UK** (including **Northern Ireland**), ☎44; **Australia,** ☎61; **Canada** or the **US,** ☎1; and for **New Zealand,** ☎64.

- **3. THE LOCAL NUMBER.** If the area code begins with a zero, you can omit that number when dialing from abroad.

BY SNAIL MAIL

Sending Mail Home from Ireland

The Irish postal service is both reliable and speedy. **Airmail** is the best way to send mail home from Ireland. Write "Par Avion - By Airmail" clearly in the top left hand corner of your envelope. Always put your return address on the reverse side of your Airmail. The maximum weight for Airmail is typically 2kg. For simple letters or postcards, airmail tends to be surprisingly cheap, but the price will go up sharply for weighty packages. **Airsure** is slightly faster and more expensive than Airmail; packages sent to the US will arrive in about six days. Surface mail is by far the cheapest, slowest, and most antiquated way to send mail. It takes one to two months to cross the Atlantic and one to three to cross the Pacific—good for heavy items you won't need for a while, like souvenirs you've acquired along the way.

Receiving Mail in Ireland

There are several ways to arrange pickup of letters sent to you while you are in Ireland, even if you do not have an address of your own. Mail can be sent via **Poste Restante** (General Delivery) to almost any city or town in Ireland with a post office and it is fairly reliable. Address Poste Restante letters like so:

Colin FARRELL
Poste Restante
Dublin, Ireland

The mail will go to a special desk in the central post office (in Dublin, it is located at 1 O'Connell St., just north of the Liffey) unless you specify a local post office by street address or postal code. It's best to use the largest post office, since mail may be sent there regardless. Bring your passport (or other photo ID) for pickup; there is no fee. If the clerks insist that there is nothing for you, ask them to check under your first name as well. *Let's Go* lists post offices in the **Practicalities** section for each city and most towns. It is usually safer and quicker, though more expensive, to send mail express or registered. If you don't want to deal with Poste Restante, consider asking your hostel or accommodation if you can have things mailed to you there. Of course, if you have your own mailing address or a reliable friend to receive mail for you, that will be the easiest solution.

essentials

TIME DIFFERENCES

The UK and Ireland are on Greenwich Mean Time (GMT). GMT is 5hr. ahead of New York, 8hr. ahead of Vancouver and Los Angeles, 10hr. behind Sydney, and 12hr. behind Auckland, although the actual time differences depend on daylight saving time. Both the UK and Ireland observe daylight saving time between the last Sunday of March and the last Sunday of October. Don't accidentally call your mom at 5am!

climate

Because Ireland is surrounded by ocean, temperature extremes are avoided, rendering this island's climate fairly mild. The southeastern coast is relatively dry and sunny, while western Ireland is considerably wetter and cloudier. July and August are the warmest months, but May and June are the sunniest. December and January are very rainy and cold. Year-round, take heart—cloudy mornings often clear by noon. But this does not mean that you should leave your slicker at home. It would be quite an anomaly to make it through a trip to Ireland without encountering a downpour of epic proportions. Whether you take note of the weather or not, though, you better be ready to put in your witty two cents, as it is a major conversation topic among the locals.

MONTH	AVG. HIGH TEMP.		AVG. LOW TEMP.		AVG. RAINFALL		AVG. NUMBER OF WET DAYS
January	7°C	45°F	2°C	36°F	71mm	2.8 in.	17
February	8°C	46°F	2°C	36°F	52mm	2.0 in.	15
March	10°C	50°F	3°C	37°F	51mm	2.0 in.	14
April	12°C	54°F	5°C	41°F	43mm	1.7 in.	14
May	14°C	57°F	7°C	45°F	62mm	2.4 in.	14
June	18°C	64°F	9°C	48°F	55mm	2.2 in.	15
July	19°C	66°F	11°C	52°F	66mm	2.6 in.	17
August	19°C	66°F	11°C	52°F	80mm	3.1in.	17
September	17°C	63°F	10°C	50°F	77mm	3.0 in.	17
October	14°C	57°F	7°C	45°F	68mm	2.7 in.	15
November	10°C	50°F	4°C	39°F	67mm	2.6 in.	17
December	8°C	46°F	3°C	37°F	77mm	3.0 in.	19

To convert from degrees Fahrenheit to degrees Celsius, subtract 32 and multiply by 5/9. To convert from Celsius to Fahrenheit, multiply by 9/5 and add 32. The mathematically challenged may use this handy chart:

°CELSIUS	-5	0	5	10	15	20	25	30	35	40
°FAHRENHEIT	23	32	41	50	59	68	77	86	95	104

measurements

Like the rest of the rational world, the Republic of Ireland uses the metric system. The basic unit of length is the meter (m), which is divided into 100 centimeters (cm) or 1000 millimeters (mm). 1000m make up one kilometer (km). Fluids are measured in liters (L), each divided into 1000 milliliters (mL). 1L of pure water weighs one kilogram (kg), the unit of mass that is divided into 1000 grams (g). One metric ton is 1000kg. Although the Republic of Ireland generally uses the metric system, beer continues to be sold by the pint, while spirits are sold by smaller imperial measures. In Northern Ireland, the British Imperial system is used. Distances are measured in inches, feet, and miles; weights are measured in ounces, pounds, and stones; and liquids are measured in pints and gallons. Gallons in the US and those in Northern Ireland are not identical: one US gallon equals 0.83 Imperial gallons. Pub aficionados will note that an Imperial pint (20oz.) is larger than its US counterpart (16 oz.).

MEASUREMENT CONVERSIONS	
1 inch (in.) = 25.4mm	1 millimeter (mm) = 0.039 in.
1 foot (ft.) = 0.305m	1 meter (m) = 3.28 ft.
1 yard (yd.) = 0.914m	1 meter (m) = 1.094 yd.
1 mile (mi.) = 1.609km	1 kilometer (km) = 0.621 mi.
1 ounce (oz.) = 28.35g	1 gram (g) = 0.035 oz.
1 pound (lb.) = 0.454kg	1 kilogram (kg) = 2.205 lb.
1 fluid ounce (fl. oz.) = 29.57mL	1 milliliter (mL) = 0.034 fl. oz.
1 gallon (gal.) = 3.785L	1 liter (L) = 0.264 gal.

language

English and Irish are the two official languages of the Republic of Ireland. Government affairs and business are generally conducted in English. Although English is the first language for the majority of Ireland's inhabitants, Irish continues to hold constitutional status as the national and first official language of the Republic. To keep Irish from dying out, all schools that receive public money in the Republic must require students to study the language. In Northern Ireland, Irish is an officially recognized minority language.

let's go online

Plan your next trip on our spiffy website, **www.letsgo.com.** It features full book content, the latest travel info on your favorite destinations, and tons of interactive features: read blogs from our trusty Researcher-Writers, browse our photo library, watch exclusive videos, check out our newsletter, find travel deals, follow us on Facebook, and buy new guides. Plus, if this Essentials wasn't enough for you, we've got even more online. We're always updating and adding new features, so check back often!

essentials

IRELAND 101

Whether or not the romantic fantasies are true, Ireland is considered the land of Saint Patrick, four leaf clovers, mad-hot drinking skills, and potato famines. But delve deeper, intrepid explorers, and what you will discover underneath the free-flowing Guinness is a land full of fascinating history, charming people, a fanatical obsession with Gaelic football, and folklore that puts the Grimm Brothers to shame. There is no need for Irish luck because your adventures and encounters here will be enough to warm both your heart and your stomach (perhaps aided by the pubs galore).

facts and figures

- **PERCENTAGE OF IRISH THAT ARE ROMAN CATHOLIC:** 88%
- **LONGEST PLACE NAME IN IRELAND:** Muckanaghederdauhaulia (it's in County Galway)
- **NUMBER OF HOURS IT TOOK A DUBLINER TO MAKE THE THEN-NONENSE WORD "QUIZ" KNOWN THROUGHOUT 1830S:** 48

history

PREHISTORY (8000 BCE-400 CE)

The first known inhabitants of Ireland arrived around 8000 BCE from continental Europe, most likely via a land bridge. These hunter-gatherers led a nomadic lifestyle until about 4000 BCE, when agriculture was introduced. These inhabitants created a great deal of pottery, earthen mounds, and other forms of primitive architecture. Especially representative of ancient Ireland are the stone, house-like structures (called cists) that were made entirely by hand and continue to decorate the country today.

Metal became the new stone during the **Bronze Age**, around 2000 BCE, and the **Iron Age**, around 600 BCE. The Bronze Age saw the production of many elaborate gold and bronze ornaments, tools, and weapons. As the Iron Age progressed, a small group of Celtic-speaking tribal societies infiltrated Ireland. The gradual blending of Celtic and pre-Celtic indigenous cultures resulted in the emergence of Gaelic culture by the fifth century. The Celts also brought to Ireland their taste for lopping off enemies' heads and nailing them over the door of their huts. Classy, right?

SAINT PATRICK, VIKINGS, AND NORMANS (400-1495)

By 400 CE, seven independent kingdoms had evolved in Ireland. These kingdoms often allied their armies to raid neighboring Roman Britain and the continent. On one of these raids, a 16 year-old lad was captured, returned to Ireland, and sold into slavery. Rather than whiling away his spare time hunting wild animals and girls (or whatever normal 16 year-old lads did back then), this boy spent his years of enslavement studying religion. Once he escaped at age 22, he began a lifelong quest of converting the Irish to Christianity. This lad was none other than Ireland's patron saint, **Saint Patrick**.

Accompanying the spread of Christianity, was an expansion in the study of Latin learning and Christian theology. Irish missionaries traveled to Continental Europe to spread their beliefs, and scholars from other countries came to Irish monasteries. This period of Insular Art produced such treasures as the Book of Kells (an illuminated Gospel book in Latin), the Ardagh Chalice (a large, two-handled silver cup), and many of the carved stone crosses that adorn the island.

In the ninth and 10th centuries, the Golden Age of Irish scholasticism was interrupted by **Viking** invasions, as scholarly work often is. Viking attacks and raids went on for over a century, destroying Saint Patrick's precious monasteries. Eventually these Vikings built settlements on the island, many of which grew into important cities, including Dublin, Limerick, Cork, and Wexford.

432 CE
Saint Patrick introduces the Roman alphabet to Ireland (or so some historians claim).

1348
Arrival of the Black Death. Gaelic Irish also becomes dominant language. No relationship between the two.

1759
Arthur Guinness starts brewing his trademark ale. Millions around the world rejoice.

The invasions, however, did not end there. In 1169, an invasion of **Norman** mercenaries marked the beginning of more than seven centuries of Norman and English rule in Ireland.

From the end of the 12th century to around 1400, many Normans from England moved to Ireland, settling in the eastern areas, particularly around Dublin. Even though some Normans assimilated, strife persisted between the native Irish and the colonists. The Kilkenny Act was enacted in 1367 to keep the two populations separate.

TUMULTUOUS ENGLISH RULE (1495-1801)

Over the next few centuries, the English increased their control over Ireland and decided to settle down for a nice, long occupation. In 1495, Henry VII extended English law to Ireland and assumed supremacy over the existing Irish government. Over the next couple of decades, however, the effective rulers of Ireland and many of their allies openly rebelled against the crown. By 1536, Henry VIII resolved once and for all to bring Ireland under English governmental control so that Ireland could not become a base for future rebellions and attacks against England. He upgraded Ireland from a lordship to a full kingdom, and Henry VIII was proclaimed King of Ireland at a meeting of the Irish parliament in 1541. As made clear by the women (and the food) in his life, Henry VIII was not easily satisfied. Next, he wanted to extend the control of the English Kingdom of Ireland over all of its claimed territory. This process took nearly a century and was marked by internal conflicts between independent Irish and Old English lords.

From the mid-16th into the early 17th century, the English government played favorites, confiscating land from Irish Catholic landowners and giving it to Protestant settlers from England and Scotland through a series of policies known as Plantations.

Alongside land reforms, the 17th century was also marked by extreme violence, with Ireland suffering 11 years of warfare. It began with the **Rebellion of 1641**, when the Irish Catholics rebelled against the domination of English and Protestant settlers. The Catholics briefly ruled the country until Oliver Cromwell reconquered Ireland on behalf of the English. By the end of the conflict, up to a third of Ireland's pre-war population was dead or in exile. Following the bloodshed, Ireland became the main arena for battle during the **Glorious Revolution of 1688**, during which the Irish Catholics fought to reverse the Penal Laws and land confiscation policy.

Irish antagonism towards the English was further aggravated by the economic situation in Ireland in the 18th century, when two frigid winters led to a **famine** between 1740 and 1741. Without the all-powerful potato or any aid from English rulers, about a million people died of starvation or disease. This led to a great migration of Irish to countries abroad, such as the US.

1800
Ireland's population almost twice as large as that of the US.

1859
Irish scientist John Tyndall correctly explains why the sky is blue.

history

1996
Divorce is now legal. Finally.

2000
US's population about 60 times as large as that of Ireland.

AUTONOMY (FINALLY?) (1801-1922)

Following the famine, Catholic Ireland gradually increased in prosperity. But along with this success came a growing awareness of the greater demand for national self-government. The Catholics slowly gained parliamentary power, and in 1801, the British and Irish parliaments enacted the Acts of Union. This merger created a new political entity called the United Kingdom of Great Britain and Ireland.

With the Irish fixated on their goal of full national sovereignty (and the sovereign potato) another potato blight, along with the political and economic factors of the time, led to the second of Ireland's "Great Famines." Again, this famine led to mass starvation and emigration. The situation got so bad that hungry Irish Catholics converted to Protestantism in exchange for British soup, earning themselves the disdainful title "soupers."

As Ireland slowly recovered from its second Great Famine, there were additional efforts to gain home rule (a demand for self-government within the United Kingdom of Great Britain and Ireland) and better living conditions (including, presumably, finding an alternative for the potato). There were also movements for land reform and efforts to make Gaelic the official language of Ireland once again.

The **Home Rule Act** was passed in 1914, which would have given Ireland some autonomy, but it was suspended for the duration of World War I. The period from 1916 to 1921 was marked by political upheaval and turmoil. From 1919 to 1921, the **Irish Republican Army (IRA)** waged a guerilla war (the Irish War of Independence). Amidst the fighting, the Fourth Government of Ireland Act of 1920 implemented Home Rule while separating the island into what was termed "Northern Ireland" and "Southern Ireland." The terms of the war-ending truce abolished the Irish Republic (Southern Ireland) and created the Irish Free State. This established the formal independence of all 26 of the Irish Free State's counties. The free state renamed itself Ireland in 1937 and declared itself a republic in 1949.

AUTONOMY (FINALLY!) (1922-1948)

But not so fast, Ireland. The Fourth Government of Ireland Act of 1920 led to even more problems. The decision to sever the Union divided the Republican movement into anti-Treaty (those who wanted to fight on until an Irish Republic was achieved) and pro-Treaty (those who accepted the Free State as a first step towards full independence) supporters. Between 1922 and 1923, the opposing sides fought the bloody **Irish Civil War,** but ultimately, the treaty stood.

From 1922 to 1937, the Irish Free State existed against the backdrop of the Great Depression and the growth of dictatorships in mainland Europe. In contrast with many contemporary European states, Ireland remained a democracy. This was reflected when power peacefully changed hands in the 1932 general election. The outcome of this election signaled a turning point and indicated that considerable parts of Irish society accepted the rule and existence of the Irish Free State.

Unlike many other states during this period, the Free State remained financially solvent as a result of low government expenditure; however, unemployment and emigration was high. The population declined to a low of 2.7 million in the 1961 census.

At the same time, the Roman Catholic Church exerted powerful influence over Irish society, forbidding divorce, pornography, contraception, and abortion, as well as encouraging the censoring and banning of many forms of media.

Ireland remained neutral during WWII, and though this saved the state from many of the horrors of the war, tens of thousands of Irishmen volunteered to serve with the British forces. Ireland was also badly hit by food rationing and coal rationing in particular.

In 1937, a new Constitution of Ireland was drawn up, re-establishing the state as Ireland. A republic in all but name, it remained formally within the British Commonwealth. This lasted only 11 years before the ties with the Commonwealth were completely severed and the **Republic of Ireland** was born (finally!) in 1948.

THE REPUBLIC TODAY (1948-PRESENT)

During the 1960s, under Taoiseach (Prime Minister of Ireland) Sean Lemass's government, Ireland underwent a series of economic reforms, including the provision of free secondary education in 1968. Additionally, Ireland sought admission to the European Economic Community, but since 90% of its exports were going to the United Kingdom, it was not admitted until the UK was in 1973.

Global economic troubles in the 1970s, augmented by a set of misjudged economic policies (including those of Prime Minister Jack Lynch) caused the Irish economy to stagnate. Along with economic troubles, there was also social and political unrest. There were sectarian conflicts in Northern Ireland between the Nationalists, Catholics who wanted Northern Ireland to unite with the Irish Republic, and the Unionists, Protestants who were loyal to Great Britain. This revived the **Provisional Irish Republican Army (PIRA)**, whose violent attempts were aimed at the creation of a new Irish Republic. The civil unrest marked a period called **The Troubles** and did not officially end until 1998, when a peace agreement was signed.

The 1980s were marked by prosperous economic and social growth, driven by solid economic policies and investment from the European Community. During this period, Ireland had one of the highest growth rates in the world, with mass immigration (particularly from Asia and Eastern Europe) in the late 1990s. This period came to be known as the **Celtic Tiger**. Property values rose by a factor of four between 1993 and 2006, in part fuelling the boom.

Economic growth accelerated alongside social liberalization. During the 1980s and 1990s, Irish society adopted liberal social policies, such as the legalization of divorce and the decriminalization of homosexuality. Major scandals within the Roman Catholic Church, both sexual and financial, coincided with a widespread decline in religious practice, which saw weekly attendance at Roman Catholic Mass fall by half over the course of 20 years.

In the last 15 years, Ireland's economy has become modern and industrial, generating substantial national income that has benefited the entire nation. Formerly an agriculture society, the "Celtic Tiger" has become a leader in high-tech industries.

However, the 2007-2008 global economic crisis led Ireland into a recession in 2008, which again produced higher unemployment and led to stagnant growth rates. The economic malaise was mostly due to a housing bubble that burst, leading to insolvent banks and bad debt that caused the financial sector to nearly collapse. In November 2010, Ireland sought and received a $113 billion (85 billion Euro) bailout package from the European Union and the IMF to shore up its funds. Due to economic pressures, Prime Minister Brian Cowen resigned as leader of his party, Fianna Fail. He was replaced with Prime Minister Enda Kenny of the Fome Gael Party in March of 2011.

customs and etiquette

In general, Irish society is relatively more conservative than other European and American countries due to its long history and connection with the Roman Catholic Church. Most people in Ireland are Roman Catholic, and up until the 1990s the church extended a wide reach into all aspects of Irish society. Even though the church's role has diminished over the past two decades, religion still impacts society's views on family, marriage, and abortion, and you will find that many of Ireland's older generations are still very orthodox in their beliefs.

MEET AND GREET

The basic greeting is a nice firm handshake and a hello (or salutation appropriate for the time of the day). It is expected that you will maintain eye contact with the person you are talking to, and even if you do not know your partner in conversation very well, the Irish are a bunch of chummy blokes (and dames), so don't be surprised when the conversation takes a friendly turn.

Of course, there are certain topics that should be avoided during casual conversation. Unless you're very familiar with your companions, steer well away from The Troubles (see the History section for more information), as well as religion. And remember that the Irish have probably come across more leprechaun jokes than they have pints of Guinness, so unless you want to participate in a pub brawl, don't reference any little green men or pots of gold. (Lucky Charms cereal may also cause trouble.)

COMMUNICATION STYLE

The Irish have turned speaking into an art form. Like your average folks, the Irish appreciate modesty and are suspicious of loudmouths and braggarts, so please don't talk to the Irish as you would talk to frat boys.

Communication styles vary from direct to indirect depending on who you are speaking to; however, there is a tendency for the Irish to view politeness as more important than absolute truth. It'll be wise to keep that rule in mind, especially after a few pints of Guinness.

Finally, while it is common in the US to flip only the middle finger to tell someone to "bug off," the Irish flip both their middle and index finger, forming a V shape. However, take note that "flipping the bird" is only insulting when you position your hand so that your palm is facing you. If your palm is facing away from you, then you've messed up and have just signaled to everyone that you're a dirty hippie.

HUMOR

The Irish have a reputation for their wit and humor, which they call "having a crack." They like to combine dry, wry humor with quick jokes, which make the Irish eloquent and well-informed speakers. They take pride in being able to find humor in nearly every situation, and they are often self-deprecating and ironic. It is not unusual for the Irish to trade well-meaning insults or to tease one another when engaged in conversation with good friends (called "slagging"). If you are teased, remember not to take it personally. And again, refrain from unleashing the pot o' leprechaun jokes you have mentally stored.

THINGS THAT WILL PISS THE IRISH OFF

Even though the Irish are relatively light-hearted and easy to share a good joke with, there are several topics that you should definitely not address. Please don't talk about homosexuality or abortion, as a majority of the Irish are very religious and conservative when it comes to social values. Never refer to the Republic of Ireland as part of the United Kingdom. And finally, never refer to someone or call someone a "mick" (a derogatory term for an Irishman) or "Briton", as this is considered a major insult.

food and drink

FOOD

Irish cuisine has revolved around the country's staple, the humble potato, for a very, very long time. Since its introduction to Ireland in the 16th century, the **potato** has been a constant feature on every Irishman's plate, with the exception of the two Great Famines. For a long time, the Irish stuck chiefly to the potato and other potato-based dishes. However, in recent decades the Irish have tried to modernize and diversify their cuisine. Nowadays, Irish cuisine is known for the freshness and quality of its ingredients. The Irish highlight these ingredients by keeping their recipes relatively simple. Most cooking is done without herbs or spices, except for salt and pepper, and food is usually served without sauce or gravy.

Along with the potato, other food staples that have played a constant role in the Irish diet are grains (especially oats), dairy products, and soups. The Irish have been accomplished cheese makers for centuries. And Irish soups are thick, hearty, and filling, made with potatoes (duh), seafood, and various meats.

Representative Irish dishes are Irish stew, bacon and cabbage, boxty, coddle, and colcannon. The most famous of these dishes would have to be the stew, as it's been the national dish for the last two centuries. Traditional Irish stew is made from lamb or mutton, as well as potatoes, carrots, onions, and parsley. Bacon and cabbage, as the name implies, consists of unsliced back bacon boiled with cabbage and potatoes. Sometimes other vegetables, such as turnips, onions, and carrots, are also added. Boxty is a traditional Irish potato pancake, similar to a latke. There are many different recipes, but they all contain finely grated, raw potatoes and all are served fried. Coddle consists of layers of roughly sliced pork sausages and rashers (thinly sliced, fatty bacon) with sliced potatoes and onions. Finally, colcannon is yet another potato-based dish that consists mainly of mashed potatoes with kale or cabbage.

In addition to their meat and potatoes, the Irish also love their bread. Be sure to try their thick, fluffy loaves of soda bread along with their soups. Soda breads are a heavy white bread made with soda instead of yeast, often with prepared with raisins or spices. Take-out has become increasingly popular in Ireland, and the most popular dish is fish and chips, which consists of battered, fried fish served with chips.

DRINKS

Let's be honest here—Ireland is not famous for its food but rather for its drinks. In 1759, Arthur Guinness began brewing his popular London "porter." He, his family, and the entire drinking world haven't looked back since. **Guinness** is known around the world for its impenetrable blackness. Although it is no longer given away free in Dublin hospitals to new mothers as a lukewarm restorative (true story), it is available on tap everywhere. Guinness is the quintessential Irish beer. It is also an acquired taste.

However, Guinness is not the only stout in town. Other popular brands are Murphy's and Beamish. In addition to stout, Irish whiskey is also immensely popular, and it comes in many forms, including single malt, single grain, and blended whiskey. True whiskey connoisseurs can make whiskey the focus of their trip through Ireland, visiting distillery after distillery and making their own whiskey trail. Other famous Irish drinks include cider (drunk by the pint like beers), mead (combines the sweetness of honey with the bite of alcohol), cream liquor, and Irish coffee.

sports and recreation

Sports in Ireland are immensely popular, for both athlete and spectator. Regardless of whether you're a sports fan or not, being a spectator (whether at the sporting arena or in your favorite pub) can be a great way to get to know the sports—and the drinking—culture.

The Irish are fanatical about their two native sports, Gaelic football and hurling (not to be confused with curling), and they are organized on an all-island basis, with a single team representing the whole of Ireland in international competitions. Other sports, such as soccer and netball, have separate organizing bodies in Northern Ireland and the Republic of Ireland.

GAELIC FOOTBALL

Gaelic football, commonly referred to as "football," "Gaelic," or "Gah," is the most popular sport in Ireland in terms of spectator attendance. A cross between British Rugby and soccer, Gaelic football is played by two teams of 15 on a rectangular grass pitch with H-shaped goals at each end. A goal is scored by kicking or striking the ball with the hand through the goals. Players advance the ball toward their goal by a combination of carrying, soloing (dropping and then toe-kicking the ball upward into the hands), kicking, and hand-passing to their teammates.

All players are amateurs, and the main national competitions are the inter-county All-Ireland Senior Football Championships and the National Football League (NFL). Every year the All-Ireland Finals in Dublin bring in crowds of 80,000 to Croke Park, the nation's largest sporting stadium. The most successful and famous "Gah" teams are Kerry, Dublin, Meath, and Cork.

HURLING

Along with Gaelic football, hurling is another one of Ireland's national sports. This fast and dangerous game has been played for at least 3,000 years and is thought to be the world's fastest field team game. The object of the game is for players to use a wooden stick (a *hurley*) to hit a small ball (the *sliotar*) between the opponent's goalposts, either over the crossbar for one point, or under the crossbar and into a net for a goal of three points. The hurley is used to hit the ball along the ground or through the air, but players can also kick the ball or hit it with the flat of their hands.

In Ireland, hurling is a fixture of life. It has been featured regularly in both film and literature, and it is continually popular among members of the expat Irish community abroad.

SOCCER

Association football, usually known as "soccer" or "football," is the team sport with the highest level of participation in the Republic of Ireland. The domestic leagues are the League of Ireland in the Republic of Ireland and the IFA Premiership in Northern Ireland. Some of the major teams in the Republic include St. Patrick's Athletic, Shamrock Rovers, and Bohemians, while Glentoran and Linfield represent Northern Ireland. On the international stage, the Republic of Ireland and Northern Ireland teams have each competed in three FIFA World Cups.

music

Traditional Irish music has remained vibrant throughout the 20th and into the 21st century. In fact, many forms of music in the US, such as country, have roots in traditional Irish music. Additionally, Irish music has occasionally been fused with other genres, including rock and roll and punk rock. Some of these fusion artists have attained mainstream attention, both domestically and abroad.

TRADITIONAL MUSIC

Traditional Irish music includes many types of songs, including drinking songs (of course), ballads, and laments. All can be sung either unaccompanied or with traditional dance music instruments, such as hornpipes and jigs and reels. But don't let the soothing melody of "Danny Boy" fool you: the Irish can cut a rug. Traditional Irish dances include the polka, set dancing, and jigs.

A revival of traditional Irish music took place around the turn of the 20th century. The button accordion and the concertina became popular, Irish stepdance was performed at many country houses and music festivals, and Irish singing was supported by the educational system and patriotic organizations. After a lull in the 1940s and 1950s, traditional Irish music experienced a second wave of revitalization in the 1960s thanks to musicians as such The Chieftains, The Clancy Brothers and Tommy Makem, The Irish Rovers, and the Dubliners.

POP/ROCK

The 1960s saw the emergence of major Irish rock bands and artists, such as Them, Van Morrison, Emmet Spiceland, Skid Row, Dr. Strangely Strange, Thin Lizzy, and Mellow Candle. Groups who formed during the emergence of punk rock in the mid-late 1970s and early 1980s include U2, The Boomtown Rats, The Understones, The Pogues, and Gavin Friday. Later in the 1980s and 1990s, Irish punk developed into new styles of alternative rock, which included bands such as That Petrol Emotion, My Bloody Valentine, and Ash. Also in the 1990s, pop bands like Boyzone, Westlife, and B*Witched emerged. Since the 2000s, the Irish pop/rock scene has continued to grow with well-established, popular acts such as Snow Patrol, The Coronas, Two Door Cinema Club, and The Script.

holidays and festivals

HOLIDAY OR FESTIVAL	DESCRIPTION	DATE
Saint Patrick's Day	Celebrated internationally, this festival commemorates Saint Patrick, one of the patron saints of Ireland, and the arrival of Christianity in Ireland. It has now become a secular celebration of Irish culture in general. The day is characterized by church services, lively street parades, the wearing of green, and massive consumption of booze.	March 17
Horseracing festivals	Horseracing, "the sport of kings," is a major tradition in Ireland. Horseracing festivals start on Easter Sunday and are located at various cities around Ireland. Key festivals include the Irish Grand National in April, the Curragh Derby in May, a weeklong Galway Summer Festival in July, the Listowel Harvest Festival in September, the Leopardstown Christmas Racing Festival in Dublin and the Guinness Christmas Racing Festival in Limerick, which are both held in December.	April to December

Midsummer's Day	Midsummer's Day is primarily a Celtic fire festival, representing the middle of summer. It involves country fairs with an abundance of singing and dancing. In rural spots, particularly in the northwest, bonfires are lit on hilltops.	June 21 or 22
Samhain	Samhain was originally the Celtic New Year and marked the end of the harvest, the end of the "lighter half" of the year and beginning of the "darker half." People and their livestock would often walk between two bonfires as part of a cleansing ritual, and the bones of slaughtered livestock were thrown into the flames.	October 31-November 1
Saint Stephen's Day	Saint Stephen's day is a national holiday in Ireland, but the celebrations have little connection to the saint. This is the day for "hunting the wren," where groups of boys would hunt for a wren and carry it from house to house while singing the Wren Boys' song.	December 26

BEYOND TOURISM

If you are reading this, then you are a member of an elite group—and we don't mean "the literate." You're a student preparing for a semester abroad. You're taking a gap year to save the trees, the whales, or the dates. You're an 80-year-old woman who has devoted her life to egg-laying platypuses and what the hell is up with that. In short, you're a traveler, not a tourist; like any good spy, you don't just observe your surroundings—you become an active part of them.

Your mission, should you choose to accept it, is to study, volunteer, or work abroad as laid out in the dossier—er, chapter—below. We leave the rest (when to go, whom to bring, and how many changes of underwear to pack) in your hands. This message will **self-destruct** in five seconds. Good luck.

greatest hits

- **INTERN** in Dublin with the Irish Parliament (p. 217).
- **BATTLE** rhododendrons for the Irish oakwood tree in Killarney National Park (p. 220).
- **STUDY** Gaelic in ancient castles at National University of Ireland in Galway (p. 217).
- **GUIDE** tourists through Aillwee Cave in County Clare (p. 224).

studying

Though you might not guess it from its stereotype as the land of Guinness and Jameson, Ireland has a plethora of summer and term-time study abroad programs. Just about every international study abroad or gap year organization has oodles of options for some quality time with tweed jackets and cool brogues (okay, there's more than that, but who doesn't want to pick up a wee lilt while yer there?). Programs tend to provide their own accommodations or have students live in dorms on campus, so it's safe to leave the cockroach spray at home. And don't feel discouraged if you don't descend from a Celtic goddess or plan to run away with **Riverdance.** Learning Gaelic? Check. Studying the sudden appearance of the white-toothed shrew (yes, this is for real)? Also check.

visa information

In the Republic of Ireland, visas are not required for most visitors, including those from the United States and Europe. Students studying abroad in Ireland may stay without a visa for a maximum of seven years if pursuing a degree at an Irish university or a maximum of three years if studying a language or other course not for a degree. Northern Ireland, however, is officially part of the UK, so students must obtain a Type 4 Student Visa if studying for longer than 6 months. For more information on Republic of Ireland visas visit www.inis.gov.ie, or visit www.ukba.homeoffice.gov.uk for information on UK visas.

UNIVERSITIES

There's more to visiting Ireland than sheep farms and raucous pubs. Well, at least more than the sheep. Universities are stashed in all corners of the island, from bustling Dublin to quaint seaside towns. Though the national language of Gaelic is understood mainly by native Irishmen and a few **leprechauns** (we never said that), English is Ireland's second official language, so most classes can be taken without an interpreter or a pot of gold. (Darn. Did it again.)

International Programs

For those feeling a little edgy about making camp overseas, an international program may help ease the pain. Study abroad or gap year organizations will do a lot of the leg work for you in registering for classes and taking care of those pesky logistics like basic sustenance (food, water, Wi-Fi; you get the drift). Many organizations offer the same or similar programs at different universities, so you'll sometimes have a pick of campus cultures to flavor your studies.

DUBLIN CITY UNIVERSITY

Collins Avenue, Dublin 9 ☎+1 800-407-8839 www.dcu.ie

If you're interested in Ireland but can't decide what to focus on, try the Irish studies program at DCU. You can't get too much broader than that. Outside of class, students take day trips to nearby castles and historic sites (read: frequent gallivanting). And if you don't return a dyed-in-the-wool Irishman (or woman) at the end of a three-week session, never fear! Just take a second one…

i Minimum GPA 2.75; 3 semester hours earned per 3-week session. $ 3-week summer session $3000, 6-week session $6000.

DUBLIN PARLIAMENTARY INTERNSHIP

Arcadia University ☎+1 866-927-2234 www.arcadia.edu/abroad

International politics junkies, here you go—an entire semester of studying under and working for some of Ireland's big shots. Students study at Ireland's Institute of Public Administration while learning the ins and outs of the Dáil (lower house) and Seanad (upper house) of Irish Parliament firsthand. Two days a week in Parliament, two days a week spent in class, seven days a week reveling in your good fortune.

i Fall and spring terms; 15 credits each semester. Minimum GPA 3.0. Program provides housing and medical insurance. $ Full program fee $15,560.

NATIONAL UNIVERSITY OF IRELAND, GALWAY

University Road, Galway

☎+1 800-266-4441 www.gowithcea.com/programs/ireland/galway.html

Think Ireland's all about rugged cliffs and seaside castles? Well, you're right. At least in Galway, that is. NUI Galway offers students courses from Gaelic to engineering and is especially well-known for its vibrant music and dance programs.

i About 18 credits per semester, exact number of credits at university's discretion. $ Semester-long programs $15,595.

QUEEN'S UNIVERSITY BELFAST

University Road Belfast, Northern Ireland, UK ☎+1 866-802-9678 www.worldendeavors.com

Despite officially singing "God Save the Queen," Belfast is as British as the Blarney Stone itself. Capital of UK-controlled Northern Ireland, the city is the site of many melding (and often clashing) cultures, languages, religions, politics, you name it. Take a few classes, watch a few rallies.

i Minimum GPA 3.0. Required 3 courses per semester. Off-campus and on-campus housing provided. $ Summer-long program $3950; semester-long $14,985; year-long $28,970; $200 application fee.

TRINITY COLLEGE DUBLIN

College Green, Dublin 2 ☎+353 1 896 1000 www.iesabroad.org

Founded in 1592, Trinity has something to brag about when it comes to staying power. Their academics aren't shabby either, ranking them consistently in the top 50 universities worldwide. International students can directly enroll at Trinity, allowing for a full college experience while being supported by a study abroad organization. Translation: all-nighters with your Celtic roommate will happen, getting abandoned in Dublin won't.

i 15-19 credits per semester. Provides off-campus housing for semester study abroad students and college housing for year-long enrollees. $ Semester-long programs $21,000-$23,000; full-year approximately $39,000.

UNIVERSITY COLLEGE DUBLIN

Belfield, Dublin 4 ☎+1 800-257-7751 http://sit.edu/studyabroad/ssa_ier.cfm

UCD, in partnership with Queen's University Belfast, University of Ulster, and Trinity College, offers the semester program Transformation of Social and Political Conflict, which explores the sectarian conflict between Northern Ireland and the Irish Republic. The course includes two homestays with Irish locals, and the final four weeks of study are approved independent study. Write your thesis, paint a mural, rub elbows with the IRA—it's really open-ended.

i 8 Credits/120 class hours. Program runs Aug-Dec. $ Tuition $15,000, room and board $5865.

UNIVERSITY OF LIMERICK

University Court, Limerick ☎+1 866-802-9678 www.worldendeavors.com

If you're the more romantic type, the University of Limerick might just be your cup of tea. Nestled only a few miles from the River Shannon and the onetime Viking city of Limerick, U Limerick is considered by many to be the most beautiful Irish campus. And considering what the rest of Ireland looks like, that's really saying something.

ℹ Minimum GPA 2.9; off-campus housing provided. $ Summer-long program $5250; semester-long $13,985; year-long $26,970; $200 application fee.

Irish Programs

For the purists out there who turn up their noses at study abroad organizations, fear not. We get you. We applaud your sense of adventure. We dig your desire to brave the rough winds of fortune and set forth on your own. You strap on your gillies and Irish step with the best of them. Your Irish Warpipes are your proud travel companions. You bravely go where few have gone before. As a token of our admiration, we humbly suggest these 100% Irish programs for your selection.

ROYAL IRISH ACADEMY OF MUSIC, DUBLIN CITY UNIVERSITY

36-38 Westland Row, Dublin 2 ☎+353 1 676 4412 www.riam.ie

James Galway is secretly your jam. Or maybe you've always been curious about what jazz would sound like with a fiddle and tin whistle. Either way, RIAM's probably got a place for you. With performing groups ranging from chamber orchestra to chorales and lots of fellow international students to hang out with between rehearsals, Dublin is practically begging you to come. RIAM also offers examination contests, where you can win cash prizes or free year-long tuition in the subject of examination. Not a bad deal.

ℹ Full-time and part-time courses and summer school provided. Application deadline Feb 1 of each year. $ Nominal cost.

UNIVERSITY COLLEGE CORK

College Road, Cork ☎+353 21 490 3000 www.ucc.ie

Medical research at UC Cork is looking up. Joining Trinity, NUI Galway, and UC Dublin, research funding at UC Cork is getting a huge boost as a newly-developed funding program, dubbed Molecular Medicine Ireland, starts working its magic on Irish university medical programs. So if you know what Bromophenol blue is and are tired of running out of it, start booking your ticket. Additionally, UCC offers a summer program in Irish studies as well as a program in the marine environment.

ℹ Irish Studies Program minimum GPA 2.85. Marine Environment Program 5 semester credits/course. $ Irish Studies Program €2200 excluding daily meals; Marine Environment Program €2500 per course, additional €500 accommodation fee.

UNIVERSITY OF ULSTER

☎+353 28 70123456 http://international.ulster.ac.uk

A Northern Ireland University with campuses in Belfast, Coleraine, Jordanstown, and Magee, University of Ulster hosts American students with the UK International Student Exchange Program (ISEP). Courses range from Spanish film study to Irish dancing (and lots in between), so we figure there's something here for almost everyone.

ℹ Course credit depends on home university. $ 1 semester £3180, 2 semesters £5840, 3 semesters £7490.

LANGUAGE SCHOOLS

As renowned novelist Gustave Flaubert once said, "Language is a cracked kettle on which we beat out tunes for bears to dance to." While we at Let's Go have absolutely no clue what he is talking about, we do know that the following are good resources for learning Gaelic.

IRISH LANGUAGE UNIVERSITY ACADEMY

National University of Ireland, Galway ☎+1 718-938-1345 www.irishamericanstudies.com

Researchers say immersion is the best way to learn a language. Universities say classes are the way to go (preferably on their campus). Trying both can't hurt. Between classes, students eat, sleep, and otherwise live in homes with Galway locals. So either learn to say "pass the potatoes" or finally lose the freshman fifteen.

ℹ Minimum GPA 2.75. Elementary, intermediate, and advanced courses offered, 6 credits each. Local housing provided. $ 3-week summer program €2395.

TRINITY COLLEGE DUBLIN

College Green, Dublin 2 ☎+353 1 896 1000 www.tcd.ie/Irish

Whether you're getting your Gaelic up to snuff with an elementary Irish course or learning to carry on with even the fiercest Vikings, Trinity will be glad to have you. And when you do learn how to pronounce ten consonants in a row, shoot us an email. We never could figure that one out.

ℹ Irish language and literature courses either semester or year-long, 15 European Credit Transfer units. Elementary Irish only offered year-long, not for credit. $ Year-long tuition €16,035 for non-EU students.

LANGUAGES ABROAD

☎+1 800 219 9924 www.languagesabroad.com/ireland/live-learn

The Live and Learn Gaelic program allows students to live in a Gaelic-speaking home while studying the language with a private tutor. Programs range from 4-week stints to year-long studying. Good Irish food guaranteed.

$ Standard program $1600-$2600, five-star program $3400-$5700, depending on number of hours of instruction.

volunteering

For many intrepid adventurers (yes, we're talking to you), observing just isn't enough. That's where volunteering comes in. Good Samaritans will have no trouble finding worthwhile ways to occupy part of their vacation, especially in fighting poverty and ecological conservation efforts. That being said, there's really no limit to the type of volunteer work international visitors can partake in, as long as said visitors have legally entered the country (always important) and are authorized to volunteer. This entails presenting 1) proof of a volunteer opportunity, 2) proof of independent medical insurance, and 3) proof of sufficient funds to cover the trip. Volunteers are also limited to a three-month stay unless registered with the Immigration Bureau (GNIB). We can't help you much with the insurance policy or necessary monies, but here are a few volunteer opportunities we like the looks of.

YOUTH

BARRETSTOWN CAMP

Ballymore Eustace, County Kildare ☎+353 4 586 4115 www.barretstown.org

Kids suffering from cancer come from all over Ireland and Europe to let their hair down at the Barretstown Castle (we know—who doesn't want to live in a castle for a summer?). Through interactive eight-day summer camps and family weekends, the camp works to help rebuild families struggling with their child's illness. Volunteers are typically assigned a specific family to work with in addition to keeping the camps running without a hitch.

ℹ Must be 19 years or older.

SOUTH WEST INNER CITY NETWORK (SWICN)

48 Hamilton Street, Dublin 8 ☎+353 1 473 2100 www.swicn.ie

Located and operating solely within the postal code Dublin 8, SWICN hosts programs ranging from drug education and prevention seminars to jewelry-making classes. They run adult and youth centers and drug education centers throughout the Dublin 8 sector.

Youth Centre on Rainsford Street. From Rainsford take first left into car park. Center is white prefab building on your left. Entrance is behind the big iron gate.

AGRICULTURE AND CONSERVATION

WORLD WIDE OPPORTUNITIES ON ORGANIC FARMS (WWOOF)

☎+353 27 512 54 www.wwoof.ie

Though it sounds more like a friendly canine welcome than a sustainable farming endeavor, WWOOF's Ireland chapter is a thriving hub of healthy organic goodliness. Aspiring WWOOFers can choose to work in just about any corner of the island and with just about every flavor of farm, from single-family plots to community cooperatives to commercial producers. Just think, you'd be helping make Ireland's Costco more eco-friendly. What more could you ask for?

i Must be 16 years or older, special restrictions for volunteers under 18.

CONSERVATION VOLUNTEERS

www.conservationvolunteers.ie

For those still muddled about whether to stroll through the countryside or rebuild it, Conservation Volunteers might be just the ticket. Hosting holiday conservation trips lasting anywhere from five days to two weeks, CV programs are really just summer camps for big kids. Younger members can also take part in the youth programs. A little bit of volunteer work plus lots of kibitzing equals a satisfying trip.

i Branches in Clare, Donegal, Dublin, Galway, Limerick, and Mayo. See site for branch directors and phone numbers.

GROUNDWORK

93A Lagan Road, Dublin 11 ☎+353 1 860 2389 www.groundwork.ie

The problem: Irish oakwood trees, which used to cloak the island, are now scarce and their numbers dwindling. The culprit: rhododendrons. That's right, your mom's favorite ornamental bush is a quiet killer. This flowery non-native species apparently also likes Killarney and has been pushing out the proud oakwood survivors. The solution: one of them's gotta go. This is where Groundwork steps in, clearing rhododendron plants from Killarney every summer to promote a victorious oakwood resurgence. It's like a small revolution, except you're armed with pruners instead of cannons.

i Work runs June-Sept each year. Office usually staffed Tu-Th 2-6pm. $ €35 for 1-week, €50 for 2 weeks.

POLITICAL AND SOCIAL ACTIVISM

GLENCREE CENTER FOR PEACE AND RECONCILIATION

Glencree, County Wicklow ☎+353 1 282 9711 www.glencree.ie

Glencree works to soothe the tensions between Northern Ireland and the Irish Republic. They host multiple peacebuilding and reconciliation programs, from networking former combatants across the North-South divide to hosting open dialogues. Glencree also has an international program, where they aim to provide the same peacebuilding strategies to foreign analogues of the Irish-English conflict, such as those in Sri Lanka, Israel/Palestine, and Colombia.

Follow Killakee Road to a fork near a small car park, take the right fork and continue until a sharp left for Glencree. The Center is about 100yds ahead on the right, after the church.

SOCIETY OF VINCENT DE PAUL

91-92 Sean MacDermott Street, Dublin 1 ☎+353 1 838 6690 www.svp.iee

SVP is a charity organization helping Irish citizens get back on their feet after economic crisis. However, they also participate in other good deeds, such as visiting hospitals and prisons and running shops for the poor, and have been known to propose legislation to help prevent poverty. Whether you're looking to ladle out soup or brush up on your Irish law, SVP is a great choice for those discovering their inner good Samaritan.

i Welcomes both long-term and short-term (1-2 days) volunteers.

SIMON COMMUNITIES OF IRELAND

28-30 Exchequer Street, Dublin 2 ☎+353 1 671 1606 www.simon.ie

If you're looking to help fight poverty in Ireland, you don't have to look far. Simon Communities are found all over the Republic of Ireland, providing housing and financial and emotional support to the homeless. Volunteers from all walks of life are welcome in helping maintain the communities and rebuild the confidence of their residents.

i Has branches throughout Irish Republic. Part-time (3-7hr. per week) and full-time (6-month minimum) volunteers. Training, accommodations, and weekly pocket money for personal expenses provided.

FOR THE UNDECIDED ALTRUIST

VOLUNTEER NOW

34 Shaftesbury Square, Belfast ☎+353 28 9023 2020 www.volunteering-ni.org

So you want to work in Northern Ireland. Maybe you enjoy tiptoeing through protesters during your coffee break. Maybe you're tired of mashed potatoes and shamrocks. Maybe you want to wear that T-shirt with the huge Union Jack without getting mugged (don't test that one out). Whatever your motives, there are plenty of volunteer opportunities awaiting you at Volunteer Now. They offer opportunities ranging from anti-poverty work to catering.

i Offices in Belfast, Broughshane, Enniskillen, and Newry. Offers volunteer training specific to volunteer program selected.

EXPERIENTIAL LEARNING INTERNATIONAL

☎+1 303-321-8278 www.eliabroad.org

Experiential Learning International provides unpaid internships and volunteer programs in and around Dublin. Projects include volunteering at animal shelters, interning at museums and art galleries, and studying hazardous waste disposal.

i Offers programs from 4-12 weeks. Office open M-F 8:30am-5pm $ Without accommodation $1250, with housing $2450-$4850, depending on length of stay; application fee $200.

VOLUNTEERS FOR INTERNATIONAL PARTNERSHIP

☎+1 802-246-1154 www.partnershipvolunteers.org/volunteer-in-ireland

VIP provides programs geared towards environmental conservation, helping those with disabilities, and aiding the poor. They also work with arts and theater projects for children, so shoot them an email if you're feeling especially whimsical during your stay.

i Food and residential accommodation at project site provided. Maximum 40hr. of work a week. Programs run from 3 weeks to a year. $ Program fee $1945-$3945 depending on length of stay.

VOLUNTARY SERVICE INTERNATIONAL

30 Mountjoy Square, Dublin 1 ☎+353 1 855 1011 www.vsi.ie

What these folks want are enthusiastic volunteers. They'll take care of the rest. From building stone walls to cooking massive meals, VSI runs 20 to 30 Irish volunteer programs each year. Participants typically work and live in small groups, so be prepared to be social. And (maybe) shower daily.

i Projects in Dublin, Galway, Limerick, Maynooth, Belfast, Waterford, and some rural areas. Fee covers food, accommodation, and insurance while on program. Program duration from 2-4 weeks. $ Costs $60-$150.

working

Ireland recognizes that jobs don't grow on trees. Employment preferences are given to fellow European Union countrymen, so non-EU citizens are allowed to work for a maximum of one year with a work visa. Irish authorities require proof of license for certain careers, like teachers, technicians, surgeons (we hope so), etc. Like most other western countries, jobs are often rare and there is some hefty competition for positions, so don't be surprised if finding a job here proves more difficult than in the US. Often, rare skills or extra qualifications are needed for foreigners to secure employment against local competition. That being said, there are many programs that specialize in international job opportunities. Though it might be hard to find a job as a heart surgeon for only a year, there are plenty of professional and pre-professional jobs to be had across the rolling green countryside of bonny Ireland. Or the blustery isles of the coast. Or the cheery streets of Dublin. You get the point.

LONG-TERM WORK

Working in Ireland long-term is fairly easy. That is, as long as your definition of "long-term" means a year. For US citizens, this is called a "work holiday" (which sounds so much nicer than a "work visa"). So, after long deliberation, you've decided that a year-long work holiday in Ireland is the thing to do. It helps that you're an English-speaker, so you won't have to learn the language to ask for directions to your first interview, but what now?

beyond tourism

more visa information

The type of work visa required varies depending on the employee's nationality. For US citizens, you must have what is called "work holiday authorization" from the Irish Embassy or Consulate General. Like with volunteer work, you must demonstrate you have a job offer in hand, your own medical insurance, sufficient funds to cover your stay, and (most importantly) sufficient funds to get you back out of Ireland after your year is up. For Northern Ireland, a Tier 1 or 2 work visa is required, depending on the employee's skill set. Visit www.dfa.ie for more information on working holiday visas, or www.ukba.homeoffice.gov.uk on UK Tier 1 and 2 visas.

Teaching

According to the Irish Teaching Council, a teaching license is a teaching license, though there is an advantage to being licensed within an EU country. Teachers licensed outside of Europe can find employment in Ireland once registered with the Teaching Council. Specific information on applying to the Irish Teaching Council can be found at www.teachingcouncil.ie. Teaching jobs are widely available, especially in fast-growing areas like suburban Dublin. However, be forewarned that teachers in Irish schools tend to be paid less than those working in American international schools (where salaries are more comparable to salaries paid stateside). Funnily enough, teachers who speak Gaelic are snapped up the quickest to teach in *gaeltachts*, the Gaelic-speaking districts sprinkled throughout the country. Science teachers and those licensed in special education might also have an easier time finding work than their fellow educators, but if your specialty is e.e. cummings's poetry, then there's plenty of room for you, too.

Google has met its match. Here is the mother of all Irish teaching job databases. Listings range from Gaelic teachers to house mothers. Whatever that means.

i Provides email alerts and newsletters to advertise new job openings. Also runs subsititute teacher database.

Au Pair Work

Frankly, au pairing in Ireland can get a little hairy. Work bureaus and au pair agencies have recently reported complaints of au pairs being forced to work longer hours and work jobs they aren't hired for (brick laying, anyone?). Irish authorities are working to pass laws protecting foreign workers, especially au pairs, but in the meantime a reputable au pair agency and a bit of caution are your best defenses. In addition, only EU citizens can legally be full-time au pairs. For non-Europeans, only part-time au pairing is an option if you're in Ireland. So for those bound and determined to au pair in Ireland, start looking into those masonry classes at DCU.

AU PAIR IRELAND

1 Victoria Villas, Clontarf, Dublin 3 ☎+353 83 392 6284 www.aupairireland.ie
Listings of available au pair work across Ireland. Jobseekers sign up for a membership online and are able to answer au pair and nanny requests when convenient.

i Free membership.

SHAMROCK AU PAIR AGENCY

County Kildare, Ireland ☎+353 56 4401 007 www.aupairireland.com
Hey gals, this one's for you—a girls-only travel party with some work on the side. If you're planning to stay in Ireland for at least half a year, au pairing just might be better than hostel-hopping. And Shamrock connects their au pairs with each other, so you'll have some buddies to go out with on your nights off.

i Must be female between 19-30 years old, minimum stay of 6 months. Previous childcare experience required. Also have summer au pair options. International Au Pair Association (IAPA) member. Ⓢ *€90 weekly pocket money, meals and private room provided.* 🕐 *30hr. per week plus 2 nights babysitting.*

SK DUBLIN AU PAIRS

4 Market Square House, Aughrim ☎+353 4 029 4695 www.skdublinaupairs.ie
Dublin is well-known for homey shops and friendly people. It's also the site of numerous Irish universities, making studying and working that much easier. Sound like a plan? We think so.

i Must be 18 or over, min. stay 2 months. Ⓢ *€100 weekly pocket money, meals and private room provided. IAPA member.* 🕐 *30hr. per week plus 2 nights babysitting or 35hr. per week plus 1 night babysitting. Su and 1 other day free.*

AU PAIR STUDY CENTRE

1 Clarinda Park North, Dun Laoghaire ☎+353 1 284 4675 www.aupairstudy.com
While providing regular au pair positions, the Study Centre also provides au pairs to senior citizens and "demi-au pair" positions for students studying and working as au pairs during evenings. Demi-au pairs typically study a language while they work.

Ⓢ *€50 per week min.* 🕐 *Demi-au pairs work 15hr. per week. Office hours M-F 9:30am-5pm.*

SHORT-TERM WORK

Some people want to squeeze out every last hour of their time overseas. Others are okay with a few solid months. If you fall into the latter category, signing up for shorter-term work commitments might behoove you. After all, you don't need a whole year to dodge sheep herds and lose your tan. Since working in Ireland is limited to only a year, short-term work is very similar to longer-term jobs—just about any job is available, as long as you get it before requesting that work holiday.

AN OIGE IRISH YOUTH HOSTEL ASSOCIATION

61 Mount Joy Street, Dublin 7 ☎+353 1 830 4555 www.anoige.ie

Yeah yeah, we know most foreign hostels aren't your first pick for a summer job. But how many hostel organizations offer boating trips or horseback riding for their customers? An Oige provides day tours and outdoor expeditions for their whippersnapper residents. We're not sure how they fit in mountain biking in the middle of Dublin, but that's another issue.

[i] 24 hostels nationwide with paid positions and summer volunteer opportunities. See "Newsroom" section of website for job listings.

AILLWEE CAVE

Ballyvaughan, County Clare ☎+353 65 707 7036 www.aillweecave.ie

One of the oldest caves in Ireland, tourists flock here year after year for cave tours and nature walks. Guides are hired for cave tours, the birds of prey center, and the hawk walk, as well as for managerial duties. So for those of you who can't get enough of extinct brown bear skeletons and a frozen waterfalls, here's your chance to strut your stuff.

 # 40min. from Galway and Shannon. [i] Hiring Mar-Dec. Workday 10am-6pm, 5 days a week. Those with geology and first aid experience preferred for cave guide positions.

BUNAC WORKING ADVENTURES WORLDWIDE

☎+1 203-264-0901 www.bunac.org/usa/workinireland

If you're looking for a quick job but aren't into the whole visa ordeal, BUNAC's four-month or twelve-month Work in Ireland programs are probably your best bet. BUNAC is authorized to allow US students to work in Ireland for four months. If you want to work longer, their twelve-month program staff will help you get the necessary paperwork.

[i] Summer jobs harder to find. Must be 18 or older and a full-time college student or recent graduate. Also has UK office. $ Program starting fee $340.

JOBS.IE

Grand Canal Quay, Dublin 2 ☎+353 1 664 2957 www.jobs.ie

Still not satisfied? Try browsing the Ireland region of Jobs.ie. New job listings are posted daily and from just about every employer imaginable. Elephant & Castle Restaurant? Louis Vuitton? Amnesty International? You see what we mean?

YOUPLANET AMBASSADOR

http://youplanet.com/ambassador/en

The saying "You can't have your cake and eat it, too" is for disgruntled souls. After all, cake is for eating. And traveling is for having fun. YouPlanet pays travelers, or what they call "ambassadors," to add listings to their travel directory. Get a new partner for YouPlanet, get paid. Ask hotels, restaurants, shop owners, pickpockets, whoever you want. Knock yourself out.

$ $100 per new partner recruited.

tell the world

If your friends are tired of hearing about that time you saved a baby orangutan in Indonesia, there's clearly only one thing to do: get new friends. Find them at our website, www.letsgo.com, where you can post your study-, volunteer-, or work-abroad stories for other, more appreciative community members to read.

INDEX

index

index

MAP INDEX

index

LET'S GO

THE STUDENT TRAVEL GUIDE

Available at bookstores and through online retailers:

EUROPE
Let's Go Budget Amsterdam, 1st ed.
Let's Go Amsterdam & Brussels, 1st ed.
Let's Go Budget Athens, 1st ed.
Let's Go Budget Barcelona, 1st ed.
Let's Go Budget Berlin, 1st ed.
Let's Go Berlin, Prague & Budapest, 2nd ed.
Let's Go Budget Florence, 1st ed.
Let's Go France, 32nd ed.
Let's Go Europe 2013, 53rd ed.
Let's Go Europe Top 10 Cities, 1st ed.
Let's Go European Riviera, 1st ed.
Let's Go Germany, 16th ed.
Let's Go Great Britain with Belfast and Dublin, 33rd ed.
Let's Go Greece, 10th ed.
Let's Go Budget Istanbul, 1st ed.
Let's Go Istanbul, Athens & the Greek Islands, 1st ed.
Let's Go Ireland, 14th ed.
Let's Go Italy, 32nd ed.
Let's Go Budget London, 1st ed.
Let's Go London, Oxford & Cambridge, 3rd ed.
Let's Go Budget Madrid, 1st ed.
Let's Go Madrid & Barcelona, 1st ed.
Let's Go Paris, 17th ed.
Let's Go Budget Paris, 1st ed.
Let's Go Paris, Amsterdam & Brussels, 1st ed.
Let's Go Budget Prague, 1st ed.
Let's Go Budget Rome, 1st ed.
Let's Go Rome, Venice & Florence, 2nd ed.
Let's Go Spain & Portugal, 27th ed.
Let's Go Western Europe, 10th ed.

UNITED STATES
Let's Go Boston, 6th ed.
Let's Go New York City, 19th ed.
Let's Go Roadtripping USA, 4th ed.

MEXICO, CENTRAL & SOUTH AMERICA
Let's Go Buenos Aires, 2nd ed.
Let's Go Central America, 10th ed.
Let's Go Costa Rica, 5th ed.
Let's Go Costa Rica, Nicaragua & Panama, 1st ed.
Let's Go Guatemala & Belize, 1st ed.
Let's Go Yucatán Peninsula, 1st ed.

ASIA & THE MIDDLE EAST
Let's Go Israel, 6th ed.
Let's Go Thailand, 5th ed.

Exam and desk copies are available for study-abroad programs and resource centers. Let's Go guidebooks are distributed to bookstores in the U.S. through Publishers Group West and in Canada through Publishers Group Canada. For more information, email letsgo.info@perseusbooks.com.

ACKNOWLEDGMENTS

MALLORY THANKS: Our RWs for their brave, bold, and badass attitude. Mark for not judging country music (or doing it quietly) and for helping me eat ALL the sushi. Clemmie for never spilling your water on my side and for being the RM to my Ed through the good, the bad, and the manstores. Michael for delicious duck, comfy beds, and a place to rest my head when silly-time rolled around. Claire for your celebrity scoops and for making me laugh over copyflow and salads. Haley for talking to strangers on buses (no wait, that's not okay). Mariel for tweets and frozen grapes. And everyone at Let's Go for a wonderful summer. Mom, Dad, Jack, and Jay for always making me laugh (LBI next year, I promise). Demetrio for a summer of country music (and we do). And all my friends scattered about for all the silliness and support.

CLEMMIE THANKS: Mark, my faithful ME, for always being there to take the weight off of our shoulders, whether with a helping hand or an off-the-cuff joke. You always make me smile. Mallory for being the most reliable, savviest editor ever and always brightening the mood. My awesomely adventurous RWs, who took everything in stride and allowed me to live vicariously through them this summer. Trailblazers. For real. Roland and Faith for prodding us along and putting up with the chaos. Michael, Haley, Claire, Lauren, Mariel, and Jess for being great at what they do and making the office a lighthearted and fun, yet productive place. Sara for holding it all together. **Bassnectar, Dillon Francis,** and **Zeds Dead** for keeping me thoroughly entertained when monotony hit. Thanks Paul for keeping me happy. Finally, thanks to **the moms.** I love you, Mum!

DIRECTOR OF PUBLISHING   Sara Plana
MANAGING EDITORS   Michael Goncalves, Mark Warren
PRODUCTION AND DESIGN DIRECTOR   Roland Yang
DIGITAL AND MARKETING DIRECTOR   Lauren Xie
PRODUCTION ASSOCIATE   Faith Zhang
MARKETING ASSOCIATES   Zi Wei Lin, Mariel Sena, Jess Stein

DIRECTOR OF IT   Calvin Tonini
PRESIDENT   Kirk Benson
GENERAL MANAGER   Jim McKellar

ABOUT LET'S GO

THE STUDENT TRAVEL GUIDE

Let's Go publishes the world's favorite student travel guides, written entirely by Harvard students. Armed with pens, notebooks, and a few changes of clothes stuffed into their backpacks, our student researchers go across continents, through time zones, and above expectations to seek out invaluable travel experiences for our readers. Because we are a completely student-run company, we have a unique perspective on how students travel, where they want to go, and what they're looking to do when they get there. If your dream is to grab a machete and forge through the jungles of Costa Rica, we can take you there. If you'd rather bask in the Riviera sun at a beachside cafe, we'll set you a table. In short, we write for readers who know that there's more to travel than tour buses. To keep up, visit our website, www.letsgo.com, where you can sign up to blog, post photos from your trips, and connect with the Let's Go community.

TRAVELING BEYOND TOURISM

We're on a mission to provide our readers with sharp, fresh coverage packed with socially responsible opportunities to go beyond tourism. Each guide's Beyond Tourism chapter shares ideas about responsible travel, study abroad, and how to give back to the places you visit while on the road. To help you gain a deeper connection with the places you travel, our fearless researchers scour the globe to give you the heads-up on both world-renowned and off-the-beaten-track opportunities. We've also opened our pages to respected writers and scholars to hear their takes on the countries and regions we cover, and asked travelers who have worked, studied, or volunteered abroad to contribute first-person accounts of their experiences.

FIFTY-THREE YEARS OF WISDOM

Let's Go has been on the road for 53 years and counting. We've grown a lot since publishing our first 20-page pamphlet to Europe in 1960, but five decades and 60 titles later, our witty, candid guides are still researched and written entirely by students on shoestring budgets who know that train strikes, stolen luggage, food poisoning, and marriage proposals are all part of a day's work. Meanwhile, we're still bringing readers fresh new features, such as a student life section with advice on how and where to meet students from around the world; a revamped, user-friendly layout for our listings; and greater emphasis on the experiences that make travel abroad a rite of passage for readers of all ages. And, of course, this year's seven titles are still brimming with editorial honesty, a commitment to students, and our irreverent style.

THE LET'S GO COMMUNITY

More than just a travel guide company, Let's Go is a community that reaches from our headquarters in Cambridge, MA, all across the globe. Our small staff of dedicated student editors, writers, and tech nerds comes together because of our shared passion for travel and our desire to help other travelers get the most out of their experience. We love it when our readers become part of the Let's Go community as well—when you travel, drop us a postcard (67 Mt. Auburn St., Cambridge, MA 02138, USA), send us an email (feedback@letsgo.com), or sign up on our website (www. letsgo.com) to tell us about your adventures and discoveries.

For more information, updated travel coverage, and news from our researcher team, visit us online at www.letsgo.com.

notes

HELPING LET'S GO. If you want to share your discoveries, suggestions, or corrections, please drop us a line. We appreciate every piece of correspondence, whether a postcard, a 10-page email, or a coconut. Visit Let's Go at **www.letsgo.com** or send an email to:

feedback@letsgo.com, subject: "Let's Go Ireland"

Address mail to:

Let's Go Ireland, 67 Mount Auburn St., Cambridge, MA 02138, USA

In addition to the invaluable travel advice our readers share with us, many are kind enough to offer their services as researchers or editors. Unfortunately, our charter enables us to employ only currently enrolled Harvard students.

Maps © Let's Go and Avalon Travel
Design Support by Jane Musser, Sarah Juckniess, Tim McGrath

Distributed by Publishers Group West.
Printed in Canada by Friesens Corp.

ISBN-13: 978-1-61237-033-0
Fourteenth edition
10 9 8 7 6 5 4 3 2 1

Let's Go Ireland is written by Let's Go Publications, 67 Mt. Auburn St., Cambridge, MA 02138, USA.

quick reference

YOUR GUIDE TO LET'S GO ICONS

👍	*Let's Go* recommends	☎	Phone numbers	🧭	Directions
i	Other hard info	$	Prices	⏰	Hours

PRICE RANGES

Let's Go includes price ranges, marked by one through four dollar signs, in accommodation and food listings. For an expanded explanation, see the chart in How To Use This Book.

REPUBLIC OF IRELAND	$	$$	$$$	$$$$
ACCOMMODATIONS	under €15	€15-29	€30-45	over €45
FOOD	under €8	€8-14	€15-20	over €20

NORTHERN IRELAND	$	$$	$$$	$$$$
ACCOMMODATIONS	under £14	£14-25	£26-45	over £45
FOOD	under £7	£7-12	£13-18	over £18

IMPORTANT PHONE NUMBERS

EMERGENCY: POLICE ☎999, FIRE ☎999, MEDICAL ASSISTANCE ☎999			
Police	☎999	Medical Emergency	☎999
Fire	☎999	Directory Assistance in Ireland	☎11811
International Operator	☎114	US Embassy in Dublin	☎+353 1 668 8777
US Consulate in Belfast	☎+44 0 75 45 50 77 38	US State Department	☎+1 317-472-2328, ☎+1 202-647-4000 (after hours)

CURRENCY CONVERSIONS

Euro

AUS$1 = €0.83	€1 = AUS$1.20	NZ$1 = €0.65	€1 = NZ$1.53
CDN$1 = €0.80	€1 = CDN$1.25	UK£1 = €1.27	€1 = UK£0.79
EUR€1 = €1	WOAH!	US$1 = €0.81	€1 = US$1.22

Pound Sterling

AUS$1 = £0.66	£1 = AUS$1.20	NZ$1 = £0.51	£1 = NZ$1.95
CDN$1 = £0.63	£1 = CDN$1.25	UK£1 = £1	WOAH!
EUR€1 = £0.79	£1 = EUR€1.27	US$1 = £0.65	£1 = US$1.55

TEMPERATURE CONVERSIONS

°CELSIUS	-5	0	5	10	15	20	25	30	35	40
°FAHRENHEIT	23	32	41	50	59	68	77	86	95	104

MEASUREMENT CONVERSIONS

1 inch (in.) = 25.4mm	1 millimeter (mm) = 0.039 in.
1 foot (ft.) = 0.305m	1 meter (m) = 3.28 ft.
1 mile (mi.) = 1.609km	1 kilometer (km) = 0.621 mi.
1 pound (lb.) = 0.454kg	1 kilogram (kg) = 2.205 lb.
1 gallon (gal.) = 3.785L	1 liter (L) = 0.264 gal.